SCIENCE AND
HUMAN BEHAVIOR

THE MACMILLAN COMPANY
NEW YORK · CHICAGO
DALLAS · ATLANTA · SAN FRANCISCO
LONDON · MANILA
IN CANADA
BRETT-MACMILLAN LTD.
GALT, ONTARIO

BY THE SAME AUTHOR

The Behavior of Organisms
Walden Two
Verbal Behavior
Schedules of Reinforcement
(with C. B. Ferster)

SCIENCE AND
HUMAN BEHAVIOR

BY

B. F. SKINNER

New York   THE MACMILLAN COMPANY

Printed in the United States of America

Sixth Printing 1960

To

F. S. KELLER

ACKNOWLEDGMENTS

The quotation from Francesco Lana (Chapter I) was brought to the attention of the readers of *Science*, August 25, 1939, by M. F. Ashley-Montagu. Permission to quote from George Bernard Shaw's *The Adventures of the Black Girl in Her Search for God* (Chapter IV) was kindly granted by the Society of Authors. The story about Dean Briggs (Chapter XIV) was reported by Mary E. Woolley in the *American Scholar*, Volume 1, Number 1, 1932. The quotation from Carl R. Rogers (Chapter XXIX) is to be found on page 212 of the *Harvard Educational Review*, Fall, 1948, and is used with permission. I am indebted to J. G. Beebe-Center for a helpful reading of the manuscript. I am also grateful for editorial assistance from Mrs. Diana S. Larsen and Miss Dorothy Cohen.

Harvard University   B.F.S.
Cambridge, Massachusetts

TABLE OF CONTENTS

SECTION IV: THE BEHAVIOR OF PEOPLE IN GROUPS

SECTION V: CONTROLLING AGENCIES

SECTION VI: THE CONTROL OF HUMAN BEHAVIOR

THE POSSIBILITY OF
A SCIENCE OF
HUMAN BEHAVIOR

CHAPTER 1

CAN SCIENCE HELP?

THE MISUSE OF SCIENCE

By the middle of the seventeenth century it had come to be understood that the world was enclosed in a sea of air, much as the greater part of it was covered by water. A scientist of the period, Francesco Lana, contended that a lighter-than-air ship could float upon this sea, and he suggested how such a ship might be built. He was unable to put his invention to a practical test, but he saw only one reason why it might not work:

. . . that God will never suffer this Invention to take effect, because of the many consequencies which may disturb the Civil Government of men. For who sees not, that no City can be secure against attack, since our Ship may at any time be placed directly over it, and descending down may discharge Souldiers; the same would happen to private Houses, and Ships on the Sea: for our Ship descending out of the Air to the sails of Sea-Ships, it may cut their Ropes, yea without descending by casting Grapples it may over-set them, kill their men, burn their Ships by artificial Fire works and Fire-balls. And this they may do not only to Ships but to great Buildings, Castles, Cities, with such security that they which cast these things down from a height out of Gun-shot, cannot on the other side be offended by those below.

3

Lana's reservation was groundless. He had predicted modern air warfare in surprisingly accurate detail—with its paratroopers and its strafing and bombing. Contrary to his expectation, God has suffered his invention to take effect.

And so has Man. The story emphasizes the irresponsibility with which science and the products of science have been used. Man's power appears to have increased out of all proportion to his wisdom. He has never been in a better position to build a healthy, happy, and productive world; yet things have perhaps never seemed so black. Two exhausting world wars in a single half century have given no assurance of a lasting peace. Dreams of progress toward a higher civilization have been shattered by the spectacle of the murder of millions of innocent people. The worst may be still to come. Scientists may not set off a chain reaction to blow the world into eternity, but some of the more plausible prospects are scarcely less disconcerting.

In the face of this apparently unnecessary condition men of good will find themselves helpless or afraid to act. Some are the prey of a profound pessimism. Others strike out blindly in counteraggression, much of which is directed toward science itself. Torn from its position of prestige, science is decried as a dangerous toy in the hands of children who do not understand it. The conspicuous feature of any period is likely to be blamed for its troubles, and in the twentieth century science must play the scapegoat. But the attack is not entirely without justification. Science has developed unevenly. By seizing upon the easier problems first, it has extended our control of inanimate nature without preparing for the serious social problems which follow. The technologies based upon science are disturbing. Isolated groups of relatively stable people are brought into contact with each other and lose their equilibrium. Industries spring up for which the life of a community may be unprepared, while others vanish leaving millions unfit for productive work. The application of science prevents famines and plagues, and lowers death rates—only to populate the earth beyond the reach of established systems of cultural or governmental control. Science has made war more terrible and more destructive. Much of this has not been done deliberately, but it has been done. And since scientists are necessarily men of some intelligence, they might have been expected to be alert to these consequences.

It is not surprising to encounter the proposal that science should be abandoned, at least for the time being. This solution appeals especially to those who are fitted by temperament to other ways of life. Some relief might be obtained if we could divert mankind into a revival of the arts or religion or even of that petty quarreling which we now look back upon as a life of peace. Such a program resembles the decision of the citizens of Samuel Butler's *Erewhon*, where the instruments and products of science were put into museum̪—as vestiges of a stage in the evolution of human culture which did not survive. But not everyone is willing to defend a position of stubborn "not knowing." There is no virtue in ignorance for its own sake. Unfortunately we cannot stand still: to bring scientific research to an end now would mean a return to famine and pestilence and the exhausting labors of a slave culture.

SCIENCE AS A CORRECTIVE

Another solution is more appealing to the modern mind. It may not be science which is wrong but only its application. The methods of science have been enormously successful wherever they have been tried. Let us then apply them to human affairs. We need not retreat in those sectors where science has already advanced. It is necessary only to bring our understanding of human nature up to the same point. Indeed, this may well be our only hope. If we can observe human behavior carefully from an objective point of view and come to understand it for what it is, we may be able to adopt a more sensible course of action. The need for establishing some such balance is now widely felt, and those who are able to control the direction of science are acting accordingly. It is understood that there is no point in furthering a science of nature unless it includes a sizable science of human nature, because only in that case will the results be wisely used. It is possible that science has come to the rescue and that order will eventually be achieved in the field of human affairs.

THE THREAT TO FREEDOM

There is one difficulty, however. The application of science to human behavior is not so simple as it seems. Most of those who advocate it are simply looking for "the facts." To them science is little more than careful observation. They want to evaluate human behavior as it really is rather than as it appears to be through ignorance or prejudice, and then to make effective decisions and move on rapidly to a happier world. But the way in which science has been applied in other fields shows that something more is involved. Science is not concerned just with "getting the facts," after which one may act with greater wisdom in an unscientific fashion. Science supplies its own wisdom. It leads to a new conception of a subject matter, a new way of thinking about that part of the world to which it has addressed itself. If we are to enjoy the advantages of science in the field of human affairs, we must be prepared to adopt the working model of behavior to which a science will inevitably lead. But very few of those who advocate the application of scientific method to current problems are willing to go that far.

Science is more than the mere description of events as they occur. It is an attempt to discover order, to show that certain events stand in lawful relations to other events. No practical technology can be based upon science until such relations have been discovered. But order is not only a possible end product; it is a working assumption which must be adopted at the very start. We cannot apply the methods of science to a subject matter which is assumed to move about capriciously. Science not only describes, it predicts. It deals not only with the past but with the future. Nor is prediction the last word: to the extent that relevant conditions can be altered, or otherwise controlled, the future can be controlled. If we are to use the methods of science in the field of human affairs, we must assume that behavior is lawful and determined. We must expect to discover that what a man does is the result of specifiable conditions and that once these conditions have been discovered, we can anticipate and to some extent determine his actions.

This possibility is offensive to many people. It is opposed to a tradition of long standing which regards man as a free agent, whose behavior is the product, not of specifiable antecedent conditions, but of spontaneous inner changes of course. Prevailing philosophies of human nature recognize an internal "will" which has the power of interfering with causal relationships and which makes the prediction and control of behavior impossible. To suggest that we abandon this view is to threaten many cherished beliefs—to undermine what appears to be a stimulating and productive conception of human nature. The alternative point of view insists upon recognizing coercive forces in human conduct which we may prefer to disregard. It challenges our aspirations, either worldly or otherworldly. Regardless of how much we stand to gain from supposing that human behavior is the proper subject matter of a science, no one who is a product of Western civilization can do so without a struggle. We simply do not want such a science.

Conflicts of this sort are not unknown in the history of science. When Aesop's lion was shown a painting in which a man was depicted killing a lion, he commented contemptuously, "The artist was obviously a man." Primitive beliefs about man and his place in nature are usually flattering. It has been the unfortunate responsibility of science to paint more realistic pictures. The Copernican theory of the solar system displaced man from his pre-eminent position at the center of things. Today we accept this theory without emotion, but originally it met with enormous resistance. Darwin challenged a practice of segregation in which man set himself firmly apart from the animals, and the bitter struggle which arose is not yet ended. But though Darwin put man in his biological place, he did not deny him a possible position as master. Special faculties or a special capacity for spontaneous, creative action might have emerged in the process of evolution. When that distinction is now questioned, a new threat arises.

There are many ways of hedging on the theoretical issue. It may be insisted that a science of human behavior is impossible, that behavior has certain essential features which forever keep it beyond the pale of science. But although this argument may dissuade many people from further inquiry, it is not likely to have any effect upon those who are willing to try and see. Another objection frequently offered is that science is appropriate up to a certain point, but that there must always remain an area in which one can act only on faith or with respect to a "value judgment": science may tell us *how* to deal with human behavior, but just *what* is to be done must be decided in an essentially nonscientific way. Or it may be argued that there is another kind of science which is compatible with doctrines of personal freedom. For example, the social sciences are sometimes said to be fundamentally different from the natural sciences and not concerned with the same kinds of lawfulness. Prediction and control may be forsworn in favor of "interpretation" or some other species of understanding. But the kinds of intellectual activities exemplified by value judgments or by intuition or interpretation have never been set forth clearly, nor have they yet shown any capacity to work a change in our present predicament.

THE PRACTICAL ISSUE

Our current practices do not represent any well-defined theoretical position. They are, in fact, thoroughly confused. At times we appear to regard a man's behavior as spontaneous and responsible. At other times we recognize that inner determination is at least not complete, that the individual is not always to be held to account. We have not been able to reject the slowly accumulating evidence that circumstances beyond the individual are relevant. We sometimes exonerate a man by pointing to "extenuating circumstances." We no longer blame the uneducated for their ignorance or call the unemployed lazy. We no longer hold children wholly accountable for their delinquencies. "Ignorance of the law" is no longer wholly inexcusable: "Father, forgive them; for they know not what they do." The insane have long since been cleared of responsibility for their condition, and the kinds of neurotic or psychotic behavior to which we now apply this extenuation are multiplying.

But we have not gone all the way. We regard the common man as the product of his environment; yet we reserve the right to give personal credit to great men for their achievements. (At the same time we take a certain delight in proving that part of the output of even such men is due to the "influence" of other men or to some trivial circumstance in their personal history.) We want to believe that right-minded men are moved by valid principles even though we are willing to regard wrong-minded men as victims of erroneous propaganda. Backward peoples may be the fault of a poor culture, but we want to regard the elite as something more than the product of a good culture. Though we observe that Moslem children in general become Moslems while Christian children in general become Christians, we are not willing to accept an accident of birth as a basis for belief. We dismiss those who disagree with us as victims of ignorance, but we regard the promotion of our own religious beliefs as something more than the arrangement of a particular environment.

All of this suggests that we are in transition. We have not wholly abandoned the traditional philosophy of human nature; at the same time we are far from adopting a scientific point of view without reservation. We have accepted the assumption of determinism in part; yet we allow our sympathies, our first allegiances, and our personal aspirations to rise to the defense of the traditional view. We are currently engaged in a sort of patchwork in which new facts and methods are assembled in accordance with traditional theories.

If this were a theoretical issue only, we would have no cause for alarm; but theories affect practices. A scientific conception of human behavior dictates one practice, a philosophy of personal freedom another. Confusion in theory means confusion in practice. The present unhappy condition of the world may in large measure be traced to our vacillation. The principal issues in dispute between nations, both in peaceful assembly and on the battlefield, are intimately concerned with the problem of human freedom and control. Totalitarianism or democracy, the state or the individual, planned society or laissez-faire, the impression of cultures upon alien peoples, economic determinism, individual initiative, propaganda, education, ideological warfare—all concern the fundamental nature of human behavior. We shall almost certainly remain ineffective in solving these problems until we adopt a consistent point of view.

We cannot really evaluate the issue until we understand the alternatives. The traditional view of human nature in Western culture is well known. The conception of a free, responsible individual is embedded in our language and pervades our practices, codes, and beliefs. Given an example of human behavior, most people can describe it immediately in terms of such a conception. The practice is so natural that it is seldom examined. A scientific formulation, on the other hand, is new and strange. Very few people have any notion of the extent to which a science of human behavior is indeed possible. In what way can the behavior of the individual or of groups of individuals be predicted and controlled? What are laws of behavior like? What over-all conception of the human organism as a behaving system emerges? It is only when we have answered these questions, at least in a preliminary fashion, that we may consider the implications of a science of human behavior with respect to either a theory of human nature or the management of human affairs.

CHAPTER II

A SCIENCE OF BEHAVIOR

The immediate tangible results of science make it easier to appraise than philosophy, poetry, art, or theology. As George Sarton has pointed out, science is unique in showing a cumulative progress. Newton explained his tremendous achievements by saying that he stood on the shoulders of giants. All scientists, whether giants or not, enable those who follow them to begin a little further along. This is not necessarily true elsewhere. Our contemporary writers, artists, and philosophers are not appreciably more effective than those of the golden age of Greece, yet the average high-school student understands much more of nature than the greatest of Greek scientists. A comparison of the effectiveness of Greek and modern science is scarcely worth making.

It is clear, then, that science "has something." It is a unique intellectual process which yields remarkable results. The danger is that its astonishing accomplishments may conceal its true nature. This is especially important when we extend the methods of science to a new field. The basic characteristics of science are not restricted to any particular subject matter. When we study physics, chemistry, or biology, we study organized accumulations of information. These are not science itself but the products of science. We may not be able

11

to use much of this material when we enter new territory. Nor should we allow ourselves to become enamored of instruments of research. We tend to think of the scientist in his observatory or laboratory, with his telescopes, microscopes, and cyclotrons. Instruments give us a dramatic picture of science in action. But although science could not have gone very far without the devices which improve our contact with the surrounding world, and although any advanced science would be helpless without them, they are not science itself. We should not be disturbed if familiar instruments are lacking in a new field. Nor is science to be identified with precise measurement or mathematical calculation. It is better to be exact than inexact, and much of modern science would be impossible without quantitative observations and without the mathematical tools needed to convert its reports into more general statements; but we may measure or be mathematical without being scientific at all, just as we may be scientific in an elementary way without these aids.

SOME IMPORTANT CHARACTERISTICS OF SCIENCE

Science is first of all a set of attitudes. It is a disposition to deal with the facts rather than with what someone has said about them. Rejection of authority was the theme of the revival of learning, when men dedicated themselves to the study of "nature, not books." Science rejects even its own authorities when they interfere with the observation of nature.

Science is a willingness to accept facts even when they are opposed to wishes. Thoughtful men have perhaps always known that we are likely to see things as we want to see them instead of as they are, but thanks to Sigmund Freud we are today much more clearly aware of "wishful thinking." The opposite of wishful thinking is intellectual honesty—an extremely important possession of the successful scientist. Scientists are by nature no more honest than other men but, as Bridgman has pointed out, the practice of science puts an exceptionally high premium on honesty. It is characteristic of science that any lack of honesty quickly brings disaster. Consider, for example, a scientist who conducts research to test a theory for which he is already well known. The result may confirm his theory, contradict it, or leave it in doubt. In spite of any inclination to the contrary, he must report a contradiction just as readily as a confirmation. If he does not, someone else will—in a matter of weeks or months or at most a few years—and this will be more damaging to his prestige than if he himself had reported it. Where right and wrong are not so easily or so quickly established, there is no similar pressure. In the long run, the issue is not so much one of personal prestige as of effective procedure. Scientists have simply found that being honest —with oneself as much as with others—is essential to progress. Experiments do not always come out as one expects, but the facts must stand and the expectations fall. The subject matter, not the scientist, knows best. The same practical consequences have created the scientific atmosphere in which statements are constantly submitted to check, where nothing is put above a precise description of the facts, and where facts are accepted no matter how distasteful their momentary consequences.

Scientists have also discovered the value of remaining without an answer until a satisfactory one can be found. This is a difficult lesson. It takes considerable training to avoid premature conclusions, to refrain from making statements on insufficient evidence, and to avoid explanations which are pure invention. Yet the history of science has demonstrated again and again the advantage of these practices.

Science is, of course, more than a set of attitudes. It is a search for order, for uniformities, for lawful relations among the events in nature. It begins, as we all begin, by observing single episodes, but it quickly passes on to the general rule, to scientific law. Something very much like the order expressed in a scientific law appears in our behavior at an early age. We learn the rough geometry of the space in which we move. We learn the "laws of motion" as we move about, or push and pull objects, or throw and catch them. If we could not find some uniformity in the world, our conduct would remain haphazard and ineffective. Science sharpens and supplements this experience by demonstrating more and more relations among events and by demonstrating them more and more precisely. As Ernst Mach showed in tracing the history of the science of mechanics, the earliest laws of science were probably the rules used by craftsmen and artisans in training apprentices. The rules saved time because the experienced craftsman could teach an apprentice a variety of details in a single formula. By learning a rule the apprentice could deal with particular cases as they arose.

In a later stage science advances from the collection of rules or laws to larger systematic arrangements. Not only does it make statements about the world, it makes statements about statements. It sets up a "model" of its subject matter, which helps to generate new rules very much as the rules themselves generate new practices in dealing with single cases. A science may not reach this stage for some time.

The scientific "system," like the law, is designed to enable us to handle a subject matter more efficiently. What we call the scientific conception of a thing is not passive knowledge. Science is not concerned with contemplation. When we have discovered the laws which govern a part of the world about us, and when we have organized these laws into a system, we are then ready to deal effectively with that part of the world. By predicting the occurrence of an event we are able to prepare for it. By arranging conditions in ways specified by the laws of a system, we not only predict, we control: we "cause" an event to occur or to assume certain characteristics.

BEHAVIOR AS A SCIENTIFIC SUBJECT MATTER

Behavior is not one of those subject matters which become accessible only with the invention of an instrument such as the telescope or microscope. We all know thousands of facts about behavior. Actually there is no subject matter with which we could be better acquainted, for we are always in the presence of at least one behaving organism. But this familiarity is something of a disadvantage, for it means that we have probably jumped to conclusions which will not be supported by the cautious methods of science. Even though we have observed behavior for many years, we are not necessarily able, without help, to express useful uniformities or lawful relations. We may show considerable skill in making plausible guesses about what our friends and acquaintances will do under various circumstances or what we ourselves will do. We may make plausible generalizations about the conduct of people in general. But very few of these will survive careful analysis. A great deal of unlearning generally takes place in our early contact with a science of behavior.

Behavior is a difficult subject matter, not because it is inaccessible, but because it is extremely complex. Since it is a process, rather than a thing, it cannot easily be held still for observation. It is changing, fluid, and evanescent, and for this reason it makes great technical demands upon the ingenuity and energy of the scientist. But there is nothing essentially insoluble about the problems which arise from this fact.

Several kinds of statements about behavior are commonly made. When we tell an anecdote or pass along a bit of gossip, we report a *single event*—what someone did upon such and such an occasion: "She slammed the door and walked off without a word." Our report is a small bit of history. History itself is often nothing more than similar reporting on a broad scale. The biographer often confines himself to a series of episodes in the life of his subject. The case history, which occupies an important place in several fields of psychology, is a kind of biography which is also concerned mainly with what a particular person did at particular times and places: "When she was eleven, Mary went to live with her maiden aunt in Winchester." Novels and short stories may be thought of as veiled biography or history, since the ingredients of even a highly fanciful work of fiction are somehow or other taken from life. The narrative reporting of the behavior of people at particular times and places is also part of the sciences of archeology, ethnology, sociology, and anthropology.

These accounts have their uses. They broaden the experience of those who have not had firsthand access to similar data. But they are only the beginnings of a science. No matter how accurate or quantitative it may be, the report of the single case is only a preliminary step. The next step is the discovery of some sort of *uniformity*. When we tell an anecdote to support an argument, or report a case history to exemplify a principle, we imply a general rule, no matter how vaguely it may be expressed. The historian is seldom content with mere narration. He reports his facts to support a theory—of cycles, trends, or patterns of history. In doing so he passes from the single instance to the rule. When a biographer traces the influence of an early event upon a man's later life, he transcends simple reporting and asserts, no matter how hesitantly, that one thing has caused another. Fable and allegory are more than storytelling if they imply some kind of uniformity in human behavior, as they generally do. Our preference for "consistency of character" and our rejection of implausible coincidences in literature show that we expect lawfulness. The "manners" and "customs" of the sociologist and anthropologist report the *general* behavior of groups of people.

A vague sense of order emerges from any sustained observation of human behavior. Any plausible guess about what a friend will do or say in a given circumstance is a prediction based upon some such uniformity. If a reasonable order was not discoverable, we could scarcely be effective in dealing with human affairs. The methods of science are designed to clarify these uniformities and make them explicit. The techniques of field study of the anthropologist and social psychologist, the procedures of the psychological clinic, and the controlled experimental methods of the laboratory are all directed toward this end, as are also the mathematical and logical tools of science.

Many people interested in human behavior do not feel the need for the standards of proof characteristic of an exact science; the uniformities in behavior are "obvious" without them. At the same time, they are reluctant to accept the conclusions toward which such proof inescapably points if they do not "sense" the uniformity themselves. But these idiosyncrasies are a costly luxury. We need not defend the methods of science in their application to behavior. The experimental and mathematical techniques used in discovering and expressing uniformities are the common property of science in general. Almost every discipline has contributed to this pool of resources, and all disciplines borrow from it. The advantages are well established.

SOME OBJECTIONS TO A SCIENCE OF BEHAVIOR

The report of a single event raises no theoretical problems and comes into no conflict with philosophies of human behavior. The scientific laws or systems which express uniformities are likely to conflict with theory because they claim the same territory. When a science of behavior reaches the point of dealing with lawful relationships, it meets the resistance of those who give their allegiance to prescientific or extrascientific conceptions. The resistance does not always take the form of an overt rejection of science. It may be transmuted into claims of limitations, often expressed in highly scientific terms.

It has sometimes been pointed out, for example, that physical science has been unable to maintain its philosophy of determinism, particularly at the subatomic level. The Principle of Indeterminacy states that there are circumstances under which the physicist cannot put himself in possession of all relevant information: if he chooses to observe one event, he must relinquish the possibility of observing another. In our present state of knowledge, certain events therefore appear to be unpredictable. It does not follow that these events are free or capricious. Since human behavior is enormously complex and the human organism is of limited dimensions, many acts may involve processes to which the Principle of Indeterminacy applies. It does not follow that human behavior is free, but only that it may be beyond the range of a predictive or controlling science. Most students of behavior, however, would be willing to settle for the degree of prediction and control achieved by the physical sciences in spite of this limitation. A final answer to the problem of lawfulness is to be sought, not in the limits of any hypothetical mechanism within the organism, but in our ability to demonstrate lawfulness in the behavior of the organism as a whole.

A similar objection has a logical flavor. It is contended that reason cannot comprehend itself or—in somewhat more substantial terms— that the behavior required in understanding one's own behavior must be something beyond the behavior which is understood. It is true that knowledge is limited by the limitations of the knowing organism.

The number of things in the world which might be known certainly exceeds the number of possible different states in all possible knowers. But the laws and systems of science are designed to make a knowledge of particular events unimportant. It is by no means necessary that one man should understand all the facts in a given field, but only that he should understand all the *kinds* of facts. We have no reason to suppose that the human intellect is incapable of formulating or comprehending the basic principles of human behavior—certainly not until we have a clearer notion of what those principles are.

The assumption that behavior is a lawful scientific datum sometimes meets with another objection. Science is concerned with the general, but the behavior of the individual is necessarily unique. The "case history" has a richness and flavor which are in decided contrast with general principles. It is easy to convince oneself that there are two distinct worlds and that one is beyond the reach of science. This distinction is not peculiar to the study of behavior. It can always be made in the early stages of any science, when it is not clear what we may deduce from a general principle with respect to a particular case. What the science of physics has to say about the world is dull and colorless to the beginning student when compared with his daily experience, but he later discovers that it is actually a more incisive account of even the single instance. When we wish to deal effectively with the single instance, we turn to science for help. The argument will lose cogency as a science of behavior progresses and as the implications of its general laws become clear. A comparable argument against the possibility of a science of medicine has already lost its significance. In *War and Peace*, Tolstoy wrote of the illness of a favorite character as follows:

Doctors came to see Natasha, both separately and in consultation. They said a great deal in French, in German, and in Latin. They criticised one another, and prescribed the most diverse remedies for all the diseases they were familiar with. But it never occurred to one of them to make the simple reflection that they could not understand the disease from which Natasha was suffering, as no single disease can be fully understood in a living person; for every living person has his individual peculiarities and always has his own peculiar, new, complex complaints unknown to medicine—not a disease of the lungs, of the kidneys, of the skin, of the heart, and so on, as described in medical books, but a disease that consists of one out of the innumerable combinations of ailments of those organs.

Tolstoy was justified in calling every sickness a unique event. Every action of the individual is unique, as well as every event in physics and chemistry. But his objection to a science of medicine in terms of uniqueness was unwarranted. The argument was plausible enough at the time; no one could then contradict him by supplying the necessary general principles. But a great deal has happened in medical science since then, and today few people would care to argue that a disease cannot be described in general terms or that a single case cannot be discussed by referring to factors common to many cases. The intuitive wisdom of the old-style diagnostician has been largely replaced by the analytical procedures of the clinic, just as a scientific analysis of behavior will eventually replace the personal interpretation of unique instances.

A similar argument is leveled at the use of statistics in a science of behavior. A prediction of what the *average* individual will do is often of little or no value in dealing with a particular individual. The actuarial tables of life-insurance companies are of no value to a physician in predicting the death or survival of a particular patient. This issue is still alive in the physical sciences, where it is associated with the concepts of causality and probability. It is seldom that the science of physics deals with the behavior of individual molecules, atoms, or subatomic particles. When it is occasionally called upon to do so, all the problems of the particular event arise. In general a science is helpful in dealing with the individual only insofar as its laws refer to individuals. A science of behavior which concerns only the behavior of groups is not likely to be of help in our understanding of the particular case. But a science may also deal with the behavior of the individual, and its success in doing so must be evaluated in terms of its achievements rather than any a priori contentions.

The extraordinary complexity of behavior is sometimes held to be an added source of difficulty. Even though behavior may be lawful, it may be too complex to be dealt with in terms of law. Sir Oliver Lodge once asserted that "though an astronomer can calculate the orbit of a planet or comet or even a meteor, although a physicist can deal with the structure of atoms, and a chemist with their possible combinations, neither a biologist nor any scientific man can calculate the orbit of a common fly." This is a statement about the limitations of scientists or about their aspirations, not about the suitability of a subject matter. Even so, it is wrong. It may be said with some assurance that if no one has calculated the orbit of a fly, it is only because no one has been sufficiently interested in doing so. The tropistic movements of many insects are now fairly well understood, but the instrumentation needed to record the flight of a fly and to give an account of all the conditions affecting it would cost more than the importance of the subject justifies. There is, therefore, no reason to conclude, as the author does, that "an incalculable element of self-determination thus makes its appearance quite low down the animal scale." Self-determination does not follow from complexity. Difficulty in calculating the orbit of the fly does not prove capriciousness, though it may make it impossible to prove anything else. The problems imposed by the complexity of a subject matter must be dealt with as they arise. Apparently hopeless cases often become manageable in time. It is only recently that any sort of lawful account of the weather has been possible. We often succeed in reducing complexity to a reasonable degree by simplifying conditions in the laboratory; but where this is impossible, a statistical analysis may be used to achieve an inferior, but in many ways acceptable, prediction. Certainly no one is prepared to say now what a science of behavior can or cannot accomplish eventually. Advance estimates of the limits of science have generally proved inaccurate. The issue is in the long run pragmatic: we cannot tell until we have tried.

Still another objection to the use of scientific method in the study of human behavior is that behavior is an anomalous subject matter because a prediction made about it may alter it. If we tell a friend that he is going to buy a particular kind of car, he may react to our prediction by buying a different kind. The same effect has been used to explain the failures of public opinion polls. In the presidential election of 1948 it was confidently predicted that a majority of the voters would vote for a candidate who, as it turned out, lost the election. It has been asserted that the electorate reacted to the prediction in a contrary way and that the published prediction therefore had an effect upon the predicted event. But it is by no means necessary that a prediction of behavior be permitted to affect the behaving individual. There may have been practical reasons why the results of the poll in question could not be withheld until after the election, but this would not be the case in a purely scientific endeavor.

There are other ways in which observer and observed interact. Study distorts the thing studied. But there is no special problem here peculiar to human behavior. It is now accepted as a general principle in scientific method that it is necessary to interfere in some degree with any phenomenon in the act of observing it. A scientist may have an effect upon behavior in the act of observing or analyzing it, and he must certainly take this effect into account. But behavior may also be observed with a minimum of interaction between subject and scientist, and this is the case with which one naturally tries to begin.

A final objection deals with the practical application of a scientific analysis. Even if we assume that behavior is lawful and that the methods of science will reveal the rules which govern it, we may be unable to make any technological use of these rules unless certain conditions can be brought under control. In the laboratory many conditions are simplified and irrelevant conditions often eliminated. But of what value are laboratory studies if we must predict and control behavior where a comparable simplification is impossible? It is true that we can gain control over behavior only insofar as we can control the factors responsible for it. What a scientific study does is to enable us to make optimal use of the control we possess. The laboratory simplification reveals the relevance of factors which we might otherwise overlook.

We cannot avoid the problems raised by a science of behavior by simply denying that the necessary conditions can be controlled. In actual fact there is a considerable degree of control over many relevant conditions. In penal institutions and military organizations the control is extensive. We control the environment of the human organism in the nursery and in institutions which care for those to whom the conditions of the nursery remain necessary in later life.

Fairly extensive control of conditions relevant to human behavior is maintained in industry in the form of wages and conditions of work, in schools in the form of grades and conditions of work, in commerce by anyone in possession of goods or money, by governmental agencies through the police and military, in the psychological clinic through the consent of the controllee, and so on. A degree of effective control, not so easily identified, rests in the hands of entertainers, writers, advertisers, and propagandists. These controls, which are often all too evident in their practical application, are more than sufficient to permit us to extend the results of a laboratory science to the inter-pretation of human behavior in daily affairs—for either theoretical or practical purposes. Since a science of behavior will continue to increase the effective use of this control, it is now more important than ever to understand the processes involved and to prepare ourselves for the problems which will certainly arise.

CHAPTER III

WHY ORGANISMS BEHAVE

The terms "cause" and "effect" are no longer widely used in science. They have been associated with so many theories of the structure and operation of the universe that they mean more than scientists want to say. The terms which replace them, however, refer to the same factual core. A "cause" becomes a "change in an independent variable" and an "effect" a "change in a dependent variable." The old "cause-and-effect connection" becomes a "functional relation." The new terms do not suggest *how* a cause causes its effect; they merely assert that different events tend to occur together in a certain order. This is important, but it is not crucial. There is no particular danger in using "cause" and "effect" in an informal discussion if we are always ready to substitute their more exact counterparts.

We are concerned, then, with the causes of human behavior. We want to know why men behave as they do. Any condition or event which can be shown to have an effect upon behavior must be taken into account. By discovering and analyzing these causes we can predict behavior; to the extent that we can manipulate them, we can control behavior.

There is a curious inconsistency in the zeal with which the doctrine of personal freedom has been defended, because men have always been fascinated by the search for causes. The spontaneity of human behavior is apparently no more challenging than its "why and wherefore." So strong is the urge to explain behavior that men have been led to anticipate legitimate scientific inquiry and to construct highly implausible theories of causation. This practice is not unusual in the history of science. The study of any subject begins in the realm of superstition. The fanciful explanation precedes the valid. Astronomy began as astrology; chemistry as alchemy. The field of behavior has had, and still has, its astrologers and alchemists. A long history of prescientific explanation furnishes us with a fantastic array of causes which have no function other than to supply spurious answers to questions which must otherwise go unanswered in the early stages of a science.

SOME POPULAR "CAUSES" OF BEHAVIOR

Any conspicuous event which coincides with human behavior is likely to be seized upon as a cause. The position of the planets at the birth of the individual is an example. Usually astrologers do not try to predict specific actions from such causes, but when they tell us that a man will be impetuous, careless, or thoughtful, we must suppose that specific actions are assumed to be affected. Numerology finds a different set of causes—for example, in the numbers which compose the street address of the individual or in the number of letters in his name. Millions of people turn to these spurious causes every year in their desperate need to understand human behavior and to deal with it effectively.

The predictions of astrologers, numerologists, and the like are usually so vague that they cannot be confirmed or disproved properly. Failures are easily overlooked, while an occasional chance hit is dramatic enough to maintain the behavior of the devotee in considerable strength. Certain valid relations which resemble such superstitions offer spurious support. For example, some characteristics of behavior can be traced to the season in which a man is born (though not to the position of the planets at his birth), as well as to climatic conditions due in part to the position of the earth in the solar system or to events in the sun. Effects of this sort, when properly validated, must not be overlooked. They do not, of course, justify astrology.

Another common practice is to explain behavior in terms of the structure of the individual. The proportions of the body, the shape of the head, the color of the eyes, skin, or hair, the marks on the palms of the hands, and the features of the face have all been said to determine what a man will do. The "jovial fat man," Cassius with his "lean and hungry look," and thousands of other characters or types thoroughly embedded in our language affect our practices in dealing with human behavior. A specific act may never be predicted from physique, but different types of personality imply predispositions to behave in different ways, so that specific acts are presumed to be affected. This practice resembles the mistake we all make when we expect someone who looks like an old acquaintance to behave like him also. When a "type" is once established, it survives in everyday use because the predictions which are made with it, like those of astrology, are vague, and occasional hits may be startling. Spurious support is also offered by many valid relations between behavior and body type. Studies of the physiques of men and women predisposed to different sorts of disorders have from time to time held the attention of students of behavior. The most recent classification of body structure—the somatotyping of W. H. Sheldon—has already been applied to the prediction of temperament and of various forms of delinquency. Valid relations between behavior and body type must, of course, be taken into account in a science of behavior, but these should not be confused with the relations invoked in the uncritical practice of the layman.

Even when a correlation between behavior and body structure is demonstrated, it is not always clear which is the cause of which. Even if it could be shown by proper statistical methods that fat men are especially likely to be jolly, it still would not follow that the physique causes the temperament. Fat people are at a disadvantage in many ways, and they may develop jolly behavior as a special competitive technique. Jolly people may grow fat because they are free of the emotional disturbances which drive other people to overwork or to neglect their diet or their health. Fat people may be jolly because they have been successful in satisfying their needs through excessive eating. Where the feature of physique can be modified, then, we must ask whether the behavior or the feature comes first.

When we find, or think we have found, that conspicuous physical features explain part of a man's behavior, it is tempting to suppose that inconspicuous features explain other parts. This is implied in the assertion that a man shows certain behavior because he was "born that way." To object to this is not to argue that behavior is never determined by hereditary factors. Behavior requires a behaving organism which is the product of a genetic process. Gross differences in the behavior of different species show that the genetic constitution, whether observed in the body structure of the individual or inferred from a genetic history, is important. But the doctrine of "being born that way" has little to do with demonstrated facts. It is usually an appeal to ignorance. "Heredity," as the layman uses the term, is a fictional explanation of the behavior attributed to it.

Even when it can be shown that some aspect of behavior is due to season of birth, gross body type, or genetic constitution, the fact is of limited use. It may help us in predicting behavior, but it is of little value in an experimental analysis or in practical control because such a condition cannot be manipulated after the individual has been conceived. The most that can be said is that the knowledge of the genetic factor may enable us to make better use of other causes. If we know that an individual has certain inherent limitations, we may use our techniques of control more intelligently, but we cannot alter the genetic factor.

The practical deficiencies of programs involving causes of this sort may explain some of the vehemence with which they are commonly debated. Many people study human behavior because they want to do something about it—they want to make men happier, more efficient and productive, less aggressive, and so on. To these people, inherited determiners—as epitomized in various "racial types" —appear to be insurmountable barriers, since they leave no course of action but the slow and doubtful program of eugenics. The evidence for genetic traits is therefore closely scrutinized, and any indication that it is weak or inconsistent is received with enthusiasm. But the practical issue must not be allowed to interfere in determining the extent to which behavioral dispositions are inherited. The matter is not so crucial as is often supposed, for we shall see that there are other types of causes available for those who want quicker results.

INNER "CAUSES"

Every science has at some time or other looked for causes of action inside the things it has studied. Sometimes the practice has proved useful, sometimes it has not. There is nothing wrong with an inner explanation as such, but events which are located inside a system are likely to be difficult to observe. For this reason we are encouraged to assign properties to them without justification. Worse still, we can invent causes of this sort without fear of contradiction. The motion of a rolling stone was once attributed to its *vis viva*. The chemical properties of bodies were thought to be derived from the *principles* or *essences* of which they were composed. Combustion was explained by the *phlogiston* inside the combustible object. Wounds healed and bodies grew well because of a *vis medicatrix*. It has been especially tempting to attribute the behavior of a living organism to the behavior of an inner agent, as the following examples may suggest.

Neural causes. The layman uses the nervous system as a ready explanation of behavior. The English language contains hundreds of expressions which imply such a causal relationship. At the end of a long trial we read that the jury shows signs of *brain fag*, that the *nerves* of the accused are *on edge*, that the wife of the accused is on the verge of a *nervous breakdown*, and that his lawyer is generally thought to have lacked the *brains* needed to stand up to the prosecution. Obviously, no direct observations have been made of the nervous systems of any of these people. Their "brains" and "nerves" have been invented on the spur of the moment to lend substance to what might otherwise seem a superficial account of their behavior.

The sciences of neurology and physiology have not divested themselves entirely of a similar practice. Since techniques for observing the electrical and chemical processes in nervous tissue had not yet been developed, early information about the nervous system was limited to its gross anatomy. Neural processes could only be inferred from the behavior which was said to result from them. Such inferences were legitimate enough as scientific theories, but they could not justifiably be used to explain the very behavior upon which they were based. The hypotheses of the early physiologist may have been sounder than those of the layman, but until independent evidence could be obtained, they were no more satisfactory as explanations of behavior. Direct information about many of the chemical and electrical processes in the nervous system is now available. Statements about the nervous system are no longer necessarily inferential or fictional. But there is still a measure of circularity in much physiological explanation, even in the writings of specialists. In World War I a familiar disorder was called "shell shock." Disturbances in behavior were explained by arguing that violent explosions had damaged the structure of the nervous system, though no direct evidence of such damage was available. In World War II the same disorder was classified as "neuropsychiatric." The prefix seems to show a continuing unwillingness to abandon explanations in terms of hypothetical neural damage.

Eventually a science of the nervous system based upon direct observation rather than inference will describe the neural states and events which immediately precede instances of behavior. We shall know the precise neurological conditions which immediately precede, say, the response, "No, thank you." These events in turn will be found to be preceded by other neurological events, and these in turn by others. This series will lead us back to events outside the nervous system and, eventually, outside the organism. In the chapters which follow we shall consider external events of this sort in some detail. We shall then be better able to evaluate the place of neurological explanations of behavior. However, we may note here that we do not have and may never have this sort of neurological information at the moment it is needed in order to predict a specific instance of behavior. It is even more unlikely that we shall be able to alter the nervous system directly in order to set up the antecedent conditions of a particular instance. The causes to be sought in the nervous system are, therefore, of limited usefulness in the prediction and control of specific behavior.

Psychic inner causes. An even more common practice is to explain behavior in terms of an inner agent which lacks physical dimensions and is called "mental" or "psychic." The purest form of the psychic explanation is seen in the animism of primitive peoples. From the immobility of the body after death it is inferred that a spirit responsible for movement has departed. The *enthusiastic* person is, as the etymology of the word implies, energized by a "god within." It is only a modest refinement to attribute every feature of the behavior of the physical organism to a corresponding feature of the "mind" or of some inner "personality." The inner man is regarded as driving the body very much as the man at the steering wheel drives a car. The inner man wills an action, the outer executes it. The inner loses his appetite, the outer stops eating. The inner man wants and the outer gets. The inner has the impulse which the outer obeys.

It is not the layman alone who resorts to these practices, for many reputable psychologists use a similar dualistic system of explanation. The inner man is sometimes personified clearly, as when delinquent behavior is attributed to a "disordered personality," or he may be dealt with in fragments, as when behavior is attributed to mental processes, faculties, and traits. Since the inner man does not occupy space, he may be multiplied at will. It has been argued that a single physical organism is controlled by several psychic agents and that its behavior is the resultant of their several wills. The Freudian concepts of the ego, superego, and id are often used in this way. They are frequently regarded as nonsubstantial creatures, often in violent conflict, whose defeats or victories lead to the adjusted or maladjusted behavior of the physical organism in which they reside.

Direct observation of the mind comparable with the observation of the nervous system has not proved feasible. It is true that many people believe that they observe their "mental states" just as the physiologist observes neural events, but another interpretation of what they observe is possible, as we shall see in Chapter XVII. Introspective psychology no longer pretends to supply direct information about events which are the causal antecedents, rather than the mere accompaniments, of behavior. It defines its "subjective" events in ways which strip them of any usefulness in a causal analysis. The events appealed to in early mentalistic explanations of behavior have remained beyond the reach of observation. Freud insisted upon this by emphasizing the role of the unconscious—a frank recognition that important mental processes are not directly observable. The Freudian literature supplies many examples of behavior from which unconscious wishes, impulses, instincts, and emotions are inferred. Unconscious thought-processes have also been used to explain intellectual achievements. Though the mathematician may feel that he knows "how he thinks," he is often unable to give a coherent account of the mental processes leading to the solution of a specific problem. But any mental event which is unconscious is necessarily inferential, and the explanation is therefore not based upon independent observations of a valid cause.

The fictional nature of this form of inner cause is shown by the ease with which the mental process is discovered to have just the properties needed to account for the behavior. When a professor turns up in the wrong classroom or gives the wrong lecture, it is because his *mind* is, at least for the moment, *absent*. If he forgets to give a reading assignment, it is because it has slipped his *mind* (a hint from the class may re*mind* him of it). He begins to tell an old joke but pauses for a moment, and it is evident to everyone that he is trying to make up his *mind* whether or not he has already used the joke that term. His lectures grow more tedious with the years, and questions from the class confuse him more and more, because his *mind* is failing. What he says is often disorganized because his *ideas* are confused. He is occasionally unnecessarily emphatic because of the force of his *ideas*. When he repeats himself, it is because he has an *idée fixe*; and when he repeats what others have said, it is because he borrows his *ideas*. Upon occasion there is nothing in what he says because he lacks *ideas*. In all this it is obvious that the mind and the ideas, together with their special characteristics, are being invented on the spot to provide spurious explanations. A science of behavior can hope to gain very little from so cavalier a practice. Since mental or psychic events are asserted to lack the dimensions of physical science, we have an additional reason for rejecting them.

Conceptual inner causes. The commonest inner causes have no specific dimensions at all, either neurological or psychic. When we say that a man eats *because* he is hungry, smokes a great deal *because* he has the tobacco habit, fights *because* of the instinct of pugnacity, behaves brilliantly *because* of his intelligence, or plays the piano well *because* of his musical ability, we seem to be referring to causes. But on analysis these phrases prove to be merely redundant descriptions. A single set of facts is described by the two statements: "He eats" and "He is hungry." A single set of facts is described by the two state-ments: "He smokes a great deal" and "He has the smoking habit." A single set of facts is described by the two statements: "He plays well" and "He has musical ability." The practice of explaining one statement in terms of the other is dangerous because it suggests that we have found the cause and therefore need search no further. More-over, such terms as "hunger," "habit," and "intelligence" convert what are essentially the properties of a process or relation into what appear to be things. Thus we are unprepared for the properties even-tually to be discovered in the behavior itself and continue to look for something which may not exist.

THE VARIABLES OF WHICH BEHAVIOR IS A FUNCTION

The practice of looking inside the organism for an explanation of behavior has tended to obscure the variables which are immediately available for a scientific analysis. These variables lie outside the organism, in its immediate environment and in its environmental history. They have a physical status to which the usual techniques of science are adapted, and they make it possible to explain behavior as other subjects are explained in science. These independent vari-ables are of many sorts and their relations to behavior are often subtle and complex, but we cannot hope to give an adequate account of behavior without analyzing them.

Consider the act of drinking a glass of water. This is not likely to be an important bit of behavior in anyone's life, but it supplies a convenient example. We may describe the topography of the behavior in such a way that a given instance may be identified quite accurately by any qualified observer. Suppose now we bring someone into a room and place a glass of water before him. Will he drink? There appear to be only two possibilities: either he will or he will not. But we speak of the *chances* that he will drink, and this notion may be refined for scientific use. What we want to evaluate is the *probability* that he will drink. This may range from virtual certainty that drinking will occur to virtual certainty that it will not. The very considerable problem of how to measure such a probability will be discussed later. For the moment, we are interested in how the probability may be increased or decreased.

Everyday experience suggests several possibilities, and laboratory and clinical observations have added others. It is decidedly not true that a horse may be led to water but cannot be made to drink. By arranging a history of severe deprivation we could be "absolutely sure" that drinking would occur. In the same way we may be sure that the glass of water in our experiment will be drunk. Although we are not likely to arrange them experimentally, deprivations of the necessary magnitude sometimes occur outside the laboratory. We may obtain an effect similar to that of deprivation by speeding up the excretion of water. For example, we may induce sweating by raising the temperature of the room or by forcing heavy exercise, or we may increase the excretion of urine by mixing salt or urea in food taken prior to the experiment. It is also well known that loss of blood, as on a battlefield, sharply increases the probability of drinking. On the other hand, we may set the probability at virtually zero by inducing or forcing our subject to drink a large quantity of water before the experiment.

If we are to predict whether or not our subject will drink, we must know as much as possible about these variables. If we are to induce him to drink, we must be able to manipulate them. In both cases, moreover, either for accurate prediction or control, we must investigate the effect of each variable quantitatively with the methods and techniques of a laboratory science.

Other variables may, of course, affect the result. Our subject may be "afraid" that something has been added to the water as a practical joke or for experimental purposes. He may even "suspect" that the water has been poisoned. He may have grown up in a culture in which water is drunk only when no one is watching. He may refuse to drink simply to prove that we cannot predict or control his behavior. These possibilities do not disprove the relations between drinking and the variables listed in the preceding paragraphs; they simply remind us that other variables may have to be taken into account. We must know the history of our subject with respect to the behavior of drinking water, and if we cannot eliminate social factors from the situation, then we must know the history of his personal relations to people resembling the experimenter. Adequate prediction in any science requires information about all relevant variables, and the control of a subject matter for practical purposes makes the same demands.

Other types of "explanation" do not permit us to dispense with these requirements or to fulfill them in any easier way. It is of no help to be told that our subject will drink provided he was born under a particular sign of the zodiac which shows a preoccupation with water or provided he is the lean and thirsty type or was, in short, "born thirsty." Explanations in terms of inner states or agents, however, may require some further comment. To what extent is it helpful to be told, "He drinks because he is thirsty"? If to be thirsty means nothing more than to have a tendency to drink, this is mere redundancy. If it means that he drinks because of a state of thirst, an inner causal event is invoked. If this state is purely inferential—if no dimensions are assigned to it which would make direct observation possible—it cannot serve as an explanation. But if it has physiological or psychic properties, what role can it play in a science of behavior?

The physiologist may point out that several ways of raising the probability of drinking have a common effect: they increase the concentration of solutions in the body. Through some mechanism not yet well understood, this may bring about a corresponding change in the nervous system which in turn makes drinking more probable. In the same way, it may be argued that all these operations make the organism "feel thirsty" or "want a drink" and that such a psychic state also acts upon the nervous system in some unexplained way to induce drinking. In each case we have a causal chain consisting of three links: (1) an operation performed upon the organism from without—for example, water deprivation; (2) an inner condition—for example, physiological or psychic thirst; and (3) a kind of behavior—for example, drinking. Independent information about the second link would obviously permit us to predict the third without recourse to the first. It would be a preferred type of variable because it would be non-historic; the first link may lie in the past history of the organism, but the second is a current condition. Direct information about the second link is, however, seldom, if ever, available. Sometimes we infer the second link from the third: an animal is judged to be thirsty if it drinks. In that case, the explanation is spurious. Sometimes we infer the second link from the first: an animal is said to be thirsty if it has not drunk for a long time. In that case, we obviously cannot dispense with the prior history.

The second link is useless in the *control* of behavior unless we can manipulate it. At the moment, we have no way of directly altering neural processes at appropriate moments in the life of a behaving organism, nor has any way been discovered to alter a psychic process. We usually set up the second link through the first: we make an animal thirsty, in either the physiological or the psychic sense, by depriving it of water, feeding it salt, and so on. In that case, the second link obviously does not permit us to dispense with the first. Even if some new technical discovery were to enable us to set up or change the second link directly, we should still have to deal with those enormous areas in which human behavior is controlled through manipulation of the first link. A technique of operating upon the second link would increase our control of behavior, but the techniques which have already been developed would still remain to be analyzed.

The most objectionable practice is to follow the causal sequence back only as far as a hypothetical second link. This is a serious handicap both in a theoretical science and in the practical control of behavior. It is no help to be told that to get an organism to drink we are simply to "make it thirsty" unless we are also told how this is to be done. When we have obtained the necessary prescription for thirst, the whole proposal is more complex than it need be. Similarly, when an example of maladjusted behavior is explained by saying that the individual is "suffering from anxiety," we have still to be told the cause of the anxiety. But the external conditions which are then invoked could have been directly related to the maladjusted behavior. Again, when we are told that a man stole a loaf of bread because "he was hungry," we have still to learn of the external conditions responsible for the "hunger." These conditions would have sufficed to explain the theft.

The objection to inner states is not that they do not exist, but that they are not relevant in a functional analysis. We cannot account for the behavior of any system while staying wholly inside it; eventually we must turn to forces operating upon the organism from without. Unless there is a weak spot in our causal chain so that the second link is not lawfully determined by the first, or the third by the second, then the first and third links must be lawfully related. If we must always go back beyond the second link for prediction and control, we may avoid many tiresome and exhausting digressions by examining the third link as a function of the first. Valid information about the second link may throw light upon this relationship but can in no way alter it.

A FUNCTIONAL ANALYSIS

The external variables of which behavior is a function provide for what may be called a causal or functional analysis. We undertake to predict and control the behavior of the individual organism. This is our "dependent variable"—the effect for which we are to find the cause. Our "independent variables"—the causes of behavior—are the external conditions of which behavior is a function. Relations between the two—the "cause-and-effect relationships" in behavior—are the laws of a science. A synthesis of these laws expressed in quantitative terms yields a comprehensive picture of the organism as a behaving system.

This must be done within the bounds of a natural science. We cannot assume that behavior has any peculiar properties which require unique methods or special kinds of knowledge. It is often argued that an act is not so important as the "intent" which lies behind it, or that it can be described only in terms of what it "means" to the behaving individual or to others whom it may affect. If statements of this sort are useful for scientific purposes, they must be based upon observable events, and we may confine ourselves to such events exclusively in a functional analysis. We shall see later that although such terms as "meaning" and "intent" appear to refer to properties of behavior, they usually conceal references to independent variables. This is also true of "aggressive," "friendly," "disorganized," "intelligent," and other terms which appear to describe properties of behavior but in reality refer to its controlling relations.

The independent variables must also be described in physical terms. An effort is often made to avoid the labor of analyzing a physical situation by guessing what it "means" to an organism or by distinguishing between the physical world and a psychological world of "experience." This practice also reflects a confusion between dependent and independent variables. The events affecting an organism must be capable of description in the language of physical science. It is sometimes argued that certain "social forces" or the "influences" of culture or tradition are exceptions. But we cannot appeal to entities of this sort without explaining how they can affect both the scientist and the individual under observation. The physical events which must then be appealed to in such an explanation will supply us with alternative material suitable for a physical analysis.

By confining ourselves to these observable events, we gain a considerable advantage, not only in theory, but in practice. A "social force" is no more useful in manipulating behavior than an inner state of hunger, anxiety, or skepticism. Just as we must trace these inner events to the manipulable variables of which they are said to be functions before we may put them to practical use, so we must identify the physical events through which a "social force" is said to affect the organism before we can manipulate it for purposes of control. In dealing with the directly observable data we need not refer to either the inner state or the outer force.

The material to be analyzed in a science of behavior comes from many sources:

(1) _Our casual observations_ are not to be dismissed entirely. They are especially important in the early stages of investigation. Generalizations based upon them, even without explicit analysis, supply useful hunches for further study.

(2) In _controlled field observation,_ as exemplified by some of the methods of anthropology, the data are sampled more carefully and conclusions stated more explicitly than in casual observation. Standard instruments and practices increase the accuracy and uniformity of field observation.

(3) _Clinical observation_ has supplied extensive material. Standard practices in interviewing and testing bring out behavior which may be easily measured, summarized, and compared with the behavior of others. Although it usually emphasizes the disorders which bring people to clinics, the clinical sample is often unusually interesting and of special value when the exceptional condition points up an important feature of behavior.

(4) Extensive observations of behavior have been made under more rigidly controlled conditions in _industrial, military, and other institutional research._ This work often differs from field or clinical observation in its greater use of the experimental method.

(5) _Laboratory studies of human behavior_ provide especially useful material. The experimental method includes the use of instruments which improve our contact with behavior and with the variables of which it is a function. Recording devices enable us to observe behavior over long periods of time, and accurate recording and measurement make effective quantitative analysis possible. The most important feature of the laboratory method is the deliberate manipulation of variables: the importance of a given condition is determined by changing it in a controlled fashion and observing the result.

Current experimental research on human behavior is sometimes not so comprehensive as one might wish. Not all behavioral processes are easy to set up in the laboratory, and precision of measurement is sometimes obtained only at the price of unreality in conditions. Those who are primarily concerned with the everyday life of the individual are often impatient with these artificialities, but insofar as relevant relationships can be brought under experimental control, the laboratory offers the best chance of obtaining the quantitative results needed in a scientific analysis.

(6) The extensive results of *laboratory studies of the behavior of animals below the human level* are also available. The use of this material often meets with the objection that there is an essential gap between man and the other animals, and that the results of one cannot be extrapolated to the other. To insist upon this discontinuity at the beginning of a scientific investigation is to beg the question. Human behavior is distinguished by its complexity, its variety, and its greater accomplishments, but the basic processes are not therefore necessarily different. Science advances from the simple to the complex; it is constantly concerned with whether the processes and laws discovered at one stage are adequate for the next. It would be rash to assert at this point that there is no essential difference between human behavior and the behavior of lower species; but until an attempt has been made to deal with both in the same terms, it would be equally rash to assert that there is. A discussion of human embryology makes considerable use of research on the embryos of chicks, pigs, and other animals. Treatises on digestion, respiration, circulation, endocrine secretion, and other physiological processes deal with rats, hamsters, rabbits, and so on, even though the interest is primarily in human beings. The study of behavior has much to gain from the same practice.

We study the behavior of animals because it is simpler. Basic processes are revealed more easily and can be recorded over longer periods of time. Our observations are not complicated by the social relation between subject and experimenter. Conditions may be better controlled. We may arrange genetic histories to control certain variables and special life histories to control others—for example, if we are interested in how an organism learns to see, we can raise an animal in darkness until the experiment is begun. We are also able to control current circumstances to an extent not easily realized in human behavior—for example, we can vary states of deprivation over wide ranges. These are advantages which should not be dismissed on the a priori contention that human behavior is inevitably set apart as a separate field.

ANALYSIS OF THE DATA

There are many ways in which data concerning human behavior may be formulated and analyzed. The plan to be followed in the present book may be summarized as follows:

Section II contains a classification of the variables of which behavior is a function and a survey of the processes through which behavior changes when any of these variables is changed.

Section III provides a broader view of the organism as a whole. Certain complex arrangements are considered in which one part of the behavior of the individual alters some of the variables of which other parts are a function. These are the activities which we describe by saying, for example, that the individual "controls himself," "thinks out a solution to a problem," or "is aware of his own behavior."

Section IV analyzes the interaction of two or more individuals in a social system. One person is often part of the environment of another, and this relationship is usually reciprocal. An adequate account of a given social episode explains the behavior of all participants.

Section V analyzes various techniques through which human behavior is controlled in government, religion, psychotherapy, economics, and education. In each of these fields the individual and the controlling agency constitute a social system in the sense of Section IV.

Section VI surveys the total culture as a social environment, and discusses the general problem of the control of human behavior.

The plan is obviously an example of extrapolation from the simple to the complex. No principle is used in any part of the book which is not discussed in Section II. The basic relations and processes of this section are derived from data obtained under conditions which most closely approximate those of an exact science. In Section V complex examples of human behavior drawn from certain established fields of knowledge are analyzed in terms of these simpler processes and relations. The procedure is often referred to as reductionism. If our interest is primarily in the basic process, we turn to material of this sort as a test of the adequacy of our analysis. If, on the other hand, our interest is primarily in the complex case, we still have much to gain in utilizing a formulation which has been worked out under more favorable circumstances. For example, historical and comparative facts about particular governments, religions, economic systems, and so on have led to certain traditional conceptions of the behaving individual, but each of these conceptions has been appropriate only to the particular set of facts from which it was derived. This restriction has proved to be a serious handicap. The conception of man which has emerged from the study of economic phenomena has been of little or no value in the field of psychotherapy. The conception of human behavior developed for use in the field of education has had little or nothing in common with that employed in explaining governmental or legal practices. A basic functional analysis, however, provides us with a common formulation of the behavior of the individual with which we may discuss issues in all these areas and eventually consider the effect upon the individual of the social environment as a whole.

Certain limitations in dealing with historical and comparative facts may be acknowledged. We are often asked to explain more about human behavior than is asked of other scientists in their respective fields. How can we account for the behavior of literary or historical figures? Why could Hamlet not kill his uncle to avenge his father's murder? What were Robespierre's real motives? How can we explain Leonardo's paintings? Was Hitler paranoid? Questions of this sort have tremendous human interest. Many psychologists, historians, biographers, and literary critics have tried to answer them, and there is therefore a strong presumption that they can be answered. But this may not be so. We lack the information needed for a functional analysis. Although we can make plausible *guesses* as to the variables which operated in each case, we cannot be sure. Comparable questions in the fields of physics, chemistry, and biology can be answered only in the same limited way. Why did the old Campanile in the Piazza San Marco collapse into a heap of brick? The physicist may know how mortar was made at the time the Campanile was built, in what atmospheric conditions it disintegrated, and so on; yet, although he may give a *plausible* explanation, he cannot with certainty account for the collapse. The meteorologist cannot account for the flood which bore Noah's ark to Mount Ararat, nor the biologist for the extinction of the dodo. The specialist may give the most plausible explanation of a historical event, but if necessary information is lacking, he cannot give a rigorous account within the framework of a science. The scientist is under greater pressure to answer comparable questions about human behavior. He may feel, or be forced to accept, the challenge of those who pretend to give valid answers. Moreover, his answers may be of great practical importance. The clinician, for example, may be urged to interpret the behavior of his patient when the available information is far from adequate, and it is often more difficult for him than for the physicist to say that he does not know.

The commonest objection to a thoroughgoing functional analysis is simply that it cannot be carried out, but the only evidence for this is that it has not yet been carried out. We need not be discouraged by this fact. Human behavior is perhaps the most difficult subject to which the methods of science have ever been applied, and it is only natural that substantial progress should be slow. It is encouraging to reflect, however, that science seldom moves at an even pace. Progress is sometimes arrested for a long time merely because the particular aspect of a subject which is emphasized proves unimportant and unproductive. A slight change in point of attack is enough to bring rapid progress. Chemistry made great strides when it was recognized that the weights of combining substances, rather than their qualities or essences, were the important things to study. The science of mechanics moved forward rapidly when it was discovered that distances and times were more important for certain purposes than size, shape, color, hardness, and weight. Many different properties or aspects of behavior have been studied for many years with varying degrees of success. A functional analysis which specifies behavior as a dependent variable and proposes to account for it in terms of observable and manipulable physical conditions is of recent advent.

It has already shown itself to be a promising formulation, and until it has been put to the test, we have no reason to prophesy failure.

Such a plan cannot be carried out at a superficial level. The engineer who builds a bridge successfully has more than a casual impression of the nature of his materials, and the time has come when we must admit that we cannot solve the important problems in human affairs with a general "philosophy of human behavior." The present analysis requires considerable attention to detail. Numerical data have been avoided, but an attempt has been made to define each behavioral process rigorously and to exemplify each process or relation with specific instances. If the reader is to participate fully in the broader interpretations of the later sections, he will have to examine these definitions and to observe the distinctions which they make between different processes. This may be hard work, but there is no help for it. Human behavior is at least as difficult a subject matter as the chemistry of organic materials or the structure of the atom. Superficial sketches of what science has to say about any subject are often entertaining, but they are never adequate for effective action. If we are to further our understanding of human behavior and to improve our practices of control, we must be prepared for the kind of rigorous thinking which science requires.

THE ANALYSIS OF
BEHAVIOR

CHAPTER IV

REFLEXES AND CONDITIONED REFLEXES

MAN A MACHINE

Behavior is a primary characteristic of living things. We almost identify it with life itself. Anything which moves is likely to be called alive—especially when the movement has direction or acts to alter the environment. Movement adds verisimilitude to any model of an organism. The puppet comes to life when it moves, and idols which move or breathe smoke are especially awe-inspiring. Robots and other mechanical creatures entertain us just because they move. And there is significance in the etymology of the *animated* cartoon.

Machines seem alive simply because they are in motion. The fascination of the steam shovel is legendary. Less familiar machines may actually be frightening. We may feel that it is only primitive people who mistake them for living creatures today, but at one time they were unfamiliar to everyone. When Wordsworth and Coleridge once passed a steam engine, Wordsworth observed that it was scarcely possible to divest oneself of the impression that it had life and volition. "Yes," said Coleridge, "it is a giant with one idea."

A mechanical toy which imitated human behavior led to the theory of what we now call reflex action. In the first part of the seventeenth century certain moving figures were commonly installed in private and public gardens as sources of amusement. They were operated hydraulically. A young lady walking through a garden might step upon a small concealed platform. This would open a valve, water would flow into a piston, and a threatening figure would swing out from the bushes to frighten her. René Descartes knew how these figures worked, and he also knew how much they seemed like living creatures. He considered the possibility that the hydraulic system which explained the one might also explain the other. A muscle swells when it moves a limb—perhaps it is being inflated by a fluid coming along the nerves from the brain. The nerves which stretch from the surface of the body into the brain may be the strings which open the valves.

Descartes did not assert that the human organism always operates in this way. He favored the explanation in the case of animals, but he reserved a sphere of action for the "rational soul"—perhaps under religious pressure. It was not long before the additional step was taken, however, which produced the full-fledged doctrine of "man a machine." The doctrine did not owe its popularity to its plausibility —there was no reliable support for Descartes's theory—but rather to its shocking metaphysical and theoretical implications.

Since that time two things have happened: machines have become more lifelike, and living organisms have been found to be more like machines. Contemporary machines are not only more complex, they are deliberately designed to operate in ways which resemble human behavior. "Almost human" contrivances are a common part of our daily experience. Doors see us coming and open to receive us. Elevators remember our commands and stop at the correct floor. Mechanical hands lift imperfect items off a conveyor belt. Others write messages of fair legibility. Mechanical or electric calculators solve equations too difficult or too time-consuming for human mathematicians. Man has, in short, created the machine in his own image. And as a result, the living organism has lost some of its uniqueness. We are much less awed by machines than our ancestors were and less likely to endow the giant with even one idea. At the same time, we have discovered more about how the living organism works and are better able to see its machine-like properties.

REFLEX ACTION

Descartes had taken an important step in suggesting that some of the spontaneity of living creatures was only apparent and that behavior could sometimes be traced to action from without. The first clear-cut evidence that he had correctly surmised the possibility of external control came two centuries later in the discovery that the tail of a salamander would move when part of it was touched or pierced, even though the tail had been severed from the body. Facts of this sort are now familiar, and we have long since adapted our beliefs to take them into account. At the time the discovery was made, however, it created great excitement. It was felt to be a serious threat to prevailing theories of the inner agents responsible for behavior. If the movement of the amputated tail could be controlled by external forces, was its behavior when attached to the salamander of a different nature? If not, what about the inner causes which had hitherto been used to account for it? It was seriously suggested as an answer that the "will" must be coexistent with the body and that some part of it must invest any amputated part. But the fact remained that an external event had been identified which could be substituted, as in Descartes's daring hypothesis, for the inner explanation.

The external agent came to be called a *stimulus*. The behavior controlled by it came to be called a *response*. Together they comprised what was called a *reflex*—on the theory that the disturbance caused by the stimulus passed to the central nervous system and was "reflected" back to the muscles. It was soon found that similar external causes could be demonstrated in the behavior of larger portions of the organism—for example, in the body of a frog, cat, or dog in which the spinal cord had been severed at the neck. Reflexes including parts of the brain were soon added, and it is now common knowledge that in the intact organism many kinds of stimulation lead to almost inevitable reactions of the same reflex nature. Many characteristics of the relation have been studied quantitatively. The time which elapses between stimulus and response (the "latency") has been measured precisely. The magnitude of the response has been studied as a function of the intensity of the stimulus. Other conditions of the organism have been found to be important in completing the account—for example, a reflex may be "fatigued" by repeated rapid elicitation.

The reflex was at first closely identified with hypothetical neural events in the so-called "reflex arc." A surgical division of the organism was a necessary entering wedge, for it provided a simple and dramatic method of analyzing behavior. But surgical analysis became unnecessary as soon as the principle of the stimulus was understood and as soon as techniques were discovered for handling complex arrangements of variables in other ways. By eliminating some conditions, holding others constant, and varying others in an orderly manner, basic lawful relations could be established without dissection and could be expressed without neurological theories.

The extension of the principle of the reflex to include behavior involving more and more of the organism was made only in the face of vigorous opposition. The reflex nature of the spinal animal was challenged by proponents of a "spinal will." The evidence they offered in support of a residual inner cause consisted of behavior which apparently could not be explained wholly in terms of stimuli. When higher parts of the nervous system were added, and when the principle was eventually extended to the intact organism, the same pattern of resistance was followed. But arguments for spontaneity, and for the explanatory entities which spontaneity seems to demand, are of such form that they must retreat before the accumulating facts. Spontaneity is negative evidence; it points to the weakness of a current scientific explanation, but does not in itself prove an alternative version. By its very nature, spontaneity must yield ground as a scientific analysis is able to advance. As more and more of the behavior of the organism has come to be explained in terms of stimuli, the territory held by inner explanations has been reduced. The "will" has retreated up the spinal cord, through the lower and then the higher parts of the brain, and finally, with the conditioned reflex, has escaped through the front of the head. At each stage, some part of the control of the organism has passed from a hypothetical inner entity to the external environment.

THE RANGE OF REFLEX ACTION

A certain part of behavior, then, is elicited by stimuli, and our prediction of that behavior is especially precise. When we flash a light in the eye of a normal subject, the pupil contracts. When he sips lemon juice, saliva is secreted. When we raise the temperature of the room to a certain point, the small blood vessels in his skin enlarge, blood is brought nearer to the skin, and he "turns red." We use these relations for many practical purposes. When it is necessary to induce vomiting, we employ a suitable stimulus—an irritating fluid or a finger in the throat. The actress who must cry real tears resorts to onion juice on her handkerchief.

As these examples suggest, many reflex responses are executed by the "smooth muscles" (for example, the muscles in the walls of the blood vessels) and the glands. These structures are particularly concerned with the internal economy of the organism. They are most likely to be of interest in a science of behavior in the emotional reflexes to be discussed in Chapter X. Other reflexes use the "striped muscles" which move the skeletal frame of the organism. The "knee jerk" and other reflexes which the physician uses for diagnostic purposes are examples. We maintain our posture, either when standing still or moving about, with the aid of a complex network of such reflexes.

In spite of the importance suggested by these examples, it is still true that if we were to assemble all the behavior which falls into the pattern of the simple reflex, we should have only a very small fraction of the total behavior of the organism. This is not what early investigators in the field expected. We now see that the principle of the reflex was overworked. The exhilarating discovery of the stimulus led to exaggerated claims. It is neither plausible nor expedient to conceive of the organism as a complicated jack-in-the-box with a long list of tricks, each of which may be evoked by pressing the proper button. The greater part of the behavior of the intact organism is not under this primitive sort of stimulus control. The environment affects the organism in many ways which are not conveniently classed as "stimuli," and even in the field of stimulation only a small part of the forces acting upon the organism elicit responses in the invariable manner of reflex action. To ignore the principle of the reflex entirely, however, would be equally unwarranted.

CONDITIONED REFLEXES

The reflex became a more important instrument of analysis when it was shown that novel relations between stimuli and responses could be established during the lifetime of the individual by a process first studied by the Russian physiologist, I. P. Pavlov. H. G. Wells once compared Pavlov with another of his distinguished contemporaries, George Bernard Shaw. He considered the relative importance to society of the quiet laboratory worker and the skillful propagandist and expressed his opinion by describing a hypothetical situation: if these two men were drowning and only one life preserver were available, he would throw it to Pavlov.

Evidently Shaw was not pleased, and, after what appears to have been a hasty glance at Pavlov's work, retaliated. His book, *The Adventures of the Black Girl in Her Search for God*, describes a girl's experiences in a jungle of ideas. The jungle is inhabited by many prophets, some of them ancient and some as modern as an "elderly myop" who bears a close resemblance to Pavlov. The black girl encounters Pavlov just after she has been frightened by a fearful roar from the prophet Micah. She pulls herself up in her flight and exclaims:

"What am I running away from? I'm not afraid of that dear noisy old man."

"Your fears and hopes are only fancies" said a voice close to her, proceeding from a very shortsighted elderly man in spectacles who was sitting on a gnarled log. "In running away you were acting on a conditioned reflex. It is quite simple. Having lived among lions you have from your childhood associated the sound of a roar with deadly danger. Hence your precipitate flight when that superstitious old jackass brayed at you. This remarkable discovery cost me twenty-five years of devoted research, during which I cut out the brains of innumerable dogs, and observed their spittle by making holes in their cheeks for them to salivate through instead of through their tongues. The whole scientific world is prostrate at my feet in admiration of this colossal achievement and gratitude for the light it has shed on the great problems of human conduct."

"Why didn't you ask me?" said the black girl. "I could have told you in twenty-five seconds without hurting those poor dogs."

"Your ignorance and presumption are unspeakable" said the old myop. "The fact was known of course to every child; but it had never been proved experimentally in the laboratory; and therefore it was not scientifically known at all. It reached me as an unskilled conjecture: I handed it on as science. Have you ever performed an experiment, may I ask?"

"Several" said the black girl. "I will perform one now. Do you know what you are sitting on?"

"I am sitting on a log grey with age, and covered with an uncomfortable rugged bark" said the myop.

"You are mistaken" said the black girl. "You are sitting on a sleeping crocodile."

With a yell which Micah himself might have envied, the myop rose and fled frantically to a neighboring tree, up which he climbed catlike with an agility which in so elderly a gentleman was quite superhuman.

"Come down" said the black girl. "You ought to know that crocodiles are only to be found near rivers. I was only trying an experiment. Come down."

But the elderly myop is unable to come down and begs the girl to perform another experiment.

"I will" said the black girl. "There is a tree snake smelling at the back of your neck."

The myop was on the ground in a jiffy.[1]

It is clear that Shaw has caught the spirit of a science of behavior. The black girl is undeniably a good behavioral engineer. In two very neat examples of stimulus control she induces clearcut responses in the elderly myop. (His behavior does not, as we shall see later, exemplify the simple reflex, conditioned or otherwise.) But if the author is fully aware of the potentialities of the practical control of behavior, he is not so strong on theory, for the passage exemplifies a common misunderstanding regarding the achievement of science.

[1] George Bernard Shaw, *The Adventures of the Black Girl in Her Search for God*, copyright, 1933, by George Bernard Shaw, and used by permission of the Public Trustee and the Society of Authors.

The facts of science are seldom entirely unknown "to every child." A child who can catch a ball knows a good deal about trajectories. It may take science a long time to calculate the position of a ball at a given moment any more exactly than the child must "calculate" it in order to catch it. When Count Rumford, while boring cannon in the military arsenal in Munich, demonstrated that he could produce any desired amount of heat without combustion, he changed the course of scientific thinking about the causes of heat; but he had discovered nothing which was not already known to the savage who kindles a fire with a spinning stick or the man who warms his hands on a frosty morning by rubbing them together vigorously.

The difference between an unskilled conjecture and a scientific fact is not simply a difference in evidence. It had long been known that a child might cry before it was hurt or that a fox might salivate upon seeing a bunch of grapes. What Pavlov added can be understood most clearly by considering his history. Originally he was interested in the process of digestion, and he studied the conditions under which digestive juices were secreted. Various chemical substances in the mouth or in the stomach resulted in the reflex action of the digestive glands. Pavlov's work was sufficiently outstanding to receive the Nobel Prize, but it was by no means complete. He was handicapped by a certain unexplained secretion. Although food in the mouth might elicit a flow of saliva, saliva often flowed abundantly when the mouth was empty. We should not be surprised to learn that this was called "psychic secretion." It was explained in terms which "any child could understand." Perhaps the dog was "thinking about food." Perhaps the sight of the experimenter preparing for the next experiment "reminded" the dog of the food it had received in earlier experiments. But these explanations did nothing to bring the unpredictable salivation within the compass of a rigorous account of digestion.

Pavlov's first step was to control conditions so that "psychic secretion" largely disappeared. He designed a room in which contact between dog and experimenter was reduced to a minimum. The room was made as free as possible from incidental stimuli. The dog could not hear the sound of footsteps in neighboring rooms or smell accidental odors in the ventilating system. Pavlov then built up a "psychic secretion" step by step. In place of the complicated stimulus of an experimenter preparing a syringe or filling a dish with food, he introduced controllable stimuli which could be easily described in physical terms. In place of the accidental occasions upon which stimulation might precede or accompany food, Pavlov arranged precise schedules in which controllable stimuli and food were presented in certain orders. Without influencing the dog in any other way, he could sound a tone and insert food into the dog's mouth. In this way he was able to show that the tone *acquired* its ability to elicit secretion, and he was also able to follow the process through which this came about. Once in possession of these facts, he could then give a satisfactory account of all secretion. He had replaced the "psyche" of psychic secretion with certain objective facts in the recent history of the organism.

The process of conditioning, as Pavlov reported it in his book *Conditioned Reflexes*, is a process of *stimulus substitution*. A previously neutral stimulus acquires the power to elicit a response which was originally elicited by another stimulus. The change occurs when the neutral stimulus is followed or "reinforced" by the effective stimulus. Pavlov studied the effect of the interval of time elapsing between stimulus and reinforcement. He investigated the extent to which various properties of stimuli could acquire control. He also studied the converse process, in which the conditioned stimulus loses its power to evoke the response when it is no longer reinforced —a process which he called "extinction."

The quantitative properties which he discovered are by no means "known to every child." And they are important. The most efficient use of conditioned reflexes in the practical control of behavior often requires quantitative information. A satisfactory theory makes the same demands. In dispossessing explanatory fictions, for example, we cannot be sure that an event of the sort implied by "psychic secretion" is not occasionally responsible until we can predict the exact amount of secretion at any given time. Only a quantitative description will make sure that there is no additional mental process in which the dog "associates the sound of the tone with the idea of food" or in which it salivates because it "expects" food to appear. Pavlov could dispense with concepts of this sort only when he could give a complete quantitative account of salivation in terms of the stimulus, the response, and the history of conditioning.

Pavlov, as a physiologist, was interested in how the stimulus was converted into neural processes and in how other processes carried the effect through the nervous system to the muscles and glands. The subtitle of his book is *An Investigation of the Physiological Activity of the Cerebral Cortex*. The "physiological activity" was inferential. We may suppose, however, that comparable processes will eventually be described in terms appropriate to neural events. Such a description will fill in the temporal and spatial gaps between an earlier history of conditioning and its current result. The additional account will be important in the integration of scientific knowledge but will not make the relation between stimulus and response any more lawful or any more useful in prediction and control. Pavlov's achievement was the discovery, not of neural processes, but of important quantitative relations which permit us, regardless of neurological hypotheses, to give a direct account of behavior in the field of the conditioned reflex.

THE "SURVIVAL VALUE" OF REFLEXES

Reflexes are intimately concerned with the well-being of the organism. The process of digestion could not go on if certain secretions did not begin to flow when certain types of food entered the stomach. Reflex behavior which involves the external environment is important in the same way. If a dog's foot is injured when it steps on a sharp object, it is important that the leg should be flexed rapidly so that the foot is withdrawn. The so-called "flexion reflex" brings this about. Similarly, it is important that dust blown into the eye should be washed out by a profuse secretion of tears, that an object suddenly moved toward the eyes should be warded off by blinking, and so on. Such biological advantages "explain" reflexes in an evolutionary sense: individuals who are most likely to behave in these ways are presumably most likely to survive and to pass on the adaptive characteristic to their offspring.

The process of conditioning also has survival value. Since the environment changes from generation to generation, particularly the external rather than the internal environment, appropriate reflex responses cannot always develop as inherited mechanisms. Thus an organism may be prepared to secrete saliva when certain chemical substances stimulate its mouth, but it cannot gain the added advantage of salivating before food is actually tasted unless the physical appearance of foodstuffs remains the same from environment to environment and from time to time. Since nature cannot foresee, so to speak, that an object with a particular appearance will be edible, the evolutionary process can only provide a mechanism by which the individual will *acquire* responses to particular features of a given environment after they have been encountered. Where inherited behaviour leaves off, the inherited modifiability of the process of conditioning takes over.

It does not follow that every conditioned reflex has survival value. The mechanism may go wrong. Certain pairs of stimuli, such as the appearance and taste of food, may occur together in a consistent way which is important to the organism throughout its life, but we have no guarantee that conditioning will not occur when the pairing of stimuli is temporary or accidental. Many "superstitions" exemplify conditioned responses arising from accidental contingencies. The behavior is due to an actual pairing of stimuli, but the resulting conditioned reflex is not useful. We call some such reflexes "irrational." A child who has been attacked by a dog may fear all dogs. The visual stimulus supplied by a dog has been paired with the terrifying stimulation of physical attack. But the pairing is not inevitable for all dogs. When the response is later elicited at the sight of a harmless dog, it serves no useful function. It is, nevertheless, due to a process which does prove valuable elsewhere. We all suffer from this miscarriage of the evolutionary process when we make stereotyped responses. Strong behavior appropriate to the sight of someone we dislike violently may be evoked by other people with the same features, wearing the same type of clothes, and so on. Minor effects of the same sort are less troublesome. A nostalgic reaction to a tune which was popular during an old love affair is a conditioned response arising from a nonfunctional pairing of stimuli, but we do not call it superstitious or irrational.

THE RANGE OF CONDITIONED REFLEXES

Although the process of conditioning greatly extends the scope of the eliciting stimulus, it does not bring all the behavior of the organism within such stimulus control. According to the formula of stimulus substitution we must elicit a response before we can condition it. All conditioned reflexes are, therefore, based upon unconditioned reflexes. But we have seen that reflex responses are only a small part of the total behavior of the organism. Conditioning adds new controlling stimuli, but not new responses. In using the principle, therefore, we are not subscribing to a "conditioned-reflex theory" of all behavior.

A fair measure of the range of the conditioned reflex is its use in the practical control of behavior. Reflexes which are concerned with the internal economy of the organism are seldom of practical importance to other people, but an occasion may arise when we are interested in making someone blush or laugh or cry, and we then resort to conditioned or unconditioned stimuli. It is frequently the business of literature to generate behavior in this way. The "tear-jerker" has a literal meaning. More subtle effects are similar: it is important in understanding the effect of a poem to note that conditioned responses may be elicited by such verbal stimuli as "death," "love," "sorrow," and so on, quite apart from the effect of the prose meaning of the poem. The emotional effects of music and painting are largely conditioned.

We also use this process to arrange for the control of behavior at a later date. In patriotic and religious education, for example, emotional responses to flags, insignia, symbols, and rituals are conditioned so that these stimuli will be effective upon future occasions. A commonly proposed "cure" for excessive drinking or smoking consists of adding substances to liquor or tobacco which generate nausea, headaches, and so on. When liquor or tobacco are later seen or tasted, similar responses are evoked as the result of conditioning. They may compete with the behavior of drinking or smoking—as by "taking all the fun out of it." Conditioning of this sort is treating a symptom rather than a cause, but it may make it easier for the patient to stop drinking or smoking for other reasons.

Training a soldier consists in part of conditioning emotional responses. If pictures of the enemy, the enemy's flag, and so on are paired with stories or pictures of atrocities, a suitable aggressive reaction will probably occur at the sight of the enemy. Favorable reactions are generated in somewhat the same way. Responses to delectable foods are easily transferred to other objects. Just as we "dislike" the liquor or tobacco which makes us ill, so we "like" stimuli which accompany delicious food. The successful salesman is likely to buy his customer a drink or take him out to dinner. The salesman is not interested in gastric reactions but in the customer's predisposition to act favorably toward him and his product which, as we shall see later, also follows from the pairing of stimuli. The free lunch at a political rally has a similar effect. So has the stick of gum which the pediatrician gives his young patient. It has been shown experimentally that people come to "like" modern music if they listen to it while eating. When the Jewish child first learns to read, he kisses a page upon which a drop of honey has been placed. The important thing is not that he will later salivate at the sight of a book, but that he will exhibit a predisposition "in favor of" books. The reinforcements which establish predispositions of this sort are not all gastric. As advertisers well know, the responses and attitudes evoked by pretty girls, babies, and pleasant scenes may be transferred to trade names, products, pictures of products, and so on.

We are sometimes interested in generating one emotional response in order to counteract or balance another. The dentist, for example, faces a practical problem in that he must administer painful stimuli. These stand in such relation to the stimuli supplied by the waiting room, the dental chair, the instruments, and the sound of the drill that eventually the latter evoke a variety of emotional reactions. Some of these we characterize roughly as anxiety. A funny picture-book in the waiting room may elicit responses which are incompatible with anxiety and which to some extent cancel it. This momentary effect exemplifies the use of stimuli which have already been conditioned. The "educational" effect of such a book in creating a less unfavorable attitude toward the dentist exemplifies the use of conditioning in the control of behavior. The flowers and music in "funeral homes" have an immediate effect in counteracting the reactions evoked by a dead body, and through the process of conditioning they create a more favorable predisposition in the future toward burial practices.

Eliminating a conditioned response is also a common practical problem. For example, we may want to reduce the fear reactions which have come to be evoked by people, animals, air raids, or military combat. Following the procedures in the conditioned-reflex experiment, we present a conditioned stimulus while omitting the reinforcing stimulus responsible for its effect. A major step in the treatment of stuttering, for example, is to extinguish reactions of anxiety or embarrassment generated by thoughtless persons who have laughed at the stutterer or grown impatient with him. A common technique is to encourage him to talk to anyone he encounters. Functional responses of anxiety and embarrassment are generally conditioned in early childhood. If the adult stutterer is no longer laughed at, the responses may undergo extinction. The therapy consists simply of encouraging the stutterer to talk so that the conditioned stimuli thus automatically generated may occur without reinforcement.

If the conditioned stimulus elicits too strong a response, it may be necessary to present it in graded doses. If a child who has been frightened by a dog is given a small puppy, the similarity between the puppy and the frightening dog is not great enough to elicit a strong conditioned fear response. Any slight response which happens to appear undergoes extinction. As the puppy grows to resemble the dog, extinction proceeds by easy stages. A similar technique is sometimes used in reducing excessive emotional reactions to air raids, combat, and similar traumatic conditions. Extinction is brought about with stimuli which are at first only slightly disturbing—vague noises, faint sirens, or distant sounds of bursting shells. Visual stimuli are presented without their auditory accompaniments in silent moving pictures of actual combat. As extinction occurs, the verisimilitude is increased. Eventually, if the treatment is successful, little or no response is elicited by a full-scale stimulus.

CHAPTER V

OPERANT BEHAVIOR

THE CONSEQUENCES OF BEHAVIOR

Reflexes, conditioned or otherwise, are mainly concerned with the internal physiology of the organism. We are most often interested, however, in behavior which has some effect upon the surrounding world. Such behavior raises most of the practical problems in human affairs and is also of particular theoretical interest because of its special characteristics. The consequences of behavior may "feed back" into the organism. When they do so, they may change the probability that the behavior which produced them will occur again. The English language contains many words, such as "reward" and "punishment," which refer to this effect, but we can get a clear picture of it only through experimental analysis.

LEARNING CURVES

One of the first serious attempts to study the changes brought about by the consequences of behavior was made by E. L. Thorndike in 1898. His experiments arose from a controversy which was then of considerable interest. Darwin, in insisting upon the continuity of species, had questioned the belief that man was unique among the animals in his ability to think. Anecdotes in which lower

59

animals seemed to show the "power of reasoning" were published in great numbers. But when terms which had formerly been applied only to human behavior were thus extended, certain questions arose concerning their meaning. Did the observed facts point to mental processes, or could these apparent evidences of thinking be explained in other ways? Eventually it became clear that the assumption of inner thought-processes was not required. Many years were to pass before the same question was seriously raised concerning human behavior, but Thorndike's experiments and his alternative explanation of reasoning in animals were important steps in that direction.

If a cat is placed in a box from which it can escape only by unlatching a door, it will exhibit many different kinds of behavior, some of which may be effective in opening the door. Thorndike found that when a cat was put into such a box again and again, the behavior which led to escape tended to occur sooner and sooner until eventually escape was as simple and quick as possible. The cat had solved its problem as well as if it were a "reasoning" human being, though perhaps not so speedily. Yet Thorndike observed no "thought-process" and argued that none was needed by way of explanation. He could describe his results simply by saying that a part of the cat's behavior was "stamped in" because it was followed by the opening of the door.

The fact that behavior is stamped in when followed by certain consequences, Thorndike called "The Law of Effect." What he had observed was that certain behavior occurred more and more readily in comparison with other behavior characteristic of the same situation. By noting the successive delays in getting out of the box and plotting them on a graph, he constructed a "learning curve." This early attempt to show a quantitative process in behavior, similar to the processes of physics and biology, was heralded as an important advance. It revealed a process which took place over a considerable period of time and which was not obvious to casual inspection. Thorndike, in short, had made a discovery. Many similar curves have since been recorded and have become the substance of chapters on learning in psychology texts.

Learning curves do not, however, describe the basic process of stamping in. Thorndike's measure—the time taken to escape—involved the elimination of other behavior, and his curve depended upon the number of different things a cat might do in a particular box. It also depended upon the behavior which the experimenter or the apparatus happened to select as "successful" and upon whether this was common or rare in comparison with other behavior evoked in the box. A learning curve obtained in this way might be said to reflect the properties of the latch box rather than of the behavior of the cat. The same is true of many other devices developed for the study of learning. The various mazes through which white rats and other animals learn to run, the "choice boxes" in which animals learn to discriminate between properties or patterns of stimuli, the apparatuses which present sequences of material to be learned in the study of human memory—each of these yields its own type of learning curve.

By averaging many individual cases, we may make these curves as smooth as we like. Moreover, curves obtained under many different circumstances may agree in showing certain general properties. For example, when measured in this way, learning is generally "negatively accelerated"—improvement in performance occurs more and more slowly as the condition is approached in which further improvement is impossible. But it does not follow that negative acceleration is characteristic of the basic process. Suppose, by analogy, we fill a glass jar with gravel which has been so well mixed that pieces of any given size are evenly distributed. We then agitate the jar gently and watch the pieces rearrange themselves. The larger move toward the top, the smaller toward the bottom. This process, too, is negatively accelerated. At first the mixture separates rapidly, but as separation proceeds, the condition in which there will be no further change is approached more and more slowly. Such a curve may be quite smooth and reproducible, but this fact alone is not of any great significance. The curve is the result of certain fundamental processes involving the contact of spheres of different sizes, the resolution of the forces resulting from agitation, and so on, but it is by no means the most direct record of these processes.

Learning curves show how the various kinds of behavior evoked in complex situations are sorted out, emphasized, and reordered. The basic process of the stamping in of a single act brings this change about, but it is not reported directly by the change itself.

OPERANT CONDITIONING

To get at the core of Thorndike's Law of Effect, we need to clarify the notion of "probability of response." This is an extremely important concept; unfortunately, it is also a difficult one. In discussing human behavior, we often refer to "tendencies" or "predispositions" to behave in particular ways. Almost every theory of behavior uses some such term as "excitatory potential," "habit strength," or "determining tendency." But how do we observe a tendency? And how can we measure one?

If a given sample of behavior existed in only two states, in one of which it always occurred and in the other never, we should be almost helpless in following a program of functional analysis. An all-or-none subject matter lends itself only to primitive forms of description. It is a great advantage to suppose instead that the *probability* that a response will occur ranges continuously between these all-or-none extremes. We can then deal with variables which, unlike the eliciting stimulus, do not "cause a given bit of behavior to occur" but simply make the occurrence more probable. We may then proceed to deal, for example, with the combined effect of more than one such variable.

The everyday expressions which carry the notion of probability, tendency, or predisposition describe the frequencies with which bits of behavior occur. We never observe a probability as such. We say that someone is "enthusiastic" about bridge when we observe that he plays bridge often and talks about it often. To be "greatly interested" in music is to play, listen to, and talk about music a good deal. The "inveterate" gambler is one who gambles frequently. The camera "fan" is to be found taking pictures, developing them, and looking at pictures made by himself and others. The "highly sexed" person frequently engages in sexual behavior. The "dipsomaniac" drinks frequently.

In characterizing a man's behavior in terms of frequency, we assume certain standard conditions: he must be able to execute and repeat a given act, and other behavior must not interfere appreciably. We cannot be sure of the extent of a man's interest in music, for example, if he is necessarily busy with other things. When we come to refine the notion of probability of response for scientific use, we find that here, too, our data are frequencies and that the conditions under which they are observed must be specified. The main technical problem in designing a controlled experiment is to provide for the observation and interpretation of frequencies. We eliminate, or at least hold constant, any condition which encourages behavior which competes with the behavior we are to study. An organism is placed in a quiet box where its behavior may be observed through a one-way screen or recorded mechanically. This is by no means an environmental vacuum, for the organism will react to the features of the box in many ways; but its behavior will eventually reach a fairly stable level, against which the frequency of a selected response may be investigated.

To study the process which Thorndike called stamping in, we must have a "consequence." Giving food to a hungry organism will do. We can feed our subject conveniently with a small food tray which is operated electrically. When the tray is first opened, the organism will probably react to it in ways which interfere with the process we plan to observe. Eventually, after being fed from the tray repeatedly, it eats readily, and we are then ready to make this consequence contingent upon behavior and to observe the result.

We select a relatively simple bit of behavior which may be freely and rapidly repeated, and which is easily observed and recorded. If our experimental subject is a pigeon, for example, the behavior of raising the head above a given height is convenient. This may be observed by sighting across the pigeon's head at a scale pinned on the far wall of the box. We first study the height at which the head is normally held and select some line on the scale which is reached only infrequently. Keeping our eye on the scale we then begin to open the food tray very quickly whenever the head rises above the line. If the experiment is conducted according to specifications, the result is invariable: we observe an immediate change in the frequency with which the head crosses the line. We also observe, and this is of some importance theoretically, that higher lines are now being crossed. We may advance almost immediately to a higher line in determining when food is to be presented. In a minute or two, the bird's posture has changed so that the top of the head seldom falls below the line which we first chose.

When we demonstrate the process of stamping in in this relatively simple way, we see that certain common interpretations of Thorndike's experiment are superfluous. The expression "trial-and-error learning," which is frequently associated with the Law of Effect, is clearly out of place here. We are reading something into our observations when we call any upward movement of the head a "trial," and there is no reason to call any movement which does not achieve a specified consequence an "error." Even the term "learning" is misleading. The statement that the bird "learns that it will get food by stretching its neck" is an inaccurate report of what has happened. To say that it has acquired the "habit" of stretching its neck is merely to resort to an explanatory fiction, since our only evidence of the habit is the acquired tendency to perform the act. The barest possible statement of the process is this: we make a given consequence contingent upon certain physical properties of behavior (the upward movement of the head), and the behavior is then observed to increase in frequency.

It is customary to refer to any movement of the organism as a "response." The word is borrowed from the field of reflex action and implies an act which, so to speak, answers a prior event—the stimulus. But we may make an event contingent upon behavior without identifying, or being able to identify, a prior stimulus. We did not alter the environment of the pigeon to *elicit* the upward movement of the head. It is probably impossible to show that any single stimulus invariably precedes this movement. Behavior of this sort may come under the control of stimuli, but the relation is not that of elicitation. The term "response" is therefore not wholly appropriate but is so well established that we shall use it in the following discussion.

A response which has already occurred cannot, of course, be predicted or controlled. We can only predict that *similar* responses will occur in the future. The unit of a predictive science is, therefore, not a response but a <u>class of responses. The word "operant" will be used to describe this class. The term emphasizes the fact that the behavior</u> <u>operates upon the environment to generate consequences.</u> The consequences define the properties with respect to which responses are called similar. The term will be used both as an adjective (operant behavior) and as a noun to designate the behavior defined by a given consequence.

A single instance in which a pigeon raises its head is a *response.* It is a bit of history which may be reported in any frame of reference we wish to use. The behavior called "raising the head," regardless of when specific instances occur, is an *operant.* It can be described, not as an accomplished act, but rather as a set of acts defined by the property of the height to which the head is raised. In this sense an operant is defined by an effect which may be specified in physical terms; the "cutoff" at a certain height is a property of behavior.

The term "learning" may profitably be saved in its traditional sense to describe the reassortment of responses in a complex situation. Terms for the process of stamping in may be borrowed from Pavlov's analysis of the conditioned reflex. Pavlov himself called all events which strengthened behavior "reinforcement" and all the resulting changes "conditioning." <u>In the Pavlovian experiment, however, a reinforcer is paired with a *stimulus;* whereas in operant behavior it is contingent upon a *response.*</u> Operant reinforcement is therefore a separate process and requires a separate analysis. In both cases, the strengthening of behavior which results from reinforcement is appropriately called "conditioning." <u>In operant conditioning we "strengthen" an operant in the sense of making a response more probable or, in actual fact, more frequent.</u> In Pavlovian or "respondent" conditioning we simply increase the magnitude of the response elicited by the conditioned stimulus and shorten the time which elapses between stimulus and response. (We note, incidentally, that these two cases exhaust the possibilities: an organism is conditioned when a reinforcer [1] accompanies another stimulus or [2] follows upon the organism's own behavior. Any event which does neither has no effect in changing a probability of response.) In the pigeon experiment, then, food is the *reinforcer* and presenting food when a response is emitted is the *reinforcement*. The operant is defined by the property upon which reinforcement is contingent— the height to which the head must be raised. The change in frequency with which the head is lifted to this height is the process of operant conditioning.

While we are awake, we act upon the environment constantly, and many of the consequences of our actions are reinforcing. Through operant conditioning the environment builds the basic repertoire with which we keep our balance, walk, play games, handle instruments and tools, talk, write, sail a boat, drive a car, or fly a plane. A change in the environment—a new car, a new friend, a new field of interest, a new job, a new location—may find us unprepared, but our behavior usually adjusts quickly as we acquire new responses and discard old. We shall see in the following chapter that operant reinforcement does more than build a behavioral repertoire. It improves the efficiency of behavior and maintains behavior in strength long after acquisition or efficiency has ceased to be of interest.

QUANTITATIVE PROPERTIES

It is not easy to obtain a curve for operant conditioning. We cannot isolate an operant completely, nor can we eliminate all arbitrary details. In our example we might plot a curve showing how the frequency with which the pigeon's head is lifted to a given height changes with time or the number of reinforcements, but the total effect is clearly broader than this. There is a shift in a larger pattern of behavior, and to describe it fully we should have to follow all movements of the head. Even so, our account would not be complete. The height to which the head was to be lifted was chosen arbitrarily, and the effect of reinforcement depends upon this selection. If we reinforce a height which is seldom reached, the change in pattern will be far greater than if we had chosen a commoner height. For an adequate account we need a set of curves covering all the possibilities. Still another arbitrary element appears if we force the head to a higher and higher position, since we may follow different schedules in advancing the line selected for reinforcement. Each schedule will yield its own curve, and the picture would be complete only if it covered all possible schedules.

We cannot avoid these problems by selecting a response which is more sharply defined by features of the environment—for example, the behavior of operating a door latch. Some mechanical indicator of behavior is, of course, an advantage—for example, in helping us to reinforce consistently. We could record the height of a pigeon's head with a photocell arrangement, but it is simpler to select a response which makes a more easily recorded change in the environment. If the bird is conditioned to peck a small disk on the wall of the experimental box, we may use the movement of the disk to close an electric circuit—both to operate the food tray and to count or record responses. Such a response seems to be different from stretching the neck in that it has an all-or-none character. But we shall see in a moment that the mechanical features of striking a key do not define a "response" which is any less arbitrary than neck-stretching.

An experimental arrangement need not be perfect in order to provide important quantitative data in operant conditioning. We are already in a position to evaluate many factors. The importance of feed-back is clear. The organism must be stimulated by the consequences of its behavior if conditioning is to take place. In learning to wiggle one's ears, for example, it is necessary to know when the ears move if responses which produce movement are to be strengthened in comparison with responses which do not. In re-educating the patient in the use of a partially paralyzed limb, it may be of help to amplify the feed-back from slight movements, either with instruments or through the report of an instructor. The deaf-mute learns to talk only when he receives a feed-back from his own behavior which can be compared with the stimulation he receives from other speakers. One function of the educator is to supply arbitrary (sometimes spurious) consequences for the sake of feed-back. Conditioning depends also upon the kind, amount, and immediacy of reinforcement, as well as many other factors.

A single reinforcement may have a considerable effect. Under good conditions the frequency of a response shifts from a prevailing low value to a stable high value in a single abrupt step. More commonly we observe a substantial increase as the result of a single reinforcement, and additional increases from later reinforcements. The observation is not incompatible with the assumption of an instantaneous change to a maximal probability, since we have by no means isolated a single operant. The increased frequency must be interpreted with respect to other behavior characteristic of the situation. The fact that conditioning can be so rapid in an organism as "low" as the rat or pigeon has interesting implications. Differences in what is commonly called intelligence are attributed in part to differences in speed of learning. But there can be no faster learning than an instantaneous increase in probability of response. The superiority of human behavior is, therefore, of some other sort.

THE CONTROL OF OPERANT BEHAVIOR

The experimental procedure in operant conditioning is straightforward. We arrange a contingency of reinforcement and expose an organism to it for a given period. We then explain the frequent emission of the response by pointing to this history. But what improvement has been made in the prediction and control of the behavior in the future? What variables enable us to predict whether or not the organism will respond? What variables must we now control in order to induce it to respond?

We have been experimenting with a *hungry* pigeon. As we shall see in Chapter IX, this means a pigeon which has been deprived of food for a certain length of time or until its usual body-weight has been slightly reduced. Contrary to what one might expect, experimental studies have shown that the magnitude of the reinforcing effect of food may not depend upon the degree of such deprivation. But the frequency of response which results from reinforcement depends upon the degree of deprivation at the time the response is observed. Even though we have conditioned a pigeon to stretch its neck, it does not do this if it is not hungry. We have, therefore, a new sort of control over its behavior: in order to get the pigeon to stretch its neck, we simply make it hungry. A selected operant has been added to all those things which a hungry pigeon will do. Our control over the response has been pooled with our control over food deprivation. We shall see in Chapter VII that an operant may also come under the control of an external stimulus, which is another variable to be used in predicting and controlling the behavior. We should note, however, that both these variables are to be distinguished from operant reinforcement itself.

OPERANT EXTINCTION

When reinforcement is no longer forthcoming, a response becomes less and less frequent in what is called "operant extinction." If food is withheld, the pigeon will eventually stop lifting its head. In general when we engage in behavior which no longer "pays off," we find ourselves less inclined to behave in that way again. If we lose a fountain pen, we reach less and less often into the pocket which formerly held it. If we get no answer to telephone calls, we eventually stop telephoning. If our piano goes out of tune, we gradually play it less and less. If our radio becomes noisy or if programs become worse, we stop listening.

Since operant extinction takes place much more slowly than operant conditioning, the process may be followed more easily. Under suitable conditions smooth curves are obtained in which the rate of response is seen to decline slowly, perhaps over a period of many hours. The curves reveal properties which could not possibly be observed through casual inspection. We may "get the impression" that an organism is responding less and less often, but the orderliness of the change can be seen only when the behavior is recorded. The curves suggest that there is a fairly uniform process which determines the output of behavior during extinction.

Under some circumstances the curve is disturbed by an emotional effect. The failure of a response to be reinforced leads not only to operant extinction but also to a reaction commonly spoken of as frustration or rage. A pigeon which has failed to receive reinforcement turns away from the key, cooing, flapping its wings, and engaging in other emotional behavior (Chapter X). The human organism shows a similar double effect. The child whose tricycle no longer responds to pedaling not only stops pedaling but engages in a possibly violent emotional display. The adult who finds a desk drawer stuck may soon stop pulling, but he may also pound the desk, exclaim "Damn it!," or exhibit other signs of rage. Just as the child eventually goes back to the tricycle, and the adult to the drawer, so the pigeon will turn again to the key when the emotional response has subsided. As other responses go unreinforced, another emotional episode may ensue. Extinction curves under such circumstances show a cyclic oscillation as the emotional response builds up, disappears, and builds up again. If we eliminate the emotion by repeated exposure to extinction, or in other ways, the curve emerges in a simpler form.

Behavior during extinction is the result of the conditioning which has preceded it, and in this sense the extinction curve gives an additional measure of the effect of reinforcement. If only a few responses have been reinforced, extinction occurs quickly. A long history of reinforcement is followed by protracted responding. The resistance to extinction cannot be predicted from the probability of response observed at any given moment. We must know the history of reinforcement. For example, though we have been reinforced with an excellent meal in a new restaurant, a bad meal may reduce our patronage to zero; but if we have found excellent food in a restaurant for many years, several poor meals must be eaten there, other things being equal, before we lose the inclination to patronize it again.

There is no simple relation between the number of responses reinforced and the number which appear in extinction. As we shall see in Chapter VI, the resistance to extinction generated by _intermittent_ reinforcement may be much greater than if the same number of reinforcements are given for consecutive responses. Thus if we only occasionally reinforce a child for good behavior, the behavior survives after we discontinue reinforcement much longer than if we had reinforced every instance up to the same total number of reinforcements. This is of practical importance where the available reinforcers are limited. Problems of this sort arise in education, industry, economics, and many other fields. Under some schedules of intermittent reinforcement as many as 10,000 responses may appear in the behavior of a pigeon before extinction is substantially complete.

Extinction is an effective way of removing an operant from the repertoire of an organism. It should not be confused with other procedures designed to have the same effect. The currently preferred technique is punishment, which, as we shall see in Chapter XII, involves different processes and is of questionable effectiveness. Forgetting is frequently confused with extinction. In forgetting, the effect of conditioning is lost simply as time passes, whereas extinction requires that the response be emitted without reinforcement. Usually forgetting does not take place quickly; sizeable extinction curves have been obtained from pigeons as long as six years after the response had last been reinforced. Six years is about half the normal life span of the pigeon. During the interval the pigeons lived under circumstances in which the response could not possibly have been reinforced. In human behavior skilled responses generated by relatively precise contingencies frequently survive unused for as much as half a lifetime. The assertion that early experiences determine the personality of the mature organism assumes that the effect of operant reinforcement is long-lasting. Thus if, because of early childhood experiences, a man marries a woman who resembles his mother, the effect of certain reinforcements must have survived for a long time. Most cases of forgetting involve operant behavior under the control of specific stimuli and cannot be discussed adequately until that control has been covered in Chapter VII.

The effects of extinction. The condition in which extinction is more or less complete is familiar, yet often misunderstood. Extreme extinction is sometimes called "abulia." To define this as a "lack of will" is of little help, since the presence or absence of will is inferred from the presence or absence of the behavior. The term seems to be useful, however, in that it implies that the behavior is lacking for a special reason, and we may make the same distinction in another way. Behavior is strong or weak because of many different variables, which it is the task of a science of behavior to identify and classify. We define any given case in terms of the variable. The condition which results from prolonged extinction superficially resembles inactivity resulting from other causes. The difference is in the history of the organism. An aspiring writer who has sent manuscript after manuscript to the publishers only to have them all rejected may report that "he can't write another word." He may be partially paralyzed with what is called "writer's cramp." He may still insist that he "wants to write," and we may agree with him in paraphrase: his extremely low probability of response is mainly due to extinction. Other variables are still operative which, if extinction had not taken place, would yield a high probability.

The condition of low operant strength resulting from extinction often requires treatment. Some forms of psychotherapy are systems of reinforcement designed to reinstate behavior which has been lost through extinction. The therapist may himself supply the reinforcement, or he may arrange living conditions in which behavior is likely to be reinforced. In occupational therapy, for example, the patient is encouraged to engage in simple forms of behavior which receive immediate and fairly consistent reinforcement. It is of no advantage to say that such therapy helps the patient by giving him a "sense of achievement" or improves his "morale," builds up his "interest," or removes or prevents "discouragement." Such terms as these merely add to the growing population of explanatory fictions. One who readily engages in a given activity is not showing an interest, he is showing the effect of reinforcement. We do not give a man a sense of achievement, we reinforce a particular action. To become discouraged is simply to fail to respond because reinforcement has not been forthcoming. Our problem is simply to account for probability of response in terms of a history of reinforcement and extinction.

WHAT EVENTS ARE REINFORCING?

In dealing with our fellow men in everyday life and in the clinic and laboratory, we may need to know just how reinforcing a specific event is. We often begin by noting the extent to which our own behavior is reinforced by the same event. This practice frequently miscarries; yet it is still commonly believed that reinforcers can be identified apart from their effects upon a particular organism. As the term is used here, however, the only defining characteristic of a reinforcing stimulus is that it reinforces.

The only way to tell whether or not a given event is reinforcing to a given organism under given conditions is to make a direct test. We observe the frequency of a selected response, then make an event contingent upon it and observe any change in frequency. If there is a change, we classify the event as reinforcing to the organism under the existing conditions. There is nothing circular about classifying events in terms of their effects; the criterion is both empirical and objective. It would be circular, however, if we then went on to assert that a given event strengthens an operant *because* it is reinforcing. We achieve a certain success in guessing at reinforcing powers only because we have in a sense made a crude survey; we have gauged the reinforcing effect of a stimulus upon ourselves and assume the same effect upon others. We are successful only when we resemble the organism under study and when we have correctly surveyed our own behavior.

Events which are found to be reinforcing are of two sorts. Some reinforcements consist of *presenting* stimuli, of adding something—for example, food, water, or sexual contact—to the situation. These we call *positive* reinforcers. Others consist of *removing* something—for example, a loud noise, a very bright light, extreme cold or heat, or electric shock—from the situation. These we call *negative* reinforcers. In both cases the effect of reinforcement is the same—the probability of response is increased. We cannot avoid this distinction by arguing that what is reinforcing in the negative case is the *absence* of the bright light, loud noise, and so on; for it is absence after presence which is effective, and this is only another way of saying that the stimulus is removed. The difference between the two cases will be clearer when we consider the *presentation* of a *negative* reinforcer or the *removal* of a *positive*. These are the consequences which we call punishment (Chapter XII).

A survey of the events which reinforce a given individual is often required in the practical application of operant conditioning. In every field in which human behavior figures prominently—education, government, the family, the clinic, industry, art, literature, and so on—we are constantly changing probabilities of response by arranging reinforcing consequences. The industrialist who wants employees to work consistently and without absenteeism must make certain that their behavior is suitably reinforced—not only with wages but with suitable working conditions. The girl who wants another date must be sure that her friend's behavior in inviting her and in keeping the appointment is suitably reinforced. To teach a child to read or sing or play a game effectively, we must work out a program of educational reinforcement in which appropriate responses "pay off" frequently. If the patient is to return for further counsel, the psychotherapist must make sure that the behavior of coming to him is in some measure reinforced.

We evaluate the strength of reinforcing events when we attempt to discover what someone is "getting out of life." What consequences are responsible for his present repertoire and for the relative frequencies of the responses in it? His responses to various topics of conversation tell us something, but his everyday behavior is a better guide. We infer important reinforcers from nothing more unusual than his "interest" in a writer who deals with certain subjects, in stores or museums which exhibit certain objects, in friends who participate in certain kinds of behavior, in restaurants which serve certain kinds of food, and so on. The "interest" refers to the probability which results, at least in part, from the consequences of the behavior of "taking an interest." We may be more nearly sure of the importance of a reinforcer if we watch the behavior come and go as the reinforcer is alternately supplied and withheld, for the change in probability is then less likely to be due to an incidental change of some other sort. The behavior of associating with a particular friend varies as the friend varies in supplying reinforcement. If we observe this covariation, we may then be fairly sure of "what this friendship means" or "what our subject sees in his friend."

This technique of evaluation may be improved for use in clinical and laboratory investigation. A direct inventory may be made by allowing a subject to look at an assortment of pictures and recording the time he spends on each. The behavior of looking at a picture is reinforced by what is seen in it. Looking at one picture may be more strongly reinforced than looking at another, and the times will vary accordingly. The information may be valuable if it is necessary for any reason to reinforce or extinguish our subject's behavior.

Literature, art, and entertainment, are contrived reinforcers. Whether the public buys books, tickets to performances, and works of art depends upon whether those books, plays, concerts, or pictures are reinforcing. Frequently the artist confines himself to an exploration of what is reinforcing to himself. When he does so his work "reflects his own individuality," and it is then an accident (or a measure of his universality) if his book or play or piece of music or picture is reinforcing to others. Insofar as commercial success is important, he may make a direct study of the behavior of others. (The interpretation of the activity of the writer and artist as an exploration of the reinforcing powers of certain media will be discussed in Chapter XVI.)

We cannot dispense with this survey simply by asking a man what reinforces him. His reply may be of some value, but it is by no means necessarily reliable. A reinforcing connection need not be obvious to the individual reinforced. It is often only in retrospect that one's tendencies to behave in particular ways are seen to be the result of certain consequences, and, as we shall see in Chapter XVIII, the relation may never be seen at all even though it is obvious to others.

There are, of course, extensive differences between individuals in the events which prove to be reinforcing. The differences between species are so great as scarcely to arouse interest; obviously what is reinforcing to a horse need not be reinforcing to a dog or man. Among the members of a species, the extensive differences are less likely to be due to hereditary endowment, and to that extent may be traced to circumstances in the history of the individual. The fact that organisms evidently inherit the capacity to be reinforced by certain kinds of events does not help us in predicting the reinforcing effect of an untried stimulus. Nor does the relation between the reinforcing event and deprivation or any other condition of the organism endow the reinforcing event with any particular physical property. It is especially unlikely that events which have *acquired* their power to reinforce will be marked in any special way. Yet such events are an important species of reinforcer.

CONDITIONED REINFORCERS

The stimulus which is presented in operant reinforcement may be paired with another in respondent conditioning. In Chapter IV, we considered the acquisition of the power to *elicit* a response; now we are concerned with the power to *reinforce*. Although reinforcement is a different stimulus function, the process resulting from the pairing of stimuli appears to be the same. If we have frequently presented a dish of food to a hungry organism, the empty dish will elicit salivation. To some extent the empty dish will also reinforce an operant.

We can demonstrate conditioned reinforcement more readily with stimuli which can be better controlled. If each time we turn on a light we give food to a hungry pigeon, the light eventually becomes a conditioned reinforcer. It may be used to condition an operant just as food is used. We know something about how the light acquires this property: the more often the light is paired with the food, the more reinforcing it becomes; the food must not follow the light by too great an interval of time; and the reinforcing power is rapidly lost when all food is withheld. We should expect all of this from our knowledge of stimulus conditioning.

Conditioned reinforcers are often the product of natural contingencies. Usually, food and water are received only after the organism has engaged in "precurrent" behavior—after it has operated upon the environment to create the opportunity for eating or drinking. The stimuli generated by this precurrent behavior, therefore, become reinforcing. Thus before we can transfer food from a plate to our mouth successfully, we must get near the plate, and any behavior which brings us near the plate is automatically reinforced. The precurrent behavior is, therefore, sustained in strength. This is important since only a small part of behavior is immediately reinforced with food, water, sexual contact, or other events of obvious biological importance. Although it is characteristic of human behavior that primary reinforcers may be effective after long delay, this is presumably only because intervening events become conditioned reinforcers. When a man puts storm windows on his house in October because similar behavior last October was followed by a warm house in January, we need to bridge the gap between the behavior in October and the effect in January. Among the conditioned reinforcers responsible for the strength of this behavior are certain verbal consequences supplied by the man himself or by his neighbors. It is often important to fill in a series of events between an act and an ultimate primary reinforcement in order to control behavior for practical purposes. In education, industry, psychotherapy, and many other fields, we encounter techniques which are designed to create appropriate conditioned reinforcers. The effect of providing immediately effective consequences where ultimate consequences are delayed is to "improve morale," to "heighten interest," to "prevent discouragement" or to correct the condition of low operant strength which we called abulia, and so on. More concretely, it is to induce students to study, employees to come to work, patients to engage in acceptable social behavior, and so on.

Generalized reinforcers. A conditioned reinforcer is generalized when it is paired with more than one primary reinforcer. The generalized reinforcer is useful because the momentary condition of the organism is not likely to be important. The operant strength generated by a single reinforcement is observed only under an appropriate condition of deprivation—when we reinforce with food, we gain control over the hungry man. But if a conditioned reinforcer has been paired with reinforcers appropriate to many conditions, at least one appropriate state of deprivation is more likely to prevail upon a later occasion. A response is therefore more likely to occur. When we reinforce with money, for example, our subsequent control is relatively independent of momentary deprivations. One kind of generalized reinforcer is created because many primary reinforcers are received only after the physical environment has been efficiently manipulated. One form of precurrent behavior may precede different kinds of reinforcers upon different occasions. The immediate stimulation from such behavior will thus become a generalized reinforcer. We are automatically reinforced, apart from any particular deprivation, when we successfully control the physical world. This may explain our tendency to engage in skilled crafts, in artistic creation, and in such sports as bowling, billiards, and tennis.

It is possible, however, that some of the reinforcing effect of "sensory feed-back" is unconditioned. A baby appears to be reinforced by stimulation from the environment which has not been followed by primary reinforcement. The baby's rattle is an example. The capacity to be reinforced in this way could have arisen in the evolutionary process, and it may have a parallel in the reinforcement we receive from simply "making the world behave." Any organism which is reinforced by its success in manipulating nature, regardless of the momentary consequences, will be in a favored position when important consequences follow.

Several important generalized reinforcers arise when behavior is reinforced by other people. A simple case is *attention.* The child who misbehaves "just to get attention" is familiar. The attention of people is reinforcing because it is a necessary condition for other reinforcements from them. In general, only people who are attending to us reinforce our behavior. The attention of someone who is particularly likely to supply reinforcement—a parent, a teacher, or a loved one—is an especially good generalized reinforcer and sets up especially strong attention-getting behavior. Many verbal responses specifically demand attention—for example, "Look," "See," or the vocative use of a name. Other characteristic forms of behavior which are commonly strong because they receive attention are feigning illness, being annoying, and being conspicuous (exhibitionism).

Attention is often not enough. Another person is likely to reinforce only that part of one's behavior of which he approves, and any sign of his *approval* therefore becomes reinforcing in its own right. Behavior which evokes a smile or the verbal response "That's right" or "Good" or any other commendation is strengthened. We use this generalized reinforcer to establish and shape the behavior of others, particularly in education. For example, we teach both children and adults to speak correctly by saying "That's right" when appropriate behavior is emitted.

A still stronger generalized reinforcer is *affection.* It may be especially connected with sexual contact as a primary reinforcer but when anyone who shows affection supplies other kinds of reinforcement as well, the effect is generalized.

It is difficult to define, observe, and measure attention, approval, and affection. They are not things but aspects of the behavior of others. Their subtle physical dimensions present difficulties not only for the scientist who must study them but also for the individual who is reinforced by them. If we do not easily see that someone is paying attention or that he approves or is affectionate, our behavior will not be consistently reinforced. It may therefore be weak, may tend to occur at the wrong time, and so on. We do not "know what to do to get attention or affection or when to do it." The child struggling for attention, the lover for a sign of affection, and the artist for professional approval show the persevering behavior which, as we shall see in Chapter VI, results from only intermittent reinforcement.

Another generalized reinforcer is the *submissiveness* of others. When someone has been coerced into supplying various reinforcements, any indication of his acquiescence becomes a generalized reinforcer. The bully is reinforced by signs of cowardice, and members of the ruling class by signs of deference. Prestige and esteem are generalized reinforcers only insofar as they guarantee that other people will act in certain ways. That "having one's own way" is reinforcing is shown by the behavior of those who control for the sake of control. The physical dimensions of submissiveness are usually not so subtle as those of attention, approval, or affection. The bully may insist upon a clear-cut sign of his dominance, and ritualistic practices emphasize deference and respect.

A generalized reinforcer distinguished by its physical specifications is the *token*. The commonest example is money. It is the generalized reinforcer par excellence because, although "money won't buy everything," it can be exchanged for primary reinforcers of great variety. Behavior reinforced with money is relatively independent of the momentary deprivation of the organism, and the general usefulness of money as a reinforcer depends in part upon this fact. Its effectiveness is also due to its physical dimensions. These permit a sharper contingency between behavior and consequence: when we are paid in money, we know what our behavior has accomplished and what behavior has accomplished it. The reinforcing effect can also be more successfully conditioned: the exchange value of money is more obvious than that of attention, approval, affection, or even submissiveness.

Money is not the only token. In education, for example, the individual behaves in part because of the marks, grades, and diplomas which he has received. These are not so readily exchanged for primary reinforcement as money, but the possibility of exchange is there. Educational tokens form a series in which one may be exchanged for the next, and the commercial or prestige value of the final token, the diploma, is usually clear. As a rule, prizes, medals, and scholarships for high marks or specialized skills or achievements are not explicitly paired with primary reinforcers, but the clear-cut physical dimensions of such awards are an advantage in arranging contingencies. Usually the ultimate reinforcement is similar to that of prestige or esteem.

It is easy to forget the origins of the generalized reinforcers and to regard them as reinforcing in their own right. We speak of the "need for attention, approval, or affection," "the need to dominate," and "the love of money" as if they were primary conditions of deprivation. But a capacity to be reinforced in this way could scarcely have evolved in the short time during which the required conditions have prevailed. Attention, affection, approval, and submission have presumably existed in human society for only a very brief period, as the process of evolution goes. Moreover, they do not represent fixed forms of stimulation, since they depend upon the idiosyncrasies of particular groups. Insofar as affection is mainly sexual, it may be related to a condition of primary deprivation which is to some extent independent of the personal history of the individual, but the "signs of affection" which become reinforcing because of their association with sexual contact or with other reinforcers can scarcely be reinforcing for genetic reasons. Tokens are of even more recent advent, and it is not often seriously suggested that the need for them is inherited. We can usually watch the process through which a child comes to be reinforced by money. Yet the "love of money" often seems to be autonomous as the "need for approval," and if we confined ourselves to the observed effectiveness of these generalized reinforcers, we should have as much reason for assuming an inherited need for money as for attention, approval, affection, or domination.

Eventually generalized reinforcers are effective even though the primary reinforcers upon which they are based no longer accompany them. We play games of skill for their own sake. We get attention or approval for its own sake. Affection is not always followed by a more explicit sexual reinforcement. The submissiveness of others is reinforcing even though we make no use of it. A miser may be so reinforced by money that he will starve rather than give it up. These observable facts must have their place in any theoretical or practical consideration. They do not mean that generalized reinforcers are anything more than the physical properties of the stimuli observed in each case or that there are any nonphysical entities which must be taken into account.

WHY IS A REINFORCER REINFORCING?

The Law of Effect is not a theory. It is simply a rule for strengthening behavior. When we reinforce a response and observe a change in its frequency, we can easily report what has happened in objective terms. But in explaining *why* it has happened we are likely to resort to theory. Why does reinforcement reinforce? One theory is that an organism repeats a response because it finds the consequences "pleasant" or "satisfying." But in what sense is this an explanation within the framework of a natural science? "Pleasant" or "satisfying" apparently do not refer to physical properties of reinforcing events, since the physical sciences use neither these terms nor any equivalents. The terms must refer to some effect upon the organism, but can we define this in such a way that it will be useful in accounting for reinforcement?

It is sometimes argued that a thing is pleasant if an organism approaches or maintains contact with it and unpleasant if the organism avoids it or cuts it short. There are many variations on this attempt to find an objective definition, but they are all subject to the same criticism: the behavior specified may be merely another product of the reinforcing effect. To say that a stimulus is pleasant in the sense that an organism tends to approach or prolong it may be only another way of saying that the stimulus has reinforced the

behavior of approaching or prolonging. Instead of defining a reinforcing effect in terms of its effect upon behavior in general, we have
simply specified familiar behavior which is almost inevitably reinforced and hence generally available as an indicator of reinforcing
power. It we then go on to say that a stimulus is reinforcing *because*
it is pleasant, what purports to be an explanation in terms of two
effects is in reality a redundant description of one.

An alternative approach is to define "pleasant" and "unpleasant"
(or "satisfying" and "annoying") by asking the subject how he "feels"
about certain events. This assumes that reinforcement has two effects
—it strengthens behavior and generates "feelings"—and that one is a
function of the other. But the functional relation may be in the other
direction. When a man reports that an event is pleasant, he may
be merely reporting that it is the sort of event which reinforces him
or toward which he finds himself tending to move because it has
reinforced such movement. We shall see in Chapter XVII that one
could probably not acquire verbal responses with respect to pleasantness as a purely private fact unless something like this were so. In any
case, the subject himself is not at an especially good point of vantage
for making such observations. "Subjective judgments" of the pleasantness or satisfaction provided by stimuli are usually unreliable and
inconsistent. As the doctrine of the unconscious has emphasized, we
may not be able to report at all upon events which can be shown to
be reinforcing to us or we may make a report which is in direct conflict with objective observations; we may report as unpleasant a type
of event which can be shown to be reinforcing. Examples of this
anomaly range from masochism to martyrdom.

It is sometimes argued that reinforcement is effective because it
reduces a state of deprivation. Here at least is a collateral effect which
need not be confused with reinforcement itself. It is obvious that
deprivation is important in operant conditioning. We used a *hungry*
pigeon in our experiment, and we could not have demonstrated operant conditioning otherwise. The hungrier the bird, the oftener it
responds as the result of reinforcement. But in spite of this connection it is not true that reinforcement always reduces deprivation.
Conditioning may occur before any substantial change can take place

in the deprivation measured in other ways. All we can say is that the *type* of event which reduces deprivation is also reinforcing.

The connection between reinforcement and satiation must be sought in the process of evolution. We can scarcely overlook the great biological significance of the primary reinforcers. Food, water, and sexual contact, as well as escape from injurious conditions (Chapter XI), are obviously connected with the well-being of the organism. An individual who is readily reinforced by such events will acquire highly efficient behavior. It is also biologically advantageous if the behavior due to a given reinforcement is especially likely to occur in an appropriate state of deprivation. Thus it is important, not only that any behavior which leads to the receipt of food should become an important part of a repertoire, but that this behavior should be particularly strong when the organism is hungry. These two advantages are presumably responsible for the fact that an organism can be reinforced in specific ways and that the result will be observed in relevant conditions of deprivation.

Some forms of stimulation are positively reinforcing although they do not appear to elicit behavior having biological significance. A baby is reinforced, not only by food, but by the tinkle of a bell or the sparkle of a bright object. Behavior which is consistently followed by such stimuli shows an increased probability. It is difficult, if not impossible, to trace these reinforcing effects to a history of conditioning. Later we may find the same individual being reinforced by an orchestra or a colorful spectacle. Here it is more difficult to make sure that the reinforcing effect is not conditioned. However, we may plausibly argue that a capacity to be reinforced by any feedback from the environment would be biologically advantageous, since it would prepare the organism to manipulate the environment successfully before a given state of deprivation developed. When the organism generates a tactual feed-back, as in feeling the texture of a piece of cloth or the surface of a piece of sculpture, the conditioning is commonly regarded as resulting from sexual reinforcement, even when the area stimulated is not primarily sexual in function. It is tempting to suppose that other forms of stimulation produced by behavior are similarly related to biologically important events.

When the environment changes, a capacity to be reinforced by a given event may have a biological *disadvantage*. Sugar is highly reinforcing to most members of the human species, as the ubiquitous candy counter shows. Its effect in this respect far exceeds current biological requirements. This was not true before sugar had been grown and refined on an extensive scale. Until a few hundred years ago, the strong reinforcing effect of sugar must have been a biological advantage. The environment has changed, but the genetic endowment of the organism has not followed suit. Sex provides another example. There is no longer a biological advantage in the great reinforcing effect of sexual contact, but we need not go back many hundreds of years to find conditions of famine and pestilence under which the power of sexual reinforcement offered a decisive advantage.

A biological explanation of reinforcing power is perhaps as far as we can go in saying why an event is reinforcing. Such an explanation is probably of little help in a functional analysis, for it does not provide us with any way of identifying a reinforcing stimulus as such before we have tested its reinforcing power upon a given organism. We must therefore be content with a survey in terms of the effects of stimuli upon behavior.

ACCIDENTAL CONTINGENCIES AND
"SUPERSTITIOUS" BEHAVIOR

It has been argued that Thorndike's experiment is not typical of the learning process because the cat cannot "see the connection" between moving a latch and escaping from a box. But seeing a connection is not essential in operant conditioning. Both during and after the process of conditioning, the human subject often talks about his behavior in relation to his environment (Chapter XVII). His reports may be useful in a scientific account, and his reaction to his own behavior may even be an important link in certain complex processes. But such reports or reactions are not required in the simple process of operant conditioning. This is evident in the fact that one may not be able to describe a contingency which has clearly had an effect.

Nor need there be any permanent connection between a response and its reinforcement. We made the receipt of food contingent upon the response of our pigeon by arranging a mechanical and electrical connection. Outside the laboratory various physical systems are responsible for contingencies between behavior and its consequences. But these need not, and usually do not, affect the organism in any other way. So far as the organism is concerned, the only important property of the contingency is temporal. The reinforcer simply *follows* the response. How this is brought about does not matter.

We must assume that the presentation of a reinforcer always reinforces something, since it necessarily coincides with some behavior. We have also seen that a single reinforcement may have a substantial effect. If there is only an accidental connection between the response and the appearance of a reinforcer, the behavior is called "superstitious." We may demonstrate this in the pigeon by accumulating the effect of several accidental contingencies. Suppose we give a pigeon a small amount of food every fifteen seconds regardless of what it is doing. When food is first given, the pigeon will be behaving in some way—if only standing still—and conditioning will take place. It is then more probable that the same behavior will be in progress when food is given again. If this proves to be the case, the "operant" will be further strengthened. If not, some other behavior will be strengthened. Eventually a given bit of behavior reaches a frequency at which it is often reinforced. It then becomes a permanent part of the repertoire of the bird, even though the food has been given by a clock which is unrelated to the bird's behavior. Conspicuous responses which have been established in this way include turning sharply to one side, hopping from one foot to the other and back, bowing and scraping, turning around, strutting, and raising the head. The topography of the behavior may continue to drift with further reinforcements, since slight modifications in the form of response may coincide with the receipt of food.

In producing superstitious behavior, the intervals at which food is given are important. At sixty seconds the effect of one reinforcement is largely lost before another can occur, and other behavior is more likely to appear. Superstitious behavior is therefore less likely to emerge, though it may do so if the experiment is carried on for a long time. At fifteen seconds the effect is usually almost immediate.

When a superstitious response has once been established, it will survive even when reinforced only infrequently.

The pigeon is not exceptionally gullible. Human behavior is also heavily superstitious. Only a small part of the behavior strengthened by accidental contingencies develops into the ritualistic practices which we call "superstitions," but the same principle is at work. Suppose we find a ten-dollar bill while walking through the park (and suppose this is an event which has a considerable reinforcing effect). Whatever we were doing, or had just been doing, at the moment we found the bill must be assumed to be reinforced. It would be difficult to prove this in a rigorous way, of course, but it is probable that we shall be more likely to go walking again, particularly in the same or a similar park, that we shall be slightly more likely to keep our eyes cast downward precisely as we did when we saw the money, and so on. This behavior will vary with any state of deprivation to which money is relevant. We should not call it superstitious, but it is generated by a contingency which is only rarely "functional."

Some contingencies which produce superstitious behavior are not entirely accidental. A response is sometimes likely to be followed by a consequence which it nevertheless does not "produce." The best examples involve a type of stimulus which is reinforcing when removed (Chapter XI). The termination of a brief stimulus of this sort may occur at just the right time to reinforce the behavior generated by its onset. The aversive stimulus appears and the organism becomes active; the stimulus terminates, and this reinforces some part of the behavior. Certain illnesses, lamenesses, and allergic reactions are of such duration that *any* measure taken to "cure" them is likely to be reinforced when the condition clears up. The measure need not actually be responsible for the cure. The elaborate rituals of nonscientific medicine appear to be explained by this characteristic of many forms of illness.

In superstitious operant behavior, as in the superstitious conditioned reflexes discussed in Chapter IV, the process of conditioning has miscarried. Conditioning offers tremendous advantages in equipping the organism with behavior which is effective in a novel environment, but there appears to be no way of preventing the acquisition of non-advantageous behavior through accident. Curiously, this diffi-culty must have increased as the process of conditioning was acceler-ated in the course of evolution. If, for example, three reinforcements were always required in order to change the probability of a response, superstitious behavior would be unlikely. It is only because organisms have reached the point at which a single contingency makes a sub-stantial change that they are vulnerable to coincidences.

Superstitious rituals in human society usually involve verbal for-mulae and are transmitted as part of the culture. To this extent they differ from the simple effect of accidental operant reinforcement. But they must have had their origin in the same process, and they are probably sustained by occasional contingencies which follow the same pattern.

GOALS, PURPOSES, AND OTHER FINAL CAUSES

It is not correct to say that operant reinforcement "strengthens the response which precedes it." The response has already occurred and cannot be changed. What is changed is the future probability of re-sponses in the same class. It is the operant as a class of behavior, rather than the response as a particular instance, which is condi-tioned. There is, therefore, no violation of the fundamental principle of science which rules out "final causes." But this principle is violated when it is asserted that behavior is under the control of an "incen-tive" or "goal" which the organism has not yet achieved or a "pur-pose" which it has not yet fulfilled. Statements which use such words as "incentive" or "purpose" are usually reducible to statements about operant conditioning, and only a slight change is required to bring them within the framework of a natural science. Instead of saying that a man behaves because of the consequences which *are* to follow his behavior, we simply say that he behaves because of the conse-quences which *have* followed similar behavior in the past. This is, of course, the Law of Effect or operant conditioning.

It is sometimes argued that a response is not fully described until its purpose is referred to as a current property. But what is meant by "describe"? If we observe someone walking down the street, we may report this event in the language of physical science. If we then add that "his purpose is to mail a letter," have we said anything which was not included in our first report? Evidently so, since a man may walk down the street "for many purposes" and in the same physical way in each case. But the distinction which needs to be made is not between instances of behavior; it is between the variables of which behavior is a function. Purpose is not a property of the behavior itself; it is a way of referring to controlling variables. If we make our report after we have seen our subject mail his letter and turn back, we attribute "purpose" to him from the event which brought the behavior of walking down the street to an end. This event "gives meaning" to his performance, not by amplifying a description of the behavior as such, but by indicating an independent variable of which it may have been a function. We cannot see his "purpose" before seeing that he mails a letter, unless we have observed similar behavior and similar consequences before. Where we have done this, we use the term simply to predict that he will mail a letter upon this occasion.

Nor can our subject see his own purpose without reference to similar events. If we ask him why he is going down the street or what his purpose is and he says, "I am going to mail a letter," we have not learned anything new about his behavior but only about some of its possible causes. The subject himself, of course, may be in an advantageous position in describing these variables because he has had an extended contact with his own behavior for many years. But his statement is not therefore in a different class from similar statements made by others who have observed his behavior upon fewer occasions. As we shall see in Chapter XVII, he is simply making a plausible prediction in terms of his experiences with himself. Moreover, he may be wrong. He may report that he is "going to mail a letter," and he may indeed carry an unmailed letter in his hand and may mail it at the end of the street, but we may still be able to show that his behavior is primarily determined by the fact that upon past occasions he has encountered someone who is important to him upon just such a walk. He may not be "aware of this purpose" in the sense of being able to say that his behavior is strong for this reason.

The fact that operant behavior seems to be "directed toward the future" is misleading. Consider, for example, the case of "looking for something." In what sense is the "something" which has not yet been found relevant to the behavior? Suppose we condition a pigeon to peck a spot on the wall of a box and then, when the operant is well established, remove the spot. The bird now goes to the usual place along the wall. It raises its head, cocks its eye in the usual direction, and may even emit a weak peck in the usual place. Before extinction is very far advanced, it returns to the same place again and again in similar behavior. Must we say that the pigeon is "looking for the spot"? Must we take the "looked for" spot into account in explaining the behavior?

It is not difficult to interpret this example in terms of operant reinforcement. Since visual stimulation from the spot has usually preceded the receipt of food, the spot has become a conditioned reinforcer. It strengthens the behavior of looking in given directions from different positions. Although we have undertaken to condition only the pecking response, we have in fact strengthened many different kinds of precurrent behavior which bring the bird into positions from which it sees the spot and pecks it. These responses continue to appear, even though we have removed the spot, until extinction occurs. The spot which is "being looked for" is the spot which has occurred in the past as the immediate reinforcement of the behavior of looking. In general, looking for something consists of emitting responses which in the past have produced "something" as a consequence.

The same interpretation applies to human behavior. When we see a man moving about a room opening drawers, looking under magazines, and so on, we may describe his behavior in fully objective terms: "Now he is in a certain part of the room; he has grasped a book between the thumb and forefinger of his right hand; he is lifting the book and bending his head so that any object under the book can be seen." We may also "interpret" his behavior or "read a meaning into it" by saying that "he is looking for something" or, more specifically, that "he is looking for his glasses." What we have added is not a further description of his behavior but an inference about some of the variables responsible for it. There is no *current* goal, incentive, purpose, or meaning to be taken into account. This is so even if we ask him what he is doing and he says, "I am looking for my glasses." This is not a further description of his behavior but of the variables of which his behavior is a function; it is equivalent to "I have lost my glasses," "I shall stop what I am doing when I find my glasses," or "When I have done this in the past, I have found my glasses." These translations may seem unnecessarily roundabout, but only because expressions involving goals and purposes are abbreviations.

Very often we attribute purpose to behavior as another way of describing its biological adaptability. This issue has already been discussed, but one point may be added. In both operant conditioning and the evolutionary selection of behavioral characteristics, consequences alter future probability. Reflexes and other innate patterns of behavior evolve because they increase the chances of survival of the *species*. Operants grow strong because they are followed by important consequences in the life of the *individual*. Both processes raise the question of purpose for the same reason, and in both the appeal to a final cause may be rejected in the same way. A spider does not possess the elaborate behavioral repertoire with which it constructs a web because that web will enable it to capture the food it needs to survive. It possesses this behavior because similar behavior on the part of spiders in the past has enabled *them* to capture the food *they* needed to survive. A series of events have been relevant to the behavior of web-making in its earlier evolutionary history. We are wrong in saying that we observe the "purpose" of the web when we observe similar events in the life of the individual.

CHAPTER VI

SHAPING AND MAINTAINING OPERANT BEHAVIOR

THE CONTINUITY OF BEHAVIOR

Operant conditioning shapes behavior as a sculptor shapes a lump of clay. Although at some point the sculptor seems to have produced an entirely novel object, we can always follow the process back to the original undifferentiated lump, and we can make the successive stages by which we return to this condition as small as we wish. At no point does anything emerge which is very different from what preceded it. The final product seems to have a special unity or integrity of design, but we cannot find a point at which this suddenly appears. In the same sense, an operant is not something which appears full grown in the behavior of the organism. It is the result of a continuous shaping process.

The pigeon experiment demonstrates this clearly. "Raising the head" is not a discrete unit of behavior. It does not come, so to speak, in a separate package. We reinforce only slightly exceptional values of the behavior observed while the pigeon is standing or moving about. We succeed in shifting the whole range of heights at which the head is held, but there is nothing which can be accurately described as a new "response." A response such as turning the latch in a problem box appears to be a more discrete unit, but only because the continuity with other behavior is more difficult to observe. In the pigeon, the response of pecking at a spot on the wall of the experimental box seems to differ from stretching the neck because no other behavior of the pigeon resembles it. If in reinforcing such a response we simply wait for it to occur—and we may have to wait many hours or days or weeks—the whole unit appears to emerge in its final form and to be strengthened as such. There may be no appreciable behavior which we could describe as "almost pecking the spot."

The continuous connection between such an operant and the general behavior of the bird can nevertheless easily be demonstrated. It is the basis of a practical procedure for setting up a complex response. To get the pigeon to peck the spot as quickly as possible we proceed as follows: We first give the bird food when it turns slightly in the direction of the spot from any part of the cage. This increases the frequency of such behavior. We then withhold reinforcement until a slight movement is made toward the spot. This again alters the general distribution of behavior without producing a new unit. We continue by reinforcing positions successively closer to the spot, then by reinforcing only when the head is moved slightly forward, and finally only when the beak actually makes contact with the spot. We may reach this final response in a remarkably short time. A hungry bird, well adapted to the situation and to the food tray, can usually be brought to respond in this way in two or three minutes.

The original probability of the response in its final form is very low; in some cases it may even be zero. In this way we can build complicated operants which would never appear in the repertoire of the organism otherwise. By reinforcing a series of successive approximations, we bring a rare response to a very high probability in a short time. This is an effective procedure because it recognizes and utilizes the continuous nature of a complex act. The total act of turning toward the spot from any point the box, walking toward it, raising the head, and striking the spot may seem to be a functionally coherent unit of behavior; but it is constructed by a continual process of differential reinforcement from undifferentiated behavior, just as the sculptor shapes his figure from a lump of clay. When we wait for a single complete instance, we reinforce a similar sequence but far less effectively because the earlier steps are not optimally strengthened.

This account is inaccurate in one respect. We may detect a discontinuity between bringing the head close to the spot and pecking. The pecking movement usually emerges as an obviously preformed unit. There are two possible explanations. A mature pigeon will already have developed a well-defined pecking response which may emerge upon the present occasion. The history of this response might show a similar continuity if we could follow it. It is possible, however, that there is a genetic discontinuity, and that in a bird such as the pigeon the pecking response has a special strength and a special coherence as a form of species behavior. Vomiting and sneezing are human responses which probably have a similar genetic unity. Continuity with other behavior must be sought in the evolutionary process. But these genetic units are rare, at least in the vertebrates. The behavior with which we are usually concerned, from either a theoretical or practical point of view, is continuously modified from a basic material which is largely undifferentiated.

Through the reinforcement of slightly exceptional instances of his behavior, a child learns to raise himself, to stand, to walk, to grasp objects, and to move them about. Later on, through the same process, he learns to talk, to sing, to dance, to play games—in short, to exhibit the enormous repertoire characteristic of the normal adult. When we survey behavior in these later stages, we find it convenient to distinguish between various operants which differ from each other in topography and produce different consequences. In this way behavior is broken into parts to facilitate analysis. These parts are the units which we count and whose frequencies play an important role in arriving at laws of behavior. They are the "acts" into which, in the vocabulary of the layman, behavior is divided. But if we are to account for many of its quantitative properties, the ultimately continuous nature of behavior must not be forgotten.

Neglect of this characteristic has been responsible for several difficult problems in behavior theory. An example is the effect sometimes spoken of as "response generalization," "transfer," or "response induction." In reinforcing one operant we often produce a noticeable increase in the strength of another. Training in one area of skilled behavior may improve performance in another. Success in one field of activity may increase the tendency to be active in other fields. By arranging optimal reinforcing contingencies in the clinic or institution, the psychotherapist strengthens behavior in the world at large. But how is this possible? What is the "transfer" which appears to strengthen behavior without reinforcing it directly? This is a good example of a pseudo problem. We divide behavior into hard and fast units and are then surprised to find that the organism disregards the boundaries we have set. It is difficult to conceive of two responses which do not have something in common. Sometimes the same muscular system is used. The effect of a reinforcement may reflect this fact rather than our arbitrary practice of calling the responses separate units. Again, when we reinforce the final response in a sequence containing many precurrent members, we may strengthen all units which contain the same precurrent members. Our skill in manipulating tools and instruments transfers from one field of reinforcement to another.

The traditional explanation of transfer asserts that the second response is strengthened only insofar as the responses "possess identical elements." This is an effort to maintain the notion of a unit of response. A more useful way of putting it is to say that the *elements* are strengthened wherever they occur. This leads us to identify the element rather than the response as the unit of behavior. It is a sort of behavioral atom, which may never appear by itself upon any single occasion but is the essential ingredient or component of all observed instances. The reinforcement of a response increases the probability of all responses containing the same elements. Verbal behavior supplies especially good examples of the need to consider these atoms. An enormous number of verbal responses are executed by the same musculature. They are responses, therefore, which are presumably composed of a fairly small number of identical elements. This is not usually recognized in the customary practice of regarding verbal behavior as composed of separate units—for example, the "words" of the grammarian. A rigorous analysis shows that the word is by no means the functional unit. Larger complexes of words—idioms,

phrases, or memorized passages—may vary together under the control
of a single variable. On the other hand, we may observe the separate
functional control of "atoms" at least as small as the separate speech
sounds. We have to recognize these small units in order to account
for such distorted verbal responses as spoonerisms and certain verbal
slips, as well as the stylistic devices of alliteration, assonance, rhyme,
and rhythm.

We lack adequate tools to deal with the continuity of behavior or
with the interaction among operants attributable to common atomic
units. The operant represents a valid level of analysis, however, because the properties which define a response are observable data. A
given set of properties may be given a functional unity. Although
methods must eventually be developed which will not emphasize
units at this level, they are not necessary to our understanding of the
principal dynamic properties of behavior.

DIFFERENTIAL REINFORCEMENT

Although operant reinforcement is always a matter of selecting certain magnitudes of response as against others, we may distinguish
between producing a relatively complete new unit and making slight
changes in the direction of greater effectiveness in an existing unit.
In the first case, we are interested in how behavior is acquired; in
the second, in how it is refined. It is the difference between "knowing
how to do something" and "doing it well." The latter is the field of
skill.

The contingency which improves skill is the differential reinforcement of responses possessing special properties. It may be supplied
automatically by the mechanical exigencies of the environment. In
learning to throw a ball well, for example, certain responses must release the ball from the fingers at the moment of its greatest forward
speed. These responses are differentially reinforced by the fact that,
when so released, the ball covers a considerable distance. Other instances in which the release comes before or after the proper moment
are not so reinforced. We are likely to forget how complex an act
this is and how much differential reinforcement is required in the
young child to produce a properly timed sequence. In games, crafts,

and certain artistic performances extremely fine differences in the execution of behavior make important differences in the consequences. (The consequences at issue are generally the conditioned reinforcers summarized in Chapter V. Primary reinforcers are seldom involved. The negative reinforcers to be considered in Chapter XI also are important. For example, the consequences which are effective in conditioning postural responses in locomotion or the maintenance of an upright position are largely the avoidance of falls, bumps, and awkward or painful postures.)

The reinforcement which develops skill must be *immediate*. Otherwise, the precision of the differential effect is lost. In many practical areas skilled behavior is encouraged by arranging a quick report of accomplishment. In rifle practice, for example, extremely small-scale properties of response are differentially reinforced by a hit or a miss. Properties of this magnitude can be selected only if the differential reinforcement is immediate. But even when a hit can be seen by the rifleman, the report is delayed by the time which the bullet takes to reach the target. Possibly this gap is bridged by conditioned reinforcement from the "feel" of the shot. The rifleman eventually "knows" before the target is hit whether the shot was good or bad. His own behavior generates a stimulating feed-back, certain forms of which are followed by hits, others by misses. The more immediate problem is to shoot in such a way as to generate the "feel" followed by a hit. In more vigorous enterprises the feed-back is clearer. Good form in bowling, for example, is reinforced by feed-back from the bowler's body. This does not mean that the rifleman will continue to shoot well, or the bowler to bowl well, even though he receives no report of the effect upon the target or pins. The report is needed to maintain the conditioned reinforcing power of the feed-back.

If the differential contingencies change, the topography of behavior changes with them. Even the very common responses which enable us to walk upright continue to be modified by the environment. When we walk on the deck of a ship at sea, a special set of contingencies prevails in maintaining our orientation in the gravitational field. The new differential reinforcement sets up "sea legs." At the end of the voyage the old contingencies work a reverse change. Contingencies of reinforcement which are arranged by society are especially likely to shift. Verbal behavior supplies many good examples. In the nursery, crude vocal responses are successful; the indulgent parent may even reinforce "baby talk" into adolescent or adult years. But eventually, verbal behavior is successful only when it generates suitable behavior in the average listener; therefore, the form of the behavior comes to correspond more and more closely to the standards of a given community. When we move from one community to another, the topography of our behavior may change.

Some differential reinforcements make a response more or less *intense* or *forceful* without appreciably altering its topography. Certain natural contingencies in the environment lead us to push or lift harder to move objects, to pull harder to break objects apart, to jump harder to reach a given height, and so on. In calling to someone at a distance or in talking to a deaf person, our verbal behavior is reinforced only when it reaches a certain level of loudness. Tests of strength and other competitive games supply examples of these differential contingencies. When a heavy ball is thrown beyond a certain mark, when a horizontal bar is cleared in vaulting or in jumping, when a ball is batted over the fence (and when, as a result, a record is broken or a match or game won), differential reinforcement is at work. It may to some extent change the topography of the behavior and produce "good form," but it has an important effect upon the mere force with which the behavior is executed.

We use differential reinforcement to shape and intensify the behavior of others in what may be spoken of, as we shall see in Chapter XX, as deliberate control. The effect may also be wholly unintentional. The mother who complains that her three-year-old child whines and cries for attention in an annoying way may not realize that her own reinforcing practices are responsible. If she is busy with other matters, she is likely not to respond to a call or request made in a quiet tone of voice. When the child raises his voice, she replies. This is differential reinforcement. The average intensity of the child's vocal behavior rises. When the mother has adapted to the new level, again only the louder instances are reinforced. Further differentiation in the direction of loud responses follows. The child's voice may also vary in intonation. What we call "whining" may be thought of as speaking with a small admixture of crying. Such speech is more likely to secure an effect and is therefore differentially strengthened. In fact, what we call annoying behavior in general is just that behavior which is especially effective in arousing another person to action. Differential reinforcement supplied by a preoccupied or negligent parent is very close to the procedure we should adopt if we were given the task of conditioning a child to be annoying.

THE MAINTENANCE OF BEHAVIOR

One reason the term "learning" is not equivalent to "operant conditioning" is that traditionally it has been confined to the process of learning *how to do something*. In trial-and-error learning, for example, the organism learns how to get out of a box or how to find its way through a maze. It is easy to see why the acquisition of behavior should be emphasized. Early devices for the study of learning did not reveal the basic process directly. The effect of operant reinforcement is most conspicuous when there is a gross change in behavior. Such a chance occurs when an organism learns how to make a response which it did not or could not make before. A more sensitive measure, however, enables us to deal with cases in which the acquisition of behavior is of minor importance.

Operant conditioning continues to be effective even when there is no further change which can be spoken of as acquisition or even as improvement in skill. Behavior continues to have consequences and these continue to be important. If consequences are not forthcoming, extinction occurs. When we come to consider the behavior of the organism in all the complexity of its everyday life, we need to be constantly alert to the prevailing reinforcements which maintain its behavior. We may, indeed, have little interest in how that behavior was first acquired. Our concern is only with its present probability of occurrence, which can be understood only through an examination of current contingencies of reinforcement. This is an aspect of reinforcement which is scarcely ever dealt with in classical treatments of learning.

INTERMITTENT REINFORCEMENT

In general, behavior which acts upon the immediate physical en~ vironment is consistently reinforced. We orient ourselves toward objects and approach, reach for, and seize them with a stable reper- toire of responses which have uniform consequences arising from the optical and mechanical properties of nature. It is possible, of course, to disturb the uniformity. In a "house of mirrors" in an amusement park, or in a room designed to supply misleading cues to the vertical, well-established responses may fail to have their usual effects. But the fact that such conditions are so unusual as to have commercial value testifies to the stability of the everyday world.

A large part of behavior, however, is reinforced only intermittently. A given consequence may depend upon a series of events which are not easily predicted. We do not always win at cards or dice, because the contingencies are so remotely determined that we call them "chance." We do not always find good ice or snow when we go skating or skiing. Contingencies which require the participation of people are especially likely to be uncertain. We do not always get a good meal in a particular restaurant because cooks are not always predictable. We do not always get an answer when we telephone a friend because the friend is not always at home. We do not always get a pen by reaching into our pocket because we have not always put it there. The reinforcements characteristic of industry and education are almost always intermittent because it is not feasible to control behavior by reinforcing every response.

As might be expected, behavior which is reinforced only inter- mittently often shows an intermediate frequency of occurrence, but laboratory studies of various schedules have revealed some surprising complexities. Usually such behavior is remarkably stable and shows great resistance to extinction. An experiment has already been men- tioned in which more than 10,000 responses appeared in the extinc- tion curve of a pigeon which had been reinforced on a special schedule. Nothing of the sort is ever obtained after continuous re- inforcement. Since this is a technique for "getting more responses out of an organism" in return for a given number of reinforcements, it is widely used. Wages are paid in special ways and betting and gambling devices are designed to "pay off" on special schedules because of the relatively large return on the reinforcement in such a case. Approval, affection, and other personal favors are frequently intermittent, not only because the person supplying the reinforcement may behave in different ways at different times, but precisely because he may have found that such a schedule yields a more stable, persistent, and profitable return.

It is important to distinguish between schedules which are arranged by a system outside the organism and those which are controlled by the behavior itself. An example of the first is a schedule of reinforcement which is determined by a clock—as when we reinforce a pigeon every five minutes, allowing all intervening responses to go unreinforced. An example of the second is a schedule in which a response is reinforced after a certain number of responses have been emitted—as when we reinforce every fiftieth response the pigeon makes. The cases are similar in the sense that we reinforce intermittently in both, but subtle differences in the contingencies lead to very different results, often of great practical significance.

Interval reinforcement. If we reinforce behavior at regular intervals, an organism such as a rat or pigeon will adjust with a nearly constant rate of responding, determined by the frequency of reinforcement. If we reinforce it every minute, the animal responds rapidly; if every five minutes, much more slowly. A similar effect upon probability of response is characteristic of human behavior. How often we call a given number on the telephone will depend, other things being equal, upon how often we get an answer. If two agencies supply the same service, we are more likely to call the one which answers more often. We are less likely to see friends or acquaintances with whom we only occasionally have a good time, and we are less likely to write to a correspondent who seldom answers. The experimental results are precise enough to suggest that in general the organism gives back a certain number of responses for each response reinforced. We shall see, however, that the results of schedules of reinforcement are not always reducible to a simple equating of input with output.

Since behavior which appears under interval reinforcement is especially stable, it is useful in studying other variables and conditions. The size or amount of each reinforcement affects the rate—more responses appearing in return for a larger reinforcement. Different kinds of reinforcers also yield different rates, and these may be used to rank reinforcers in the order of their effectiveness. The rate varies with the immediacy of the reinforcement: a slight delay between response and the receipt of the reinforcer means a lower over-all rate. Other variables which have been studied under interval reinforcement will be discussed in later chapters. They include the degree of deprivation and the presence or absence of certain emotional circumstances.

Optimal schedules of reinforcement are often of great practical importance. They are often discussed in connection with other variables which affect the rate. Reinforcing a man with fifty dollars at one time may not be so effective as reinforcing him with five dollars at ten different times during the same period. This is especially the case with primitive people where conditioned reinforcers have not been established to bridge the temporal span between a response and its ultimate consequence. There are also many subtle interactions between schedules of reinforcement and levels of motivation, immediacy of reinforcement, and so on.

If behavior continues to be reinforced at fixed intervals, another process intervenes. Since responses are never reinforced just after reinforcement, a change, to be described in Chapter VII, eventually takes place in which the rate of responding is low for a short time after each reinforcement. The rate rises again when an interval of time has elapsed which the organism presumably cannot distinguish from the interval at which it is reinforced. These changes in rate are not characteristic of the effect of wages in industry, which would otherwise appear to be an example of a fixed-interval schedule. The discrepancy is explained by the fact that other reinforcing systems are used to maintain a given level of work, as we shall see in Chapter XXV. Docking a man for time absent guarantees his presence each day by establishing a time-card entry as a conditioned reinforcer. The aversive reinforcement (Chapter XI) supplied by a supervisor or boss is, however, the principal supplement to a fixed-interval wage.

A low probability of response just after reinforcement is eliminated with what is called *variable-interval* reinforcement. Instead of reinforcing a response every five minutes, for example, we reinforce every five minutes *on the average*, where the intervening interval may be as short as a few seconds or as long as, say, ten minutes. Reinforcement occasionally occurs just after the organism has been reinforced, and the organism therefore continues to respond at that time. Its performance under such a schedule is remarkably stable and uniform. Pigeons reinforced with food with a variable interval averaging five minutes between reinforcements have been observed to respond for as long as fifteen hours at a rate of from two to three responses per second without pausing longer than fifteen or twenty seconds during the whole period. It is usually very difficult to extinguish a response after such a schedule. Many sorts of social or personal reinforcement are supplied on what is essentially a variable-interval basis, and extraordinarily persistent behavior is sometimes set up.

Ratio reinforcement. An entirely different result is obtained when the schedule of reinforcement depends upon the behavior of the organism itself—when, for example, we reinforce every fiftieth response. This is reinforcement at a "fixed ratio"—the ratio of reinforced to unreinforced responses. It is a common schedule in education, where the student is reinforced for completing a project or a paper or some other specific amount of work. It is essentially the basis of professional pay and of selling on commission. In industry it is known as piecework pay. It is a system of reinforcement which naturally recommends itself to employers because the cost of the labor required to produce a given result can be calculated in advance.

Fixed-ratio reinforcement generates a very high rate of response provided the ratio is not too high. This should follow from the input-output relation alone. Any slight increase in rate increases the frequency of reinforcement with the result that the rate should rise still further. If no other factor intervened, the rate should reach the highest possible value. A limiting factor, which makes itself felt in industry, is simple fatigue. The high rate of responding and the long hours of work generated by this schedule can be dangerous to health. This is the main reason why piecework pay is usually strenuously opposed by organized labor.

Another objection to this type of schedule is based upon the possibility that as the rate rises, the reinforcing agency will move to a larger ratio. In the laboratory, after first reinforcing every tenth response and then every fiftieth, we may find it possible to reinforce only every hundredth, although we could not have used this ratio in the beginning. In industry, the employee whose productivity has increased as the result of a piecework schedule may receive so large a weekly wage that the employer feels justified in increasing the number of units of work required for a given unit of pay.

Under ratios of reinforcement which can be sustained, the behavior eventually shows a very low probability just after reinforcement, as it does in the case of fixed-interval reinforcement. The effect is marked under high fixed ratios because the organism always has "a long way to go" before the next reinforcement. Wherever a piecework schedule is used—in industry, education, salesmanship, or the professions—low morale or low interest is most often observed just after a unit of work has been completed. When responding begins, the situation is improved by each response and the more the organism responds, the better the chances of reinforcement become. The result is a smooth gradient of acceleration as the organism responds more and more rapidly. The condition eventually prevailing under high fixed-ratio reinforcement is not an efficient over-all mode of responding. It makes relatively poor use of the available time, and the higher rates of responding may be especially fatiguing.

The laboratory study of ratio reinforcement has shown that for a given organism and a given measure of reinforcement there is a limiting ratio beyond which behavior cannot be sustained. The result of exceeding this ratio is an extreme degree of extinction of the sort which we call abulia (Chapter V). Long periods of inactivity begin to appear between separate ratio runs. This is not physical fatigue, as we may easily show by shifting to another schedule. It is often called "mental" fatigue, but this designation adds nothing to the observed fact that beyond a certain high ratio of reinforcement the organism simply has no behavior available. In both the laboratory study of ratio reinforcement and its practical application in everyday life, the first signs of strain imposed by too high a ratio are seen in these breaks. Before a pigeon stops altogether—in complete "abulia"—it will often not respond for a long time after reinforcement. In the same way, the student who has finished a term paper, perhaps in a burst of speed at the end of the gradient, finds it difficult to start work on a new assignment.

Exhaustion can occur under ratio reinforcement because there is no self-regulating mechanism. In interval reinforcement, on the other hand, any tendency toward extinction is opposed by the fact that when the rate declines, the next reinforcement is received in return for fewer responses. The variable-interval schedule is also self-protecting: an organism will stabilize its behavior at a given rate under any length of interval.

We get rid of the pauses after reinforcement on a fixed-ratio schedule by adopting essentially the same practice as in variable-interval reinforcement: we simply vary the ratios over a considerable range around some mean value. Successive responses may be reinforced or many hundreds of unreinforced responses may intervene. The probability of reinforcement at any moment remains essentially constant and the organism adjusts by holding to a constant rate. This "variable-ratio reinforcement" is much more powerful than a fixed-ratio scedule with the same mean number of responses. A pigeon may respond as rapidly as five times per second and maintain this rate for many hours.

The efficacy of such schedules in generating high rates has long been known to the proprietors of gambling establishments. Slot machines, roulette wheels, dice cages, horse races, and so on pay off on a schedule of variable-ratio reinforcement. Each device has its own auxiliary reinforcements, but the schedule is the important characteristic. Winning depends upon placing a bet and in the long run upon the number of bets placed, but no particular payoff can be predicted. The ratio is varied by any one of several "random" systems. The pathological gambler exemplifies the result. Like the pigeon with its five responses per second for many hours, he is the victim of an unpredictable contingency of reinforcement. The long-term net gain or loss is almost irrelevant in accounting for the effectiveness of this schedule.

A combined schedule. It is fairly easy to combine ratio and interval reinforcement in a laboratory experiment so that reinforcement is determined both by the passage of time and by the number of unreinforced responses emitted. In such a case, if the organism is responding rapidly, it responds many times before being reinforced, but if it is responding slowly, only a few responses occur before the next reinforcement. Such a schedule resembles either interval or ratio reinforcement, depending upon the values chosen in the combination, but there is some evidence that there is a middle ground in which neither schedule predominates and that the resulting behavior is unstable. Although this combined schedule may seem quite arbitrary, it is exemplified by many social situations where, as we shall see in Chapter XIX, the reinforcing agent may be affected by the level of the behavior reinforced.

We can reinforce an organism only when responses are occurring at a specified rate. If we reinforce only when, say, the four preceding responses have occurred within two seconds, we generate a very high rate. This is maintained even when we reinforce only at varying intervals with a fairly long mean interval. The rates exceed those which prevail under a variable-ratio schedule for the same net rate of reinforcement. Reinforcing a *low* rate of responding at variable intervals has the opposite effect of generating a sustained low rate. These studies have yielded many facts, too detailed to be discussed here, which explain why a given schedule of reinforcement has the effect it has. The effects of a schedule are due to the contingencies which prevail at the moment of reinforcement under it. Such schedules are, in other words, *simply rather inaccurate ways of reinforcing rates of responding.* They are often the most convenient way of doing this, and this may explain their widespread use in the practical control of behavior. But with proper instrumentation it should be possible to improve upon established practices in all these fields. Thus gambling devices could be "improved"—from the point of view of the proprietor—by introducing devices which would pay off on a variable-interval basis, but only when the rate of play is exceptionally high. The device would need to be more complex than the slot machine or roulette wheel but would undoubtedly be more effective in inducing play. Schedules of pay in industry, salesmanship, and the professions, and the use of bonuses, incentive wages, and so on, could also be improved from the point of view of generating maximal productivity.

Whether these improvements should be permitted is a matter to be discussed later. A schedule of reinforcement not only increases productivity, it also increases the interest, morale, and happiness of the worker. Any decision concerning a choice of schedules is complicated by this fact. In any event, we can act intelligently in this area only if we are in possession of clear-cut information regarding the nature and effect of the devices responsible for the maintenance of behavior in strength. We have much to gain from a close study of the results of experimental analyses.

CHAPTER VII

OPERANT DISCRIMINATION

DISCRIMINATIVE STIMULI

Operant conditioning may be described without mentioning any stimulus which acts before the response is made. In reinforcing neck-stretching in the pigeon it was necessary to wait for the stretching to occur; we did not elicit it. When a baby puts his hand to his mouth, the movement may be reinforced by the contact of hand and mouth, but we cannot find any stimulus which elicits the movement and which is present every time it occurs. Stimuli are always acting upon an organism, but their functional connection with operant behavior is not like that in the reflex. Operant behavior, in short, is *emitted*, rather than *elicited*. It must have this property if the notion of probability of response is to make sense.

Most operant behavior, however, acquires important connections with the surrounding world. We may show how it does so in our pigeon experiment by reinforcing neck-stretching when a signal light is on and allowing it to be extinguished when the light is off. Eventually stretching occurs only when the light is on. We can then demonstrate a stimulus-response connection which is roughly comparable to a conditioned or unconditioned reflex: the appearance of the light will be quickly followed by an upward movement of the head. But the relation is fundamentally quite different. It has a different history and different current properties. We describe the contingency by saying that a _stimulus_ (the light) is the occasion upon which a _response_ (stretching the neck) is followed by _reinforcement_ (with food). We must specify all three terms. The effect upon the pigeon is that eventually the response is more likely to occur when the light is on. The process through which this comes about is called _discrimination._ Its importance in a theoretical analysis, as well as in the practical control of behavior, is obvious: when a discrimination has been established, we may alter the probability of a response instantly by presenting or removing the discriminative stimulus.

Operant behavior almost necessarily comes under this kind of stimulus control, since only a few responses are automatically reinforced by the organism's own body without respect to external circumstances. Reinforcement achieved by adjusting to a given environment almost always requires the sort of physical contact which we call stimulation. The environmental control has an obvious biological significance. If all behavior were equally likely to occur on all occasions, the result would be chaotic. It is obviously advantageous that a response occur only when it is likely to be reinforced.

The three-term contingencies which produce discriminative operants are of many kinds. We develop the behavior with which we adjust to the spatial world because visual stimulation from an object is the occasion upon which certain responses of walking, reaching, and so on lead to particular tactual consequences. The visual field is the occasion for effective manipulatory action. The contingencies responsible for the behavior are generated by the relations between visual and tactual stimulation characteristic of physical objects. Other connections between the properties of objects supply other sorts of contingencies which lead to similar changes in behavior. For example, in an orchard in which red apples are sweet and all others sour, the behavior of picking and eating comes to be controlled by the redness of the stimulus.

The social environment contains vast numbers of such contingencies. A smile is an occasion upon which social approach will meet with approval. A frown is an occasion upon which the same approach will not meet with approval. Insofar as this is generally true, approach comes to depend to some extent upon the facial expression of the person approached. We use this fact when by smiling or frowning we control to some extent the behavior of those approaching us. The ringing of a telephone is an occasion upon which answering will be followed by hearing a voice. The young child may pick up and speak into the telephone at any time, but eventually he will do so only when it has been ringing. The verbal stimulus "Come to dinner" is an occasion upon which going to a table and sitting down is usually reinforced with food. The stimulus comes to be effective in increasing the probability of that behavior and is produced by the speaker because it does so. Bells, whistles, and traffic signals are other obvious occasions upon which certain actions are generally followed by certain consequences.

Verbal behavior fits the pattern of the three-term contingency and supplies many illuminating examples. We learn to name objects by acquiring an enormous repertoire of responses each of which is appropriate to a given occasion. A chair is the occasion upon which the response "chair" is likely to be reinforced, a cat is the occasion upon which the response "cat" is likely to be reinforced, and so on. When we read aloud, we respond to a series of visual stimuli with a series of corresponding vocal responses. The three-term contingency is evident in teaching a child to read, when a given response is reinforced with "right" or "wrong" according to the presence or absence of the appropriate visual stimulus.

Many verbal responses are under the control of *verbal* discrimination stimuli. In memorizing the multiplication table, for example, the stimulus "9 × 9" is the occasion upon which the response "81" is appropriately reinforced, either by an instructor or by the successful outcome of a calculation. Historical "facts" and many other types of information fit the same formula. When the student writes an examination, he emits, insofar as it has become part of his repertoire, the behavior which is reinforced upon the special occasion established by the examination question.

We use operant discrimination in two ways. In the first place, stimuli which have already become discriminative are manipulated in order to change probabilities. We do this explicitly and almost con-tinuously when we direct constructive work, control the behavior of children, issue orders, and so on. We do it more subtly when we arrange stimuli whose effectiveness has not been specifically estab-lished for such purposes. In displaying merchandise in a large store the behavior of the customer is controlled through existing dis-criminative operants. The purchase of certain types of merchandise may be assumed to be strongly determined by conditions which com-monly bring customers to the store. It is a mistake to exhibit this merchandise in the front of the store, since the customer will then buy and leave. Instead, goods are displayed which are more likely to be purchased "on the spur of the moment" rather than as the result of deprivations sufficient to bring the customer into the store. The display serves as a "reminder" in the sense of making the occa-sion optimal for the emission of weak behavior.

In the second place, we may set up a discrimination in order to make sure that a future stimulus will have a given effect when it appears. Education is largely a matter of establishing such discrimina-tive repertoires, as we shall see in Chapter XXVI. We set up con-tingencies which generate behavior as the result of which children will look before crossing streets, will say "Thank you" upon the proper occasions, will give correct answers to questions about his-torical events, will operate machines in the proper manner, will buy books, attend concerts, plays, and moving pictures identified in cer-tain ways, and so on.

VOLUNTARY AND INVOLUNTARY BEHAVIOR

The relation between the discriminative operant and its controlling stimulus is very different from elicitation. Stimulus and response occur in the same order as in the reflex, but this does not warrant the inclusion of both types in a single "stimulus-response" formula. The discriminative stimulus does not elicit a response, it simply alters a probability of occurrence. The relation is flexible and continuously graded. The response follows the stimulus in a more leisurely fashion, and it may be intense or feeble almost without respect to the intensity of the stimulus. This difference is at the root of the classical distinction between voluntary and involuntary behavior.

In the early history of the reflex, an effort was made to distinguish between reflexes and the rest of the behavior of the organism. One difference frequently urged was that a reflex was *innate,* but the principle of conditioning made such a distinction trivial. It was also said that reflexes were different because they were *unconscious.* This did not mean that the individual could not report upon his own reflex behavior, but that the behavior made its appearance whether he could do so or not. Reflex action might take place when a man was asleep or otherwise "unconscious." As we shall see in Chapter XVII, this too is no longer considered a valid difference; behavior which is clearly not reflex may occur under such circumstances. A third classical distinction held that reflexes were not only innate and unconscious, but "involuntary." They were not "willed." The evidence was not so much that they could not be willed as that they could not be willed against. A certain part of the behavior of the organism cannot, so to speak, be helped. We may not be able to keep from winking when something moves close to our eyes. We may not be able to help flinching at gunfire or salivating at the taste of a lemon or (through a conditioned reflex) at the sight of a lemon. Before the discovery of the reflex such behavior was reconciled with a scheme of inner causation by postulating separate causes. It was attributed to seditious selves or foreign spirits temporarily invading the body. The involuntary sneeze, for example, revealed the presence of the Devil. (We still take the precaution of saying "God bless you" when someone sneezes.) With the advent of the notion of the reflex the issue of controllability became less crucial.

In the present analysis we cannot distinguish between involuntary and voluntary behavior by raising the issue of who is in control. It does not matter whether behavior is due to a willing individual or a psychic usurper if we dismiss all inner agents of whatever sort. Nor can we make the distinction on the basis of control or lack of control, since we assume that no behavior is free. If we have no reason to distinguish between being able to do something and doing it, such expressions as "not being able to do something" or "not being able to help doing something" must be interpreted in some other way. When all relevant variables have been arranged, an organism will or will not respond. If it does not, it cannot. If it can, it will. To ask whether someone *can* turn a handspring is merely to ask whether there are circumstances under which he will do so. A man who *can* avoid flinching at gunfire is a man who will not flinch under certain circumstances. A man who *can* hold still while a dentist works on his teeth is one who holds still upon certain occasions.

The distinction between voluntary and involuntary behavior is a matter of the *kind* of control. It corresponds to the distinction between eliciting and discriminative stimuli. The eliciting stimulus appears to be more coercive. Its causal connection with behavior is relatively simple and easily observed. This may explain why it was discovered first. The discriminative stimulus, on the other hand, shares its control with other variables, so that the inevitability of its effect cannot be easily demonstrated. But when all relevant variables have been taken into account, it is not difficult to guarantee the result—to force the discriminative operant as inexorably as the eliciting stimulus forces its response. If the manner in which this is done and the quantitative properties of the resulting relation warrant such a distinction, we may say that voluntary behavior is operant and involuntary behavior reflex.

It is natural that the "will" as an inner explanation of behavior should have survived longer in the study of operant behavior, where the control exercised by the environment is more subtle and indirect. In the case of the operation we call reinforcement, for example, the current strength of behavior is due to events which have occurred in the past history of the organism—events which are not observed at the moment their effect is felt. Deprivation is a relevant variable, but one which has a history of which we may have little or no information. When a discriminative stimulus has an effect upon the probability of a response, we see that the present environment is indeed relevant, but it is not easy to prove the inevitability of the control without an adequate account of the history of reinforcement and deprivation.

Consider, for example, a hungry guest who hears his host say,

"Won't you come to dinner?" (We assume that the guest has undergone the elaborate conditioning responsible for the behavior described as "knowing English.") As the result of respondent conditioning, this verbal stimulus leads to a certain amount of "involuntary" secretion of saliva and other gastric juices and perhaps contraction of the smooth muscles in the walls of the stomach and intestines. It may also induce the guest to approach and sit down at the table, but this behavior is certainly of another sort. It appears to be less sharply determined, and we predict it less confidently. Both the salivary reflex and the operant response occur because they have usually been reinforced with food, but this history lies in the past, much of it in the remote past. In the absence of an appropriate state of deprivation they may not occur; the guest may instead reply, "Thank you, I'm not hungry." But even if the history of reinforcement and deprivation is satisfactory, the operant responses may be displaced by other behavior involving the same musculature. If our guest has been offended by undue delay in the preparation of the meal, for example, he may take revenge by creating a further delay—perhaps by asking to wash his hands and remaining out of the room a long time. The behavior has been acquired because it has been reinforced by its damaging effect upon other persons—because the guest has "learned how to annoy people." Before we can predict that he will come to the table as surely as we predict that he will salivate, we must have information about all relevant variables—not only those which increase the probability of the response but also those which increase the probability of competing responses. Since we ordinarily lack anything like adequate knowledge of all these variables, it is simpler to assume that the behavior is determined by the guest's will—that he will come if he wants to and wills to do so. But the assumption is of neither theoretical nor practical value, for we still have to predict the behavior of the "will." The inner explanation is no short cut to the information we need. If many variables are important, many variables must be studied.

The distinction between voluntary and involuntary behavior, or operant and reflex behavior, parallels another distinction. Reflexes are primarily concerned, as we have seen, with the internal economy of the organism, where glands and smooth muscles are most important. Reflexes employing the striped muscles are chiefly involved in maintaining posture and in other responses to the more stable properties of the surrounding world. This is the only area in which well-defined responses are effective enough to be acquired as part of the genetic equipment of the organism. Operant behavior, on the other hand, is largely concerned with that part of the environment in which the conditions for effective action are quite unstable and where a genetic or "instinctive" endowment is much less probable, if not actually impossible.

Reflex behavior is extended through respondent conditioning and apparently cannot be conditioned according to the operant pattern. Glands and smooth muscles do not naturally produce the kinds of consequences involved in operant reinforcement, and when we arrange such consequences experimentally, operant conditioning does not take place. We may reinforce a man with food whenever he "turns red," but we cannot in this way condition him to blush "voluntarily." The behavior of blushing, like that of blanching or secreting tears, saliva, sweat, and so on cannot be brought directly under the control of operant reinforcement. If some technique could be worked out to achieve this result, it would be possible to train a child to control his emotions as readily as he controls the positions of his hands.

A result which resembles the voluntary control of glands or smooth muscles is achieved when operant behavior creates appropriate stimuli. If it is not possible to alter the rate of the pulse directly through operant reinforcement, other behavior—violent exercise, for example—can generate a condition in which the pulse rate changes. If we reinforce a certain critical rate, we may in fact, though inadvertently, simply reinforce operant behavior which produces it. This effect appears to be the explanation of apparent exceptions to the rule. Cases have been reported in which a man could raise the hair on his arm "voluntarily." Other subjects have been able to slow their pulse on command. But there is reasonable evidence for supposing that in every case an intervening step occurs and that the response of the gland or smooth muscle itself is not an operant. Other examples in which an operant and a reflex are chained together in this way will be described in Chapter XV.

It is not so easy to determine whether we can condition purely reflex responses in striped muscles through operant reinforcement. The difficulty is that an operant response may arise which simply imitates the reflex. One may sneeze, for example, not only because of the pepper but because of special social consequences—"He only does it to annoy, because he knows it teases." Whether the facsimile sneeze resembles the reflex response in every particular is hard to say, but it probably does not. In any case, the controlling variables are sufficiently different to warrant a distinction. The little boy who sneezes to annoy is unmasked when we set up conditions for incompatible operant behavior. If we offer him candy and the sneezing stops, we may be pretty sure that it was not reflex. We need not say that the sneezing must have been voluntary "because he could stop it when he wanted to." A more acceptable translation reads, "He stopped sneezing when variables were introduced which strengthened competing behavior."

The distinction between voluntary and involuntary behavior is further complicated by the fact that the two muscular systems sometimes overlap. The sphincters of the eliminative system and the muscles of the eyelid take part in certain well-known reflexes. In the young child the reflex control sometimes acts alone, but operant behavior is later acquired which may become powerful enough to oppose reflex action. Ordinarily, breathing is reflex, but we "voluntarily" stop breathing under suitable conditions of operant reinforcement—for example, to win a bet or to escape the aversive stimulation of water in the nose when we dive. How long we stop will depend upon the strength of the breathing reflexes, which become more and more powerful as carbon dioxide accumulates in the blood. Eventually a point is reached at which we "cannot help breathing."

The distinction between voluntary and involuntary behavior bears upon our changing concept of personal responsibility. We do not hold people responsible for their reflexes—for example, for coughing in church. We hold them responsible for their operant behavior—for example, for whispering in church or remaining in church while coughing. But there are variables which are responsible for whispering as well as for coughing, and these may be just as inexorable. When we recognize this, we are likely to drop the notion of responsibility altogether and with it the doctrine of free will as an inner causal agent. This may make a great difference in our practices. The doctrine of personal responsibility is associated with certain techniques of controlling behavior—techniques which generate "a sense of responsibility" or point out "an obligation to society." These techniques are relatively ill-adapted to their purpose. Those who suffer are the first to speak out for the inevitability of their behavior. The alcoholic insists that he can't help drinking and the "victim of a bad temper" that he can't help kicking the cat or speaking his mind. We have every reason to agree. But we can improve our understanding of human behavior and greatly strengthen our control by designing alternative practices which recognize the importance of reinforcement as well as other variables of which behavior is a function.

DISCRIMINATIVE REPERTOIRES

We have seen that any *unit* of operant behavior is to a certain extent artificial. Behavior is the coherent, continuous activity of an integral organism. Although it may be analyzed into parts for theoretical or practical purposes, we need to recognize its continuous nature in order to solve certain common problems. Discriminative behavior offers many examples. In the behavior of reaching toward and touching a spot in the visual field, each position which the spot may occupy requires a particular combination of reaching and touching movements. Each position becomes the distinguishing property of a discriminative stimulus which raises the probability of the appropriate response. Eventually a spot in any position evokes the movement which achieves contact with it. At the very edges of the field the behavior may be defective, and unusual cases may need special conditioning—for example, reaching for an object seen in a mirror or from an unusual posture—but in the central area all positions of the spot comprise a continuous field and all possible combinations of movements leading to contact form a corresponding field. The behavior is acquired upon specific occasions when specific responses toward specific locations are reinforced, but the organism almost inevitably acquires a coherent repertoire which can be described without referring to the punctate origins of the two fields.

If we wish to specify the smallest possible unit of correspondence between stimulus and response, we use the dimensions in which the two fields are described. The correspondence is between points. But in many repertoires the minimal units fall considerably short of points in continuous fields. The stimuli and responses may not compose fields. When we learn the names of a large number of people, we do not expect either the visual patterns which the people present or their names to form continuous fields. The repertoire remains a collection of discrete units. Even when stimuli and responses can be described as fields, the behavior may not be developed to that point. In several of the discriminative repertoires now to be considered, the functional unit is much smaller than the stimulus or response which appears upon any given occasion and with which we characteristically deal, but it is by no means always so small as to be expressed as an instance of the correspondence between fields.

Drawing from copy. Our behavior in response to the spatial field in which we live is so familiar that we are likely to forget how it is acquired. There are certain less familiar forms of behavior in which the origin of a discriminative repertoire can sometimes be clearly traced. In drawing "from copy"—or, less obviously, from an object—our behavior is the product of a set of three-term contingencies. A given line in the material to be copied is the occasion upon which certain movements with pencil and paper produce a similar line. All such lines and all such movements comprise fields, but the behavior may not reach a condition in which it can be dealt with as a field. This is easily seen in the behavior of the young child learning to draw. A small number of standardized responses are evoked by the highly complex stimulus field. The behavior of the skilled copyist is composed of a much larger number of responses and may seem as "natural" as our responses to spatial positions. It does not reach the point at which it comprises a continuous field if a given line in the copy is not reproduced exactly but rather with a characteristic response in the "individual style" of the artist. An extreme case, in which behavior is divided into clearly identifiable discrete units even though the stimulus has the characteristics of a field, is the behavior of the electrical engineer who "draws a picture" of a radio set using perhaps twenty or thirty unit responses.

There are great individual differences in the ability to draw from copy. The contingencies responsible for the behavior are by no means so universal as those responsible for spatial behavior with respect to the visual field, and very different amounts of instruction are received by different individuals. Moreover, a small difference in early instruction may make a big difference in the eventual result. The child who develops at an early age a repertoire with which he successfully copies drawings and objects is likely to continue to use it and to receive further differential reinforcement. The special training of the artist includes many highly sensitive differential contingencies, supplied by a teacher or automatically by the artist himself as he becomes "discriminating." A man who cannot draw well is likely to be puzzled by one who can. He cannot see "how it is done." By no "effort of will" can he produce a comparable achievement. The basic minimal repertoire is simply lacking. It can be established only through discriminative reinforcement. The behavior is under the control of the copy, not of the artist, and until the copy has been put into control through differential reinforcement based upon it as a discriminative stimulus, the behavior will not occur.

Singing or playing by ear. Drawing from copy is like responding to the spatial world insofar as both stimuli and responses approach continuous fields in the same way in both cases. In playing an instrument or singing a tune "by ear," however, spatial dimensions are lacking. Here appropriate repertoires are set up by similar three-term contingencies. A tone is the occasion upon which certain complex behavior in the vocal apparatus will be reinforced by generating a matching tone. The reinforcement is either automatic, depending upon previous conditioning of the singer with respect to good matches, or supplied by someone—an instructor, for example—whose behavior also reflects goodness of match. Such a repertoire may also include responses to intervals, each heard interval being the occasion upon which a complex response generating a corresponding interval is reinforced. Melodies, harmonic progressions, and so on, may form the bases for similar repertoires. The same kind of relationships may govern the playing of a musical instrument, where the topography of the behavior which generates the tones or patterns is entirely different.

The ultimate unit in singing or playing by ear may stop at the level of the half-tone scale. Both stimuli and responses usually show this "grain." A singer with poor pitch is one whose response system has a poorly defined grain which does not match the stimulus system. On the other hand, a singer with good pitch may correctly sing a melody which is itself defective. Here the response repertoire is in better focus than the stimulus. The half-tone scale is not, of course, a natural limit. The successful vocal mimic has a repertoire which approaches a continuous field and which permits him to duplicate nonmusical sounds. The successful imitation of bird song or of the noise of machines requires this sort of fine-grained repertoire.

We easily lose sight of the conditioning required to develop such behavior. The individual who cannot mimic an auditory pattern or who cannot sing or play by ear is likely to be puzzled by one who can. He finds it quite impossible to sing a matching pitch or to hum a corresponding tune or to imitate the noise of a locomotive, and he has no conception of how the successful mimic does so. He cannot be a successful mimic by any "act of will." The difference lies in the histories of reinforcement. If the repertoire with which one reproduces a melody has never been established, it will not be brought into play by the appropriate circumstances.

Imitation. It is only a short step from these discriminative repertoires to the field of imitation. So far as we know, imitative behavior does not arise because of any inherent reflex mechanism. Such a mechanism would require that the stimulus generated by a given pattern of behavior in another organism elicit a series of responses having the same pattern—for example, the visual stimulus of a running dog would elicit running in another dog. This would be an extremely complex mechanism and, in spite of a strong belief to the contrary, it seems not to exist. Imitation develops in the history of the individual as the result of discriminative reinforcements showing our same three-term contingency. The visual stimulation of someone waving a hand is the occasion upon which waving a hand will probably receive reinforcement. The auditory stimulus "Da-Da" is the occasion upon which the complicated verbal response which produces a matching auditory pattern is reinforced by the delighted parent. We see this sort of conditioning taking place in everyday life, and we can also set it up in the laboratory. For example, we can condition a pigeon to execute any one of several acts according to whether another pigeon is executing that particular act. When the imitatee is pecking a key in a certain position, the imitator pecks a corresponding key. When the imitatee pecks a key in a different position, the imitator behaves accordingly. When the imitatee moves to the opposite side of the cage, the imitator follows. Such imitative behavior occurs only when specific discriminative reinforcement has taken place. Pigeons do not appear to imitate each other "naturally." The necessary three-term contingency often occurs in nature, however. Thus, if a pigeon is scratching in a leaf-strewn field, this is an occasion upon which another pigeon is likely to be reinforced for similar behavior. The human parallel is not far distant. When we see people looking into a shop window, we are likely to look, too—not because there is an instinct of imitation, but because windows into which other people are looking are likely to reinforce such behavior. So well developed is the imitative repertoire of the average person that its origins are forgotten, and it is easily accepted as an inherent part of his behavior.

Imitative repertoires are often developed in relatively discrete sets of responses. In learning to dance, a set of more or less stereotyped responses is acquired by virtue of which a step executed by the instructor is duplicated by the pupil. The good dancer possesses a large imitative repertoire of dance steps. When this repertoire is faulty, the imitation is poor, and the novice finds it very difficult to match a complicated step. In dancing, as in singing by ear, the imitative ability of a good performer seems almost magical to the untutored.

A good actor possesses an imitative repertoire of attitudes, postures, and facial expressions which enable him to follow the suggestions of a director or to duplicate behavior observed in everyday life. The attempts of the unskilled actor may be ludicrously wide of the mark because the essential repertoire is lacking. Although imitative responses approach a continuous field, that condition is probably never reached. The duplication of the stimulus is often not precise, and the "grain" of the repertoire with which even the good mimic duplicates behavior may be apparent.

The similarity of stimulus and response in imitation has no special function. We could easily establish behavior in which the "imitator" does exactly the opposite of the "imitatee." Our second pigeon could be conditioned to peck always in a different position. Something of this sort is involved in ballroom dancing where the behavior of instructor and pupil in an "imitative" repertoire are not the same. In ballroom dancing a step backward on the part of the instructor is the occasion for a step forward on the part of the pupil. This kind of inverse imitation can become as smooth as behavior having the same properties, as the good "follower" shows.

Other noncorresponding repertoires are found in the field of sport. The behavior of the tennis player is controlled in large measure by the behavior of his opponent, but the corresponding patterns are not imitative in the usual sense. There is, nevertheless, a three-term contingency: subtle stimuli from the behavior of the opponent which are correlated with a forthcoming placement of the ball are the occasion for appropriate defensive behavior. The good tennis player becomes extremely sensitive to this kind of stimulation, and it is only because of this that he is able to get into proper defensive positions. Fencing offers an especially good example of the integrated behavior of two individuals in which a response on the part of one constitutes a discriminative stimulus for a *different* response on the part of the other. The behavior may be as closely integrated as that of two dancers executing the *same* steps at the same time.

These inverse "imitative" repertoires cannot approach continuous fields from which new instances will automatically emerge. To some extent, skilled dancers may *improvise* a dance in which one introduces a series of steps and the other follows, just as a tennis player is to some extent automatically in possession of the proper reply to a new offensive maneuver, but the corresponding fields which provide for the duplication of behavior in true imitation are lacking.

ATTENTION

The control exerted by a discriminative stimulus is traditionally dealt with under the heading of attention. This concept reverses the direction of action by suggesting, not that a stimulus controls the behavior of an observer, but that the observer *attends* to the stimulus and thereby controls it. Nevertheless, we sometimes recognize that the object "catches or holds the attention" of the observer.

What we usually mean in such a case is that the observer continues to look at the object. An animated billboard is dangerous, for example, if it holds the attention of a motorist too long. The behavior of the motorist in attending to the sign is simply the behavior of looking at it rather than at the road ahead of him. The behavior involves conditioning, and, in particular, the special conditioning of the discriminative operant. The variables are not always obvious, but they can usually be detected. The fact that people read billboards instead of looking at the surrounding countryside shows how effectively reading is usually reinforced—not only by billboards, but by stories, novels, letters, and so on. Powerful reinforcements are arranged by thousands of writers in every field of the written or printed word. All of these stimuli have common typographical properties, which induce the reading of new material. Some reinforcement may also occur on the spot if the particular material is "interesting." (We saw in Chapter VI that "taking an interest" is only another way of expressing the consequences of operant reinforcement.)

We may study this relation in a simple experiment. We arrange to reinforce a pigeon when it pecks a key but only when a small light above the key is flickering. The pigeon forms a discrimination in which it responds to the key when the light flickers and not otherwise. We also note that the pigeon begins to watch the light. We might say that it is attending to it or that it holds its attention. The behavior is easily explained in terms of conditioned reinforcement.

Looking toward the light is occasionally reinforced by seeing the light flicker. The behavior is comparable to looking for an object (Chapter V).

A steady orientation of the eyes is not the only possible result. The behavior of a lookout in the dark or in a heavy fog is an example of looking with orientation to the whole visual field. The behavior of searching the field—or responding to every part of it in some exploratory pattern—is the behavior which is most often reinforced by the discovery of important objects; hence it becomes strong. We can usually observe that the behavior with which a child looks for a misplaced toy is specifically conditioned. If some patterns of looking are reinforced by the discovery of objects more often than others, they emerge as standard behavior. We may study this in the pigeon experiment by arranging a series of lights, any one of which may begin to flicker as a discriminative stimulus. The pigeon comes to look at all the spots in a more or less random order. It may be said to be "looking for the flickering spot," as in the example discussed in Chapter V. If the light begins to flicker while the pigeon is looking elsewhere, the flicker is seen at one side of the visual field. The behavior of looking directly toward the light is then optimally reinforced. We say that the light "captures the undivided attention" of the bird.

But attention is more than looking at something or looking at a class of things in succession. As everyone knows, we may look at the center of a page while "attending to" details at the edges. Attempts to account for this in terms of "incipient eye movements" have failed; and in any case no comparable orientation appears to occur in attending to features of an auditory pattern. Thus, when we listen to a phonograph recording of a symphony while attending particularly to the clarinets, it is apparently not possible to demonstrate any special orientation of the ear. But if attention is not a form of behavior, it does not follow that it is, therefore, outside the field of behavior. Attention is a controlling *relation*—the relation between a response and a discriminative stimulus. When someone is paying attention he is under special control of a stimulus. We detect the relation most readily when receptors are conspicuously oriented, but this is not essential. An organism is attending to a detail of a stimulus, whether or not its receptors are oriented to produce the most clear-cut reception, if its behavior is predominantly under the control of that detail. When our subject describes an object at the edge of the page even though we are sure he is not looking at it, or when he tells us that the clarinets have fallen a beat behind the violins, we need not demonstrate any spatial arrangement of stimulus and response. It is enough to point to the special controlling relation which makes such a response possible. Similarly, in our experiment, we can say that the pigeon is attending to the light, even though it is not looking at it, if it consistently makes the correct discriminative reaction—if it strikes the key when the light is flickering and does not strike it when the light is still. It will probably look at the light because the contingency responsible for the "attention" is also responsible for the reinforcement of such behavior, but it need not do so.

When we enjoin someone to pay particular attention to a feature of the environment, our injunction is itself a discriminative stimulus which supplements the stimulus mentioned in controlling the behavior of the observer. The observer is conditioned to look at or listen to a particular stimulus when he is told to "pay attention" to it because under such conditions he is reinforced for doing so. People generally say "watch that man" only when that man is up to something interesting. They generally say "Listen to the conversation in the seat in back of you" only when something interesting is being said.

Just as we may attend to an object without looking at it, so we may look at an object without attending to it. We need not conclude that we must then be looking with an inferior sort of behavior in which the eyes are not correctly used. The criterion is whether the stimulus is exerting any effect upon our behavior. When we stare at someone without noticing him, listen to a speech without attending to what is said, or read a page "absent-mindedly," we are simply failing to engage in some of the behavior which is normally under the control of such stimuli.

TEMPORAL RELATIONS BETWEEN STIMULUS,
RESPONSE, AND REINFORCEMENT

The environment is so constructed that certain things tend to happen together. The organism is so constructed that its behavior changes when it comes into contact with such an environment. There are three principal cases. (1) Certain events—like the color and taste of ripe fruit—tend to occur together. Respondent conditioning is the corresponding effect upon behavior. (2) Certain activities of the organism effect certain changes in the environment. Operant conditioning is the corresponding effect upon behavior. (3) Certain events are the occasions upon which certain actions effect certain changes in the environment. Operant discrimination is the corresponding effect upon behavior. As a result of these processes, the organism which finds itself in a novel environment eventually comes to behave in an efficient way. The result could not be achieved by inherited mechanisms because the environment it not sufficiently constant from one generation to another.

It is also characteristic of the normal environment that events occur together *in certain temporal relations.* A stimulus may precede another stimulus by a given interval, as when lightning precedes thunder. A response may produce a consequence only after a given interval, as when the ingestion of alcohol is followed by typical effects after a certain delay. A response may achieve its consequence when executed at a given time after the appearance of a discriminative stimulus, as when a ball can be hit only by swinging at it after it has come within reach and before it goes out of reach.

The first two of these characteristics raise no special problem. The effect of an interval of time between the stimuli in respondent conditioning is easily stated. If we give food to an organism ten seconds after a neutral stimulus has been presented, the process of conditioning follows essentially the usual pattern: the dog salivates to the previously neutral stimulus. But eventually a temporal discrimination is established. The dog does not salivate when the conditioned stimulus is first presented but only after an interval has elapsed which gradually approaches the interval after which the unconditioned stimulus usually appears. We may deal with this result simply by defining the conditioned stimulus as a given event *plus the lapse of so many units of time.* The introduction of an interval of time between response and reinforcer in operant conditioning is also of little interest here. The effectiveness of the reinforcement is reduced, but the behavior is not otherwise greatly changed.

When temporal properties are added to the three-term contingency of the discriminative operant, however, special effects follow. A response is sometimes reinforced only if it is made *as rapidly as possible* after the appearance of a given stimulus. A contingency of this sort is responsible for the speed with which many people rush to answer the telephone. Picking up the telephone and saying "Hello" is reinforced only if the response is made quickly. The runner responds to the starting gun in the same way for the same reason. In a typical "reaction-time" experiment a subject is instructed to lift a finger off a key as soon as a light has appeared or a tone has sounded, with the result that the behavior comes to occur "as soon as possible." Although the instructions given the subject in a reaction-time experiment or to the runner starting a race are complex, the effect upon behavior is due to the simple three-term contingency with an added temporal specification. This same contingency will cause a pigeon to behave "as quickly as possible" also. The pigeon's reaction time is of approximately the same magnitude as man's.

A response may also be reinforced only if it is *delayed* by a given interval of time after presentation of the stimulus. Thus, a pigeon is reinforced for pecking a key only if it waits, say, six seconds after the key is presented. Many social and commercial reinforcements are of this sort—where, for example, the net effect is reduced if one replies too quickly or agrees too readily to an arrangement or where an optimal reinforcement follows only after "due deliberation." Under contingencies of this sort, the maximal probability of response is characteristically reached a little before the required interval has elapsed.

A characteristic effect of a delay is sometimes referred to as "expectancy" or "anticipation." Let us suppose that a frequent visitor makes it a practice to give a child a bit of candy a few minutes after arrival. How can we formulate the behavior of the child in "antici-pating" the gift of candy? We may note, first of all, that the arrival of the visitor serves as a conditioned stimulus and that the child's mouth will possibly water. If the interval which elapses between the arrival and the presentation of candy is fairly uniform, a temporal discrimination may develop so that this conditioned response will not appear until the interval has almost elapsed. If certain move-ments on the part of the visitor have usually preceded the presenta-tion of candy, any movement on the part of the visitor will be rein-forcing. The child will therefore "attend" to the visitor, as that term has just been defined. He will watch the visitor closely. If any verbal stimuli have been especially correlated with the candy, he will also listen to whatever the visitor is saying, since listening will have been reinforced by such stimuli. Any behavior on the part of the child which has made the appearance of candy more probable has also been reinforced and will be strong. The child may make himself conspicuous by "showing off," for example. For the same reason he may refer to former gifts and thus supply a "hint" to the visitor (Chapter XV).

Much of the child's behavior will be emotional. It is easier to observe this when the "anticipated" stimulus is aversive. As we shall see in Chapter XI, the emotional state in such a case is called "anxiety." When the anticipated stimulus is positively reinforcing, there is a general change in the behavior of the child in the direction of greater excitement and responsiveness. These are to some extent the strengthening aspects of "joy" or "delight." (We shall see in Chapter X that these terms must be used with caution.)

There is still another ingredient in "anticipation." The behavior of the runner in response to the words "Get ready, get set . . ." shows all the effects so far listed: (1) conditioned reflexes involving pulse, respiration, sweating, and so on, (2) a special controlling rela-tion to the voice of the starter which we call "close attention," and (3) emotional changes which, if the race is to be a grueling one, will be more characteristic of anxiety than of joy. In addition to all this, the runner tenses his muscles and adopts just that posture which will make his response to the signal "Go!" most effective. This kind of behavior, sometimes called "preparatory set," is reinforced by the increased speed of the response which follows. The behavior may be nothing more than a partial execution of the response of "going," sometimes revealed in the false start, or it may consist of any other form of behavior which receives the net reinforcement of a more successful start—for example, holding still rather than rocking back and forth on one's toes.

CHAPTER VIII

THE CONTROLLING ENVIRONMENT

THE IMPORTANCE OF THE ENVIRONMENT

No matter what our philosophy of behavior may be, we are not likely to deny that the world about us is important. We may disagree as to the nature or extent of the control which it holds over us, but some control is obvious. Behavior must be appropriate to the occasion. Failure to keep in touch with reality leads to the kinds of difficulties often observed in psychotic behavior. Even when a man is engaged in rejecting the world, in systematically reducing certain forms of its control over him, he is physically interacting with it.

Many theories of human behavior, nevertheless, neglect or ignore the action of the environment. The contact between the organism and the surrounding world is wholly disregarded or at best casually described. This is almost always true in clinical psychology, for example. The clinician often speaks of people, places, and things as "facts" entering into the interpretation of his patient's behavior, without further specifying their action. This practice may be adequate for certain purposes of communication, but it must be expected to fail at some point. Some of the problems of clinical psychology show that that point is often reached. A case history may inform us,

129

for example, that on a given day the patient saw an acquaintance who was approaching him cross the street, and this event may be regarded as significant in interpreting the patient's behavior. But the report "X saw Y cross the street" does not prepare us for many possibly relevant questions. For example, what are the important properties of visual patterns which lead X to say, "That is Y"? Was X's report of this event determined by a clear visual stimulus possessing these properties—in other words, was it really Y or did X merely "think it was Y"? In the latter case how plausible was the mistake? How much of the effect upon X was due to the appearance of Y as a person and how much to Y's behavior in crossing the street? Upon what past occasions had similar stimuli affected X, and what conditioning had taken place with respect to people who cross streets, whether or not they were Y? To what extent was X's reaction due to a condition which we may describe by saying that X was "afraid that Y was avoiding him"? Did earlier conditioning with respect to people who cross streets really involve Z, who resembles Y, and if so, may we say that Y was serving as a "symbol" for Z?

Questions of this sort are frequently treated in the later discussion of a case history, but often they would not arise if the earlier analysis of the contact between organism and environment had been adequate. An improved analysis would mean, not necessarily more information in any particular instance, but rather an understanding of the ways in which stimuli generally work. The casual account ignores many important points.

THE ANALYSIS OF STIMULI

In studying the extremely important independent variables which lie in the immediate environment, we may begin with a physical description. What is the structure of the world which we see, hear, touch, smell, and taste? We should not prejudge these events from their effects upon the organism. They are to be described in the usual terms of the physics of light and sound, the chemistry of odorous or tasteful substances, and so on. We are interested, of course, only in conditions or events which have an effect upon behavior. The electromagnetic radiation of radio and television has no effect upon the unequipped organism, except perhaps at very high energy levels. We do not say that the radiation is "not a stimulus because it does not stimulate." We simply ignore it just as we ignore the color of the apparatus we use in the study of mechanics as soon as we find it to be irrelevant.

The kinds of events which stimulate the organism are effective only within certain limits. We hear sound, but only of certain pitches and intensities. We see light, but only of certain intensities and wave lengths. The limits of stimulation, and also the smallest differences in stimuli which make detectable differences in behavior, have been extensively investigated. The normal individual differs from the blind or color-blind in his reaction to visible radiation, from the deaf or partially deaf in his reaction to tones, from the anosmic in his reaction to odors, and so on. Smaller differences between normal individuals may be equally important. Research of this sort often emphasizes the action of the organ where the interchange with the environment takes place—the eye, the ear, the taste buds in the tongue, and so on—but the whole organism may be involved. What appear to be simple sensory reactions often depend upon variables in the fields of conditioning, motivation, and emotion.

Several important problems concerning stimulation are relatively independent of the particular physical properties of stimuli and of their range of effectiveness. In attacking these problems it does not matter whether the receiving organ is the eye or ear, for example, and we may work with values of stimuli which do not raise the problem of limits. In discussing the stimulus functions of elicitation, discrimination, and reinforcement, it was not always necessary to specify the nature of the stimulation, and we shall see in Chapter IX that this is also true of another function of stimuli in the field of emotion. There are even more general processes which may be studied not only without considering the particular form of energy exchange at the periphery of the organism, but also without specifying whether the stimuli are eliciting, discriminative, reinforcing, or emotional. In the following discussion the discriminative stimulus will be emphasized, but each process could presumably be demonstrated in the other functions as well.

INDUCTION

When we have once brought behavior under the control of a given stimulus, we frequently find that certain other stimuli are also effective. If a pigeon has been conditioned to peck a red spot on the wall of the experimental chamber, the response will also be evoked, though not with the same frequency, by an orange or even a yellow spot. The property of redness is important, but not exclusively so. Spots of different shapes or sizes, or spots against different colors of background, also may be effective. To evaluate the full extent of the change brought about through reinforcement, we need to survey the effects of a large number of stimuli. The spread of the effect to other stimuli is called generalization or induction. The process suggests that a discrete stimulus is as arbitrary a notion as a discrete operant. The "identical elements" of a response have their parallels in the values or properties of a stimulus which are separately effective. If we reinforce a response to a round, red spot one square inch in area, a yellow spot of the same size and shape will be effective because of the common properties of size and shape; a square, red spot of the same area will be effective because of its color and size; and a round, red spot half a square inch in area will be effective because of the common properties of color and shape.

The effectiveness of a single property of a stimulus when combined with novel properties is shown when we are uneasy in the presence of a new acquaintance because he resembles someone whom we dislike. The very subtle property responsible for the resemblance is sufficient to arouse an emotional reaction. The Freudian argument that early emotional conditioning affects later personal adjustment presupposes such a process, in which the subtle property by virtue of which an acquaintance resembles one's father or mother, for example, is said to be independently effective. The Freudian "symbol" presupposes the same process: a piece of abstract sculpture which generates an emotional response because it resembles the human body demonstrates the effectiveness of the property responsible for the resemblance. As Freud pointed out, the resemblance may be effective whether or not it is recognized by the individual.

In literature the same process is exemplified by the device of metaphor. The emphasis in the usual rhetorical analysis is inverted, for the active control is assigned to the organism rather than to the stimulus. The speaker is said to *transfer* a description from one state of affairs to another which resembles it. We should say here that the metaphorical response is evoked by a stimulus which shares some of the properties of the stimulus to which the response is normally appropriate. Thus when Romeo compares Juliet to the sun, we need not suppose that he is engaging in an act of creative imagination; we need only suppose that Juliet's effect upon him shares some of the properties of the effect of the sun and that the verbal response "sun" is therefore strengthened. (The elaboration of the metaphor must be distinguished from an explanation of its ingredients. The first step is to account for the appearance of the metaphorical term. This can usually be done by pointing to a property of a current stimulus which is possessed also by the customary stimulus for the verbal response.)

We check the importance of any dimension of a stimulus by examining the effect of different values. After building up a strong tendency to respond to a red spot, we may examine the rate of response during extinction to orange-red, orange, yellow-orange, and yellow. An experiment of this sort yields a generalization or induction gradient. The responding during extinction is most rapid whenever the spot is red. It is slightly slower to orange-red and much slower to yellow. An experimental animal such as the pigeon may not respond at all if the color is as different as, say, green, even though the two spots have common properties of shape, position, illumination, and being visual rather than, say, auditory stimuli. For the pigeon, therefore, color is obviously an important property. A color-blind organism, on the other hand, would not show this gradient; the rate would not change with color, if differences in brightness, texture, and so on were eliminated. Other properties of stimuli yield similar gradients when systematically explored. This procedure enables us to answer such a question as whether a given change in color is as important for the organism as a given change in size, or even whether color is as important a property of visual stimuli as pitch is of auditory stimuli. Not all the dimensions of stimuli, however, are continuous in this way.

DISCRIMINATION

Induction (or generalization) is not an activity of the organism; it is simply a term which describes the fact that the control acquired by a stimulus is shared by other stimuli with common properties or, to put it another way, that control is shared by all the properties of the stimulus taken separately. A particular combination of properties comprises what we speak of as *a* stimulus, but the expression does not represent the control exercised by the environment very accurately.

The discrimination described in Chapter VII is also not a form of action on the part of the organism. When we establish a discrimination between red and orange spots of light, we simply sharpen a natural gradient. By continuing to reinforce red spots while extinguishing orange spots, the control of the property of redness is consistently strengthened, while that of the property of orange is consistently weakened. In such an experiment, other properties of the stimuli—for example, size, shape, and location—are both reinforced and extinguished. Those who work with pigments, dyes, or other colored materials are affected by contingencies in which slight differences in color make a great deal of difference in the consequences of behavior. We say that they become "highly discriminating" with respect to color. But their behavior shows only processes of conditioning and extinction.

ABSTRACTION

Behavior may be brought under the control of a single property or a special combination of properties of a stimulus while being freed from the control of all other properties. The characteristic result is known as abstraction. The relation to discrimination may be shown by an example. By reinforcing responses to a circular red spot while extinguishing responses to circular spots of all other colors, we may give the red spot exclusive control over the behavior. This is discrimination. Since spots of other colors apparently have no effect, it would appear that the other dimensions which they possess—for example, size, shape, and location—are unimportant. But this is not quite true, since it is less likely that the response will be made to a red object of another size and shape. We have, in other words, brought the response under the control of circular red spots but not of the "property of redness" alone. To achieve the latter, we must reinforce responses to many objects, all of which are red, but which differ widely in their other properties. Eventually, the organism responds only to the property of redness. The case is exemplified by the verbal response "red." It should be remembered, however, that a perfectly abstract response is probably never achieved. Stimuli which possess the required property but which are quite extraordinary in other respects may not evoke the response. Stimuli without the required property which resemble especially common instances which possess it may also exert some control.

Abstraction, too, is not a form of action on the part of the organism. It is simply a narrowing of the control exercised by the properties of stimuli. The controlling property cannot be demonstrated upon a single occasion. In other words, a single instance of an abstract response will not tell us very much about its "referent." The controlling relation can be discovered only through a survey of a large number of instances.

We are likely to overlook the history required for an abstract response, and we make many mistakes in interpreting behavior when we do so. When a child is taught to call a red ball red, we are surprised to find him calling a green ball red. In our own behavior, the response has long since come under the control of a particular color, but in the behavior of the child the properties of size, shape, and manipulability remain important until a program of differential reinforcement rules them out.

An organism will not acquire an abstract response until a reinforcing agency sets up the required contingency. There are no "natural" contingencies which reinforce a response in the presence of a single property without respect to other properties. The necessary contingency apparently requires the mediation of other organisms. Abstraction, therefore, appears to have become possible only with the development of verbal behavior. It does not follow that, if this was the case, abstract responses could never have arisen; for it is not impossible to conceive of events in a group of individuals which could have given rise to the rudiments of a verbal environment from which abstract verbal behavior could then have sprung. The matter, however, is highly speculative.

We are in a better position to see how abstractions grow and change. Verbal behavior, perpetuated by the verbal community, has succeeded in isolating more and more subtle properties of nature. Sometimes we can watch this happen. Sometimes we can make plausible speculations as to how it might have happened. Etymology often supplies valuable clues. The word "chance," for example, comes from a word which referred to the *fall* of a die or coin. A conspicuous feature of such an event is the indeterminacy of the result, which is similar to the indeterminacy of other events in which nothing falls—for example, of the suit of a card drawn from a deck. The metaphorical transfer of the term for falling, on the basis of indeterminacy, is the first step in isolating this important property. The referent of the term is further refined—perhaps through centuries of changing practices in a verbal community—until in the hands of the modern mathematician the term comes under the control of a very special property of nature, the modern referent of the word "chance."

SOME TRADITIONAL PROBLEMS
IN STIMULUS CONTROL

Cross-modal induction. We sometimes find that a response is under the control of two stimuli which have no physical properties in common. If it has been conditioned to each of the stimuli separately, no explanation is required; but apparently this is not always the case. "Induction" appears to occur although common properties are lacking. Sometimes an intermediate connection can be discovered. Pins and pains are both called "sharp." That sharp pins cause sharp pains may be relevant. It is only a short step from "the pin is sharp" to "the pain caused by the pin is sharp." Once this verbal practice has been established in a community, the response is usually learned separately in the two cases and is then no longer an issue.

Common mediating behavior supplies another possible explanation. When Samuel Butler once saw the Wetterhorn, he caught himself humming an aria from Handel. "The big shoulder of the Wetterhorn seemed to fall just like the run on [the word] 'shoulder.'" Here an auditory response appears to have been made to a visual stimulus which in some way resembled it. Presumably Butler had not heard the one while looking at the other; and we may suppose, for the sake of the example, that he had also not seen the musical phrase in visual form. We may account for the result if we assume that the two stimuli were capable of generating similar behavior. If Butler had learned to execute certain spatial responses to the "ups" and "downs" of pitch—say, in playing an instrument—and if, as the amateur artist he was, he had learned to respond to visual patterns with the copying responses described in Chapter VII, then the two stimuli could have evoked a common form of behavior, self-stimulation from which might have served as the basis for the response. The melodic line of the aria could have evoked a response which generated stimulation often followed by the response "Wetterhorn." Conversely, the profile of the Wetterhorn could have evoked a response which in turn generated stimulation often followed by imitative humming or the verbal response "Handel." In this particular instance the verbal response "shoulder" provides a clear cut example of mediating behavior. The shoulder of the mountain strengthens the verbal response "shoulder" which has been part of the auditory pattern of the aria. Speculation of this sort proves nothing, but it does suggest a possible solution of the problem of induction from one sensory field to another. An adequate solution would require an experimental analysis of the various auxiliary processes through which stimulus control can be extended.

Responding to a relation. If an organism has been conditioned to choose a five-inch disk rather than a three-inch disk when the two are presented together, it may choose a seven-inch disk if this is paired with the five-inch. This fact has frequently been offered as a criticism of the principle of the stimulus. If the five-inch disk is the controlling stimulus, why is it not effective in the new combination? Actually it is possible to condition an organism either to choose the larger of two objects or to choose a particular size no matter what the size of an accompanying object. Similar conditioning begins very early in the history of the individual, and the behavior which predominates when a test is made will depend upon such a history. The *relational* case is important in most environments. As the organism moves about in space, reinforcements are generally contingent upon relative, rather than absolute, size.

Stimulus induction on the basis of a "relation" presents no difficulty in a natural science if the relation can be described in physical terms. Where this appears not to be the case, we have to turn to other possibilities—for example, the mediating behavior just discussed. Even such relatively simple organisms as the pigeon may respond appropriately to new stimuli on the basis of relative size, relative intensity, relative position, and so on. They can also be conditioned to ignore any of these properties and to transfer a response on the basis of some other property. The relevant properties are all capable of physical specification.

The "interpreted" stimulus. Another problem in stimulus control has attracted more attention than it deserves because of metaphysical speculations on what is "really there" in the outside world. What happens when an organism responds "as if" a stimulus had other properties? Such behavior seems to indicate that the "perceptual" world—the world as the organism experiences it—is different from the real world. But the difference is actually between responses—between the responses of two organisms or between the responses of one organism under different modes of stimulation from a single state of affairs. Thus I may "think" I have found my coat on the coat rack of a restaurant, though I discover upon examining the contents of the pockets that I am wrong. I may "think" that an object in the sky is a plane only to see a moment later that it is a soaring bird. I may "think" that an object is square only to find when I shift my position that it is not. I may "think" that a spot of light has moved from one point to another, although an examination of the wiring circuit which has produced the spot convinces me that it merely disappeared from one position and reappeared at the other. There is no reason to regard the first of each of these pairs of reactions as "perceptual" and the second as a form of contact with the real world. They are different responses made at different times to a common source of stimulation.

Usually, objects are capable of generating many different kinds of stimuli which are related to each other in certain ways. Responses to some forms of stimulation are more likely to be "right" than responses to others, in the sense that they are more likely to lead to effective behavior. Naturally these modes are favored, but any suggestion that they bring us closer to the "real" world is out of place here. As we saw in Chapter VII, the visual and tactual properties of objects in space lead us to develop an effective repertoire in which we approach and reach for objects successfully. To take a specific case, the visual stimuli generated by a square object are usually accompanied by other visual stimuli when the object is seen from another angle or placed alongside measuring scales, as well as by certain tactual stimuli when the object is manipulated. Now, we can construct an object which, seen from a given point of view, supplies the stimulation characteristic of a square object, although it supplies very different stimuli when handled, measured, or viewed from other angles. Once we have responded to such an object in apparently inconsistent ways, we may be less confident in saying "square" to any one set of visual stimuli, but we have no reason to argue that our original visual response was not to the object "as it really is." We operate in one world—the world of physics. Organisms are part of that world, and they react to it in many ways. Responses may be consistent with each other or inconsistent, but there is usually little difficulty in accounting for either case.

To take another example, suppose we observe a faint haze in the distance at the edge of a forest. This stimulus is appropriate to either of two large classes to which we emit the verbal responses "fog" and "smoke," respectively. The appropriate nonverbal responses are very different: in one case we simply pass on; in the other we dash to give the alarm. We may do neither until we have "decided which it really is." We "interpret" the stimulus before taking specific overt action. But "interpretation" is like the "attention" discussed in Chapter VII; we need not find a particular form of *behavior* to be identified with it. We "interpret" a stimulus as smoke insofar as we tend to respond with behavior appropriate to smoke. We "interpret" it as fog insofar as the probability of a different repertoire is increased. It is only when specific behavior has occurred that we can say that a stimulus has been "interpreted" in a given way, but we may still speak meaningfully of both probabilities. A given stimulus may have two different effects simultaneously when they are compatible, and two different effects in rapid alternation when they are not. A complex condition of indecision may prevail until the matter is resolved either by clarifying the stimulus or in some other way. (What happens when we make a decision will be discussed in Chapter XVI.)

The functional control exerted by a stimulus enables us to distinguish between *sensing* and certain other activities suggested by such terms as "seeing," "perceiving," or "knowing." "Sensing" may be taken to refer to the mere reception of stimuli. "Seeing" is the "interpretive" behavior which a stimulus controls. The term "seeing" characterizes a special relation between behavior and stimuli. It is different from "sensing" just as responding is different from being stimulated. Our "perception" of the world—our "knowledge" of it —is our *behavior* with respect to the world. It is not to be confused with the world itself or with other behavior with respect to the world or with the behavior of others with respect to the world.

CHAPTER IX

DEPRIVATION AND SATIATION

The discovery that part of the behavior of an organism was under the control of the environment led, as we have seen, to an unwarranted extension of the notion of the stimulus. Writers began to infer stimuli where none could be observed and to include various internal conditions in a "total stimulating situation." The principle of the stimulus was weakened by this extension and often abandoned in favor of other formulations of a less specific nature. It may be restored to usefulness in its proper sphere by distinguishing, as we have done, between the several functions of stimuli. We have now to note that some effects of the environment are not usefully classified as stimulation at all. When we deprive an organism of food, for example, we may stimulate it, but this is incidental to the main effect.

DEPRIVATION

We saw in Chapter III that the probability of drinking becomes very high under severe water deprivation and very low under excessive satiation. It is reasonable to assume that the probability always lies somewhere between these two extremes and that if the deprivation is changed, it simply moves toward one or the other. The biological significance of the change in probability is obvious. Water is constantly being lost through excretion and evaporation, and

141

an equal amount must be taken in to compensate for this loss. Under ordinary circumstances an organism drinks intermittently and maintains a fairly steady and presumably optimal state. When this interchange is disturbed—when the organism is deprived of the opportunity to drink—it is obviously important that drinking should be more likely to occur at the first opportunity. In the evolutionary sense this "explains" why water deprivation strengthens all conditioned and unconditioned behavior concerned with the intake of water. In a similar way we explain why an organism deprived of the opportunity to get rid of carbon dioxide breathes more rapidly and more deeply, why the feeding reflexes of the newborn baby grow more powerful as time elapses after feeding, and why a pet dog hovers about its feeding place in the kitchen as mealtime grows near.

The adaptive character of the increase in probability is sometimes expressed in another way. Deprivation is said to disturb some kind of equilibrium which the strengthened behavior tends to restore. The tendency of living systems to maintain or restore equilibrium, which W. B. Cannon called homeostasis, has been of special interest to physiologists. The notion of equilibrium is compatible with a functional analysis, but the two should not be confused. A study of equilibrium may enable us to predict the *direction* in which behavior will change as the result of a change in an independent variable, but it will not tell us much more. Equilibrium is hard to define and even harder to observe and measure. A much more clear-cut program is to show how deprivation affects the probability of relevant behavior, and this may be done without mentioning equilibrium.

Not all deprivation or satiation is concerned with the conspicuous interchange of materials. A man may be "deprived of physical exercise" if he is kept indoors by bad weather; as a result he is especially likely to be active when the weather clears. Here deprivation consists merely of preventing the occurrence of behavior, and the emission of the behavior is itself satiating. Sexual satiation appears to be the result of the mere exercise of sexual behavior as well as of the special consequence known as the orgasm. Each mode of satiation must be dealt with in terms of the relevant economy of the organism, and its biological significance must be interpreted accordingly.

Certain other kinds of operations which, as we saw in Chapter III, have effects similar to deprivation and satiation are conveniently included under the common heading of "motivation."

A given act of deprivation usually increases the strength of many kinds of behavior simultaneously. As the newborn baby goes unfed, reflex sucking increases in strength, and movements of the head in response to tactual stimuli at the cheeks and in the region of the mouth (by virtue of which the head is turned so that the breast is more readily received) become more vigorous. Eventually, many other forms of behavior are added to this group. Similarly, when an adult goes without water for a long time, a large group of operants are strengthened. Not only does he drink more readily when a glass of water is presented, he also will engage in many other activities which lead to the ingestion of water—going to the kitchen, operating a drinking fountain, asking for a glass of water, and so on.

NEEDS AND DRIVES

In traditional terms an organism drinks because it *needs* water, goes for a walk because it *needs* exercise, breathes more rapidly and deeply because it *wants* air, and eats ravenously because of the promptings of *hunger*. Needs, wants, and hungers, are good examples of the inner causes discussed in Chapter III. They are said to have various dimensions. Needs and wants are likely to be thought of as psychic or mental, while hungers are more readily conceived of as physiological. But the terms are freely used when nothing with these dimensions has been observed. Sometimes the inner operation is inferred from the operation responsible for the strength of the behavior—as when we say that someone who has had nothing to drink for several days "must be thirsty" and probably will drink. On the other hand, it is sometimes inferred from the behavior itself—as when we observe someone drinking large quantities of water and assert without hesitation that he possesses a great thirst. In the first case, we infer the inner event from a prior independent variable and predict the dependent variable which is to follow. In the second case, we infer the inner event from the event which follows, and attribute it to a preceding history of deprivation. So long as the inner event is inferred, it is in no sense an explanation of the behavior and adds nothing to a functional account.

Needs and wants are convenient terms in casual discourse, and many students of behavior have been interested in setting up similar hypothetical intervening states as legitimate scientific concepts. A need or want could simply be redefined as a condition resulting from deprivation and characterized by a special probability of response. Since it is difficult to lay the ghosts which hover about these older terms, there is a certain advantage in using a term which has fewer connotations. "Drive" is sometimes used. A drive need not be thought of as mental or physiological. The term is simply a convenient way of referring to the effects of deprivation and satiation and of other operations which alter the probability of behavior in more or less the same way. It is convenient because it enables us to deal with many cases at once. There are many ways of changing the probability that an organism will eat; at the same time, a single kind of deprivation strengthens many kinds of behavior. The concept of hunger as a drive brings these various relations together in a single term.

The simplicity of the concept of drive is only apparent. This is true as well of need and want. No concept can eliminate an actual diversity of data. A drive is a verbal device with which we account for a state of strength, and it cannot answer experimental questions. We cannot control the behavior of an organism by directly changing its hunger, its thirst, or its sex drive. In order to change these states indirectly, we must deal with the relevant variables of deprivation and satiation and must face all the complexity of these operations.

A drive is not a stimulus. A common belief is that deprivation affects the organism by creating a stimulus. The classic example is hunger pangs. When an organism has been without food for a sufficient time, the contractions of the empty stomach stimulate it in a characteristic way. This stimulation is often identified with the hunger drive. But such stimulation is not closely correlated with the probability of eating. Hunger pangs are characteristic of only a small part of the range through which that probability varies continuously. We usually eat our meals without reaching the condition of deprivation in which pangs are felt, and we continue to eat long after the first few mouthfuls have stopped any pangs which may have occurred. The attempt to find comparable stimulation in other drives has proved futile and occasionally even ludicrous. Dryness of the throat does not vary continuously with a tendency to drink through the entire range of deprivation. Any comparable stimulation under sexual deprivation is poorly correlated with the probability of sexual behavior. In any case a drive, as defined above, cannot be a stimulus.

A drive is not a physiological state. Certain internal conditions probably result from any given degree of deprivation. Adequate independent knowledge of them might enable us to dispense with a history of deprivation in predicting behavior; but we are not likely to have such knowledge about a given organism at the moment when it would be useful in prediction; and we are even less likely to be able to create such an appropriate state directly in order to control behavior. Insofar as we infer the state from the history of deprivation or generate it by creating such a history, it is of no value in enabling us to dispense with that history. Even when it is directly observed, it may still be useless in control. We have seen that in laboratory research the weight of an organism is often used as an index of food deprivation. To maintain a given level of drive, the organism is kept at a given percentage of its weight when well fed. The weight is easily observed, and as a fairly direct result of a history of deprivation it can generally be used as a substitute for such a history. But since we change the weight only by changing the history, it cannot be used as a substitute in practical control. In any case, we do not assert that the weight of the organism *is* the hunger drive.

A drive is not a psychic state. A parallel argument applies to the mental or psychic states with which drives are often identified. Here the possibility of independent evidence is more doubtful. What people "feel" when they are deprived of food, oxygen, and so on, will be considered in Chapter XVII. Since deprivation affects behavior, whether or not anything is "felt," the feeling is not a secure basis for prediction. Direct manipulation of a psychic condition for purposes of control seems even more doubtful.

A drive is not simply a state of strength. A strong "drive to chew gum" is sometimes attributed to a person, not with reference to any history of deprivation, but simply because he tends to chew gum. It is possible that some relevant deprivation which would alter the tendency to chew gum could be uncovered, but no reference is made to such an operation in this use of the term. The possibility remains that the strength of the behavior is due to other kinds of variables not in the field of motivation. Other terms which often do nothing more than report the unusual strength of behavior are "desire" ("He has a strong desire to go to Europe"), "wish" ("He wishes his father were dead"), and "complex" ("He has a sex complex"). The probability of response may be due to many different kinds of variables, where deprivation plays a minor role. For example, the strong "drive" of the gambler, his gambling "complex," or his "desire" to gamble may not be primarily due to a condition of deprivation at all, since a carefully arranged schedule of variable-ratio reinforcement will lead to a high probability of responding at a relatively low level of deprivation.

THE PRACTICAL USE OF DRIVES

Some examples of how behavior is actually controlled through deprivation and satiation will show how easily concepts referring to intervening states may be avoided.

Deprivation is put to practical use when a child is made more likely to drink milk by restriction of his water intake; when guests are induced to eat a modest meal with greater gusto by a delay in serving the meal; when the prisoner is made more likely to talk to interrogators by being put in "solitary" ("depriving him of talking" as in the case of the "need for exercise" discussed above); when a population is made more likely to cooperate with the authorities who control food supplies by reducing rations; and when a child is kept interested in his toys by being given only one at a time. Operations which have a similar effect are put to practical use when guests are induced to consume more cocktails at a party at which salty hors d'oeuvres are served, and when sexual behavior is intensified by the administration of certain hormones or aphrodisiacs. Extensive engineering control is obviously necessary to achieve some of these conditions for either theoretical or practical purposes. It is sometimes possible to use conditions which arise fortuitously. For example, waterfront brothels and other amusement enterprises take advantage of the deprivations suffered by sailors at sea. Wartime shortages generate large-scale deprivations, and these are frequently exploited for both theoretical and commercial purposes.

Satiation is put to practical use when a *table d'hôte* restaurant serves a large supply of good bread while a meal is being prepared in order to serve small portions of the rest of the meal without complaint (it is obviously a bad practice to serve bread if the customer has still to order *à la carte*); when an abundance of hors d'oeuvres is used to conceal the scantiness of the dinner which follows; when legalized prostitution is recommended on the ground that it reduces the probability of sexual behavior in members of the population who might, if unsatiated, otherwise attack innocent women; when bread lines are set up to reduce the violence which would otherwise result from meager rations; and when a clinic reduces aggressive or otherwise undesirable behavior by giving the individual attention, approval, or even affection. An effect comparable to satiation is obtained when a drug is administered to reduce the probability of sexual behavior.

All these examples could be described by reference to "drives." We could say that the eating of salty hors d'oeuvres makes a guest thirsty and that his thirst then drives him to drink. It is simpler, in both theory and practice, to restrict ourselves to the fact that consuming salty hors d'oeuvres leads to drinking.

These operations are not to be confused with operant conditioning through which behavior is brought under the control of a different deprivation. A government which offers a bonus for having a baby in a program designed to raise the birth rate is not increasing the deprivation which controls procreation. By reinforcing the behavior of procreation with money, the behavior is brought under the control of a larger set of deprivations. The behavior can then be strengthened by depriving an individual of money or of anything money will buy —as by severe taxation. The effect may be canceled by satiating the individual directly with money or indirectly with whatever money will buy. This might be done by an employer who responded to such a bonus by increasing wages in order to keep the families of his employees small. So long as such a bonus is offered, an increase in relief or unemployment insurance may affect the birth rate. The level of sexual deprivation meanwhile has not necessarily been changed.

SOME QUESTIONS CONCERNING DRIVE

How many drives are there? Is the maternal drive stronger than sex or hunger? Will satiating such a drive as hunger partially reduce a drive like sex? Can all drives be reduced to sex? Questions of this sort are more easily answered when restated in terms of deprivation and satiation.

How many drives are there? The question has two translations. When we are inferring drives from histories of deprivation, we may ask in how many ways an organism can be deprived. We can answer this only by exploration—by interfering with the exchange between organism and environment and observing the result. When we reduce the proportions of certain inert gases in the air breathed by the organism, we observe no change in its behavior. In such a case we do not speak of the "need" for such gases, or of any "drive" to get them. In translation, we do not list what we have done as an instance of deprivation. The fact that a gas has no biological value is irrelevant. We might deprive an organism of an essential food substance and still observe no change in its behavior, even though it might become ill or even die. The physiologist speaks of nutritional "needs," but deprivation as here defined requires an effect upon behavior. Our explorations would, of course, uncover many important cases, each of which might lead us to speak of a drive.

A second translation is needed when we speak of a drive simply because the probability of behavior varies. The child who does not eat well is said to be suffering from anorexia—a lack of hunger. If he eats spasmodically, it is because his hunger is unpredictable—he is sometimes hungry and sometimes not. Here we use the concept of drive, not to refer to a history of ingestion, but simply to account (spuriously) for unexplained changes in probability. (Characteristically, we do not postulate a drive if the probability does not change.

The reflex secretion of tears in response to irritation does not vary from moment to moment in any way which cannot otherwise be explained, and hence we do not speak of a drive to rid the eyes of foreign substances.) Our question thus becomes: How many kinds of behavior vary in strength independently of each other? On this basis we can distinguish between eating, drinking, sexual behavior, and so on, as well as between subdivisions of each of these fields. If the probabilities of eating two kinds of food always vary together, we assume a common hunger; but if at certain times an organism eats salt more readily than sugar and at other times sugar more readily than salt, we find it necessary to speak of separate salt- and sugar-hungers. Presumably, separate operations of satiation and deprivation have accompanied these changes although they are not described by this use of the term "hunger."

What are the drives of conditioned responses? Satiation and deprivation are obviously related to operant reinforcement. To a hungry organism food is both reinforcing and satiating. As we shall see in Chapter XIV, it is necessary, although sometimes difficult, to distinguish between these effects. In reinforcement the presentation of food is contingent upon a response; we can satiate without consistently reinforcing if we avoid this contingency. We can also reinforce without substantial satiation or at least before satiation has taken place. But there is an inevitable connection between the two processes: the effect of operant reinforcement will not be observed if the organism has not been appropriately deprived. The net result of reinforcement is not simply to strengthen behavior but to strengthen it *in a given state of deprivation*. Reinforcement thus brings behavior under the control of an appropriate deprivation. After we have conditioned a pigeon to stretch its neck by reinforcing with food, the variable which controls neck-stretching is food deprivation. The response of stretching the neck has merely joined that group of responses which vary with this operation. We can describe the effect of reinforcement in no simpler way.

By conditioning and extinguishing a response under different degrees of deprivation, it is possible to see the effect of deprivation in detail. If we reinforce a response in a group of organisms at the same level of deprivation and extinguish it in subgroups at different levels, we find that the number of responses in the extinction curve is a function of deprivation. The hungrier the organism, the more responses it will emit during extinction. If, on the other hand, we condition at different levels of deprivation and extinguish at the same level, we find, surprisingly enough, that the two extinction curves contain approximately the same number of responses. The effect of deprivation is felt during extinction, not during conditioning.

Behavior which has been strengthened by a conditioned reinforcer varies with the deprivation appropriate to the primary reinforcer. The behavior of going to a restaurant is composed of a sequence of responses, early members of which (for example, going along a certain street) are reinforced by the appearance of discriminative stimuli which control later responses (the appearance of the restaurant, which we then enter). The whole sequence is ultimately reinforced by food, and the probability varies with food deprivation. We increase the chances that someone will go to a restaurant, or even walk along a particular street, by making him hungry. We do not say that there are special drives associated with the early responses in the sequence, because there are no parallel operations of deprivation. Such traditional terms as "needs," "wants," and so on recognize these subsidiary steps. For example, we might say that a man first *wants* a taxi, that he then *wants* the driver to take him to Fifty-sixth Street, that he then *wants* to find a particular restaurant, that he then *wants* to open the door, that he then *wants* a table, a menu, and the roast beef. But since there are no processes of satiation and deprivation appropriate to the behavior which is involved here, except for the last item, we have no reason to set up corresponding drives. A man does not need a taxi in the sense of not having had a taxi for a long time. Certain behavior which requires a taxi for its execution is strong and occurs as soon as a taxi is available. The appearance of the taxi reinforces any behavior which brings it about. It is also an enabling event which makes a later response possible and hence brings the earlier behavior to an end. It would only confuse the issue, however, to say that the appearance of the taxi had satiated the behavior of hailing taxis. The practical use of the relation reveals its essentials. If for some reason we want to induce a man to hail a taxi, we strengthen any behavior requiring a taxi; we do not deprive him of taxis. He will not hail a taxi if he already has one because other behavior then intervenes.

Generalized reinforcers raise this issue in a more acute form. They are important precisely because they are effective under a number of deprivations, some of which are likely to be present at any given time. The lack of a specific deprivation encourages us to assume a separate drive for the immediate generalized reinforcer. Although we may be willing to give up the notion of a "taxi drive," we are likely to insist upon a drive for attention, approval, affection, domination, or money. In order to justify assigning separate drives to the behavior so reinforced, we should have to show that it is possible to deprive or satiate an organism with given amounts of attention, approval, and so on, but we should also have to make sure that no satiation or deprivation is taking place in any of the primary areas associated with the generalized reinforcer. For example, we should have to reduce a "need for affection" by supplying an abundance of affection without supplying any of the primary reinforcers associated with it. Only then would we have evidence of an autonomous drive. But although generalized reinforcers may reinforce when primary reinforcement is not forthcoming—a case exemplified by the behavior of the miser in poring over his gold—we have no reason to assume a corresponding drive. It is one of the more obvious characteristics of the miser that he is not actually satiated by money. The reinforcing effect of money is extraordinarily great, so that most of his behavior which is strong is strong for that reason, but a separate drive implies a separate operation of deprivation or satiation, for which we have little evidence in the behavior of the miser. There are other kinds of misers who specialize in attention, affection, approval, or domination. Although we may show that they are strongly *reinforced* by these generalized reinforcers, even in the absence of primary reinforcement, we do not speak of separate drives because there are no appropriate operations of deprivation or satiation.

The drives appropriate to conditioned reinforcers are not to be confused with acquired drives for nicotine, alcohol, morphine, or other drugs. The effects induced by drugs of this sort reinforce the behavior of consuming them. The drug may bring release from some aversive condition such as anxiety, fear, or a sense of guilt (Chapter XI), or it may produce some condition which is positively reinforcing. The reinforcement may become more and more powerful if repeated use leads to physiological changes which increase the aversive condition which the drug reduces. This sort of "addiction" is an acquired drive for which well-marked processes of deprivation and satiation are evident. A potent technique of control is the development of an addiction. A drug is administered repeatedly until its reinforcing power becomes great. It is then used to reinforce desired behavior—for example, the behavior of a prisoner of war in answering questions. The drug is then withheld, and the probability of the behavior increases greatly.

In Chapter V we saw that an event could be a positive reinforcer even though it did not reduce a level of deprivation. There is a related point to be made here: behavior which is strengthened through deprivation need not reduce that deprivation. The Freudian process of *sublimation* raises this issue. Through either stimulus or response induction an operation which strengthens a response also strengthens other responses having similar properties or the same response upon similar occasions. Deprivation is an example of such an operation. Thus a childless couple may "sublimate" their parental behavior by treating a pet dog as a child. The artist "sublimates" sexual behavior in working on pictures or models of the human body. If we believe that behavior always takes place "for good reason"— that is, because of some conceivable biological advantage—many instances of this sort seem puzzling. But a response strengthened through induction may very well have no effect upon the deprivation, even though the response from which it borrows its strength does have such an effect. In many examples of sublimation the behavior itself is automatically satiating.

Are drives interrelated? There is another area in which it is advantageous to deal with the processes of satiation and deprivation rather than with any drive. Efforts have been made to reduce all motivation to one primary drive. Freud, for example, emphasized sex. The contention that a given activity is "essentially sexual in nature" may be translated in either of two ways depending upon whether we emphasize the dependent or the independent variable. To say that artistic and musical activities "express sexual impulses" may mean that characteristic behavior in this field *resembles* sexual behavior in topography. The sculptor modeling a human figure is behaving to some extent as he would behave toward a human body; certain temporal aspects of musical behavior resemble the temporal pattern of sexual behavior. This is simply induction from one stimulus to another or from one response to another on the basis of similarity. But it is often difficult to decide whether two situations or two actions are similar enough to warrant such an explanation. Often we have to infer the importance of a point of similarity from its effect upon behavior. On the other hand the issue may be expressed in a question of this form: Does the probability of an act which is asserted to be sexual in nature change with sex deprivation or satiation? If so, it may be regarded as sexual even though it is not topographically similar to obviously sexual behavior.

An alternative contention is that the basic human drive is "domination." This generalized reinforcer is certainly very important. The more specific biological reinforcers are frequently received only after precurrent behavior has been effective in "dominating" the physical or social environment, and to this extent we may bring all behavior together under the rubric of domination. We have seen, however, that a corresponding *drive* is not required when the reinforcer is generalized. Domination may be *reinforcing* and hence very important as a controlling variable. A man may come to dominate "for the sake of dominating," just as the miser collects money for its own sake. But apparently there is no independent deprivation or satiation concerned with domination itself. To deprive a man of domination would mean to arrange circumstances in which he dominated neither physical nature nor society, but under such circumstances he would presumably suffer other deprivations, to which any general strengthening of his behavior could then be attributed. Conversely, when we change a man's behavior by "letting him have his own way," we may appear to be satiating his "need for domination," but we almost certainly also change some primary deprivations or some of the aversive conditions to be described in Chapter XI. The surprisingly general effect of many specific satiations or deprivations makes the generality of the drive to dominate questionable. A man who tends to dominate in many walks of life may undergo an extensive change as the result of a successful marriage or, on a shorter time scale, a satisfying meal.

Attempts to reduce all human motivation to a single need for approval, affection, and so on, are subject to the same criticism.

Which drive is strongest? Is the maternal drive stronger than sex? Is sex stronger than hunger? We might answer questions of this sort by bringing some arbitrarily chosen response under the control of different deprivations (by reinforcing it in different ways) and then observing the maximal frequency under extreme values of each. How does the rate at which an extremely hungry male rat emits a response which is reinforced with food on a given schedule compare with the rate of the same rat under extreme sexual deprivation when the response has been reinforced on the same schedule with access to a receptive female? But there is little point in comparing deprivations unless situations arise naturally in which the relative magnitudes of their effects are important. By depriving an organism of both food and sexual contact, we can observe which behavior emerges when appropriate stimuli are presented together. These conditions are not easily satisfied, however. Many organisms suffering severe water deprivation cannot eat dry food; when we limit the ingestion of water, therefore, we create an effect similar to that of satiation with food. In the same way, sexual behavior is weakened when an organism is severely deprived of food for a long time.

TIME AS A VARIABLE

The mere emission of behavior is sometimes satiating, and we then "deprive" the organism simply by making the behavior impossible. As we have seen, the "need for exercise" shows this pattern: the organism confined within narrow limits is more than usually active when the limits are first removed. The behavior which ensues reduces the level of activity as a form of satiation. When the behavior is possible at all times, it shows a periodicity. If a rat is confined in a small cage and given continuous access to a running-wheel, its behavior in the wheel may be taken as a fair measure of its activity. A rat usually alternates between active and inactive phases with considerable regularity. A similar periodicity is seen when an interchange with the environment is not restricted—as in eating, drinking, or behaving sexually under conditions of unlimited opportunity. When the period can be established, we may use time as an independent variable in predicting the behavior.

A fairly drastic periodic change is exemplified by sleeping and waking. During sleep, much of the activity of the organism reaches an extremely low point. This is not all that happens, however. We may conveniently regard sleep as a special form of behavior which occurs periodically and with fair regularity in the lives of most organisms. Usually, the periodicity coincides with the night-day cycle, with obvious advantages. We deprive an organism of sleep by preventing the behavior—for example, we keep it on a slowly revolving platform where it must move constantly in order to keep from falling into a tank of water. The tendency to sleep increases as a function of this deprivation. Just as we induce a child to eat more readily at mealtime by making sure that he does not eat between meals, so we induce him to go to bed at night by making sure that he does not sleep during the day. To some extent we may also satiate an organism with sleep. We do this when we send a child to bed early to prepare him for a particularly long or exhausting day. Under unrestricted conditions, the periodicity of sleeping and waking permits us to use time as a variable in predicting behavior.

Time appears to be the principal experimental variable in certain slower periodic changes. Behavior during the menstrual cycle is an example. This may be altered by administering hormones or in other ways, but our principal opportunity to predict a given response lies in studying such cyclic changes. Strength cannot be changed by interfering in a cycle, as in activity or sleep, because the periodicity is not the result of automatic deprivation and satiation. Time as a variable cannot be manipulated experimentally.

Many behavioral changes, especially in the instinctive behavior of lower organisms, follow an annual cycle. Migratory patterns, for example, coincide fairly accurately with the seasons of the year. Some condition varying with time may be more important than time itself. We can interfere with the normal periodicity by, so to speak, changing the season—by keeping the organism at a temperature or length of day characteristic of a different time of year. If the behavior responds to the unseasonal condition, the mere passage of time can scarcely be the primary variable. Under normal conditions the time of year may be an important bit of information.

When changes in behavior extend over longer periods, we speak of the independent variable as the age of the organism. A response may appear at a given age and later disappear. The increase in probability as a function of age is often spoken of as maturation. We achieve some degree of prediction by discovering these developmental schedules. Various forms of so-called instinctive behavior, especially in species other than man, usually appear at characteristic ages, and the age may be our only useful variable. Since these changes are usually not cyclic, prediction must be made on the basis of information obtained with other organisms. Individual differences may be great; we cannot predict accurately when an individual will engage in a certain kind of sexual behavior by establishing the average age of onset in a population. Usually, therefore, practical problems of this kind are not solved by appeal to schedules of maturation. Certain instructional procedures are most effective when a child is ready for them, but in planning an educational program for young children chronological age may be of little value in determining readiness. The presence or absence of the relevant behavior may have to be determined by direct observation of each child.

THE INDIVIDUAL AND THE SPECIES

At any given time in its life, an individual displays certain behavior in certain states of probability. This is the background against which we study selected operants and explore the effects of independent variables. These variables are seldom relevant in accounting for the *existence* of the behavior chosen for study; they merely affect its *probability*. Its existence is taken for granted. When we examine different individuals, however, we find certain differences in behavior —in their repertoires, in the frequencies with which given responses are emitted, and in the extent to which the behavior responds to reinforcement, deprivation, and other operations. Between species these differences may be very large. The concept of "instinct" has been used to account for them. Behavior which is characteristic of a species is attributed to an instinct (of uncertain location or properties) said to be possessed by all members of the species. This is a flagrant example of an explanatory fiction. The term, like "drive," may be given respectable scientific status by being defined as a tendency to respond in a way which is characteristic of a species, but so defined it cannot be used as an explanation. If the instinct of nest-building refers only to the observed tendency of certain kinds of birds to build nests, it cannot explain why the birds build nests.

A tendency of the members of species to behave in a certain way is no more remarkable than a tendency to exhibit certain features of anatomy and internal physiology. Behavior is as much a part of the organism as are its anatomical features. Species-status itself is a variable to be taken into account in evaluating the probability of any kind of behavior. Since we cannot change the species of an organism, the variable is of no importance in extending our control, but information about species-status enables us to predict characteristic behavior and, in turn, to make more successful use of other techniques of control.

The problem of individual differences within the species must be solved in the same way. If we are interested in sexual behavior, for example, we cannot make use of probabilities characteristic of a species unless we know where our subject stands in the population. The individual capacity or level of ability is the same kind of datum as species-status itself. We arrive at species-status as a relevant variable by surveying the incidence of a particular form of behavior in the species; we arrive at the position of the individual in the species by a similar survey of characteristic tendencies. The problem of individual differences will be discussed again in Chapter XIII.

SUMMARY

We may summarize the kinds of independent variables considered in this chapter by listing the questions which we must answer in order to account for the probability of a response.

1. Is the behavior in question characteristic of the species to which the individual belongs?

2. If so, is the current age of the individual within the range in which the behavior is observed?

3. If the behavior varies considerably between individuals, what is the relative position of the individual we are studying?

4. If the behavior shows any long-range cyclic change, what is the current position of the individual in the cycle? If the cycle can be shown to correspond to a change in some external condition—for example, the mean temperature—this variable may permit a more explicit prediction and may possibly be useful in control.

5. If the behavior shows cyclic changes on a smaller scale—for example, a diurnal change—at what time are we to predict or control the response? If we are dealing with a nocturnal animal, for example, and if the day-night cycle is a part of our experimental conditions, then we must note the time of day.

6. What is the history of the individual with respect to sleep? If there has been no interference with sleep, what is the present point in the cycle? If the organism has been deprived of or satiated with sleep, how has this been done?

7. What is the history of the organism with respect to relevant deprivations and satiations? If the behavior in which we are interested is conditioned, to what deprivation was the reinforcement related? What is the recent history of this deprivation? In studying behavior which is characteristically reinforced with food, we must have some record of the history of ingestion or some contemporary measure, such as body weight, which varies with that history. We must also know whether any variable in the recent history of the organism—for example, the administration of a drug—has had an effect similar to that of deprivation or satiation.

There are other variables of which the behavior may be a function.

Reinforcement has not been included in the list, and we have still to consider other variables in the fields of emotion, aversive stimulation, and punishment. All in all, therefore, the list may seem dishearteningly long. In actual practice, however, many of these conditions are easily arranged. In routine laboratory research it is not difficult to set up a procedure which assures considerable stability from day to day with respect to most or all of them. We can then study a very few variables at a time. In practical applications as well, many of the points which have just been raised prove to be trivial. The effective variables are easily isolated.

CHAPTER X

EMOTION

WHAT IS AN EMOTION?

The "emotions" are excellent examples of the fictional causes to which we commonly attribute behavior. We run away because of "fear" and strike because of "anger"; we are paralyzed by "rage" and depressed by "grief." These causes are in turn attributed to events in our history or present circumstances—to the things which frighten or enrage us or make us angry or sad. The behavior, the emotion, and the prior external event comprise the three links of our familiar causal chain. The middle link may be taken to be either psychic or physiological. In the psychic case, it is argued that an external circumstance makes an individual *feel emotional* and that the feeling leads him to take appropriate action. The famous James-Lange theory—developed by the American psychologist William James and the Danish physician C. G. Lange—asserted, however, that one did not feel the inner cause of emotion, but simply some part of the emotional behavior itself. James cast this assertion in classical form by saying "that we feel sorry because we cry, angry because we strike, afraid because we tremble, and not that we cry, strike, or tremble because we are sorry, angry, or fearful, as the case may be." This theory emphasized the study of the physiological

160

changes which we "feel" in emotion and to some extent identified the psychic middle link with the physiological. The most obvious changes which are present when the layman says he "feels an emotion" are the responses of smooth muscles and glands—for example, blushing, blanching, weeping, sweating, salivating, and contracting the small muscles in the skin which produce goose flesh in man and elevate the fur of animals. Many of these are familiar in the form recorded by the "lie detector," which detects, not dishonesty, but the emotional responses generated when the individual engages in behavior for which he has previously been punished.

In spite of extensive research it has not been possible to show that each emotion is distinguished by a particular pattern of responses of glands and smooth muscles. Although there are a few characteristic patterns of such responses, the differences between emotions are often not great and do not follow the usual distinctions. Nor are such responses diagnostic of emotion in general, since they also occur under other circumstances—for example, after heavy exercise or in a chill wind.

Certain responses executed by the facial and postural muscles are commonly said to "express" emotion. Laughing, growling, snarling, baring the teeth, and the muscular responses which accompany the secretion of tears are examples. The lower organisms generally have a more extensive repertoire of this sort. Emotional expressions can be imitated by operant behavior, as in the theater, and are frequently modified by the social environment to conform to cultural specifications. To some extent a given culture has its own way of laughing, its own cries of pain, and so on. It has not been possible to specify given sets of expressive responses as characteristic of particular emotions, and in any case such responses are not said to *be* the emotion.

In the search for what is happening "in emotion" the scientist has found himself at a peculiar disadvantage. Where the layman identifies and classifies emotions not only with ease but with considerable consistency, the scientist in focusing upon responses of glands and smooth muscles and upon expressive behavior has not been sure that he could tell the difference between even such relatively gross emotions as anger and fear. Some means of identification available to the layman appears to have been overlooked. The layman does not say that a man is angry simply because the small blood vessels enlarge so that he becomes red or because his pulse accelerates, or because certain muscles set his jaw and lips in a position reminiscent of the snarl of the uncivilized animal. All of this may happen "without emotion," and the layman frequently judges a man to be angry when he has no knowledge of such responses whatsoever—for example, when he says that the writer of a letter must have been angry when he wrote it. He knows that a companion is afraid as he walks with her through a dark street even though he does not see her turning pale or know that the secretion of her digestive juices has been suppressed or that her pulse has accelerated. Under other circumstances all of this might be happening when he would not call her afraid at all.

EMOTION AS PREDISPOSITION

When the man in the street says that someone is afraid or angry or in love, he is generally talking about predispositions to act in certain ways. The "angry" man shows an increased probability of striking, insulting, or otherwise inflicting injury and a lowered probability of aiding, favoring, comforting, or making love. The man "in love" shows an increased tendency to aid, favor, be with, and caress and a lowered tendency to injure in any way. "In fear" a man tends to reduce or avoid contact with specific stimuli—as by running away, hiding, or covering his eyes and ears; at the same time he is less likely to advance toward such stimuli or into unfamiliar territory. These are useful facts, and something like the layman's mode of classification has a place in a scientific analysis.

The names of the so-called emotions serve to classify behavior with respect to various circumstances which affect its probability. The safest practice is to hold to the adjectival form. Just as the hungry organism can be accounted for without too much difficulty, although "hunger" is another matter, so by describing behavior as fearful, affectionate, timid, and so on, we are not led to look for *things* called emotions. The common idioms, "in love," "in fear," and "in anger," suggest a definition of an emotion as a conceptual state, in which a special response is a function of circumstances in the history of the individual. In casual discourse and for many scientific purposes some such way of referring to current strength in terms of the variables of which it is a function is often desirable. But so defined, an emotion, like a drive, is not to be identified with physiological or psychic conditions.

THE RESPONSES WHICH VARY
TOGETHER IN EMOTION

We have no guarantee that the vocabulary of the layman will survive unchanged in a scientific study. In the following discussion, however, terms taken from casual discourse are used to refer to familiar observations and to point up certain essential problems.

Some emotions—joy and sorrow, for example—involve the whole repertoire of the organism. We recognize this when we say that an emotion is exciting or depressing. Some emotions involve the whole repertoire, but in more specific ways. Probably no behavior remains unchanged when the organism becomes afraid or angry, but responses related to specific features of the environment (the "object" of the fear or anger) are especially affected. Some of the milder emotions, such as embarrassment, sympathy, and amusement, may be localized more narrowly in small subdivisions of a repertoire.

Responses which vary together in an emotion do so in part because of a common consequence. The responses which grow strong in anger inflict damage upon persons or objects. This process is often biologically useful when an organism competes with other organisms or struggles with the inanimate world. The grouping of responses which define anger thus depends in part upon conditioning. Behavior which inflicts damage is reinforced in anger and is subsequently controlled by the conditions which control anger. Just as food is reinforcing to a hungry organism, so damage inflicted upon another is reinforcing to an angry one. Just as a hungry man exclaims "Good!" when he receives food, so the angry man exclaims "Good!" when his opponent is damaged in any way.

Some of the behavior involved in an emotion is apparently unconditioned, however, and in that case the grouping must be explained in terms of evolutionary consequences. For example, in some species biting, striking, and clawing appear to be strengthened during anger before conditioning can have taken place. These responses generate cries of pain and other evidences of damage which then reinforce other responses to bring them within the class of "angry behavior." For example, if an angry child attacks, bites, or strikes another child —all without prior conditioning—and if the other child cries or runs away, then these same consequences may reinforce other behavior of the angry child which can scarcely be innate—for example, teasing the other child, taking toys away from him, destroying his work, or calling him names. The adult possesses a full-fledged repertoire of obviously conditioned verbal responses which inflict injury, all of which are strong "in anger" and co-vary with unconditioned behavior as a function of the same variables.

EMOTIONAL OPERATIONS

We discover the variables of which emotional states are a function —as we discover any variables—by looking for them. Many cases are familiar. A sudden loud noise often induces "fear." Continued physical restraint or other interference with behavior may generate "rage." Failure to receive an accustomed reinforcement is a special case of restraint which generates a kind of rage called "frustration." Behavior which has frequently been punished may be emitted in a form called "timid" or "embarrassed." We must not expect too much, however, from these everyday terms. They have grown out of circumstances which emphasize typical cases and have never been tested under conditions which require precise definition. Even an apparently well-marked emotion like anger may not be reducible to a single class of responses or attributable to a single set of operations. The anger produced by one circumstance may not be the same as that produced by another. Again, the interruption of an established sequence of responses usually has an emotional effect, but when one cannot write a letter because a pen is missing or cannot open a door because it is bolted on the other side or cannot converse with someone who is totally deaf or does not speak the same language, the resulting effects may differ in as many ways as the circumstances differ. To group them all together as "frustrating conditions" and to describe all the changes in behavior as "rage" is a misleading simplification. The recognition of mixed emotions suggests that the usual classification makes distinctions which do not always correspond to the facts.

The subtle emotions are still more difficult. The condition which the layman calls loneliness, for example, appears to be a mild form of frustration due to the interruption of an established sequence of responses which have been positively reinforced by the social environment. The lonely man has no one to talk to. No matter where he turns, powerful behavior has no chance to be effective. Loneliness which is due to the absence of a single person who has supplied reinforcement in the form of affection may be especially profound, as the lovesick individual demonstrates. The loneliness of the amiable man who finds himself among strangers for a long time will be of a different character. A child lost in a large crowd suffers in still a different way: all the behavior which has been previously reinforced by the appearance of his mother or father now fails; he looks about but does not see them; he calls and cries, but they do not answer. Depending upon a variety of circumstances, the result may be close to fear or rage or sorrow. At the moment there appears to be no over-all classification which will be applicable to all these examples.

We have noted that the fields of motivation and emotion are very close. They may, indeed, overlap. Any extreme deprivation probably acts as an emotional operation. The starving man is almost necessarily frustrated and afraid. Nostalgia includes both a drive and an emotion. If we remove a man from his characteristic surroundings, a large part of his social behavior cannot be emitted and may therefore become more and more probable: he will return to his old surroundings whenever possible and will be particularly "sociable" when he does so. Other parts of his behavior become strong because they are automatically reinforced under the prevailing deprivation; he will talk to anyone who will listen about his old surroundings, his old friends, and what he used to do. This is all a result of deprivation. But nostalgia is also an emotional condition in which there is a general weakening of other forms of behavior—a "depression," which may be quite profound. We cannot classify this as the result of deprivation because the behavior which is thus affected has not been specifically restrained. Distinctions of this sort may seem a little forced, but they are worth making whenever we are interested in understanding or altering such conditions.

THE TOTAL EMOTION

We define an emotion—insofar as we wish to do so—as a particular state of strength or weakness in one or more responses induced by any one of a class of operations. We may make as many distinctions as we wish between separate emotions, although this endeavor usually exhausts itself in the endless number of distinctions which are actually possible. Methods and practices are available for surveying the effects of any given operation in which we may be interested, and a statement of the relation appears to leave nothing of importance out of account. The reflex responses which accompany many of these states of strength are not to be completely disregarded. They may not help us to refine our distinctions, but they add characteristic details to the final picture of the effect of a given emotional circumstance. In describing the fact that criticism of his work "makes an employee mad," for example, we may report: (1) that he turns red, that the palms of his hands sweat, and, if the evidence is available, that he stops digesting his lunch; (2) that his face takes on a characteristic "expression" of anger; and (3) that he tends to slam doors, to kick the cat, to speak curtly to his fellow workers, to get into a fight, and to watch a street fight or boxing match with special interest. The operant behavior under (3) appears to hang together *via* a common consequence—someone or something is damaged. The "total emotion"—if this is of any importance—is the total effect of the criticism of his work upon his behavior.

The so-called phobias provide extreme examples. Phobias are generally named after the circumstances which give rise to the emotional condition: in claustrophobia, for example, a possibly violent change in behavior is the result of confining the organism in a small space; in agoraphobia a similar effect follows from placing the organism in a large, open space. Many phobias are generated by more specific circumstances: a man with otherwise normal behavior may show an excessive fear of dead birds, for example. How should we describe the latter "emotion"? We could probably show that the unexpected sight of a dead bird elicits very considerable reflex responses—blanching, sweating, change of pulse rate, and so on, as well as various expressions executed by the musculature of the face and body. If this were the extent of the phobia, we could give a complete description of it as a set of conditioned reflexes evoked by sight of a dead bird, but there are other important effects. The behavior of escape will be very powerful. Some of this—such as turning or running away—may be unconditioned or conditioned very early in the history of the organism. Some of it—calling upon someone to take the bird away, for example—is obviously of later origin. The rest of the repertoire undergoes a general change. If our subject was in the course of eating his dinner, we observe that he stops eating or eats less rapidly. If he was engaged in some other task, we observe a change which might be described as "losing interest." We see that he is more likely to jump at sudden noises and to look about him cautiously upon entering new territory. He will be less likely to talk at a natural rate, to laugh, to joke, and so on. He will be predisposed to "see" a dead bird in place of an old hat lying on the ground, in the sense that this stimulus, which to some extent resembles a dead bird, may reinstate all the emotional conditions just described. These changes may persist for a considerable period of time after the stimulus has been removed. A complete account of the phobia would need to refer to all of them, and this would obviously require a description of the whole behavorial repertoire of the individual.

EMOTIONS ARE NOT CAUSES

As long as we conceive of the problem of emotion as one of inner states, we are not likely to advance a practical technology. It does not help in the solution of a practical problem to be told that some feature of a man's behavior is due to frustration or anxiety; we also need to be told how the frustration or anxiety has been induced and how it may be altered. In the end, we find ourselves dealing with two events—the emotional behavior and the manipulable conditions of which that behavior is a function—which comprise the proper subject matter of the study of emotion.

There are certain cases in which three separate stages can be identified. A chronic emotional condition sometimes leads to certain forms of illness. For example, a man whose business is failing may be subject to a long series of circumstances which generate a chronic condition of frustration or anxiety. Part of the total emotion may be reflex responses in the alimentary tract, as a result of which the man may become physically ill—he may develop ulcers, for example. Here it is legitimate to attribute the illness to an "emotion" as a cause, because we define the emotion as a pattern of behavior. We might in the same way attribute a cracked skull to emotion if the injury was suffered as the result of reckless behavior. But this is very different from arguing that emotional behavior is due to an emotion. A man does not neglect his business *because of* anxiety or worry. Such a statement is at best merely a way of classifying a particular kind of neglect. The only valid cause is the external condition of which the behavior of neglect, as part of an emotional pattern known as anxiety or worry, can be shown to be a function. A similar neglect which might be attributed to a preoccupying love affair would not be "due to a different emotion," it would simply be the effect of a different set of circumstances. In order to remedy the neglectful behavior in either case, we must attack the external circumstances which are responsible for it.

The behavior observed during an emotion is not to be confused with emotion as a hypothetical "state," any more than eating is to be confused with hunger. An angry man, like a hungry man, shows a disposition to act in a certain way. He may never act in that way, but we may nevertheless deal with the probability that he will do so. Just as we infer from a history of deprivation that a man is probably hungry even though he is unable to eat, so we infer that he is probably angry by showing that he generally behaves in an angry fashion upon similar occasions. Just as we infer that a man is hungry from his preoccupation with displays of food, so we infer that he is angry because of relatively unimportant responses which co-vary in that emotion. In neither of these cases need our subject emit the important ultimate behavior for which he is predisposed.

The layman makes a further distinction between an emotion and a predisposition toward emotion. He speaks of the latter as a *mood* when the state is temporary ("He is in a jolly mood") and as a *disposition* when it is of longer standing ("He has a mean disposition"). Moods and dispositions represent a kind of second-order probability—the probability that a given circumstance will raise the probability of a given response.

THE PRACTICAL USE OF EMOTION

Emotional behavior and the conditions which generate it are most easily examined when they are put to practical use. Sometimes we wish to elicit the *reflexes* which commonly occur in emotion. Reflexes, as we have seen, cannot be executed upon demand as "voluntary behavior." The poet who exclaims, "Oh, weep for Adonais!" does not actually expect the reader to respond in this way upon request. There is no interpersonal relationship which permits one person to evoke emotional behavior in another according to this formula. The only possibility is to use an eliciting stimulus, either conditioned or unconditioned. The "tear-jerker," as we have noted, is a piece of writing which is designed literally to induce the secretion of tears. Other verbal repertoires are designed to evoke laughter. The use of conditioned stimuli to elicit emotional responses in this way is of great practical importance to professional entertainers.

When we wish to eliminate responses of this sort, we adopt procedures appropriate to the conditioned reflex. When we control a companion's tendency to laugh upon a solemn occasion by drawing his attention away from a funny event, we simply remove the stimulus for laughter. When we achieve the same effect by kicking him in the shins, we simply present the stimulus for an incompatible response. Practical use is also made of certain drugs which induce or eliminate emotional reactions. For example, in the military services a drug which reduces the responses characteristic of anxiety or fear is obviously of great value under battle conditions.

Frequently it is also desirable to change emotional *predispositions*. In a "pep talk" a coach may take advantage of the fact that players exert themselves more aggressively against their opponents if they have been made angry. The skilled cross-examiner may use the same procedure to lead a witness to emit verbal responses which would otherwise be withheld. Soldiers and civilian populations are aroused to aggressive action with stories of atrocities, reminders of present or past injuries, and so on. Since individual histories are involved, the effective operations are to be found, not in a theoretical analysis, but in a study of each case as it arises; a clear understanding of what is being done, however, may make such practices more effective.

A particularly important emotional predisposition is that in which the individual *favors* a particular person, group, or state of affairs. It is hard to define the particular consequences of "favorable" behavior, but a fairly specific effect can often be discovered. A politician may arrange political rallies, kiss babies, publish favorable autobiographical details, and so on, only to strengthen one very specific response on the part of the electorate—placing a mark on a ballot opposite his name. An author or playwright generates favorable responses toward his characters by depicting them in situations which strengthen such behavior or which counteract opposing, unfavorable behavior, and in this way he increases the chances that his book or play will be "liked"; but the behavior at issue may be nothing more than the purchase of books or tickets or the spreading of favorable reports. Part of the effect here is reinforcement, but we may also distinguish a kind of operation which must be classed as emotional. The advertiser interested in generating "good will" for his product employs the same procedures, where the specific behavior at issue is the purchase of the product.

CHAPTER XI

AVERSION, AVOIDANCE, ANXIETY

AVERSIVE BEHAVIOR

The kind of stimuli which are usually called unpleasant, annoying, or, more technically, aversive are not distinguished by particular physical specifications. Very strong stimuli are often aversive, but some weak stimuli are aversive also. Many aversive stimuli damage tissue or otherwise threaten the well-being of the individual, but this is not always true. Painful stimuli are generally aversive, but not necessarily so—as a counterirritant shows. Stimuli which have acquired their aversive power in the process of conditioning are especially unlikely to possess identifying physical properties. A stimulus is known to be aversive only if its removal is reinforcing. In Chapter V such a stimulus was called a negative reinforcer. We define both positive and negative reinforcers in terms of the *strengthening* of a response. What happens when a positive reinforcer is withdrawn or a negative reinforcer presented will not be considered until the following chapter.

Behavior which is followed by the withdrawal of an aversive stimulus is called escape. We weaken an aversive noise by putting fingers in our ears, by moving away from the source, by closing intervening doors or windows, by stopping it at the source, and so on. Similarly, we escape from a bright light by shutting our eyes, turning our head away, or turning off the light. We cannot say that these responses are positively reinforced with "freedom from" noise, light, and so on, since it is the change from one situation to another which is effective, and this is the reduction of a condition prevailing before reinforcement.

In the laboratory we condition a rat to press a lever by reducing the intensity of a light when it does so. The level of illumination is critical. A weak light may be ineffective and a very strong light may lead to aversive behavior acquired earlier in the history of the rat, such as shutting the eyes or covering the head with other parts of the body. A loud noise or a light shock delivered through the floor of the box is less likely to evoke previously established aversive behavior, but the use of such stimuli is complicated by other factors. Aversive stimuli elicit reflexes and generate emotional predispositions which often interfere with the operant to be strengthened. It is then difficult to observe the effect of negative reinforcement alone.

Aversive stimuli are often used, both in the laboratory and in the practical control of behavior, because of the immediacy of the result. When we present an aversive stimulus, any behavior which has previously been conditioned by the withdrawal of the stimulus immediately follows, and the possibility of conditioning other behavior is immediately provided. The presentation of the aversive stimulus therefore resembles a sudden increase in deprivation (Chapter IX); but since deprivation and satiation differ in many respects from the presentation or removal of an aversive stimulus, it is advisable to consider the two kinds of operations separately. We study aversive behavior in accordance with our definition: by presenting an aversive stimulus, we create the possibility of reinforcing a response by withdrawing the stimulus. When conditioning has already taken place, the aversive stimulus provides an immediate mode of control.

Hunger pangs are a possible source of confusion between deprivation and aversive stimulation. Since hunger is the commonest drive, we have tended to model our formulation of all drives upon it. But we have seen that pangs are not representative of drives in general and that, even in the case of hunger, they call for a separate formulation. Insofar as one eats in order to reduce hunger pangs, the behavior is aversive. Whether pangs ever lead to eating before negative reinforcement has taken place would be difficult to determine, since pangs are produced by the very conditions which produce a heightened probability of eating regardless of the presence or absence of pangs. It is possible, however, to separate the producing of pangs from the increase in likelihood that eating will take place. When stimulation which resembles a hunger pang arises from other sources —for example, an inflammation—aversive eating may take place without deprivation. On the other hand, when we drink water, chew an indigestible substance, or take certain drugs in order to reduce hunger pangs, we are emitting behavior which otherwise may not vary with food deprivation. Similarly, although an individual may engage in certain sex practices because they reduce the time wasted in other sexual preoccupations, it does not follow that this result or the reduction of any other aversive consequence is essential to the normal variation in sexual behavior with deprivation or satiation.

Just as we did not define a positive reinforcer as pleasant or satisfying, so in defining a negative reinforcer in terms of its power to reinforce when withdrawn we do not assert that the stimulus is unpleasant or annoying. It would be as difficult to show that the reinforcing power of an aversive stimulus is due to its unpleasantness as to show that the reinforcing power of a positive reinforcer is due to its pleasantness. The arguments given in Chapter V on this point could be repeated step by step for the negative case. There is also a parallel explanation in terms of biological significance. It is not difficult to show that an organism which is reinforced by the withdrawal of certain conditions should have an advantage in natural selection.

Conditioned aversive stimuli. The formula of stimulus substitution applies to the function of negative reinforcement. Neutral events which accompany or precede established negative reinforcements become negatively reinforcing. Thus we move to escape from an annoying or offensive person even though he is not annoying or offensive at the moment. The so-called cures for smoking and drinking mentioned in Chapter IV follow this formula. By pairing the taste of tobacco or alcohol with a condition of nausea, the aversive behavior appropriate to nausea, perhaps including vomiting, is transferred to the tobacco or alcohol.

THE PRACTICAL USE OF AVERSIVE STIMULI

We use negative reinforcement in several different ways. An aversive stimulus which has already been withdrawn to reinforce a desired operant offers, as we have seen, an immediate mode of control. One boy holds another on the ground until the victim cries "Uncle." An arm is twisted until a gun is dropped. A horse is whipped until it moves at a given speed. We use conditioned aversive stimuli in the same way—when, for example, we "shame" someone into acting. The boy who does not dive from the high board is called a sissy; and he can escape from this conditioned verbal stimulus only by diving. His companions present the stimulus to increase the probability that he will dive. "Daring" is a similar practice. (The inverse case, as we shall see in the next chapter, is to prevent behavior from occurring by branding it shameful. Shameful behavior is behavior which one may be "shamed out of." Escape from the aversive shame is achieved by not engaging in the behavior or, more obviously, by engaging in conspicuously incompatible behavior.)

We extend the effectiveness of the technique when we condition behavior so that future aversive stimuli will have an effect. We may plan to present these stimuli upon later occasions, or we may simply prepare for them whenever they may occur. Conditioning is an important stage in the exploiting of aversive control in ethics, religion, and government, as we shall see in Section V.

We also condition aversive stimuli in order to provide for negative reinforcement. A neutral stimulus which is likely to occur on some later occasion is made aversive by being paired with aversive stimuli. Escape is then automatically reinforced. For example, the spread of venereal disease is to some extent controlled by educational programs which provide for the future reinforcement of aversive behavior to prostitutes or "easy pickups." Descriptions or pictures of such people are paired with aversive information about venereal disease. One result is a strong emotional response at the sight of a prostitute which may be effective from the point of view of the educational program by being incompatible with sexual behavior: the individual may be too frightened to participate. To this extent the effect is emotional rather than aversive. Another object of such a program, however, is to guarantee the reinforcement of aversive behavior. When the individual looks away, turns away, or walks away from the prostitute, his behavior will be reinforced by the reduction of a conditioned aversive stimulus.

An important example of this use of aversive conditioning is the practice of branding an act wrong or sinful. Any behavior which reduces the stimulation arising from the early stages of such an act is then negatively reinforced. A single pairing of two stimuli may be sufficient to transfer aversive power, and a conditioned reinforcer may continue to be effective long after the basic unconditioned reinforcers have disappeared from the environment. Many problems in psychotherapy arise from the strength and duration of this effect, as we shall see in Chapter XXIV.

The withdrawal of a positive reinforcer has by definition the same effect as the presentation of a negative. Taking away privileges is not very different from establishing aversive conditions. We occasionally remove a positive reinforcer for practical purposes. What is removed is, more precisely, a conditioned positive reinforcer—a discriminative stimulus or, in other words, the occasion for successful action. There are several subtle distinctions here which are perhaps more important for the theory of behavior than for its practical control. Suppose we have deprived a man of permission to leave a military camp until a certain task has been performed, and suppose that upon past occasions the performance of similar tasks has been followed by the restoration of this privilege. Have we generated a state of deprivation, in which behavior which has been reinforced by the return of privileges will be strong, or have we presented an aversive condition from which the individual can escape only by performing the required task? It is possible, of course, that we have done both. Practically, the distinction may appear to be of little importance, but certain collateral results depend upon the extent to which each is involved.

AVOIDANCE

Escaping from an aversive condition is clearly not the same as avoiding it, since the aversive condition which is avoided does not directly affect the organism. Although avoidance suggests that behavior may be influenced by an event which does not occur, we may account for the effect without violating any fundamental principle of science with the concept of conditioned negative reinforcement. In avoidance the conditioned and unconditioned aversive stimuli are separated by an appreciable interval of time. The required temporal relation is commonly encountered in nature. A rapidly approaching object *precedes* painful contact. The sputter of the fuse *precedes* the explosion of the firecracker. The sound of the dentist's drill *precedes* painful stimulation in the tooth. The interval separating the two stimuli may be definitely fixed, or it may vary widely. In any case, the individual comes to execute behavior which prevents the occurrence or reduces the magnitude of the second stimulus. He dodges the object, puts his fingers in his ears to soften the sound of the explosion, and jerks his head away from the drill. Why?

When stimuli occur in this order, the first stimulus becomes a conditioned negative reinforcer, and henceforth any action which reduces it is strengthened through operant conditioning. When we *avoid* the painful stimulation of the tooth, we merely *escape* from the sound of the drill. That the behavior of avoidance appears to be "directed" toward a future event may be explained as in operant behavior in general: it is always past occurrences of conditioned negative reinforcers and past instances of their reduction which are responsible for the probability of the escape response. The fact that the future event does not occur when the behavior is emitted would raise a puzzling issue if the behavior did in fact continue in strength. But if an occasion for avoidance behavior arises often enough, the conditioned aversive situation grows progressively weaker. The behavior is no longer reinforced, and eventually not emitted. When this happens, the primary negative reinforcer is received. A single instance may suffice to recondition the reinforcing power of the earlier stimulus. Thus when certain visual stimuli generated by a rapidly approaching object are followed by injury, any behavior which converts the stimuli into more harmless forms will be strengthened. Moving out of the way, dodging, and putting up a guard are cases in point. By virtue of these responses the individual is successful in avoiding injury, but he is reinforced only in escaping from the conditioned aversive stimuli which we call the "threat" of injury. If injury is always avoided, the threat grows weaker, and the behavior is less and less strongly reinforced. Eventually a response is not made, an injury is received, and the visual pattern is re-established as a negative reinforcer. Similarly, if the stimulation incidental to the eating of a particular food always precedes a severe allergic headache, it may become aversive. As a result the food is not eaten, the headaches do not occur, and the original conditioning of the negative reinforcer suffers extinction. Eventually the food is no longer aversive. When it is eaten again, another headache occurs, the conditioned nega- tive reinforcer is again established, and another cycle is begun. The "absence of a headache" has had an effect upon behavior only in furthering the extinction of the conditioned aversive stim- ulus.

The practical use of a "threat" is familiar to everyone. The bandit threatens his victim by creating a condition which has preceded physical injury, and the victim reduces this threat by turning over his pocketbook. Escape—running away—may also be highly probable, but it is only the behavior with respect to the pocketbook which fits the present formula. A threat is something more than daring or sham- ing because of the special temporal relation between conditioned and unconditioned negative reinforcers. Nothing else happens if a dare is not taken; the aversive condition simply continues.

Any stimulus which consistently precedes the aversive withdrawal of a positive reinforcer may come to act as a conditioned negative reinforcer. We *avoid* an aversive condition when we act to reduce any indication that an entertaining program will be brought to an end or that any advantage in a competitive affair will be reduced or that we shall lose the affection or love or services of someone who is important to us. The behavior reinforced by reducing such threats will not necessarily be the same as that which is positively reinforced by the entertaining program, by the advantage, or by love, affection, or services.

ANXIETY

A stimulus which characteristically precedes a strong negative reinforcer has a far-reaching effect. It evokes behavior which has been conditioned by the reduction of similar threats and also elicits strong emotional responses. The bandit's victim not only turns over his pocketbook and displays a high probability of running away, he also undergoes a violent emotional reaction which is characteristic of all stimuli leading to avoidance behavior. One who has been severely seasick will tend to escape from conditioned aversive stimuli which occur while planning a trip, while going up the gang-plank, and so on—for example, he will tend to cancel his trip or turn and rush off the ship. He will also exhibit strong conditioned reflexes transferred from the original stimulation of the ship in motion. Some of these may be simple gastric responses which we should not call emotional. Others may be of the sort commonly seen in fear. Operant behavior will be also markedly changed. The individual may seem "preoccupied"—which may mean nothing more than that he is not normally occupied. He may find it impossible to engage in normal conversation or to attend to the simplest practical affairs. He may speak curtly and show none of his usual interests. These are emotional effects upon probability which might have been considered in Chapter X. They can occur, however, only when a stimulus characteristically *precedes* an aversive stimulus by an interval of time sufficiently great to permit behavioral changes to be observed. The condition which results is usually called anxiety.

Almost every strong aversive stimulus is preceded by a characteristic stimulus which may come to generate anxiety. Contingencies of this sort are arranged in the practical control of behavior, often in connection with punishment. Although the biological advantage of avoidance is obvious, the emotional pattern of anxiety appears to serve no useful purpose. It interferes with the normal behavior of the individual and may even disorganize avoidance behavior which would otherwise be effective in dealing with the circumstances. For this reason anxiety is an important problem in psychotherapy, as we shall see in Chapter XXIV. In the design of controlling techniques the possibility of generating anxiety as an unfortunate by-product must constantly be kept in mind.

Since conditioning may take place as the result of one pairing of stimuli, a single aversive event may bring a condition of anxiety under the control of incidental stimuli. The sudden death of a close friend, for example, is sometimes followed by a sustained depression which may be verbalized as a feeling that "something is going to happen," as a "feeling of doom," and so on. It is hard to deal with such a case. When we say that a death was sudden or occurred without warning, we mean that no prior stimulus was particularly associated with it. The stimuli which received the force of the conditioning were therefore the undistinguished elements of daily life. It is not likely that there are any successful forms of escape appropriate to these stimuli, although other forms of escape may, through induction, be strengthened. Conditioned emotional reflexes, as well as conditioned emotional predispositions, may be almost constantly activated. In the case of an "expected" death—for example, the death of someone who has been ill for a long time—the event may be equally aversive, but the anxiety is conditioned to the specific stimuli which precede it. Anxiety is not so likely to arise again unless these stimuli are reinstated—for example, through the illness of another friend.

Although the emotional aspect of anxiety may be distinguished from the conditioned aversive effect responsible for avoidance behavior, it is possible that the emotion is also aversive. Avoidance responses may be interpreted as in part an escape from the emotional components of anxiety. Thus we avoid the dentist's office, not only because it precedes painful stimulation and is therefore a negative reinforcer, but because, having preceded such stimulation, it arouses a complex emotional condition which is also aversive. The total effect may be extremely powerful. A problem of great military importance is the behavior of avoiding battle. Malingering, desertion, or a "nervous breakdown" may reach a very high probability. Successful preparation of the fighting man requires a clear understanding of the effect of the stimuli which precede the more aversive stimuli of combat. The man may be avoiding, not merely battle, but his own reactions of anxiety.

ANXIETY AND ANTICIPATION

A counterpart of anxiety arises when a stimulus precedes a *positive* reinforcement by an appreciable interval. If an envelope received through the mail contains bad news, a similar envelope received later will, before it is opened, generate the anxiety just described. But envelopes also contain good news—perhaps a check or the offer of a good job. Here the avoidance behavior strengthened by bad news— turning away from the mail box, throwing the envelope down unopened, losing the envelope before it is opened, and so on—has its parallel in the increased probability of looking in the box, opening the letter in haste, and so on. Emotional reflexes in response to the unopened envelope will be appropriate to bad news in the one case and to good news in the other. Instead of responses commonly observed in grief, sorrow, or fear, we may observe responses characteristic of elation or joy. Emotional predispositions also stand in the same polar opposition: the general depression of activity in the one case is matched by a general heightening of activity in the other. Instead of growing silent and reserved, our subject speaks to everyone, reacts in an exaggerated fashion, walks faster and seemingly more lightly, and so on. This is particularly obvious in the behavior of young children—for example, on the eve of a holiday or festival.

The effect of stimuli which characteristically precede positive reinforcement may be chronic in a world in which "good" things frequently happen. It is not seen in the clinic because it is not troublesome. Anxiety, which is chronic in a world in which "bad" things frequently happen, has resulting disadvantages both to the individual and to society.

ANXIETY NOT A CAUSE

Anxiety, as a special case of emotion, should be interpreted with the usual caution. When we speak of the *effects of anxiety*, we imply that the state itself is a cause, but so far as we are concerned here, the term merely classifies behavior. It indicates a set of emotional predispositions attributed to a special kind of circumstance. Any therapeutic attempt to reduce the "effects of anxiety" must operate upon these circumstances, not upon any intervening state. The middle term is of no functional significance, either in a theoretical analysis or in the practical control of behavior.

PUNISHMENT

A QUESTIONABLE TECHNIQUE

The commonest technique of control in modern life is punishment. The pattern is familiar: if a man does not behave as you wish, knock him down; if a child misbehaves, spank him; if the people of a country misbehave, bomb them. Legal and police systems are based upon such punishments as fines, flogging, incarceration, and hard labor. Religious control is exerted through penances, threats of excommunication, and consignment to hell-fire. Education has not wholly abandoned the birch rod. In everyday personal contact we control through censure, snubbing, disapproval, or banishment. In short, the degree to which we use punishment as a technique of control seems to be limited only by the degree to which we can gain the necessary power. All of this is done with the intention of reducing tendencies to behave in certain ways. Reinforcement builds up these tendencies; punishment is designed to tear them down.

The technique has often been analyzed, and many familiar questions continue to be asked. Must punishment be closely contingent upon the behavior punished? Must the individual know what he is being punished for? What forms of punishment are most effective and under what circumstances? This concern may be due to the realization that the technique has unfortunate by-products. In the long run, punishment, unlike reinforcement, works to the disadvantage of both the punished organism and the punishing agency. The aversive stimuli which are needed generate emotions, including predispositions to escape or retaliate, and disabling anxieties. For thousands of years men have asked whether the method could not be improved or whether some alternative practice would not be better.

DOES PUNISHMENT WORK?

More recently, the suspicion has also arisen that punishment does not in fact do what it is supposed to do. An immediate effect in reducing a tendency to behave is clear enough, but this may be misleading. The reduction in strength may not be permanent. An explicit revision in the theory of punishment may be dated by the changes in the theories of E. L. Thorndike. Thorndike's first formulation of the behavior of his cats in a puzzle box appealed to two processes: the stamping in of rewarded behavior, or operant conditioning, and a converse process of stamping out as the effect of punishment. Thorndike's later experiments with human subjects required a change in this formulation. The rewards and punishments he used were the relatively mild, verbal conditioned reinforcers of "right" and "wrong." Thorndike found that although "right" strengthened the behavior that preceded it, "wrong" did not weaken it. The relatively trivial nature of the punishment was probably an advantage, since the collateral effects of severe punishment could be avoided and the absence of a weakening effect could therefore be observed without interference from other processes.

The difference between immediate and long-term effects of punishment is clearly shown in animal experiments. In the process of extinction the organism emits a certain number of responses which can be reasonably well predicted. As we have seen, the rate is at first high and then falls off until no significant responding occurs. The cumulative extinction curve is one way of representing the net effect of reinforcement, an effect which we may describe as a predisposition to emit a certain number of responses without further reinforcement. If we now punish the first few responses emitted in extinction, the theory of punishment would lead us to expect that the rest of the extinction curve would contain fewer responses. If we could choose a punishment which subtracted the same number of responses as are added by a reinforcement, then fifty reinforced responses followed by twenty-five punished responses should leave an extinction curve characteristic of twenty-five reinforced responses. When a similar experiment was performed, however, it was found that although punishing responses at the beginning of an extinction curve reduced the momentary rate of responding, the rate rose again when punishment was discontinued and that eventually all responses came out. The effect of punishment was a temporary suppression of the behavior, not a reduction in the total number of responses. Even under severe and prolonged punishment, the rate of responding will rise when punishment has been discontinued, and although under these circumstances it is not easy to show that all the responses originally available will eventually appear, it has been found that after a given time the rate of responding is no lower than if no punishment had taken place.

The fact that punishment does not permanently reduce a tendency to respond is in agreement with Freud's discovery of the surviving activity of what he called repressed wishes. As we shall see later, Freud's observations can be brought into line with the present analysis.

THE EFFECTS OF PUNISHMENT

If punishment is not the opposite of reward, if it does not work by subtracting responses where reinforcement adds them, what does it do? We can answer this question with the help of our analysis of escape and of avoidance and anxiety. The answer supplies not only a clear-cut picture of the effect of punishment but an explanation of its unfortunate by-products. The analysis is somewhat detailed, but it is essential to the proper use of the technique and to the therapy required to correct some of its consequences.

We must first define punishment without presupposing any effect. This may appear to be difficult. In defining a reinforcing stimulus we could avoid specifying physical characteristics by appealing to the effect upon the strength of the behavior. If a punishing consequence is also defined without reference to its physical characteristics and if there is no comparable effect to use as a touchstone, what course is open to us? The answer is as follows. We first define a positive reinforcer as any stimulus the *presentation* of which strengthens the behavior upon which it is made contingent. We define a negative reinforcer (an aversive stimulus) as any stimulus the *withdrawal* of which strengthens behavior. Both are reinforcers in the literal sense of reinforcing or strengthening a response. Insofar as scientific definition corresponds to lay usage, they are both "rewards." In solving the problem of punishment we simply ask: What is the effect of *withdrawing* a *positive* reinforcer or *presenting* a *negative*? An example of the former would be taking candy from a baby; an example of the latter, spanking a baby. We have not used any new terms in posing these questions and hence need not define any. Yet insofar as we are able to give a scientific definition of a lay term, these two possibilities appear to constitute the field of punishment. We do not presuppose any effect; we simply raise a question to be answered by appropriate experiments. The physical specifications of both kinds of consequences are determined in the case in which behavior is strengthened. Conditioned reinforcers, including the generalized reinforcers, fit the same definition: we punish by *dis*approving, by taking money away, as in a legal fine, and so on.

Although punishment is a powerful technique of social control, it is not necessarily administered by another individual. The burned child has been punished for touching flame. Eating unsuitable food is punished by indigestion. It is not necessary that the contingency represent an established functional relation, such as that between flames and burns or certain foods and indigestion. When a salesman in a midwestern city once approached a house and rang the doorbell, the rear of the house exploded. There was only an accidental and very rare contingency: gas had escaped into the kitchen, and the explosion was set off by sparks from the electric doorbell. The effect upon the subsequent behavior of the salesman as he rang other doorbells nevertheless falls within the present field.

A FIRST EFFECT OF PUNISHMENT

The first effect of the aversive stimuli used in punishment is confined to the immediate situation. It need not be followed by any change in behavior upon later occasions. When we stop a child from giggling in church by pinching it severely, the pinch elicits responses which are incompatible with laughing and powerful enough to suppress it. Although our action may have other consequences, we can single out the competing effect of the responses elicited by the punishing stimulus. The same effect is obtained with a conditioned stimulus when we stop the child with a threatening gesture. This requires earlier conditioning, but the current effect is simply the elicitation of incompatible behavior—the responses appropriate, for example, to fear. The formula can be extended to include emotional predispositions. Thus we may stop a man from running away by making him angry. The aversive stimulus which makes him angry may be unconditioned (for example, stamping on his toe) or conditioned (for example, calling him a coward). We may stop someone from eating his dinner by frightening him with a sudden deafening noise or a gruesome story.

It is not essential to this effect that the aversive stimulus be contingent upon behavior in the standard punishing sequence. When that sequence is observed, however, the effect still occurs and must be considered as one of the results of punishment. It resembles other effects of punishment in bringing undesirable behavior to an end; but since this is temporary, it is not likely to be accepted as typical of control through punishment.

A SECOND EFFECT OF PUNISHMENT

Punishment is generally supposed to have some abiding effect. It is hoped that some change in behavior will be observed in the future, even though further punishment is withheld. One enduring effect, also not often considered as typical, resembles the effect just considered. When a child who has been pinched for giggling starts to giggle upon a later occasion, his own behavior may supply conditioned stimuli which, like the mother's threatening gesture, evoke opposed emotional responses. We have seen an adult parallel in the use of drugs which induce nausea or other aversive conditions as consequences of drinking alcoholic beverages. As a result later drinking generates conditioned aversive stimuli which evoke responses incompatible with further drinking. As an effect of the severe punishment of sexual behavior, the early stages of such behavior generate conditioned stimuli giving rise to emotional responses which interfere with the completion of the behavior. One difficulty with the technique is that punishment for sexual behavior may interfere with similar behavior under socially acceptable circumstances—for example, in marriage. In general, then, as a second effect of punishment, behavior which has consistently been punished becomes the source of conditioned stimuli which evoke incompatible behavior.

Some of this behavior involves glands and smooth muscles. Let us say, for example, that a child is consistently punished for lying. The behavior is not easily specified, since a verbal response is not necessarily in itself a lie but can be defined as such only by taking into account the circumstances under which it is emitted. These circumstances come to play a conspicuous role, however, so that the total situation stimulates the child in a characteristic fashion. For reasons which we shall examine in Chapter XVII, an individual is in general able to tell when he is lying. The stimuli to which he responds when he does so are conditioned to elicit responses appropriate to punishment: his palms may sweat, his pulse may speed up, and so on. When he later lies during a lie-detection test, these conditioned responses are recorded.

Strong emotional *predispositions* are also rearoused by the beginnings of severely punished behavior. These are the main ingredient of what we speak of as guilt, shame, or a sense of sin. Part of what we feel when we feel guilty are conditioned responses of glands and smooth muscles of the kind reported by the lie detector, but we may also recognize a displacement of the normal probabilities of our behavior. This is often the most conspicuous feature of the guilt of others. The furtive look, the skulking manner, the guilty way of speaking are emotional effects of the conditioned stimuli aroused by punished behavior. Comparable effects are observed in lower animals:

the guilty behavior of a dog which is behaving in a way which has previously been punished is a familiar spectacle. A case may be easily set up in the laboratory. If a rat has been conditioned to press a lever by being reinforced with food and is then punished by being lightly shocked as it presses the lever, its behavior in approaching and touching the lever will be modified. The early stages in the sequence generate conditioned emotional stimuli which alter the behavior previously established. Since the punishment is not directly administered by another organism, the pattern does not resemble the more familiar behavior of guilt in the pet dog.

A condition of guilt or shame is generated not only by previously punished behavior but by any consistent external occasion for such behavior. The individual may feel guilty in a situation in which he has been punished. We gain control by introducing stimuli for just this effect. For example, if we punish a child for any behavior executed after we have said "No, no!" this verbal stimulus will later evoke an emotional state appropriate to punishment. When this policy has been followed consistently, the behavior of the child may be controlled simply by saying "No, no!" since the stimulus arouses an emotional condition which conflicts with the response to be controlled.

Although the rearousal of responses appropriate to aversive stimuli is again not the main effect of punishment, it works in the same direction. In none of these cases, however, have we supposed that the punished response is permanently weakened. It is merely temporarily suppressed, more or less effectively, by an emotional reaction.

A THIRD EFFECT OF PUNISHMENT

We come now to a much more important effect. If a given response is followed by an aversive stimulus, any stimulation which accompanies the response, whether it arises from the behavior itself or from concurrent circumstances, will be conditioned. We have just appealed to this formula in accounting for conditioned emotional reflexes and predispositions, but the same process also leads to the conditioning of aversive stimuli which serve as negative reinforcers. *Any behavior which reduces this conditioned aversive stimulation will be reinforced.*

In the example just considered, as the rat approaches the lever to which its recent responses have been punished, powerful conditioned aversive stimuli are generated by the increasing proximity of the lever and by the rat's own behavior of approach. Any behavior which reduces these stimuli—turning or running away, for example—is reinforced. Technically we may say that further punishment is avoided.

The most important effect of punishment, then, is to establish aversive conditions which are avoided by any behavior of "doing something else." It is important—for both practical and theoretical reasons—to specify this behavior. It is not enough to say that what is strengthened is simply the opposite. Sometimes it is merely "doing nothing" in the form of actively holding still. Sometimes it is behavior appropriate to other current variables which are not, however, sufficient to explain the level of probability of the behavior without supposing that the individual is also acting "for the sake of keeping out of trouble."

The effect of punishment in setting up behavior which competes with, and may displace, the punished response is most commonly described by saying that the individual *represses* the behavior, but we need not appeal to any activity which does not have the dimensions of behavior. If there is any repressing force or agent, it is simply the incompatible response. The individual contributes to the process by executing this response. (In Chapter XVIII we shall find that another sort of repression involves the individual's knowledge of the repressed act.) No change in the strength of the punished response is implied.

If punishment is repeatedly avoided, the conditioned negative reinforcer undergoes extinction. Incompatible behavior is then less and less strongly reinforced, and the punished behavior eventually emerges. When punishment again occurs, the aversive stimuli are reconditioned, and the behavior of doing something else is then reinforced. If punishment is discontinued, the behavior may emerge in full strength.

When an individual is punished for *not* responding in a given way, conditioned aversive stimulation is generated when he is doing anything else. Only by behaving in a given way may he become free of "guilt." Thus one may avoid the aversive stimulation generated by "not doing one's duty" by simply doing one's duty. No moral or ethical problem is necessarily involved: a draft horse is kept moving according to the same formula. When the horse slows down, the slower pace (or the crack of a whip) supplies a conditioned aversive stimulus from which the horse escapes by increasing its speed. The aversive effect must be reinstated from time to time by actual contact with the whip.

Since punishment depends in large part upon the behavior of other people, it is likely to be intermittent. The action which is always punished is rare. All the schedules of reinforcement described in Chapter VI are presumably available.

SOME UNFORTUNATE BY-PRODUCTS
OF PUNISHMENT

Severe punishment unquestionably has an immediate effect in reducing a tendency to act in a given way. This result is no doubt responsible for its widespread use. We "instinctively" attack anyone whose behavior displeases us—perhaps not in physical assault, but with criticism, disapproval, blame, or ridicule. Whether or not there is an inherited tendency to do this, the immediate effect of the practice is reinforcing enough to explain its currency. In the long run, however, punishment does not actually eliminate behavior from a repertoire, and its temporary achievement is obtained at tremendous cost in reducing the over-all efficiency and happiness of the group.

One by-product is a sort of conflict between the response which leads to punishment and the response which avoids it. These responses are incompatible and they are both likely to be strong at the same time. The repressing behavior generated by even severe and sustained punishment often has very little advantage over the behavior it represses. The result of such a conflict is discussed in Chapter XIV. When punishment is only intermittently administered, the conflict is especially troublesome, as we see in the case of the child who "does not know when he will be punished and when he will get away with it." Responses which avoid punishment may alternate with punished responses in rapid oscillation or both may blend into an uncoordinated form. In the awkward, timorous, or "inhibited" person, standard behavior is interrupted by distracting responses, such as turning, stopping, and doing something else. The stutterer or stammerer shows a similar effect on a finer scale.

Another by-product of the use of punishment is even more unfortunate. Punished behavior is often strong, and certain incipient stages are therefore frequently reached. Even though the stimulation thus generated is successful in preventing a full-scale occurrence, it also evokes reflexes characteristic of fear, anxiety, and other emotions. Moreover, the incompatible behavior which blocks the punished response may resemble external physical restraint in generating rage or frustration. Since the variables responsible for these emotional patterns are generated by the organism itself, no appropriate escape behavior is available. The condition may be chronic and may result in "psychosomatic" illness or otherwise interfere with the effective behavior of the individual in his daily life (Chapter XXIV).

Perhaps the most troublesome result is obtained when the behavior punished is reflex—for example, weeping. Here it is usually not possible to execute "just the opposite," since such behavior is not conditioned according to the operant formula. The repressing behavior must therefore work through a second stage, as in the operant control of "involuntary behavior" discussed in Chapter VI. Some examples will be considered in Chapter XXIV where the techniques of psychotherapy will be shown to be mainly concerned with the unfortunate by-products of punishment.

ALTERNATIVES TO PUNISHMENT

We may avoid the use of punishment by weakening an operant in other ways. Behavior which is conspicuously due to *emotional* circumstances, for example, is often likely to be punished, but it may often be more effectively controlled by modifying the circumstances. Changes brought about by *satiation*, too, often have the effect which is contemplated in the use of punishment. Behavior may often be eliminated from a repertoire, especially in young children, simply by allowing time to pass in accordance with a *developmental schedule.*

If the behavior is largely a function of age, the child will, as we say, outgrow it. It is not always easy to put up with the behavior until this happens, especially under the conditions of the average household, but there is some consolation if we know that by carrying the child through a socially unacceptable stage we spare him the later complications arising from punishment.

Another way of weakening a conditioned response is simply to let time pass. This process of *forgetting* is not to be confused with extinction. Unfortunately it is generally slow and also requires that occasions for the behavior be avoided.

The most effective alternative process is probably *extinction*. This takes time but is much more rapid than allowing the response to be forgotten. The technique seems to be relatively free of objectionable by-products. We recommend it, for example, when we suggest that a parent "pay no attention" to objectionable behavior on the part of his child. If the child's behavior is strong only because it has been reinforced by "getting a rise out of" the parent, it will disappear when this consequence is no longer forthcoming.

Another technique is to *condition incompatible behavior*, not by withdrawing censure or guilt, but through positive reinforcement. We use this method when we control a tendency toward emotional display by reinforcing stoical behavior. This is very different from punishing emotional behavior, even though the latter also provides for the indirect reinforcement of stoical behavior through a reduction in aversive stimuli. Direct positive reinforcement is to be preferred because it appears to have fewer objectionable by-products.

Civilized man has made some progress in turning from punishment to alternative forms of control. Avenging gods and hell-fire have given way to an emphasis upon heaven and the positive consequences of the good life. In agriculture and industry, fair wages are recognized as an improvement over slavery. The birch rod has made way for the reinforcements naturally accorded the educated man. Even in politics and government the power to punish has been supplemented by a more positive support of the behavior which conforms to the interests of the governing agency. But we are still a long way from exploiting the alternatives, and we are not likely to make any real advance so long as our information about punishment and the alternatives to punishment remains at the level of casual observation. As a consistent picture of the extremely complex consequences of punishment emerges from analytical research, we may gain the confidence and skill needed to design alternative procedures in the clinic, in education, in industry, in politics, and in other practical fields.

CHAPTER XIII

FUNCTION VERSUS ASPECT

Frequently we describe behavior not with verbs which specify action but with adjectives describing characteristics or aspects of action. Instead of saying, "He shook hands and said, 'Hello, hello,'" we may say, "He was most cordial." The adjective "cordial" is one of a list of about 4,500 English words compiled by Allport and Odbert which refer to more or less enduring *traits* of human behavior. If we add terms which refer to temporary conditions, such as "embarrassed" or "hazy," the number is about doubled. Most of these trait-names are nontechnical words which we use in our daily affairs. They are an essential tool of the novelist; literature is, in fact, responsible for adding many of them to the language. By describing human behavior in characteristic situations, the storyteller creates convenient expressions for later use—such as "dog in the manger" or "a Daniel come to judgment." The list has also been extended by the invention of such technical terms as "phlegmatic" and "melancholic" or, more recently, "inhibited," "introverted," and "cerebrotonic."

Staying at a single letter in the Allport and Odbert list, a biographer might describe the behavior of a subject as follows: "There was a remarkable change in his behavior. Where he had been *happy-go-lucky*, he grew *hesitant* and *heavy-handed*. His natural *humility* gave

194

way to a sustained *haughtiness*. Once the most *helpful* of men, he became *heedless* and *hard-hearted*. A sort of *histrionic horseplay* was all that remained of his fine sense of *humor*." A passage of this sort tells us something important. If it were a description of an old friend, for example, it would prepare us to deal with him more effectively when we saw him again. But it may come as something of a surprise to discover that no behavior has actually been described. Not a single action has been mentioned. The passage might be describing a series of letters—of a colleague or business acquaintance, perhaps. On the other hand, it might be describing a wholly nonverbal scene from a ballet. It might concern a shopkeeper, a plant foreman, a salesman, a diplomat, a schoolboy—in short, any one of dozens of different kinds of people whose behavior would have nothing in common except those aspects to which the passage refers.

There are practical circumstances under which it is useful to know that a man will behave in a given manner even though we may not know precisely what he will do. To be able to predict, for example, that a proposal will probably be "received favorably" is valuable even though the specific form of the reception remains to be seen. Under certain circumstances everything else about the behavior may be irrelevant, and a description in terms of traits is then highly economical. But are terms of this sort valuable in a functional analysis? And if they are, how are they related to the variables which we have so far considered?

WHAT ARE TRAITS?

A common and unchanging property of the behavior of all members of a species would not usefully be referred to as a trait at all. It is only because people differ from moment to moment or from person to person that trait-names arise. We may look for the equivalents of traits in a functional analysis, therefore, by asking in how many ways we should expect a person to differ from other persons or from himself from time to time.

Differences in variables. Some differences are due to the differences in the independent variables to which people are exposed. Although we may be struck by the effect upon behavior, the original individuality lies outside the organism. Differences in experience between the "ignorant" and the "learned," the "naive" and the "sophisticated," or the "innocent" and the "worldly" refer mainly to differences in histories of reinforcement. Such terms as "enthusiastic," "interested," and "discouraged" describe the effects of different schedules of reinforcement. People are "inhibited," "timid," or "cowed" because of special contingencies involving punishment. The "discriminating" individual has made distinctions among stimuli which are not made by the "undiscriminating." Differences in deprivation lead us to distinguish between the "voracious" and the "finicky," the "libidinous" and the "sexless." Differences in hereditary endowment, which are too conspicuous to be overlooked when we compare different species but presumably are also present to a lesser extent between members of a single species, account for other differences in repertoire, as do differences in age ("youthful," "senile") or in development ("infantile," "adolescent"). The field of emotion has scarcely advanced beyond an aspect-description, where more or less transitory differences in behavior are attributed to various exciting circumstances ("frightened," "angry," and "embarrassed").

Traits of this sort are simply a way of representing the repertoire of an organism, with some indication of the relative strength of its parts and with certain inferences regarding relevant variables. The "tests" which measure such traits are inventories, which list responses falling within certain classes and estimate their relative frequencies of occurrence. Surveys of attitudes and opinions are usually of this sort, as are tests of achievement. The Kinsey reports on sexual behavior are surveys of frequencies of certain types of responses from which we may infer certain conditions of deprivation, a history of sexual reinforcement, and the health and hereditary endowment of the organism.

Differences in processes. A second kind of difference in behavior arises from a difference in the rate at which changes in behavior take place. The "intelligent" individual, for example, is commonly supposed to show more rapid conditioning and extinction, to form discriminations more rapidly, and so on. The resulting effect upon

behavior is not always distinguishable from that of "experience."
When an individual scores high on an achievement test, the result
may be traced either to an exposure to certain variables or to the rate
at which these variables have taken effect or to both. Vocabulary
tests, for example, presumably reflect differences both in exposure
and in rate of conditioning. When we distinguish between the
"phlegmatic" and the "sanguine" or "the slow-to-anger" and the
"truculent," the differences are not in degree of deprivation or emotional circumstances but in the speed with which behavior changes
as a function of such circumstances.

Traits of this second sort cannot be measured by an inventory.
If we want to know simply whether a given set of conditions will
make a man angry or lead him to take any other sort of action, a
survey of his behavior under those conditions will suffice. If, however, we want to know how quickly he becomes angry or how alertly
he takes action, we need a measure appropriate to a functional process. Differences of this second sort can eventually be expressed in
quantitative form as differences in the values of certain constants in
the equations describing the appropriate processes. Once these values
are available, they will *characterize* an individual just as the physical
constants of thermal conductivity, electrical conductivity, specific
gravity, and so on characterize materials. (It is significant that these
"individual differences" among physical objects were once attributed
to essences or principles which strongly resemble traits as the term
is now commonly used.)

Traits which can be reduced to inventories of behavior, to the relative strengths of parts of a repertoire, or to the speed with which
behavioral processes take place have acceptable scientific dimensions,
and their relation to a functional analysis is clear. Those who are
currently engaged in the study of traits, however, almost always
quantify their data in a quite different way. The intelligence test is
a classic example. When a man takes such a test, he makes a score.
This is numerical, but it is not an acceptable measure of a trait
because it is arbitrary: it depends upon the length of the test, its
nature, the time allowed in taking it, and so on. To obtain a less
arbitrary measure, the same test is given to a number of people under

comparable conditions, and each raw score is converted into a standard score which gives the position of the individual with respect to the group. Even this standard score is not a quantitative measure of a trait; it simply shows that the performance of an individual exceeds that of a certain percentage of the group. But the group is, like the original score, arbitrary. Trouble will arise when we try to use such a measure in a different group.

The difference between a measure based upon a population and a measure based upon frequency of response is clear when we consider a population of only one man. Robinson Crusoe, before the advent of his man Friday, must have shown a certain repertoire of behavior, certain frequencies of response, and certain rates of change in frequency. Occasionally he must have been hungry in the sense of being inclined to eat at a given rate, angry in the sense of being disposed to injure animals or objects, and intelligent in the sense of being quick to solve the problems of his daily life. His behavior must have been modified at given rates as the result of certain contingencies. He must have been able to discriminate stimuli of given complexities or subtleties. All this he himself might have observed and measured in a quantitative way. He could not, however, have measured his own I.Q., since he could not have devised a test on which his score would be divested of the arbitrary features of length, level of difficulty, or allotted time.

The use of a population to measure a trait is illustrated by a scale commonly used to designate the hardness of minerals. The scale ranges from 1 (talc) to 10 (diamond). When we say that quartz has a hardness of 7, we mean that it will scratch or cut all minerals having a hardness of 6 or less, and that it in turn can be cut by minerals of hardness 8, 9, or 10. If the world were constructed of quartz alone, the number 7 would have no significance. Such a scale is unquestionably useful for technological purposes, but it does not greatly advance the study of the hardness of minerals. The physicist accounts for different positions on the scale as differences in molecular structure. A measure of the hardness of quartz expressed in terms of structure is meaningful without reference to minerals of other hardnesses. Insofar as we can express differences in intelligence as differences in repertoire, in exposure to variables, or in rates of change, our measure is similarly independent of a population.

PREDICTION IN TERMS OF TRAITS

A test is simply a convenient opportunity to observe behavior—to survey or sample our dependent variable. The score may be used to predict some aspect of the larger universe of behavior from which the test is drawn. Thus a test of mechanical ability, or intelligence, or extroversion may enable us to predict success or failure in a job in which these traits are important. But the causal relation invoked in this kind of prediction is not the same as that which appears in a functional analysis. Certain variables in the history of the individual and in the current environment are responsible for the behavior in the test situation, and they also determine the behavior in the larger situation. The prediction is not from cause to effect, but *from one effect to another*. This is shown by the fact that we use tests as a basis for prediction without knowing what variables are responsible for the score obtained or for the behavior predicted. It is shown also by the fact that if we extend a test without limit, adding more and more items, it eventually coincides with the behavior to be predicted. No true prediction then survives. There is no way in which we could extend a true independent variable so that it would become identical with the dependent variable in a functional analysis.

A prediction from effect to effect is, of course, sometimes useful. It may enable us to dispense with the direct observation of variables. This is particularly important when the variables are clearly out of reach. For example, whether an individual shows certain patterns of behavior characteristic of his species or where he stands with respect to other members of his species in relative frequency of response, as in the Kinsey reports, can at the moment be determined only through a survey, since we have no direct control over the independent variables. A complete survey of such behavior would be easily understood; an incomplete survey constitutes a "test" from which the result of a complete survey may be inferred.

We may also find it convenient to survey the current effects of variables which, though manipulable, lie in the remote history of the individual. We use body weight as a current indication of a history of food deprivation in predicting the probability that an experimental animal will eat, and we might use some collateral test of the "trait of voracity" for the same purpose. Rate of eating in a test situation would enable us to predict rate of eating in a larger experimental situation. Similarly, by making an inventory of current aggressive tendencies, we may dispense with the possibly difficult study of early environmental factors responsible for aggressive behavior.

The principal advantages of a functional analysis are lost, however, when we resort to these alternative practices. Perhaps the most conspicuous feature of an aspect-description is its failure to advance the control of behavior. By measuring a set of traits, we judge the suitability of an individual to a given task, but the only practical step is to accept or reject him. The measurement of the trait does not suggest a way of altering his suitability to the task, for it does not bring us into contact with variables which may be manipulated in generating or eliminating the behavior which it describes. The only practical advantage we gain is that we may make better use of relevant variables already in our possession.

Instead of predicting performance from the test of a trait, we may be interested in predicting one trait from another or from some other sort of variable. Thus a personality in all its manifestations is often attributed to the physique of the organism, a relation which is presumably capable of being expressed trait by trait. Often personality is attributed to variables which are immediately controllable. For example, the "oral," "anal," and "erotic" personalities of Freud refer to groups of traits which are assumed to have been generated by the early history of the individual—a history which is presumably modifiable, if taken in time, or at least capable of being masked by a later history superimposed upon it. A similar controlling relation is suggested for a single trait when it is asserted that aggressiveness is a function of frustration. There are, however, certain inherent limitations in a functional analysis in which the dependent variable is a trait.

The usefulness of any lawful relation depends upon the sharpness of reference of the terms in which it is stated. We may predict and control only as much as we specify in our laws. We have seen that there are practical circumstances under which it may be useful to predict traits, but in general the trait-name tells us little about behavior. It is not only lack of specificity, however, which makes the trait-name unsuitable for a functional analysis. In the chapters which follow we shall turn to certain complex processes. Interlocking systems of responses will be traced to complex arrangements of variables, and a workable conception of the individual as a responding system will be set up. The trait-name does not refer to a unit of behavior which makes such an analysis possible.

The fact that a conception of the individual as a behaving system seems to lie beyond the reach of an aspect-description is exemplified by a practical problem in current clinical psychology. Through an extensive use of tests and other measurements of aspects of behavior the individual is characterized for diagnostic purposes. But the resulting information is of little or no help in therapy—in dealing with the individual as a dynamic system. The clinician must turn from a "psychograph" of the personality to "common sense" or to an entirely different conceptual system—such as that of psychoanalysis, which, as we shall see later, is similar to a functional analysis. Currently, little or no effort is being made to reconcile these two ways of dealing with human behavior, perhaps because a reconciliation seems hopeless. The measurement of aspects of behavior is likely to be associated with the belief that the business of science is primarily to supply information which is then used to further the *art* of dealing with people, not only in the clinic, but in salesmanship, education, family counseling, labor problems, diplomacy, and so on. But the special wisdom which this art presupposes, the special insight into human behavior which is needed to make effective use of such information, is precisely what a *functional analysis* supplies.

We are all thoroughly familiar with descriptions of behavior in terms of traits, and trait-names are an extensive part of our daily vocabulary. As a result, we feel at home in describing behavior in this way. But the familiarity is misleading. The fact is that we can predict and control a *response* much more readily than a *trait*. A response is easier to define and identify, and its probability varies more sensitively. Even when we define a trait as a group of responses, the unity or coherence of the group needs to be proved. Do all the responses which are taken to be evidences of aggressiveness, for example, vary together with a given condition of frustration? And are all conditions of frustration equally effective? In order to be sure of the unity of the trait, we have to show that each of the acts which "expresses" it is controlled by each of the conditions specified as its cause—that each aggressive act, for example, is controlled to the same degree by every condition which can be described as frustrating. But this is the program of a functional analysis. We have not reduced the labor of such an analysis by resorting to summary statements in terms of traits.

Almost any characteristic may be set up as a dimension of the personality, but this extended coverage is of little value until something is achieved beyond mere naming. The additional work required to establish traits as scientific categories is just as laborious and just as detailed as the analysis of discrete responses. The effort required to make any account comprehensive is determined by the subject matter itself. Unfortunately, behavior is complex.

TRAITS ARE NOT CAUSES

Trait-names usually begin as adjectives—"intelligent," "aggressive," "disorganized," "angry," "introverted," "ravenous," and so on—but the almost inevitable linguistic result is that adjectives give birth to nouns. The things to which these nouns refer are then taken to be the active causes of the aspects. We begin with "intelligent behavior," pass first to "behavior which *shows* intelligence," and then to "behavior which *is the effect of* intelligence." Similarly, we begin by observing a preoccupation with a mirror which recalls the legend of Narcissus; we invent the adjective "narcissistic," and then the noun "narcissism"; and finally we assert that the thing presumably referred to by the noun is the cause of the behavior with which we began. But at no point in such a series do we make contact with any event But at no point in such a series do we make contact with any event outside the behavior itself which justifies the claim of a causal connection.

Efforts have been made to put the matter in better scientific order by establishing the validity of the trait as a conceptual cause. A search for the smallest number of traits which will "explain" behavior has worked in this direction. Since trait-names come from many sources and may be multiplied at will, the kinds of behavior to which they refer often overlap. The overlap may be discovered by analyzing the forms of behavior specified in tests of two traits or by showing that the result on one test enables us to predict the result on another. When two traits are found to be almost identical, one is simply dropped. When the overlap is not complete, we appear to be measuring a trait which is common to both tests, yet not measured exclusively by either one. The trait therefore appears to have different dimensions from the behavior from which it is inferred, and this fact has encouraged those who are concerned with finding a minimal set of these causes.

The smallest number of traits needed to account for the performances of a group of people on a number of tests may be determined through certain mathematical procedures. From such a result we may say that a given individual does well in one group of tests because he possesses a certain amount of a certain trait, and on another group of tests because he possesses a certain amount of a different trait. Since these procedures take us some distance away from the observed data, it is tempting to identify the resulting traits or factors with physiological states or psychological faculties and to give them additional dimensions not found in the measures of behavior from which they were inferred. Regardless of the length of the mathematical procedure, however, a trait or factor is derived from the observation of the dependent variable only. This limitation is not changed by any mathematical operation. A fairly exhaustive set of tests may enable us to evaluate traits and to predict performances in a wide range of situations, but the prediction is still from effect to effect. The mathematical refinement has not brought the trait under control. We do **not** change behavior by manipulating a trait.

CHAPTER XIV

THE ANALYSIS OF COMPLEX CASES

"OVERSIMPLIFICATION"

In a scientific analysis it is seldom possible to proceed directly to complex cases. We begin with the simple and build up to the complex, step by step. In its early years any science is vulnerable to the charge that it neglects important instances. Boyle's Law, relating the volume of a gas to its pressure, was a significant advance in knowledge, but a contemporary critic could easily have denounced it as a flagrant oversimplification. It was only necessary to vary the temperature to show that volume was not simply a function of pressure. When the temperature was specified in a new version of the law, more precise measurements could still show that there were discrepancies between different gases, and a "gas constant" had to be added to the equation. There is nothing wrong with this sort of patchwork; it is the way scientific knowledge grows.

In a science of behavior we begin in the simplest way. We study relatively simple organisms with relatively simple histories and under relatively simple environmental conditions. In this way we obtain the degree of rigor necessary for a scientific analysis. Our data are as uniform and reproducible as, say, the data of modern biology. It is true that the simplicity is to some extent artificial. We do not often find anything like it outside the laboratory—especially in the field of human behavior, which is of primary interest. As a result those who are impatient to get on to bigger issues are inclined to object to the "oversimplified" formulations of the laboratory. Their objections take the form, as in the example of Boyle's Law, of setting forth apparent exceptions to the rule. Such criticism is useful if it points to facts which have been unseen or ignored. But very often the exceptions are only apparent; the existing formulation is capable of giving a good account of them when properly applied.

A common source of misunderstanding is the neglect of what happens when variables are combined in different ways. Although a functional analysis begins with relatively isolated relations, an important part of its task is to show how its variables interact. Several important cases will be discussed in the present chapter.

MULTIPLE EFFECTS OF A SINGLE VARIABLE

A given event may have two or more kinds of effects upon behavior at the same time. In the analysis of punishment in Chapter XII it was seen that a single aversive stimulus contingent upon a response has at least *four* effects. (1) It elicits reflexes, often of an emotional nature. (2) It alters emotional predispositions to act in various ways. (3) It serves as a reinforcing stimulus in respondent conditioning when paired with stimuli which precede or accompany it; these stimuli eventually evoke the responses and predispositions of (1) and (2), and any *avoidance* behavior which brings the stimuli to an end is reinforced. (4) It makes possible the reinforcement of any *escape* behavior which brings the punishing stimulus itself to an end. In this example, then, a single event serves as an eliciting stimulus, an emotional operation, a reinforcing stimulus in respondent conditioning, and a negative reinforcer in operant conditioning.

It would be meaningless to say that an event has two or more effects if we could not separate them. When the effects are felt at different times, this is not difficult. For example, a reinforcement may be of such magnitude that considerable satiation takes place. The strengthening effect of the reinforcement may be temporarily concealed by the weakening effect of satiation. Thus a single, relatively large payment of wages may produce such a degree of satiation that the worker does not work again for some time, but the reinforcing effect of the wage will become evident when a sufficient deprivation again arises.

A common objection to the Law of Effect provides another example. The doctrine of "need-gratification" in psychotherapy is based upon the fact that behavior which has been strengthened by deprivation is weakened by satiation. Satiation thus becomes a clinical procedure. For example, behavior which is strong because it has been reinforced with personal attention may be weakened if the individual receives attention or if the primary deprivations responsible for the reinforcing power of attention are reduced. Similarly, behavior which is strong because it gets affection can be weakened by giving affection or appropriate primary reinforcers. It has been argued that these results contradict the Law of Effect, which appears to predict that the behavior should be strengthened rather than weakened. But the case is easily formulated in terms of the multiple effects of giving attention or affection. A child who is behaving in an asocial fashion to draw attention to himself may be "cured" by a sizable measure of attention if satiation takes precedence over reinforcement, as it may. But what will happen when deprivation again arises? If the "cure" sends the patient back for more attention or affection, a reinforcing effect is obvious. (This can be avoided. If a certain "need-gratification" is prescribed, it should be given when the patient is not misbehaving. This will produce satiation without reinforcing undesirable behavior.)

An objection which has been raised to the principle of satiation supplies an example of a different set of multiple effects. Suppose we approach a child who is playing happily by himself and give him a small piece of candy. We may observe the sudden emergence of a great deal of objectionable behavior—asking and teasing for more candy, then crying, and perhaps even a temper tantrum. We appear to have *increased* his candy-hunger, although our definition of satiation implies that we have decreased it, at least by a small amount. The explanation is that the candy has had a second effect. The sight and taste of candy are *discriminative stimuli* under which the behavior of asking or reaching for candy is frequently effective. There is no likelier occasion for the reinforcement of such behavior than the immediate presence of candy. By giving the child a small amount of candy, we establish a common situation in which powerful behavior under the control of candy-deprivation is usually effective and hence strong. We have not made the child any hungrier in terms of deprivation. With a given history of deprivation the behavior of begging for candy shows two levels of strength under the control of two stimuli. In our experiment we change from the stimulus which controls the low level to that which controls the high. Another result then follows. A small piece of candy, as a discriminative stimulus, evokes behavior which is usually reinforced, but we have specified that it is not further reinforced in the present case. Not only does the child ask for candy; he asks unsuccessfully. This is the condition for an emotional reaction of "frustration," in which the child begins to cry and perhaps ends with a temper tantrum (Chapter X). It is obvious that the child was free of these behaviors before seeing the candy, but this does not mean that he was not hungry. If we were to define hunger in terms of strength of behavior regardless of the presence or absence of discriminative stimuli, we should have to agree that a small amount of food increases it. But the case is not an exception to the present formulation.

We can separate the discriminating and satiating effects of the candy in several ways. For example, a regimen in which a child is never given more than a single piece of candy at a time will eventually extinguish the behavior of asking for more. As a result, the condition responsible for crying or a temper tantrum will not arise. A single piece of candy will have none of the disturbing effects described in this example, and it should be possible to demonstrate a small measure of satiation.

A somewhat more important parallel also shows how easily "drive" is identified with probability of response rather than with a probability due to deprivation. An individual in whom sexual behavior is at the moment not conspicuous may be aroused by exciting conversations, pictures, performances, and so on. It is not correct to say that his sex drive has then been strengthened. Sexual behavior has been strengthened, but by the presentation of stimuli appropriate to such behavior rather than by deprivation.

An operation may have two effects which change the probability of behavior in the same direction. For example, when a response has been reinforced consistently with food but now goes unreinforced for the first time, the probability due to previous reinforcement is decreased and emotional changes in behavior characteristic of frustration are generated. Since the latter include the weakening of any behavior reinforced with food, the first few responses in extinction will be followed by a reduction in rate *for two reasons*. For a time very few responses will be emitted and hence very few will go unreinforced. The emotional effect will therefore not be sustained, and the rate will rise, only to fall again as further responses go unreinforced. The result is, as we have seen, an oscillation in rate which gives the extinction curve a wavelike character.

At first blush it may seem difficult to separate these effects experimentally. We may, however, demonstrate the emotional effect by frustrating the organism in some other connection. We may also make use of the fact that emotional reactions eventually "adapt out." By repeatedly extinguishing and reconditioning a response, particularly on a schedule of intermittent reinforcement, we obtain extinction curves with little or no interference from emotional effects. We may also use the fact that an emotional effect involves the whole repertoire of the organism, while extinction is fairly narrowly localized in the response not reinforced. It is possible to record the frequency of emission of two responses in the same organism at the same time. If the responses do not use the same musculature to any great extent, their changes in rate may show a surprising independence. In the pigeon experiment pecking a key and stepping on a pedal satisfy these conditions reasonably well. A somewhat more convenient arrangement is to suspend the pigeon in a harness with one leg free; the pecking response and the flexion of the leg can then be separately but simultaneously studied. When these two responses have been conditioned, they can be extinguished at the same time except for a slight delay in one process. The extinction curves, recorded separately, are slightly displaced in time, but the major oscillations occur simultaneously. This suggests that the rise and fall of frustration is a single process in the whole organism, while the change due to extinction is separately determined in each response.

MULTIPLE CAUSES

Another way in which independent variables may interact is of greater importance. *Two or more operations may combine in a common effect.* We have already discussed several examples. An operant may be reinforced in more than one way, with the result that it varies with more than one deprivation. This is, in fact, the effect of a generalized reinforcer. A response so conditioned is not only more likely to be strong at any given time, because at least one state of deprivation is likely to prevail, but it may have an especially high probability of emission if two or more states of deprivation prevail at the same time. A similar result is achieved if two or more reinforcements are directly applied to a single operant. The principle is used when attendance at the business meeting of a club is encouraged by the serving of refreshments. Although a member may not attend because of the refreshments alone or because of participation in the business meeting alone, he will be more likely to attend if the probabilities due to both of these reinforcements are combined.

Emotional variables are frequently combined with variables in the fields of motivation and conditioning. Contrary to several well-established views there is no fundamental opposition between emotion and the "intellectual" behavior of the discriminated operant. Behavior is often most vigorous and effective when an emotional predisposition works in the same direction as a contingency of reinforcement. This is implied when we say that "a man's heart is in his work," where "heart" refers to emotional variables and "work" to contingencies of reinforcement. The individual in whom aggressive or brutal behavior is particularly strong may work especially well in certain kinds of employment—for example, in certain kinds of police or military work. An actress whose role required her to slap another person in a play slapped with unusual force when she became angry with him for extraneous reasons. The individual with an "affectionate" disposition may be especially successful at jobs which are concerned with helping other people.

In an important application of this principle, one discriminative stimulus is combined with another discriminative stimulus or with other variables. The effects are of various sorts. Some are commonly called "suggestion," others are dealt with as "projective techniques," while still others are important in the field of perception. Verbal behavior supplies particularly good examples.[1] A single verbal response is especially likely to be a function of more than one variable because it may be part of several different repertoires. In simple imitative or echoic behavior the response is controlled by a verbal stimulus of similar form—the verbal stimulus "house" evokes the verbal response "house." When the verbal stimulus is of different form—as in the word-association experiment—we may speak of an intraverbal repertoire—the stimulus "home" evokes the response "house." In reading, the stimulus is a text—the printed stimulus "HOUSE" evokes the vocal response "house." A great deal of verbal behavior is controlled by nonverbal stimuli, as when we name or describe objects and the properties of objects—an actual house evokes the response "house." Since a single verbal response usually comes under the control of variables in all these fields, in addition to its relation to emotional and motivational conditions, it is likely to be a function of more than one variable at a time.

The presence of more than one stimulus variable in verbal behavior is sometimes dealt with as "multiple meaning." The term is too narrow for our present purposes, for we must include contributions of strength from variables which are usually not included in the "meaning" of a response—for example, in the echoic response or the textual response to a printed word. A newspaper article about a convention of dentists reported that, in order to improve their profession, the dentists were urging the passage of certain laws "with teeth

---

[1] For an extensive analysis of verbal behavior from this point of view see B. F. Skinner, *Verbal Behavior*, New York, Appleton-Century-Crofts, Inc., 1957.

in them." The circumstances under which this was written might have led to alternative responses such as "laws with appropriate penalties" or "laws which could be enforced." These responses might have been equally probable if another profession had been under discussion. The response "with teeth in them" probably emerged because of the additional strength of the response "teeth"; a particular synonym had taken precedence over equivalent forms because of a multiple causation. Similarly, when a writer discussing a man who had been in China hunting for pandas reported that his plans had not "panned out," the expression appears to have taken precedence over such synonyms as "worked out," "come to anything," or "materialized," because of a contribution of strength from the variables responsible for "panda."

The multiple determination of verbal behavior is the basis of much wit. The witty response differs from the unconsciously amusing to the extent that the speaker is able to respond to the multiple sources of strength and to point them up by a proper elaboration. We are concerned here merely with the multiple sources of the witty element, not with the complete joke. An example is a story told of Dean Briggs of Harvard. The Dean was speaking at a dinner on an uncomfortably hot evening. The chairs had recently been varnished, and when the Dean rose to speak, he found his coat stuck to the chair. There was a good deal of laughter as he pulled it loose. When he was at last able to speak, he began, "I had expected to bring to you this evening an unvarnished tale, but circumstances make it impossible to fulfill my expectations." The multiple sources of "unvarnished tale" are essentially the same as those in the preceding examples, but the Dean was able to construct a sentence which made the multiple causation of the response clear to everyone.

All sustained verbal behavior is multiply determined. When a man begins to speak or write, he creates an elaborate set of stimuli which alter the strength of other responses in his repertoire. It is impossible to resist these supplementary sources of strength. We cannot, for example, call out a random series of numbers. Various sequences of numbers are reinforced as we learn to count by ones, twos, threes, or fives, to recite multiplication tables, to give telephone numbers, and so on. When we call out a first number, therefore, we alter the probabilities determining the next call. When a series of some length has been emitted, later numbers may be extremely powerfully determined.

In the same way, any sustained sample of verbal behavior establishes strong predispositions among the responses still to come. Our imitative or echoic repertoire produces rhyme, rhythm, assonance, and alliteration, which may appear simply as a disturbing singsong or, as in the parallel case of wit, may be elaborated into poetry. Verbal material we have memorized and familiar collocations of words in everyday use establish intraverbal tendencies which add other supplementary strengths. The literary artist exploits these when he fashions a poem or constructs a convincing argument. He builds multiple tendencies in the reader by virtue of which the reader finds himself unaccountably predisposed to "chime in" with the rhyming word of a poem or the clinching word of an argument.

Occasionally, verbal behavior is actually distorted by this sort of multiple determination. We may be able to give a plausible account of the variables responsible, but the speech itself is not always effective. Many years ago a young woman was asked to speak at a dinner advocating the repeal of the Prohibition Amendment. It was her first public appearance, and she was extremely ill at ease. As she rose to speak, someone placed a microphone in front of her. It was an unfamiliar and frightening instrument. She decided to throw herself on the mercy of the audience and plead her inexperience. Her first words were, "This is the first time I have ever faced a speakeasy." The intruding "speakeasy," which was as much a surprise to the speaker as to her delighted audience, may be traced to several contributing variables: her subject was in part the evils of the *speakeasy*, she was concerned with her own ability to *speak easily*, and a microphone could be called a *speakeasy* in the sense that it enables one to speak to many people with little effort. We shall see later that the intruding response may also have reduced aversive stimulation from the incipient response "microphone." We could presumably have shown that the stimulus "microphone" would elicit some of the emotional reflexes which, as in the case of the lie detector, are typical of aversive stimuli. We do not say that the response "microphone" had a tendency "not to be emitted," but rather that any response which displaced it would be strong for that reason. Because of this overwhelming strength, the response broke into the speech in progress. In spite of the disruption the sources of strength were so obvious that the total response was not without an effect, and it was accepted as wit.

A different kind of distortion arises when two or more fairly similar forms of response are strengthened. One may prevail as the result of both sources of strength, or a combined form may be generated. Folk etymologies ("sparrow grass" for "asparagus") and blends ("smog" for "smoke" and "fog") or the portmanteau words of Lewis Carroll ("frumious" for "furious" and "fuming") are examples. Some distortions are sufficiently effective to survive in the verbal behavior of the community, but others (such as "urving" for "urge" and "craving" or "heritage" for "heresy" and "sacrilege") suffer a sadder fate.

THE PRACTICAL USE OF MULTIPLE CAUSATION

Supplementary variables are often used in controlling behavior. A familiar case is "suggestion," which may be defined as the use of a stimulus to raise the probability of a response already assumed to exist at some low value. Verbal suggestions may be classified according to the kind of supplementary stimulation. In the imitative or echoic case, we strengthen a response by supplying stimulation of the same form. We may call this *formal suggestion*. When we strengthen a response with nonverbal stimuli or verbal stimuli of different form, the suggestion is *thematic*. A cross-classification may be set up according to whether the response can or cannot be identified in advance. If we call the first a "prompt" and the second a "probe," then we have to consider formal prompts, formal probes, thematic prompts, and thematic probes.

The *formal prompt* is the common practice in the theater. A word whispered in the wings strengthens the verbal behavior of the actor by setting up an echoic response which combines with the imperfectly memorized behavior. If the part has not been memorized at all, the actor repeats what he hears from the prompter merely as an echoic response. Since there is then only one source of strength, it is not prompting in the present sense. It is difficult to be sure of multiple sources if the prompter supplies the whole passage, but two variables are obviously at work if he does not. The relative strength of learned material is shown by how much of a prompt is required: if the passage has been fairly well memorized, a very small echoic contribution will suffice. Radio and television quiz programs use a kind of concealed formal prompt. The contestant who finds it difficult to answer a question may be helped if the master of ceremonies makes a remark containing a word which is similar to the answer. If the answer is, say, "Washington," the concealed prompt might contain the word "washing."

A *thematic prompt* having the same effect would be a remark containing the words, "Father of his Country." When we acquire intraverbal behavior like "Washington was the Father of his Country," we show an increased tendency to say "Washington" when "the Father of his Country" is heard. Neither the formal nor the thematic prompt will be effective if the response "Washington" does not already exist in some strength. If the contestant is simply told the answer and says "Washington," this is echoic behavior, and no prompting in the present sense has taken place. The thematic prompt is ordinarily called a "hint." Hinting, as a type of suggestion, always involves the use of a supplementary variable in rendering a given response more probable.

A *formal probe* which supplements verbal behavior of unknown form utilizes a process which has long been familiar. We may be interested in the behavior which it reveals because of the light which is thrown on other variables. Ambitious young Dick Whittington, discouraged by his failure in London, leaves the city, but as he walks away he hears Bow Bells tolling the words, "Turn again, Whittington, thrice Lord Mayor of London town." The stimulus from the bells must have been only vaguely similar to this response. No one else would have heard them saying the same thing. The words represent strong responses in the ambitious Whittington's own behavior, to which the echoic supplement supplied by the sound of the bells gave the strength needed for emission. (The fact that Whittington heard the *bells* speak is a separate point to which we shall return later. The only speaker was Whittington himself.) The effect has often been used in literature: a young girl running away from home hears the click of the wheels of the train saying, "Why are you here? Why are you here?"; the lapping of water against the side of a boat whispers, "He speaks the truth. He speaks the truth."

A device called the Verbal Summator, which is used experimentally and clinically to probe latent verbal behavior, uses the same process. Vague speech patterns—*"eye-uh-ah-uh"* or *"oo-ee-uh-uh,"* for example—are repeated by a phonograph so softly or against so noisy a background that they resemble barely audible speech. The subject is asked to listen to each repeated pattern until he hears "what is said." The feeble echoic response generated by the repeated auditory stimulus combines with a verbal response already in some strength. The resulting response is often emitted with great confidence. A subject may respond to hundreds of different patterns while remaining convinced that they are genuine speech and that he is usually identifying them correctly. An extensive sample of latent verbal behavior may thus be collected which, since it bears little relation to the stimulating situation, must be the product of other variables in the behavior of the subject. The clinical use of the material is based upon the assumption that these variables—in the fields of reinforcement, motivation, or emotion—are probably important in interpreting other behavior of the individual.

A *thematic probe* is exemplified by the so-called word-association experiment. This is similar to the Verbal Summator except that the supplementary strength is derived from intraverbal responses. A stimulus word is spoken or shown to the subject, and he is asked to report "the first word he thinks of" or, as we should say here, to emit aloud the first verbal response which appears in his behavior. Many different responses are strengthened by an intraverbal stimulus. For example, the stimulus "house" may evoke "home," "building," "keeper," and so on. Which of these is emitted at a particular time is presumably determined by a relatively effective additional source of strength. When verbal behavior is collected in this way, it is possible to infer some of the verbal history of the subject, as well as current variables responsible for his interests, his emotional predispositions, and so on. The clinical use of this material is based upon the assumption that these variables are relevant in interpreting other behavior. The supplementary strength of the thematic probe is not always intraverbal. We may strengthen verbal behavior simply by presenting pictures, objects, or events and asking our subject to talk about them.

By asking our subject to talk in a minimal stimulating situation we generate the condition for what is known as free association, which does not necessarily exemplify the present process. The verbal behavior obtained may be maximally controlled by variables in his history, and inferences about these variables may be of optimal value; but since no supplementary source of strength is used, the case is not classified as either a formal or thematic probe. A great deal of self-probing may go on, however, when parts of such a verbal production alter other parts through supplementary stimulation.

PROJECTION AND IDENTIFICATION

Formal and thematic probes are frequently called "projective tests," but the word "projection" has a broader significance. Freud described the process to which it refers as a way in which repressed wishes work themselves out (Chapter XXIV). A similar mechanism is called "identification." Quite apart from any analysis of wishes, we may classify the behavior in terms of its relevant variables: certain occasions for verbal or nonverbal behavior join forces with behavior already in some strength. When we "identify" ourselves with the hero of a novel, movie, or play, or "throw ourselves into a character," we simply *behave in the same way*—that is, imitatively (Chapter VII). When our imitative behavior is so microscopic as to be wholly private, a special problem may arise, as we shall see in Chapter XVII. The imitative supplement may be either verbal or nonverbal, but the verbal behavior has several advantages. For example, in reading a novel we can more easily identify ourselves with the character who is speaking than with someone behaving nonverbally because the recorded speech provides a direct source of strength for verbal responses and because these responses can be executed in any environment. A widespread preference for conversation in novels seems to be due to this fact.

The behavior which is executed in identification must have some strength for other reasons. If the strength is considerable, we have to explain why the response is not emitted without supplementation. In a common case the behavior cannot be emitted in everyday life because the opportunity is lacking or because the behavior is restrained or punished. A tendency to identify oneself with, say, a fictional character may be clinically significant as evidence of the strength of the behavior. It is often the case, however, that a story simply builds up a tendency; the author *forces* a sort of identification, which is evident in the fact that interest in a character grows as the story unfolds. Such an identification may have little bearing upon variables operating elsewhere in the reader's life.

We speak of projection, rather than identification, when the behavior is less specifically controlled by the supplementary stimulus. A classic example is the lover who accuses his beloved of coolness or unfaithfulness because he himself has grown cool or unfaithful. The lover has reacted with a response which is formally imitative of the behavior of the other person but which is controlled by quite different variables in his own behavior. For example, remaining silent for some trivial reason is imitated and combined with a gesture of boredom; a passing comment is echoed and combined with a critical remark. In what is sometimes called the "old maid's neurosis," a response which imitates the behavior of an innocent person is combined with a sexually aggressive response. The fact that the projector attributes similar aggressive behavior to the other person is an additional detail (Chapter XVII).

The possibility of identifying oneself with animals or even with inanimate objects offers an interesting opportunity to study the formal properties of behavior. In what way can a man's behavior resemble the behavior of a cloud or wave or falling tree so that the imitative response will summate with other parts of his behavior?

MULTIPLE VARIABLES IN PERCEPTION

It is only a short step to an issue of some importance in the field of perception. Our reactions are determined not only by stimuli, but by supplementary variables in the fields of emotion, motivation, and reinforcement. If we are expecting an important telephone call, we may rush to the phone at the faint sound of a doorbell. This is an example of stimulus generalization, which can easily be duplicated in the rat or pigeon. By increasing the deprivation we increase the range of effective stimuli or, to put it another way, reduce the importance of differences in stimuli. When a young man deeply in love mistakes a stranger passing in the street for his beloved, the strong motivation has made a wider range of stimuli effective in controlling the response of seeing his beloved. (We may report that the doorbell "sounded like" the telephone, and the lover may insist that the girl in the street "looked like" his beloved, just as Dick Whittington heard the bells speak rather than himself. What this means we shall see later.)

VARIABLES WITH INCOMPATIBLE EFFECTS

Two responses which use the same parts of the body in different ways cannot be emitted together. When two such responses are strong at the same time, the condition is often called "conflict." When the incompatible responses are due to different kinds of deprivation, we speak of a conflict of motives; when they are due to different reinforcing contingencies, we speak of a conflict of goals; and so on. The term suggests an active struggle of some sort inside the organism— evidently between some of the hypothetical precursors of behavior. The conflict can scarcely be among the independent variables since these are physical events, and any conflict would be resolved at the physical level. From the present point of view, we must suppose that the conflict is between *responses* and that any "struggle" will be evident in the behavior. If we want to study conflict, then, we simply strengthen incompatible responses and observe the result.

Algebraic summation. When incompatible responses resemble each other in topography except for sign—when, in other words, they are diametrically opposed to each other—the result may be "algebraic summation." Simple examples are observed in the postural reflexes. One reflex may call for the extension of a leg, another for its flexion. Under certain circumstances the occurrence of both stimuli at the same time produces an intermediate position of the leg. A similar opposition is possible in the discriminative behavior of the whole organism. A dog approaching a strange object, or a soldier going into battle, possesses diametrically opposed kinds of behavior—approach and withdrawal. If no other variables are to be taken into account, the resulting movement will be in one direction or the other but at a qualified speed: the individual will move cautiously forward or slowly retreat. The combination of variables may, of course, have other effects; the behavior may be poorly integrated, less skillfully executed, or, as is always the case with behavior of low strength, easily disturbed by extraneous variables.

If the resulting movement changes the relative strength of the variables, the behavior may oscillate. Thus if the stimulus which induces the dog to approach a strange object is stronger than that which controls withdrawal, the dog will approach slowly, but if this strengthens the variable controlling withdrawal, the direction may at some point be reversed. If withdrawal in turn weakens the variables controlling withdrawal or strengthens the variables controlling approach, a second reversal will occur—and so on. The oscillation will be slow or rapid depending upon the extent to which the variables are modified. The hand of the chess player reaching toward the piece to be moved may oscillate either slowly with a period of several seconds or almost as rapidly as in tremor, depending upon the pressure of the game.

The variables responsible for algebraic summation need not be stimuli. A man whose "heart is not in his work" exemplifies an opposition between reinforcing contingencies and variables in the field of motivation or emotion. Some of his behavior is due to reinforcement, possibly of an economic sort, which keeps him at his job. Opposed to this is behavior which is strong for different reasons. We see this in the tender-hearted thug, in the idealist caught up in a profession in which he must exploit or injure people, or in the pacifist drafted into military service.

Prepotency. Only rarely will the topography of incompatible responses permit algebraic summation since in general one response cannot simply be subtracted from another. In general, when two responses are strong at the same time, only one can be emitted. The appearance of one response is called "prepotency." The term, like algebraic summation, is borrowed from the study of simple reflexes, but the principle applies to operant behavior as well. We appealed to this principle in noting, as an alternative to extinction or punishment, that we may prevent the occurrence of a response simply by creating circumstances which evoke an incompatible response which is prepotent over it.

The prepotent response does not, merely by virtue of its having been emitted, alter the strength of the dispossessed response. It may, however, change some of the variables controlling this response, and oscillation may then follow. This is all the more likely because the execution of the prepotent response usually weakens it—through partial satiation, for example. A simple instance is the selection of a necktie. The satiation which follows when a tie is worn is clearly evident when it reaches the point at which we are "tired of the tie," but a smaller measure of satiation must be supposed to occur in a shorter time. In choosing between two ties, an oscillation may arise since putting on one tie increases the *relative* probability of putting on the other. The oscillation may under certain circumstances become pathological, as in *folie du doute*. More important examples are frequently dealt with in literary works. An ancient example is the conflict between behavior strengthened by "love" and behavior due to the ethical pressure which we speak of as "duty" (Chapter XXI). The execution of behavior appropriate to either variable changes the relative strength of the opposed behavior, which then becomes momentarily prepotent.

The oscillation is rapid if only a slight step in either direction makes a significant change in probability, as in the case of the individual who "cannot make up his mind" in ordering at a restaurant. A very slow oscillation is exemplified by the individual who turns from one field of interest to another and back again, perhaps remaining for years in one field. Sometimes a fairly acceptable solution to the problem of incompatible behavior is to engage primarily in one type of response but to interlace one's activity with responses of another type. This is especially feasible when the latter are relatively independent of the external environment: torn between love and duty, one may do one's duty while continuing to talk about love. The alternative response may also be executed "in fantasy," as we shall see in Chapter XVII.

To do or not to do. We are often interested in whether a response will be emitted in competition with alternative behavior which is of no importance to us and which we dismiss as "doing nothing" or as "doing something else." Such behavior (defined merely as incompatible with a specified response) appears in the analysis of punishment. Any response which interferes with punished behavior reduces a conditioned aversive stimulus and is reinforced for that reason, but we may have little interest in what the response is.

There are several kinds of conflict generated by punishment. An example of a response which is first reinforced and then punished is eating a delicious but indigestible food. The two consequences follow from the chemical properties of the food, which are positively reinforcing on contact with the tongue but eventually aversive in the stomach. In eating someone else's food without his permission, aversive consequences may possibly be arranged by the owner of the food or by society. The aversive stimulus may *precede* the positive reinforcement—for example, when we swim in cold water for the effect of the invigorating glow which follows—but in both cases the aversive stimulus is avoided if the response is not emitted. The aversive stimulus may follow *unless* a response is emitted. When an individual takes steps to prepare for a bad storm, his behavior reduces the threat of strong aversive consequences or "avoids" the consequences of the storm, in the sense of Chapter XI; but a conflict will arise if the behavior has its own aversive consequences.

It is tempting to formulate these cases without mentioning the incompatible behavior. We are interested in whether the indigestible food is eaten, or the plunge taken, or the preparation for the storm made, not in what may be done instead. This may lead us to speak of a negative tendency to engage in the act which is supplanted. One variable increases the probability of a response while another appears to reduce it. But for both theoretical and practical purposes it is important to remember that we are always dealing with positive probabilities. Punishment, as we have seen, does not create a negative probability that a response will be made but rather a positive probability that incompatible behavior will occur.

Another example in which it is tempting to speak of negative probabilities is "Freudian forgetting." The instances usually described involve punishment. Let us say that an aversive appointment—with the dentist, for example—is forgotten. The observed fact is simply that the behavior of keeping the appointment does not appear under appropriate circumstances. The theory of Freudian forgetting asserts that the aversive consequences of such appointments are relevant. Any step toward keeping the appointment generates conditioned aversive stimulation because of earlier painful stimulation in the dentist's chair. Any behavior which reduces the aversive stimulation by displacing such a response is automatically reinforced in accordance with the analysis of Chapter XII. Two mutually exclusive kinds of behavior are therefore strong, and the issue is one of prepotency. We have no interest, however, in specifying the incompatible response. Hence we are likely to suppose that forgetting means that the probability of keeping the appointment has reached zero or has passed through zero to a negative value. But we need not deal with any behavior called "not keeping the appointment." One response has simply lost out to another in the matching of probabilities. If the same result were achieved without "forgetting" by canceling the appointment, the action which supplanted the behavior would be clearly specified, and the principle of prepotency would be obvious. Forgetting is ordinarily attributed to an inner organism which "represses" the behavior of keeping the appointment, but the only repressing agent is the incompatible response.

Just as an additional source of strength may select one response from a group of responses otherwise all equally strong, so a sort of "negative selection" may arise from the strength of behavior which is incompatible with one response in a group. In the example described above, the intruding response "speakeasy" could be explained in part by its effect in displacing the aversive response "microphone."

When we are concerned simply with whether a single response will or will not be emitted, the incompatible behavior may remain unspecified. The basic process, emphasized by Freud, has long been recognized. In *Barchester Towers*, Anthony Trollope described the behavior of his hero Mr. Arabin as follows:

> But he never could have loved the Signora Neroni as he felt that he now loved Eleanor! And so *he flung stones into the brook, instead of flinging himself in,* and sat down on its margin as sad a gentleman as you shall meet in a summer's day.

We cannot account for suicide as a simple response. We cannot, for example, measure its frequency. No one jumps into a brook to bring his life to an end because the same behavior has had a similar consequence in the past. But the general behavior of throwing objects into water is another matter. It has a specifiable result: the objects disappear. This behavior is readily generalized; having thrown an old hat into a brook, we get rid of a pair of shoes in the same way. It is not impossible that throwing oneself into a brook may be merely a dramatic example of destroying oneself with the behavior which has destroyed other things. Fortunately we need not decide this issue to make the present point. Both Trollope and Freud agree that Mr. Arabin in flinging stones into the brook was to some extent flinging himself in. Circumstances had given rise to a strong tendency to "throw things into brooks," but aversive consequences were also attached to some responses in this class. Mr. Arabin does not fling himself into the brook (or, with less aversive consequences, his watch or his pocketbook); he flings stones. This response may have only a tenuous membership in the strengthened group, but at least it has no aversive consequences and hence is emitted. (The same aversive consequences generate the familiar oscillation of the potential suicide, as Hamlet demonstrated.)

In these examples of incompatible behavior, we have considered the outcome when nothing intervenes. Obviously a sudden change in circumstances might yield a different result, and, as we shall see in a moment, the individual himself may effect such a change. Before analyzing how he does so, it is necessary to consider another way in which variables may be arranged.

CHAINING

A response may produce or alter some of the variables which control another response. The result is a "chain." It may have little or no organization. When we go for a walk, roaming the countryside or wandering idly through a museum or store, one episode in our behavior generates conditions responsible for another. We look to one side and are stimulated by an object which causes us to move in its direction. In the course of this movement we receive aversive stimulation from which we beat a hasty retreat. This generates a condition of satiation or fatigue in which, once free of aversive stimulation, we sit down to rest. And so on. Chaining need not be the result of movement in space. We wander or roam verbally, for example, in a casual conversation or when we "speak our thoughts" in free association.

Some chains have a functional unity. The links have occurred in more or less the same order, and the whole chain has been affected by a single consequence. We often deal with a chain as a single "response." When a cat pounces on a mouse, for example, this complicated act is an intricate network of postural reflexes, as the physiologist Magnus first showed. We often emphasize the initiating member (to jump or not to jump), overlooking the fact that it precedes by several stages the response which is actually reinforced by contact with the mouse. Long chains organized as simple sequences are exhibited as we pick our way through streets to a particular spot, or recite a poem, or play a piece of music. Other examples have been discussed in connection with conditioned reinforcement. Organized chains are not necessarily confined to the production of stimuli since other sorts of variables may be altered by behavior. In drinking a glass of water we change an important condition of deprivation which has the usual effect of making further drinking less probable, and behavior which has been suppressed by behavior which has led to drinking may then be released. A special kind of chaining is represented by *behavior which alters the strength of other behavior and is reinforced because it does so.* Such behavior could almost be said to distinguish the human organism from all others. In Section III we shall consider some of the more important problems which it raises.

THE INDIVIDUAL AS A WHOLE

CHAPTER XV

"SELF-CONTROL"

THE "SELF-DETERMINATION" OF CONDUCT

Implicit in a functional analysis is the notion of control. When we discover an independent variable which can be controlled, we discover a means of controlling the behavior which is a function of it. This fact is important for theoretical purposes. Proving the validity of a functional relation by an actual demonstration of the effect of one variable upon another is the heart of experimental science. The practice enables us to dispense with many troublesome statistical techniques in testing the importance of variables.

The practical implications are probably even greater. An analysis of the techniques through which behavior may be manipulated shows the kind of technology which is emerging as the science advances, and it points up the considerable degree of control which is currently exerted. The problems raised by the control of human behavior obviously can no longer be avoided by refusing to recognize the possibility of control. Later sections of this book will consider these practical implications in more detail. In Section IV, for example, in an analysis of what is generally called social behavior, we shall see how one organism utilizes the basic processes of behavior to control another. The result is particularly impressive when the individual is under the concerted control of a group. Our basic processes are responsible for the procedures through which the ethical group controls the behavior of each of its members. An even more effective control is exerted by such well-defined agencies as government, religion, psychotherapy, economics, and education; certain key questions concerning such control will be considered in Section V. The general issue of control in human affairs will be summarized in Section VI.

First, however, we must consider the possibility that the individual may control his own behavior. A common objection to a picture of the behaving organism such as we have so far presented runs somewhat as follows. In emphasizing the controlling power of external variables, we have left the organism itself in a peculiarly helpless position. Its behavior appears to be simply a "repertoire"—a vocabulary of action, each item of which becomes more or less probable as the environment changes. It is true that variables may be arranged in complex patterns; but this fact does not appreciably modify the picture, for the emphasis is still upon behavior, not upon the behaver. Yet to a considerable extent an individual does appear to shape his own destiny. He is often able to do something about the variables affecting him. Some degree of "self-determination" of conduct is usually recognized in the creative behavior of the artist and scientist, in the self-exploratory behavior of the writer, and in the self-discipline of the ascetic. Humbler versions of self-determination are more familiar. The individual "chooses" between alternative courses of action, "thinks through" a problem while isolated from the relevant environment, and guards his health or his position in society through the exercise of "self-control."

Any comprehensive account of human behavior must, of course, embrace the facts referred to in statements of this sort. But we can achieve this without abandoning our program. When a man controls himself, chooses a course of action, thinks out the solution to a problem, or strives toward an increase in self-knowledge, he is *behaving*. He controls himself precisely as he would control the behavior of anyone else—through the manipulation of variables of which behavior is a function. His behavior in so doing is a proper object of analysis, and eventually it must be accounted for with variables lying outside the individual himself.

It is the purpose of Section III to analyze how the individual acts to alter the variables of which other parts of his behavior are functions, to distinguish among the various cases which arise in terms of the processes involved, and to account for the behavior which achieves control just as we account for behavior of any other kind. The present chapter concerns the processes involved in *self-control*, taking that term in close to its traditional sense, while Chapter XVI concerns behavior which would traditionally be described as *creative thinking*. The two sets of techniques are different because in self-control the individual can identify the behavior to be controlled while in creative thinking he cannot. The variables which the individual utilizes in manipulating his behavior in this way are not always accessible to others, and this has led to great misunderstanding. It has often been concluded, for example, that self-discipline and thinking take place in a nonphysical inner world and that neither activity is properly described as behavior at all. We may simplify the analysis by considering examples of self-control and thinking in which the individual manipulates *external* variables, but we shall need to complete the picture by discussing the status of private events in a science of behavior (Chapter XVII). A purely private event would have no place in a study of behavior, or perhaps in any science; but events which are, for the moment at least, accessible only to the individual himself often occur as links in chains of otherwise public events and they must then be considered. In self-control and creative thinking, where the individual is largely engaged in manipulating his own behavior, this is likely to be the case.

When we say that a man controls himself, we must specify who is controlling whom. When we say that he knows himself, we must also distinguish between the subject and object of the verb. Evidently selves are multiple and hence not to be identified with the biological organism. But if this is so, what are they? What are their dimensions in a science of behavior? To what extent is a self an integrated personality or organism? How can one self act upon another? The interlocking systems of responses which account for self-control and thinking make it possible to answer questions of this sort satisfactorily, as we shall see in Chapter XVIII. We can do this more conveniently, however, when the principal data are at hand. Meanwhile, the term "self" will be used in a less rigorous way.

"SELF-CONTROL"

The individual often comes to control part of his own behavior when a response has conflicting consequences—when it leads to both positive and negative reinforcement. Drinking alcoholic beverages, for example, is often followed by a condition of unusual confidence in which one is more successful socially and in which one forgets responsibilities, anxieties, and other troubles. Since this is positively reinforcing, it increases the likelihood that drinking will take place on future occasions. But there are other consequences—the physical illness of the "hang-over" and the possibly disastrous effects of overconfident or irresponsible behavior—which are negatively reinforcing and, when contingent upon behavior, represent a form of punishment. If punishment were simply the reverse of reinforcement, the two might combine to produce an intermediate tendency to drink, but we have seen that this is not the case. When a similar occasion arises, the same or an increased tendency to drink will prevail; but the occasion as well as the early stages of drinking will generate conditioned aversive stimuli and emotional responses to them which we speak of as shame or guilt. The emotional responses may have some deterrent effect in weakening behavior—as by "spoiling the mood." A more important effect, however, is that any behavior which weakens the behavior of drinking is automatically reinforced by the resulting reduction in aversive stimulation. We have discussed the behavior of simply "doing something else," which is reinforced because it displaces punishable behavior, but there are other possibilities. The organism may make the punished response less probable by altering the variables of which it is a function. Any behavior which succeeds in doing this will automatically be reinforced. We call such behavior self-control.

The positive and negative consequences generate two responses which are related to each other in a special way: one response, the *controlling response,* affects variables in such a way as to change the probability of the other, the *controlled response.* The controlling response may manipulate any of the variables of which the controlled response is a function; hence there are a good many different forms of self-control. In general it is possible to point to parallels in which the same techniques are employed in controlling the behavior of others. A fairly exhaustive survey at this point will illustrate the process of self-control and at the same time serve to summarize the kind of control to be emphasized in the chapters which follow.

TECHNIQUES OF CONTROL

Physical restraint and physical aid. We commonly control behavior through physical restraint. With locked doors, fences, and jails we limit the space in which people move. With strait-jackets, gags, and arm braces we limit the movement of parts of their bodies. The individual controls his own behavior in the same way. He claps his hand over his mouth to keep himself from laughing or coughing or to stifle a verbal response which is seen at the last moment to be a "bad break." A child psychologist has suggested that a mother who wishes to keep from nagging her child should seal her own lips with adhesive tape. The individual may jam his hands into his pockets to prevent fidgeting or nail-biting or hold his nose to keep from breathing when under water. He may present himself at the door of an institution for incarceration to control his own criminal or psychotic behavior. He may cut his right hand off lest it offend him.

In each of these examples we identify a controlling response, which imposes some degree of physical restraint upon a response to be controlled. To explain the existence and strength of the controlling behavior we point to the reinforcing circumstances which arise when the response has been controlled. Clapping the hand over the mouth is reinforced and will occur again under similar circumstances because it reduces the aversive stimulation generated by the cough or the incipient bad break. In the sense of Chapter XII, the controlling response *avoids* the negatively reinforcing consequences of the controlled response. The aversive consequences of a bad break are supplied by a social environment; the aversive consequences of breathing under water do not require the mediation of others.

Another form of control through physical restraint is simply to move out of the situation in which the behavior to be controlled may take place. The parent avoids trouble by taking an aggressive child away from other children, and the adult controls himself in the same way. Unable to control his anger, he simply walks away. This may not control the whole emotional pattern, but it does restrain those features which are likely to have serious consequences.

Suicide is another form of self-control. Obviously a man does not kill himself because he has previously escaped from an aversive situation by doing so. As we have already seen, suicide is not a form of behavior to which the notion of frequency of response can be applied. If it occurs, the components of the behavior must have been strengthened separately. Unless this happens under circumstances in which frequency is an available datum, we cannot say meaningfully that a man is "likely or unlikely to kill himself"—nor can the individual say this of himself (Chapter XVII). Some instances of suicide, but by no means all, follow the pattern of cutting off one's right hand that it may not offend one; the military agent taken by the enemy may use this method to keep himself from divulging secrets of state.

A variation on this mode of control consists of removing the situation, so to speak, rather than the individual. A government stops inflationary spending by heavy taxation—by removing the money or credit which is a condition for the purchase of goods. A man arranges to control the behavior of his spendthrift heir by setting up a trust fund. Non-coeducational institutions attempt to control certain kinds of sexual behavior by making the opposite sex inaccessible. The individual may use the same techniques in controlling himself. He may leave most of his pocket money at home to avoid spending it, or he may drop coins into a piggy bank from which it is difficult to withdraw them. He may put his own money in trust for himself. H. G. Wells's Mr. Polly used a similar procedure to distribute his funds over a walking trip. He would mail all but a pound note to himself at a village some distance along his route. Arriving at the village, he would call at the post office, remove a pound note, and readdress the balance to himself at a later point.

In a converse technique we increase the probability of a desirable form of behavior by supplying physical *aid*. We facilitate human behavior, make it possible, or expand and amplify its consequences with various sorts of equipment, tools, and machines. When the problem of self-control is to generate a given response, we alter our own behavior in the same way by obtaining favorable equipment, making funds readily available, and so on.

Changing the stimulus. Insofar as the preceding techniques operate through physical aid or restraint, they are not based upon a behavioral process. There are associated processes, however, which may be analyzed more accurately in terms of stimulation. Aside from making a response possible or impossible, we may create or eliminate the occasion for it. To do so, we manipulate either an eliciting or a discriminative stimulus. When a drug manufacturer reduces the probability that a nauseous medicine will be regurgitated by enclosing it in tasteless capsules—or by "sugar-coating the pill"—he is simply removing a stimulus which elicits unwanted responses. The same procedure is available in the control of one's own reflexes. We swallow a medicine quickly and "chase" it with a glass of water to reduce comparable stimuli.

We remove *discriminative* stimuli when we turn away from a stimulus which induces aversive action. We may forcibly look away from a wallpaper design which evokes the compulsive behavior of tracing geometrical patterns. We may close doors or draw curtains to eliminate distracting stimuli or achieve the same effect by closing our eyes or putting fingers in our ears. We may put a box of candy out of sight to avoid overeating. This sort of self-control is described as "avoiding temptation," especially when the aversive consequences have been arranged by society. It is the principle of "Get thee behind me, Satan."

We also *present* stimuli because of the responses they elicit or make more probable in our own behavior. We rid ourselves of poisonous or indigestible food with an emetic—a substance which generates stimuli which elicit vomiting. We facilitate stimulation when we wear eyeglasses or hearing aids. We arrange a discriminative stimulus to encourage our own behavior at a later date when we tie a string on our finger or make an entry in a date book to serve as the occasion for action at an appropriate time. Sometimes we present stimuli because the resulting behavior displaces behavior to be controlled—we "distract" ourselves just as we distract others from a situation which generates undesirable behavior. We amplify stimuli generated by our own behavior when we use a mirror to acquire good carriage or to master a difficult dance step, or study moving pictures of our own behavior to improve our skill in a sport, or listen to phonograph recordings of our own speech to improve pronunciation or delivery.

Conditioning and extinction provide other ways of changing the effectiveness of stimuli. We arrange for the future effect of a stimulus upon ourselves by pairing it with other stimuli, and we extinguish reflexes by exposing ourselves to conditioned stimuli when they are not accompanied by reinforcement. If we blush, sweat, or exhibit some other emotional response under certain circumstances because of an unfortunate episode, we may expose ourselves to these circumstances under more favorable conditions in order that extinction may take place.

Depriving and satiating. An impecunious person may make the most of an invitation to dinner by skipping lunch and thus creating a high state of deprivation in which he will eat a great deal. Conversely, he may partially satiate himself with a light lunch before going to dinner in order to make the strength of his ingestive behavior less conspicuous. When a guest prepares himself for an assiduous host by drinking a large amount of water before going to a cocktail party, he uses self-satiation as a measure of control.

Another use is less obvious. In *Women in Love*, D. H. Lawrence describes a practice of self-control as follows:

A very great doctor . . . told me that to cure oneself of a bad habit, one should force oneself to do it, when one would not do it;—make oneself do it—and then the habit would disappear. . . . If you bite your nails, for example, then when you don't want to bite your nails, bite them, make yourself bite them. And you would find the habit was broken.

This practice falls within the present class if we regard the behavior of "deliberately" biting one's finger nails, or biting a piece of celluloid or similar material, as automatically satiating. The practice obviously extends beyond what are usually called "bad habits." For example, if we are unable to work at our desk because of a conflicting tendency to go for a walk, a brisk walk may solve the problem—through satiation.

A variation on this practice is to satiate one form of behavior by engaging in a somewhat similar form. Heavy exercise is often recommended in the control of sexual behavior on the assumption that exercise has enough in common with sexual behavior to produce a sort of transferred satiation. (The effect is presumed to be due to topographical overlap rather than sheer exhaustion.) A similar overlap may account for a sort of transferred deprivation. The practice of leaving the table while still hungry has been recommended as a way of generating good work habits. Presumably for the same reason the vegetarian may be especially alert and highly efficient because he is, in a sense, always hungry. Self-deprivation in the field of sex has been asserted to have valuable consequences in distantly related fields—for example, in encouraging literary or artistic achievements. Possibly the evidence is weak; if the effect does not occur, we have so much the less to explain.

Manipulating emotional conditions. We induce emotional changes in ourselves for purposes of control. Sometimes this means simply presenting or removing stimuli. For example, we reduce or eliminate unwanted emotional reactions by going away for a "change of scene" —that is, by removing stimuli which have acquired the power to evoke emotional reactions because of events which have occurred in connection with them. We sometimes prevent emotional behavior by eliciting incompatible responses with appropriate stimuli, as when we bite our tongue to keep from laughing on a solemn occasion.

We also control the *predispositions* which must be distinguished from emotional *responses* (Chapter X). A master of ceremonies on a television program predisposes his studio audience toward laughter before going on the air—possibly by telling jokes which are not permissible on the air. The same procedure is available in self-control.

We get ourselves into a "good mood" before a dull or trying appointment to increase the probability that we shall behave in a socially acceptable fashion. Before asking the boss for a raise, we screw our courage to the sticking place by rehearsing a history of injustice. We reread an insulting letter just before answering it in order to generate the emotional behavior which will make the answer more easily written and more effective. We also engender strong emotional states in which undesirable behavior is unlikely or impossible. A case in point is the practice described vulgarly as "scaring the hell out of someone." This refers almost literally to a method of controlling strongly punished behavior by reinstating stimuli which have accompanied punishment. We use the same technique when we suppress our own behavior by rehearsing past punishments or by repeating proverbs which warn of the wages of sin.

We reduce the extent of an emotional reaction by delaying it—for example, by "counting ten" before acting in anger. We get the same effect through the process of adaptation, described in Chapter X, when we gradually bring ourselves into contact with disturbing stimuli. We may learn to handle snakes without fear by beginning with dead or drugged snakes of the least disturbing sort and gradually moving on to livelier and more frightening kinds.

Using aversive stimulation. When we set an alarm clock, we arrange for a strongly aversive stimulus from which we can escape only by arousing ourselves. By putting the clock across the room, we make certain that the behavior of escape will fully awaken us. We *condition* aversive reactions in ourselves by pairing stimuli in appropriate ways—for example, by using the "cures" for the tobacco and alcohol habits already described. We also control ourselves by creating verbal stimuli which have an effect upon us because of past aversive consequences paired with them by other people. A simple command is an aversive stimulus—a threat—specifying the action which will bring escape. In getting out of bed on a cold morning, the simple repetition of the command "Get up" may, surprisingly, lead to action. The verbal response is easier than getting up and easily takes precedence over it, but the reinforcing contingencies established by the verbal community may prevail. In a sense the individual "obeys himself." Continued use of this technique may lead to a finer discrimination between commands issued by oneself and by others, which may interfere with the result.

We prepare aversive stimuli which will control our own future behavior when we make a resolution. This is essentially a prediction concerning our own behavior. By making it in the presence of people who supply aversive stimulation when a prediction is not fulfilled, we arrange consequences which are likely to strengthen the behavior resolved upon. Only by behaving as predicted can we escape the aversive consequences of breaking our resolution. As we shall see later, the aversive stimulation which leads us to keep the resolution may eventually be supplied automatically by our own behavior. The resolution may then be effective even in the absence of other people.

Drugs. We use drugs which simulate the effect of other variables in self-control. Through the use of anesthetics, analgesics, and soporifics we reduce painful or distracting stimuli which cannot otherwise be altered easily. Appetizers and aphrodisiacs are sometimes used in the belief that they duplicate the effects of deprivation in the fields of hunger and sex, respectively. Other drugs are used for the opposite effects. The conditioned aversive stimuli in "guilt" are counteracted more or less effectively with alcohol. Typical patterns of euphoric behavior are generated by morphine and related drugs, and to a lesser extent by caffeine and nicotine.

Operant conditioning. The place of operant reinforcement in self-control is not clear. In one sense, all reinforcements are self-administered since a response may be regarded as "producing" its reinforcement, but "reinforcing one's own behavior" is more than this. It is also more than simply generating circumstances under which a given type of behavior is characteristically reinforced—for example, by associating with friends who reinforce only "good" behavior. This is simply a chain of responses, an early member of which (associating with a particular friend) is strong because it leads to the reinforcement of a later member (the "good" behavior).

Self-reinforcement of operant behavior presupposes that the individual has it in his power to obtain reinforcement but does not do so until a particular response has been emitted. This might be the case if a man denied himself all social contacts until he had finished a particular job. Something of this sort unquestionably happens, but is it operant reinforcement? It is certainly roughly parallel to the procedure in conditioning the behavior of another person. But it must be remembered that the individual may at any moment drop the work in hand and obtain the reinforcement. We have to account for his not doing so. It may be that such indulgent behavior has been punished—say, with disapproval—except when a piece of work has just been completed. The indulgent behavior will therefore generate strong aversive stimulation except at such a time. The individual finishes the work in order to indulge himself free of guilt (Chapter XII). The ultimate question is whether the consequence has any strengthening effect upon the behavior which precedes it. Is the individual more likely to do a similar piece of work in the future? It would not be surprising if he were *not*, although we must agree that he has arranged a sequence of events in which certain behavior has been followed by a reinforcing event.

A similar question arises as to whether one can extinguish one's own behavior. Simply emitting a response which is not reinforced is not self-control, nor is behavior which simply brings the individual into circumstances under which a particular form of behavior will go unreinforced. Self-extinction seems to mean that a controlling response must arrange the lack of consequence; the individual must step in to break the connection between response and reinforcement. This appears to be done when, for example, a television set is put out of order so that the response of turning the switch is extinguished. But the extinction here is trivial; the primary effect is the removal of a source of stimulation.

Punishment. Self-punishment raises the same question. An individual may stimulate himself aversively, as in self-flagellation. But punishment is not merely aversive stimulation; it is aversive stimulation which is contingent upon a given response. Can the individual arrange this contingency? It is not self-punishment simply to engage in behavior which is punished, or to seek out circumstances in which certain behavior is punished. The individual appears to punish himself when, having recently engaged in a given sort of behavior, he injures himself. Behavior of this sort has been said to show a "need for punishment." But we can account for it in another way if in stimulating himself aversively, the individual escapes from an even more aversive condition of guilt (Chapter XII).

There are other variations in the use of aversive self-stimulation. A man concerned with reducing his weight may draw his belt up to a given notch and allow it to stay there in spite of a strong aversive effect. This may directly increase the conditioned and unconditioned aversive stimuli generated in the act of overeating and may provide for an automatic reinforcement for eating with restraint. But we must not overlook the fact that a very simple response—loosening the belt —will bring escape from the same aversive stimulation. If this behavior is not forthcoming, it is because it has been followed by even more aversive consequences arranged by society or by a physician— a sense of guilt or a fear of illness or death. The ultimate question of aversive self-stimulation is whether a practice of this sort shows the effect which would be generated by the same stimulation arranged by others.

"Doing something else." One technique of self-control which has no parallel in the control of others is based upon the principle of prepotency. The individual may keep himself from engaging in behavior which leads to punishment by energetically engaging in something else. A simple example is avoiding flinching by a violent response of holding still. Holding still is not simply "not-flinching." It is a response which, if executed strongly enough, is prepotent over the flinching response. This is close to the control exercised by others when they generate incompatible behavior. But where another person can do this only by arranging external variables, the individual appears to generate the behavior, so to speak, simply by executing it. A familiar example is talking about something else in order to avoid a particular topic. Escape from the aversive stimulation generated by the topic appears to be responsible for the strength of the verbal behavior which displaces it (Chapter XXIV).

In the field of emotion a more specific form of "doing something else" may be especially effective. Emotions tend to fall into pairs--

fear and anger, love and hate—according to the direction of the behavior which is strengthened. We may modify a man's behavior in fear by making him angry. His behavior is not simply doing something else; it is in a sense doing the opposite. The result is not prepotency but algebraic summation. The effect is exemplified in self-control when we alter an emotional predisposition by practicing the opposite emotion—reducing the behavorial pattern in fear by practicing anger or nonchalance, or avoiding the ravages of hatred by "loving our enemies."

THE ULTIMATE SOURCE OF CONTROL

A mere survey of the techniques of self-control does not explain why the individual puts them into effect. This shortcoming is all too apparent when we undertake to engender self-control. It is easy to tell an alcoholic that he can keep himself from drinking by throwing away available supplies of alcohol; the principal problem is to get him to do it. We make this controlling behavior more probable by arranging special contingencies of reinforcement. By punishing drinking—perhaps merely with "disapproval"—we arrange for the automatic reinforcement of behavior which controls drinking because such behavior then reduces conditioned aversive stimulation. Some of these additional consequences are supplied by nature, but in general they are arranged by the community. This is indeed the whole point of ethical training (Chapter XXI). It appears, therefore, that society is responsible for the larger part of the behavior of self-control. If this is correct, little ultimate control remains with the individual. A man may spend a great deal of time designing his own life—he may choose the circumstances in which he is to live with great care, and he may manipulate his daily environment on an extensive scale. Such activity appears to exemplify a high order of self-determination. But it is also behavior, and we account for it in terms of other variables in the environment and history of the individual. It is these variables which provide the ultimate control.

This view is, of course, in conflict with traditional treatments of the subject, which are especially likely to cite self-control as an important example of the operation of personal responsibility. But an analysis which appeals to external variables makes the assumption of an inner originating and determining agent unnecessary. The scientific advantages of such an analysis are many, but the practical advantages may well be even more important. The traditional conception of what is happening when an individual controls himself has never been successful as an educational device. It is of little help to tell a man to use his "will power" or his "self-control." Such an exhortation may make self-control slightly more probable by establishing additional aversive consequences of failure to control, but it does not help anyone to understand the actual processes. An alternative analysis of the *behavior* of control should make it possible to teach relevant techniques as easily as any other technical repertoire. It should also improve the procedures through which society maintains self-controlling behavior in strength. As a science of behavior reveals more clearly the variables of which behavior is a function, these possibilities should be greatly increased.

It must be remembered that formulae expressed in terms of personal responsibility underlie many of our present techniques of control and cannot be abruptly dropped. To arrange a smooth transition is in itself a major problem. But the point has been reached where a sweeping revision of the concept of responsibility is required, not only in a theoretical analysis of behavior, but for its practical consequences as well. We shall return to this point in Sections V and VI.

CHAPTER XVI

THINKING

THE BEHAVIOR OF
MAKING A DECISION

In self-control the alternative courses of action are specifiable in advance, and the issue is resolved before control is exerted. The techniques of control can be efficiently designed to achieve a particular state of affairs. There are instances of the manipulation of one's own behavior, however, in which the outcome cannot be predicted. Some sort of "self-determination" is involved, for example, in deciding *which* of two courses of action is to be followed. The task is not simply to make a selected course of action probable but to decide an issue. The individual sometimes does this by manipulating some of the variables of which his behavior is a function. The techniques are more limited than in self-control because the outcome cannot be specified in advance.

In making a decision, as in self-control, the manipulated variables are often private events within the organism. As such they present a special problem, to which we shall return in Chapter XVII. Familiar instances in which the variables are accessible to everyone will suffice here. The processes appear to be the same whether the variables are public or private. "Making a decision" also resembles self-control in that some of the techniques are used in essentially the same way in controlling the behavior of others. This is not true when we *persuade* someone to behave in a given way since our variables operate in favor of a single alternative, and no decision is involved. When we attempt to help someone "make up his mind" without prejudice to any course of action, however, we employ the techniques which the individual may use upon himself in reaching a decision.

Although variables in the field of motivation and conditioning are used in making a decision, they are less specific and their effect is often delayed. For more direct results we resort to the manipulation of stimuli. If all relevant courses of action show some strength before we decide among them, our techniques consist of finding *supplementary* sources of strength which, when applied to the behavior of others, would be classified as prompting or probing (Chapter XIV). In deciding whether to spend our vacation in the mountains or at the seashore, for example, we may pore over travel magazines and vacation booklets, find out where our friends are going and what weather is predicted for each place, and so on. This material may, if we are unlucky, simply maintain the balance between the two courses of action, but it is more likely to lead to the prepotent emergence of one of them. "Deciding," as the term will be used here, is not the execution of the act decided upon but the preliminary behavior responsible for it.

The process of deciding may come to an end before the act is executed when some relatively irrevocable step is taken—for example, we may decide about the vacation by making a down payment to hold a reservation. A common conclusion is simply to announce our decision. By saying that we are going to the seashore, we insure aversive consequences if this prediction of our future behavior is not fulfilled. The new variable may prevent the reinstatement of any conflict and hence of any further behavior of deciding. Deciding is also brought to an end when the techniques begin to be applied toward a single outcome—when we throw away the pamphlets describing the seashore and continue to work to strengthen the behavior of going to the mountains. We are then behaving as if we had been told to go to the mountains for our health and were simply accumulating material which made it possible to carry out the order (perhaps in competition with aversive variables which strengthened staying home or going elsewhere).

ORIGIN AND MAINTENANCE OF THE BEHAVIOR OF DECIDING

The individual manipulates relevant variables in making a decision because the behavior of doing so has certain reinforcing consequences. One of these is simply escape from indecision. Conflicting alternatives lead to an oscillation between incomplete forms of response which, by occupying a good deal of the individual's time, may be strongly aversive. Any behavior which brings this conflict to an end will be positively reinforced. What we may distinguish as "due deliberation" has other consequences. When we look a situation over carefully in the course of making a decision, we presumably increase the probability that the response eventually made will achieve maximal reinforcement. In the long run the net gain may be enough to maintain the strength of the behavior of looking over the situation.

Escape from indecision or the net advantage of a deliberated response may seem inadequate to explain the origin and maintenance of the behavior of deciding. They are certainly defective reinforcers, for they may be long delayed and their connection with a response may be obscure. We may readily admit these deficiencies, however, for the *behavior* of making decisions is also usually deficient. It is not present in any degree in the behavior of lower organisms or of many people. When present, it is usually the result of special reinforce- ments applied by the community. Though the individual may accidentally hit upon various ways of deciding, it is more likely that he will be taught relevant techniques. We teach a child to "stop and think" and to "consider all the consequences" by supplying additional, and to some extent irrelevant or spurious, reinforcements (Chapter XXVI). Even these may not be successful. The child may still find it difficult to "make up his mind" and may occasionally experience the pathological condition of *folie du doute* or some version of the plight of Buridan's ass.

THE BEHAVIOR OF RECALL

In making a decision the alternative courses of action can be specified in advance, even though the outcome cannot be foreseen. Are there circumstances under which an individual manipulates variables to affect a response which he cannot identify until it is emitted? At first glance this may seem not only improbable but impossible. Nevertheless it is done—and done extensively. Let us suppose that we have forgotten the name of a man we must shortly introduce to someone. Since the response cannot be specified in advance, the usual techniques of self-determination may seem not to apply. There is, indeed, nothing we can do unless we have a lead of some sort. But not being able to identify a response does not mean that we cannot make other statements about it or manipulate conditions relevant to it. We may be able to say, for example, that it is a name we once knew, that it is a name which will be correct in introducing a particular person, that we shall probably recognize it at once as correct, or that it is the name of a man whom we met on a particular occasion and with whom we discussed a particular subject. With these extra specifications it is not impossible to work upon oneself in order to strengthen the response. The available techniques should be classified as self-probes (Chapter XIV). (A self-prompt would presuppose that we could identify the response.)

The techniques are familiar. We use thematic probes when we review a conversation we had with the man in question, when we describe the circumstances under which we were introduced to him, or when we review thematic classifications (was it a German name, an Irish name, an unusual name, and so on?). We use formal probes when we try various stress patterns—ta-*da*-ta-*dada*—or recite the alphabet repetitively in a form of verbal summation. We may even set up an aversive condition from which we can escape only by emitting the name. This is done in rehearsing a formal introduction—"I'd like to have you meet Mr. . . ."—or by embarking upon the actual introduction, counting upon the powerful pressure which will arise when the appropriate point is reached to produce the name. If, as the result of any of these procedures, the name "suddenly pops into our head," then a response has been strengthened which could not be specified in advance.

PROBLEMS AND SOLUTIONS

In recalling a name it is assumed that the response exists in some strength and that other information is available as a source of supplementary stimulation. These are the essential features of a broader and generally more complex activity commonly called "problem-solving," "thinking," or "reasoning." The analysis of recalling a name thus serves as a preface to a much more important field of human behavior.

The language in which problem-solving is usually discussed does not differ much from the layman's vocabulary. The rigorous concepts and methods developed in other areas of human behavior are commonly abandoned when this field is reached. It is easy to give an example of a problem, but it is difficult to define the term rigorously. There appears to be no problem for the organism which is not in a state of deprivation or aversive stimulation, but something more is involved. The hungry organism eating ravenously is perhaps disposing of a problem, but only in a trivial sense. In the true "problem situation" the organism has no behavior immediately available which will reduce the deprivation or provide escape from aversive stimulation. This condition may be expressed more generally. We need not specify the deprivation or aversive condition if we can demonstrate that *a response exists in strength which cannot be emitted*. Discriminative stimulation may be needed to determine the form or direction of the response (the golfer cannot shoot for the green until he finds the green); or the response may require external support or instrumentation which is lacking (the golfer cannot shoot for the green until he finds the ball). We may demonstrate the strength of the response in several ways but usually by showing that it occurs as soon as the occasion is suitable.

A locked drawer presents a problem if behavior requiring an open drawer is strong and if the individual does not have the key or other means of opening it. The strength of the behavior is inferred from the presence of responses which have previously opened the drawer or from the appearance of the behavior as soon as the drawer has been opened. We can say that a stalled car presents a problem if no behavior which succeeds in starting it is immediately available and if behavior which has previously succeeded in starting it is strong or if we have other evidence that behavior which depends upon a started car is strong. Interlocked wire rings are a problem if the behavior of demonstrating them apart is strong and no available response makes this possible. A murder mystery presents a problem if we are strongly inclined to name the murderer—to show that one name fits all statements in the story consistently—and cannot do so. Buying wallpaper for a room is a problem if we cannot say how many rolls we need; it is another type of problem if we have measured the room but have not converted our measurements into rolls of paper. Mathematics is rich in problems, but the motivation of the mathematician is often obscure. The deprivation or aversive stimulation responsible for the strength of writing a formula which always generates a prime number or of proving that a given formula never fails to generate a prime number is by no means clear.

In any case, the solution to a problem is simply a response which alters the situation so that the strong response can be emitted. Finding the key to the locked drawer, putting gasoline into the car, twisting the wire rings in a certain way, emitting a name which fits all the statements in the murder mystery, and writing a formula which always generates a prime number are solutions in this sense. Once the solution has occurred, the problem vanishes simply because the essential condition has been eliminated. (The same problem is not likely to recur since the situation will no longer be novel. Henceforth, the response which appeared as a solution will occur because it has been reinforced under similar circumstances.)

Simply emitting a solution, however, is not solving a problem. We are concerned here with the process of "finding the solution." Problem-solving may be defined as any behavior which, through the manipulation of variables, makes the appearance of a solution more probable. This definition seems to embrace the activities most commonly described as problem-solving, and it permits a fairly rigorous analysis of procedures or techniques. We may solve the problems of other people in this way, but we shall limit the discussion here to the case in which the individual solves his own problems.

The appearance of a solution does not guarantee that problem-solving has taken place. An accidental change in the environment often brings about a similar result—the key may be found or the car suddenly respond to the starter. A more subtle example, which has already been mentioned, is Descartes's explanation of the behavior of the living organism. The problem arose from a strong disposition to emit explanatory remarks concerning the operation of the living body. We must assume the strength of such behavior even though at this late date we cannot account for it. The explanation was a metaphor; a response based upon certain fountain figures which were constructed to resemble living organisms was simply extended through stimulus induction to the living organism itself. We need not suppose that at the moment this occurred, Descartes was engaged in solving the problem in any active sense. The availability of the information about the fountain figures may have been wholly accidental. We need not, therefore, treat any particular part of Descartes's behavior as problem-solving. It was simply "hitting upon a solution."

For the same reason, so-called trial-and-error learning is not problem-solving. The state of deprivation or aversive stimulation required by a problem implies the high probability of many responses. Some of these may be emitted because the situation resembles other situations in which they have been reinforced. It is possible that one of these will be a solution—that it will solve the problem by disposing of the essential condition. But this requires no special treatment. Another kind of behavior likely to be observed is random exploration. In the presence of a problem the organism is simply active. Here again the solution may follow by accident.

An example of problem-solving in the sense of finding a solution appears in connection with trial-and-error learning when the organism "learns how to try." It emits responses in great numbers because of previous success and perhaps according to certain features of the problem. Suppose we challenge an individual to identify a word selected from a list. Our challenge provides aversive stimulation, and our statement that we have chosen a word from a particular list provides a discriminative stimulus increasing the probability of a corresponding set of responses. The individual's only recourse is to emit words on the list until he hits upon the effective response. He may have discovered ways of ordering his behavior, however, to avoid repetition, to avoid omissions, and so on. He may progress rapidly toward a solution if we reinforce him with descriptive categories. He may then run through the alphabet for the initial letter ("Is it a word beginning with . . .?"), then for the second letter, and so on. A formal prompt will soon be generated which will strengthen responses having a reasonable chance of success. Or he may guess thematic or grammatical categories—animal or vegetable, noun or verb, and so on. The approach to the solution may be very skillful when profitable categories have once been reinforced. But in spite of the fact that one learns to use such a technique and in spite of the apparent direction of the process, the behavior is scarcely more than a trial-and-error performance. We can account for the emergence of each trial response in terms of the current occasion and the past history of the individual. There is a minimum of "self-determination."

One way to encourage the emission of a response which may prove to be a solution is to manipulate stimuli. A simple example is a survey of the problem situation. This is often the effect of random exploratory behavior and is therefore grouped loosely with trial-and-error learning. But the effect is not to emit a response which will prove to be a solution but to hit upon stimuli which may control such a response. Improving or amplifying available stimulation is especially effective; we increase the chances of a solution when we look a problem over carefully, when we get all the facts, or when we point up relevant stimuli by stating a problem in its clearest terms. A further step is to arrange or rearrange stimuli. In the game of anagrams, for example, the problem is to compose words from a miscellaneous assortment of letters; the solution is simply spelling out an acceptable word. It is helpful to rearrange the available letters since some arrangements may resemble parts of words in the individual's repertoire and hence serve as formal prompts. The experienced anagram player learns to group letters efficiently, especially in certain subgroups which enable him to make profitable larger groups. He learns to put "q" and "u" together, to try various combinations of "sl," "sh," "sp," "th," and so on.

The logical syllogism is a way of arranging stimuli. The logician possesses a verbal repertoire in which certain conclusions are likely to be made upon the statement of certain premises, but a particular problem may not present itself in the required order. Solving the problem consists of arranging the materials in syllogistic form. If the solution is obtained wholly by applying a formula (*Barbara celarent* . . .), the arrangement does not merely facilitate a response but actually determines it, and the process is not problem-solving as here defined. But there are less mechanical cases in which the arrangement is made primarily to encourage the appearance of a response which has other sources of strength. In the same way the mathematician is trained to transpose, factor, clear fractions, and so on, until an expression appears in a form which suggests a solution. Much of this may be relatively mechanical, but in true problem-solving the procedures are used to encourage the appearance of a novel response which has other sources of strength.

Scientific knowledge often advances as the result of the arrangement of stimuli. The Linnaean classification of species was an arrangement of data which led, among other results, to Darwin's solution of the problem of the origin of species. Mendelyeev's table of the elements was an arrangement of the data of chemistry which necessarily preceded modern atomic theory. The marshalling of relevant information is now so obvious a step in the solution of any problem that it is a matter of routine where problems are to be solved by groups and where the different functions of problem-solving are delegated to different people. The "fact researcher" is a familiar figure in the organized problem-solving of science and industry.

Another technique of problem-solving consists essentially of the self-probe. Tentative solutions, perhaps assembled for this purpose, are systematically reviewed. There are also certain practices which are not to be overlooked even though they are not directed toward specific solutions and hence are not ordinarily included in problem-solving. An example is a certain type of self-probe which is so general that it must be used repetitively in the manner of the verbal summator. Repetition is, of course, helpful in increasing the effect of more specific techniques, as when we repeatedly survey relevant material or restate a problem again and again. But something like a formal probe which has no specific reference to a given solution appears to be exemplified by people who can "think better" in a noisy or otherwise apparently distracting environment. Features of the noisy background appear to operate like speech patterns of the verbal summator to contribute strength to solutions. Visual materials in the form of ink blots, "doodlings," or the ambiguous stimulation of a crystal ball contribute to some kinds of solutions.

The person who is skilled in "how to think" often manipulates his levels of deprivation. He may know how to generate interests relevant to a problem. He may generate an adequate energy level by arranging a satisfactory program of sleep or rest. He may arrange aversive schedules which keep his behavior at an efficient pace. He may follow a rigid routine to achieve the same result. Solving a problem may also be facilitated by eliminating responses which conflict with the solution. The techniques for doing this do not, of course, depend upon a particular solution. In recalling a name, for example, a wrong name may seem to stand in the way of the right one. Here the response to be controlled, the intruding response, can be identified, and any of the devices employed in weakening behavior described in Chapter XV may be used.

The "difficulty" of a problem is the availability of the response which constitutes the solution. We may not need to increase the strength very much. This is the case when the problem closely resembles an earlier one: the wire ring puzzle is like one which has previously been solved, the murder mystery uses a standard plot, and the scientific problem parallels a problem in another field. As the similarity with earlier instances increases, and with it the availability of an adequate response, a point is reached at which it is idle to speak of problem-solving at all. At the other extreme there may be little or nothing in the present situation which strengthens appropriate responses, and in this case the individual must industriously manipulate the variables of which his behavior is a function. If no behavior at all is available, no matter what is done by way of changing the variables, the problem is insoluble so far as he is concerned.

"HAVING AN IDEA"

The result of solving a problem is the appearance of a solution in the form of a response. The response alters the situation so that the problem disappears. The relation between the preliminary behavior and the appearance of the solution is simply the relation between the manipulation of variables and the emission of a response. Until the functional relations in behavior had been analyzed, this could not be clearly understood; and meanwhile a great many fictional processes were invented. Conspicuous examples are the "thought processes" called thinking and reasoning. A functional analysis removes much of the mystery which surrounds these terms. We need not ask, for example, "where a solution comes from." A solution is a response which exists in some strength in the repertoire of the individual, if the problem is soluble by him. The appearance of the response in his behavior is no more surprising than the appearance of any response in the behavior of any organism. It is either meaningless or idle to ask where the response resides until it summons strength enough to spring out into the open. We may also easily represent the activities by virtue of which the thinker gets an idea—at least so long as the behavior is overt. Special problems undoubtedly arise when it is not, but they are not peculiar to the analysis of thinking.

Instances have been described in which a mathematician abandons a problem after working on it for a long time, only to have the solution "pop into his head" quite unexpectedly at a later date. It is tempting to suppose that he has continued to work on the problem "unconsciously" and that his solution follows immediately upon some successful manipulation of variables. But variables will change automatically during a period of time. Variables which have interfered with a solution may grow weak, and supporting variables may turn up. We need not, therefore, suppose that any problem-solving occurred after overt work on the problem was dropped. The fact that the solution comes as a surprise to the individual himself does not alter this conclusion. We shall see in Chapter XVIII that genuine problem-solving may well take place when the individual himself cannot observe it, but many instances of "unconscious thought" can be accounted for simply as changes leading to a solution which ensue with the passage of time.

It is not only in problem-solving that one "suddenly has an idea" in the sense of emitting a response. In a metaphor, for example, we have seen that a response is evoked by a stimulus which shares only certain tenuous properties with the stimulus originally in control. One suddenly "sees the similarity" between repeated misfortune and the repeated assault of waves against a rocky coast in the sense that a response appropriate to the one is now made to the other. This may occur with or without external aid. The metaphor may "come to us" as we are speaking or writing, or we may "see the point" when someone else emits the transferred response. On a broader scale we "get new ideas from a book" in the sense that we acquire many responses to a situation which we did not possess before reading it. In this sense the book may "clear up our thinking" about a given situation.

We often manipulate materials in the world about us to generate "new ideas" when no well-defined problem is present. A child of six, playing with a badminton bird and a white rubber ball, put the ball in the feathered end of the bird. This "gave her an idea." She began to lick the ball as if the whole assemblage were an ice cream cone and immediately spoke of it as such. There is nothing mysterious about this "act of thought." The manipulative and verbal responses appropriate to an ice cream cone were brought out by similar geometrical features of the bird and ball. There was no significant problem; an idle manipulation of nature simply generated a novel pattern which, through stimulus induction, evoked a response characteristically in some strength in a child of six.

The artist may manipulate a medium simply to generate ideas in much the same way. It is true that he may mix or place colors on a palette or canvas to solve a specific problem—for example, that of producing a likeness. The trained artist has already solved some of the subsidiary problems and possesses a repertoire, similar to those discussed in Chapter VII, which generates patterns resembling the properties of the object to be copied. There may also be certain novel features in the object which call for the preliminary behavior which we should here designate as problem-solving. The artistic exploration of a medium may, however, proceed in the absence of any explicit problem. This behavior is most obvious when the task is delegated to mechanical devices. The artist may generate novel geometrical designs by following an arbitrary formula, such as that of "dynamic symmetry," or by "doodling." In the same way the writer may generate novel plots by manipulating stock characters in stock situations, just as the composer may generate new melodies or rhythms by changing the settings on a mechanical device or by manipulating symbols on paper or by allowing his cat to walk across the keyboard. All this may be done, not to solve a specific problem, but to enlarge an artistic repertoire. The general problem is simply to come up with something new.

ORIGINALITY IN IDEAS

We saw that self-control rests ultimately with the environmental variables which generate controlling behavior and, therefore, originates outside the organism. There is a parallel issue in the field of ideas. Is an idea ever original?

We do not call original that response which is obviously imitative or controlled by explicit verbal stimuli, as in following spoken or written instructions. We are not wholly inclined to call a response original, even though it has never been made before, when it is the result of some established procedure of manipulating variables—as in routine mathematical operations or the use of syllogistic formulae. When a pattern of manipulation has never been applied to a particular case before, the result is, in a sense, new. For example, the individual learns to count as the result of explicit educational reinforcement, but he may be original in what he counts. The observation that a cube has six faces must at one time have been an original idea.

We reserve the term "original" for those ideas which result from manipulations of variables which have not followed a rigid formula and in which the ideas have other sources of strength. A given procedure in problem-solving may never have been used in precisely the same way before or in connection with the same material, and it does not lead to the conclusion by itself. Some additional strength is supplied by stimulus induction from similar situations. This induction, however, is also the result of a particular personal history and of well-defined behavioral processes. We may, therefore, acknowledge the emergence of novel ideas, in the sense of responses never made before under the same circumstances, without implying any element of originality in the individuals who "have" them.

Man is now in much better control of the world than were his ancestors, and this suggests a progress in discovery and invention in which there appears to be a strong element of originality. But we could express this fact just as well by saying that the environment is now in better control of man. Reinforcing contingencies shape the behavior of the individual, and novel contingencies generate novel forms of behavior. Here, if anywhere, originality is to be found. As time passes men react to more and more subtle features of the world about them and in more and more effective ways. The accumulation of behavior is made possible by the growth of a social environment which forces modern man to respond to differences which only very slowly gained control of the behavior of his ancestors (Chapters XIX and XXVIII). Educational agencies established by the group provide for the transmission of the results of environmental contingencies from one individual to another, and it becomes possible for the individual to acquire effective behavior on a vast scale.

We cannot rigorously account for the origin of important ideas in the history of science because many relevant facts have long since become unavailable. The question of originality can be disposed of, however, by providing plausible accounts of the way in which a given idea might have occurred. The study of the history of science has made this task somewhat more feasible than it once seemed, since it has tended to minimize the contribution made by any one man. It is much easier to account for Harvey's discovery that the blood passes from the right to the left ventricle by way of the lungs and not through the septum when we learn that the view had already been proposed that *some* of the blood passed this way. James Watt's invention of the steam engine seems much less miraculous when we have once learned about the earlier forms of the engine upon which his contribution was based.

A formulation of creative thinking within the framework of a natural science may be offensive to those who prize their conception of the individual in control of the world about him (Chapter XXIX), but the formulation may have compensating advantages. So long as originality is identified with spontaneity or an absence of lawfulness in behavior, it appears to be a hopeless task to teach a man to be original or to influence his process of thinking in any important way. The present analysis should lead to an improvement in educational practices. If our account of thinking is essentially correct, there is no reason why we cannot teach a man how to think. There is also no reason why we cannot greatly improve methods of thinking to utilize the full potentialities of the thinking organism—whether this is the individual or the organized group or, indeed, the highly complex mechanical device.

CHAPTER XVII

PRIVATE EVENTS
IN A NATURAL SCIENCE

THE WORLD WITHIN ONE'S SKIN

When we say that behavior is a function of the environment, the term "environment" presumably means any event in the universe capable of affecting the organism. But part of the universe is enclosed within the organism's own skin. Some independent variables may, therefore, be related to behavior in a unique way. The individual's response to an inflamed tooth, for example, is unlike the response which anyone else can make to that particular tooth, since no one else can establish the same kind of contact with it. Events which take place during emotional excitement or in states of deprivation are often uniquely accessible for the same reason; in this sense our joys, sorrows, loves, and hates are peculiarly our own. With respect to each individual, in other words, a small part of the universe is *private*.

We need not suppose that events which take place within an organism's skin have special properties for that reason. A private event may be distinguished by its limited accessibility but not, so far as we know, by any special structure or nature. We have no reason to suppose that the stimulating effect of an inflamed tooth is essentially different from that of, say, a hot stove. The stove, however, is capable of affecting more than one person in approximately the same way. In studying behavior we may have to deal with the stimulation from a tooth as an inference rather than as a directly observable fact. But if some of the independent variables of which behavior is a function are not directly accessible, what becomes of a functional analysis? How are such variables to be treated?

These questions may not be of interest to all readers. The issue is an ancient one, which has occupied the attention of philosophers and others for more than two thousand years. It has never been satisfactorily resolved, and perhaps the present inclination on the part of educated laymen to avoid it represents simple extinction. Fortunately, the issue is seldom crucial in the practical control of human behavior. The reader whose interests are essentially practical and who may now prefer to move on to later chapters may do so without serious trouble. Nevertheless, the issue is important and must sometime be faced. Modern science has attempted to put forth an ordered and integrated conception of nature. Some of its most distinguished men have concerned themselves with the broad implications of science with respect to the structure of the universe. The picture which emerges is almost always dualistic. The scientist humbly admits that he is describing only half the universe, and he defers to another world—a world of mind or consciousness—for which another mode of inquiry is assumed to be required. Such a point of view is by no means inevitable, but it is part of the cultural heritage from which science has emerged. It obviously stands in the way of a unified account of nature. The contribution which a science of behavior can make in suggesting an alternative point of view is perhaps one of its most important achievements. No discussion of the implications of science for an understanding of human behavior would be complete without at least a brief review of this contribution.

VERBAL RESPONSES TO PRIVATE EVENTS

The verbal response "red" is established as a discriminative operant by a community which reinforces the response when it is made in the presence of red stimuli and not otherwise. This can easily be done if the community and the individual both have access to red stimuli. It cannot be done if either the individual *or the community* is color-blind. The latter case resembles that in which a verbal response is based upon a private event, where, by definition, common access by both parties is impossible. How does the community present or with-hold reinforcement appropriately in order to bring such a response as "My tooth aches" under the control of appropriate stimulation? It may easily establish the response "My tooth is broken" because both the individual and the community have access to the stimulus for "broken," but the community has no comparable access to the stimu-lus eventually controlling "aches." Nevertheless, verbal behavior of this sort is obviously set up.

The community may resort to public accompaniments of the pri-vate event. For example, it may establish a verbal response to an aching tooth by presenting or withholding reinforcement according to a special condition of the tooth which almost certainly accom-panies the private event or according to violent collateral responses such as holding the jaw or crying out. Thus we teach a child to say "That itches" or "That tickles" because we observe either public events which accompany such private stimulation ("the kinds of things which itch or tickle") or some such identifying response as scratching or squirming. This method of circumventing the privacy of the individual is not foolproof because the public and private events may not be perfectly correlated.

There is another possibility. Verbal responses which are acquired with respect to public events may be transferred to private events on the basis of common properties. It has often been pointed out that many subjective terms are metaphorical, at least in origin. The lan-guage of emotion, for example, is almost wholly metaphorical; its terms are borrowed from descriptions of public events in which both the individual and the reinforcing community have access to the same stimuli. Here again the community cannot guarantee an accu-rate verbal repertoire because the response may be transferred from public event to private event on the basis of irrelevant properties.

The techniques which guarantee the reliability of a verbal report cannot be brought to bear upon a private description. The science of introspective psychology met this difficulty whenever it departed from the study of responses to controllable stimuli. The psychologist can, for example, manipulate the color, brightness, or saturation of a spot of light in order to establish a sensitive verbal repertoire in his subject with respect to these properties. Such an experimental situation does not raise the problem of privacy at all. But establishing a comparable repertoire to distinguish between various "states of emotion," for example, is a task of a very different sort. Unless the psychologist can manipulate the events reported during emotion as he manipulates the properties of a patch of light, he must resort to imperfect public accompaniments.

The layman also finds the lack of a reliable subjective vocabulary inconvenient. Everyone mistrusts verbal responses which describe private events. Variables are often operating which tend to weaken the stimulus control of such descriptions, and the reinforcing community is usually powerless to prevent the resulting distortion. The individual who excuses himself from an unpleasant task by pleading a headache cannot be successfully challenged, even though the existence of the private event is doubtful. There is no effective answer to the student who insists, after being corrected, that that was what he "meant to say," but the existence of this private event is not accepted with any confidence.

The individual himself also suffers from these limitations. The environment, whether public or private, appears to remain undistinguished until the organism is forced to make a distinction. Anyone who has suddenly been required to make fine color discriminations will usually agree that he now "sees" colors which he had not previously "seen." It is hard to believe that we should not distinguish between the primary colors unless there were some reason for doing so, but we are conditioned to do this so early in our history that our experience is probably not a safe guide. Experiments in which organisms are raised in darkness tend to confirm the view that discriminative behavior waits upon the contingencies which force discriminations. Now, self-observation is also the product of discriminative contingencies, and if a discrimination cannot be forced by the community, it may never arise. Strangely enough, it is the community which teaches the individual to "know himself."

Some contingencies involving inner stimulation do not, of course, have to be arranged by a reinforcing community. In throwing a ball we time a sequence of responses by the stimulation which our own movements generate. Here the reinforcing contingencies are determined by the mechanical and geometrical exigencies of throwing a ball, and since a reinforcing community is not involved, the question of accessibility to the behaving individual does not arise. But "knowledge," as we saw in Chapter VIII, is particularly identified with the verbal behavior which arises from social reinforcement. Apparently, conceptual and abstract behavior are impossible without such reinforcement. The kind of self-knowledge represented by discriminative verbal behavior—the knowledge which is "expressed" when we talk about our own behavior—is strictly limited by the contingencies which the verbal community can arrange. The deficiencies which generate public *mistrust* lead, in the case of the individual himself, to simple *ignorance*. There appears to be no way in which the individual may sharpen the reference of his own verbal repertoire in this respect. This is particularly unfortunate because he probably has many reasons for distorting his own report to himself (Chapter XVIII).

VARIETIES OF PRIVATE STIMULATION

It is customary to distinguish between two types of internal stimulation. *Interoceptive* stimuli arise mainly in the digestive, respiratory, and circulatory systems. A full or inflamed stomach, a stomach contracting in hunger, a gallstone distending the bile duct, the contractions or relaxations of small blood vessels in blushing and blanching, and a pounding heart all generate interoceptive stimuli. These are the principal stimuli to which one reacts in "feeling an emotion." *Proprioceptive* stimuli, on the other hand, are generated by the position and movement of the body in space and by the position and movement of parts of the body with respect to other parts. We usually respond to stimuli of this sort in combination with *exteroceptive* stimulation from the surrounding environment, and we do not always correctly identify the source of stimulation. Thus when we run our hand over a surface and judge it to be sticky, gummy, or slippery, our response is in part to the resistance encountered in moving our hand, even though we appear to be talking about the surface as a public event. The important point here, however, is not the locus of stimulation but the degree of accessibility to the community.

An important verbal repertoire describes one's own *behavior*. It is generated by a community which insists upon answers to such questions as "What did you say?" "What are you doing?" "What are you going to do?" or "Why are you doing that?" Although these questions are usually practical ones, the theoretical implications are equally important. Since the individual may often observe his own behavior as a public event, the public-private distinction does not always arise. In that case the accuracy of the self-descriptive repertoire may be adequate. If a man says, "I went home at three o'clock," there are ways in which this may be checked and his behavior reinforced to insure future accuracy. But part of the stimulation which the individual receives from his own behavior is different from that available to the community.

A description of behavior which has not been executed appears to depend upon private events only. For example, a man may say, "I was on the point of going home at three o'clock," though he did not go. Here the controlling stimuli are not only private, they appear to have no public accompaniments. Such responses as "I'm strongly inclined to go home" or "I shall go home in half an hour" also describe states of affairs which appear to be accessible only to the speaker. How can the verbal community establish responses of this sort?

A possible explanation is that the terms are established as part of a repertoire when the individual is behaving publicly. Private stimuli, generated in addition to the public manifestations, then gain the necessary degree of control. Later when these private stimuli occur alone, the individual may respond to them. "I was on the point of going home" may be regarded as the equivalent of "I observed events in myself which characteristically precede or accompany my going home." What these events are, such an explanation does not say.

Comparable expressions may describe the momentary probability of behavior as well as its particular form.

Another possibility is that when an individual appears to describe unemitted behavior, he is actually describing a history of variables which would enable an independent observer to describe the behavior in the same way if a knowledge of the variables were available to him. The question, "*Why* did you do that?" is often important to the community, which establishes a repertoire of responses based upon the external events of which behavior is a function, as well as upon the functional relation itself. We are usually able to report that a particular stimulating situation, a special contingency of reinforcement, a condition of deprivation, or some emotional circumstance is responsible for our own behavior: "I often drop in on X because he serves excellent drinks," "I spanked the brat because he had been thoroughly annoying," "I generally take the early train because it is less crowded," and so on. It is possible that the same data may be used to predict our own future behavior. The statement, "I shall probably go abroad next summer," may be due to variables of a wholly public nature which make it equivalent to the statement, "Circumstances have arisen which make it highly probable that I shall go abroad." This is not a description of behavior-to-be-emitted but of the conditions of which that behavior is a function. The individual himself is, of course, often in an advantageous position for observing his own history.

One important sort of stimulus to which the individual may possibly be responding when he describes unemitted behavior has no parallel among other forms of private stimulation. It arises from the fact that the behavior may actually occur but on such a reduced scale that it cannot be observed by others—at least without instrumentation. This is often expressed by saying that the behavior is "covert." Sometimes it is said that the reduced form is merely the beginning of the overt form—that the private event is incipient or inchoate behavior. A verbal repertoire which has been established with respect to the overt case might be extended to covert behavior because of similar self-stimulation. The organism is generating the same effective stimuli, albeit on a much smaller scale.

The appeal to covert or incipient behavior is easily misused. If the statement, "I was on the point of going home," is a response to stimuli generated by a covert or incipient response of actually going home, how may the response of going home be executed covertly? In such a case, one of the other interpretations may well be preferred. Verbal behavior, however, can occur at the covert level because it does not require the presence of a particular physical environment for its execution. Moreover, it may remain effective at the covert level because the speaker himself is also a listener and his verbal behavior may have private consequences. The covert form continues to be reinforced, even though it has been reduced in magnitude to the point at which it has no appreciable effect on the environment. Most people observe themselves talking privately. A characteristic report begins "I said to myself . . ." where the stimuli which control the response "I said" are presumably similar, except in magnitude, to those which in part control the response, "I said to him . . ."

RESPONSES TO ONE'S OWN
DISCRIMINATIVE BEHAVIOR

When a man says, "There is a rainbow in the sky" or "The clock is striking twelve," we can give a reasonable interpretation of his behavior in terms of a stimulating situation and certain characteristic conditioning procedures with which the community has set up verbal responses. But if he says, "*I see* a rainbow in the sky" or "*I hear* the clock striking twelve," additional terms have to be taken into account. Their importance is easily demonstrated. The group usually benefits when an individual responds verbally to events with which he alone is in contact. In so doing, he broadens the environment of those who hear him. But it is also important that he report the conditions under which he is responding. In so doing he reveals, so to speak, the "source of his information." The response, "*I see* a rainbow in the sky," is of a different order of importance from the response, "*They say there is* a rainbow in the sky." Other reasons why the group may be interested in the nature of the behavior of the speaker are suggested by such familiar questions as "Do you see that man over by the window?" "Can you hear me?" or "Do you smell smoke?"

When the community conditions the individual to say, "I see . . ." "I hear . . ." "I smell . . ." and so on, it must have some evidence of *discriminative* behavior. In certain cases it may rely upon the inevitability of a response to a conspicuous stimulus—"You see, it's raining after all." At other times it may rely upon the orientation of receptors: we tell a child that he is seeing a dog when we are sure that his eyes are oriented toward the dog, or that he is feeling the texture of a piece of cloth when we run his fingers over the cloth. But we cannot always or safely count upon evidence that a stimulus is merely being received. We have no comparable evidence for faint odors or tastes, or for visual or auditory stimuli to which receptors need not be especially oriented. How, for example, can the community teach the individual to report correctly that he is seeing the *color* of a piece of cloth or hearing the *oboe* in a full orchestra? Here there must be clear evidence that a discriminative reaction is being made. "Do you see that bird in the bush?" "Yes." "What kind is it?" Only when collateral information is correctly given does the community appropriately reinforce the response "Yes."

A verbal repertoire which describes the discriminative behavior of the individual appears, then, to be established on external evidence that a discriminative response is taking place, rather than that stimuli are present or received. When the individual comes to describe his *own* discriminative behavior, presumably he does so, at least initially, on comparable evidence. He observes himself as he executes some identifying response. The private events correlated with the public events used by the community are also the result of discriminative behavior, not simple stimulation. The response, "I see a rainbow," is, therefore, not equivalent to "There is a rainbow." If it were, a single discriminative stimulus—the rainbow—would account for both forms, but "I see a rainbow" is a description of the response of seeing a rainbow. When the rainbow is actually present, the distinction may be of little moment.

But the rainbow is not always present. Perhaps the most difficult problem in the analysis of behavior is raised by responses beginning

"I see . . .," "I hear . . .," and so on, *when the customary stimuli are lacking.* Here an accurate formulation of responses which describe one's own discriminative behavior is essential. We may approach this problem by surveying the circumstances under which a man "sees something." Presumably these will also be the circumstances under which he says, "I see something." (Parallel cases for "I hear . . .," "I taste . . .," need not be explicitly discussed.) No special problem is raised when an appropriate stimulus is present. We are also prepared for instances in which the stimulus is not the customary one but has enough in common with it to control the response. The process of abstraction also provides examples in which the complete stimulus is not available but of which an adequate account may nevertheless be given. When there are no stimuli present which resemble the usual stimuli, a response beginning "I see . . ." must be explained in terms of conditioning. There are two major possibilities corresponding to the distinction between respondent and operant conditioning.

CONDITIONED SEEING

A man may see or hear "stimuli which are not present" on the pattern of the conditioned reflex: he may see X, not only when X is present, but when any stimulus which has frequently accompanied X is present. The dinner bell not only makes our mouth water, it makes us see food. In the Pavlovian formula we simply substitute "seeing food" for "salivating." Originally both of these responses were made to food, but through a process of conditioning they are eventually made in response to the bell. When a man reports that the dinner bell makes him see food (he is more likely to say that it "reminds him of food" or "makes him think of food"), we may suppose that he is reporting a response which is similar to the response made in the presence of food. It is only an unfortunate tradition, apparently due to the Greeks, which leads us to ask *what* he is seeing in such a case. When he reports that the bell makes his mouth water, we do not feel compelled to ask *what* he is salivating to. A stimulus function has been assumed by a different stimulus, which may control seeing food as well as salivating.

The effect of a conditioned stimulus in evoking the response of seeing something helps to explain the character of responses to stimuli which are present but which are at variance with "what is seen." Conditioned seeing may combine with responses to unconditioned stimuli. We see familiar objects more readily and easily than unfamiliar objects; the stimuli actually present upon a given occasion may be effective both as conditioned and unconditioned stimuli at the same time. In catching only a passing glimpse of a bird, we see it distinctly if it is a familiar bird and indistinctly if it is not. The fragmentary stimuli have served to evoke conditioned seeing, which combines with the unconditioned seeing of the immediate stimulus. A poetic description of the sound of the sea is especially effective if one reads it while listening to the sea, for the verbal and nonverbal stimuli combine to produce an especially strong response. In a pack of playing cards, the shape of a heart or diamond is correlated with the color red. While playing cards one is especially likely to see a heart or diamond, rather than a spade or club, if one catches a glimpse of red. The verbal stimulus "heart" is likely to evoke seeing red as well as seeing a heart. It has been shown experimentally that if one who is familiar with playing cards is very briefly shown a heart printed in black ink, the heart is sometimes seen as red or as a mixture of red and black, perhaps reported as purple. If the card remains in view for a longer time, the current stimulus will completely mask the conditioned response of seeing red, but a brief exposure of appropriate duration leads to a fusion of conditioned and unconditioned responses.

In more general terms, conditioned seeing explains why one tends to see the world according to one's previous history. Certain properties of the world are responded to so commonly that "laws of perception" have been drawn up to describe the behavior thus conditioned. For example, we generally see completed circles, squares, and other figures. An incomplete figure presented under deficient or ambiguous circumstances may evoke seeing a completed figure as a conditioned response. For example, a ring with a small segment missing when very briefly exposed may be seen as a completed ring. Seeing a completed ring would presumably not be inevitable in an individual whose daily life was concerned with handling incompleted rings—as might be the case in manufacturing certain types of piston rings, for example. Some of the so-called synesthesias are also examples of a fusion of conditioned and unconditioned seeing. In a common example numbers are seen as colored. Something of this sort could arise if a child first learned to respond to numbers in a book in which geometric form and color were systematically paired. The geometric form would then lead to the conditioned response of seeing the corresponding color. The spoken stimulus "Seven" would lead to two conditioned responses: seeing the form **7** and seeing the associated color.

All those circumstances under which a mature individual will exhibit the response of seeing something may be arranged in a continuum. At one extreme the momentary stimulation is optimal. If, for example, the individual is listening to a stormy sea, the sound is primarily in control. "Hearing the sea" is not a wholly unconditioned response, however, since it depends upon previous experience. If we now reduce the momentary stimulation by transporting our individual farther and farther from the sea, we increase the role played by conditioned stimuli. A faint distant roar is heard "as the sound of the sea" only because of a particular history. Any sound similar to that of the sea may have this effect—for example, that of traffic in the street. If we now begin to introduce conditioned stimuli of a clearly different form—for example, nonauditory stimuli—we may be able to show the fusion of two distinct effects. If our subject examines a picture of heavy surf, current auditory stimuli resembling the sound of surf will make the total response of seeing and hearing the sea more powerful. At the other extreme of our continuum is the purely conditioned response—hearing appropriate sounds in a quiet room while observing a painting of the sea. If such an effect occurs, it must be due to conditioning, since what is heard is an auditory stimulus but what is present is visual.

There are, of course, great differences in the extent to which individuals exhibit conditioned seeing, hearing, and so on. Francis Galton first surveyed this form of human behavior in the nineteenth century. Some of his subjects showed an exceptional ability to see things which he described to them, while others found it almost impossible. Some subjects showed special abilities in certain fields only. Congenital defects of sensory equipment are sometimes responsible —as, for example, in the color-blind or tone-deaf. Other individual differences may be traced to the histories of the individuals. One difference depends upon the extent to which the requisite conditioning has taken place. In a world in which visual stimuli are extremely important one would expect many conditioned responses of this sort to be set up. It is not surprising to find that the composer is especially likely to be able to "hear music which is not present," while the artist is especially able to "see forms which are not present," and so on. It is possible, of course, that a man may become an artist or musician because of special abilities of this sort, but the obvious differences in personal history are almost certainly relevant. Another difference depends upon whether the individual is able to respond to his conditioned discriminative responses, and this in turn depends upon whether the community has forced verbal responses to them. A society which breeds introspective people would probably have more data of this sort to account for, not because more private seeing occurs, but because more of it comes into the public domain through self-description. In a group which seldom insists upon such behavior, the problem might never arise at all.

When an individual reports that he sees an object which is actually before him, we can distinguish between his response to the object and his response to his response. The individual himself makes the same distinction. It is usually possible for him to say that there is or is not a rainbow present when he reports that he sees one and that this is the variable of which his behavior is primarily a function. When the stimulus only partially resembles the usual stimulus, the subject may report that it "reminds him" of it. When the "stimulus seen" is actually lacking but the subject cannot report that fact, we say that he is suffering from a hallucination. He sees something and reports that he sees something, and from these events alone he may assert that something is there. When the current situation is further clarified, he may revise this report and conclude that he "only thought" he saw it. On the other hand he may refuse to make a response to the current situation which is incompatible with his conditioned response and may insist that what he sees is "really there." There are certain areas in which a collateral check on the presence or absence of an appropriate stimulus is not easily made. In such a case, we are much less likely to insist upon the distinction. Since we do not ordinarily confirm the presence or absence of bitter substances in the mouth, we are not likely to argue that the response, "My mouth tastes bitter," is hallucinatory.

The practical importance of conditioned seeing. A private event is not wholly without practical importance. Stimuli which generate conditioned seeing are often reinforcing because they do so, and they extend the range of reinforcing stimuli available in the control of human behavior. The practical task of generating conditioned stimuli of special effectiveness is an important one, as the artist, writer, and composer know. If it is possible to reinforce a man with the "beauties of nature," it is usually possible to reinforce him also with conditioned stimuli which evoke responses of seeing the beauties of nature. It is the function of the "word picture" to generate such conditioned seeing. By fusing conditioned and unconditioned seeing the artist makes the observer see the same thing in another way. Nostalgic music is effective if it "reminds one" of happier days, a return to which would also be reinforcing. The extent to which this process is used in art varies from period to period but is always considerable. It is not to be identified with realism or naturalism since the responses appropriate to the effect of pure design are also largely dependent upon experience. We shall return later to other practical applications of conditioned seeing, hearing, and so on. In evaluating the effect of a given culture it is important to note the extent to which conditioned responses of this sort are set up and the extent to which discriminative responses of self-knowledge are established with respect to them.

OPERANT SEEING

There are many ways of showing that the discriminative operant "seeing X" is strong. One kind of evidence is the strength of precurrent behavior which makes seeing X possible. This may be nothing more than the behavior of looking at X, which the individual may engage in at every opportunity or for long periods of time. Another sort of precurrent behavior is *looking for* X—looking about in ways which in the past have led to seeing X. Suppose we strongly reinforce a person when he finds a four-leaf clover. The increased strength of "seeing a four-leaf clover" will be evident in many ways. The person will be more inclined to look at four-leaf clovers than before. He will look in places where he has found four-leaf clovers. Stimuli which resemble four-leaf clovers will evoke an immediate response. Under slightly ambiguous circumstances he will mistakenly reach for a three-leaf clover. If our reinforcement is effective enough, he may even see four-leaf clovers in ambiguous patterns in textiles, wallpaper, and so on. He may also "see four-leaf clovers" when there is no similar visual stimulation—for example, when his eyes are closed or when he is in a dark room. If he has acquired an adequate vocabulary for self-description, he may report this by saying that four-leaf clovers "flash into his mind" or that he "is thinking about" four-leaf clovers.

We frequently observe strong behavior without knowing much about the circumstances which account for its strength. Consider, for example, a person who is interested in dogs. One characteristic of such a person is that the response "seeing dogs" is especially strong. He looks at dogs at every opportunity and engages in behavior which makes it possible to do so—for example, he visits kennels and dog shows. He arranges stimuli which resemble dogs—he hangs pictures of dogs on his walls, puts statues of dogs on his desk, and buys books containing pictures of dogs. If he is an artist, photographer, or sculptor, he may create similar pictures or statues himself. But the presence of a dog or of a reasonable facsimile is not essential. Conditioned stimuli which have accompanied dogs—leashes, feeding equipment, and so on—easily "remind him of dogs." Certain verbal stimuli—for example, stories or descriptions of dogs—lead him to "picture dogs to himself," and he may obtain or even compose such stimuli. The same strength is manifested when he sees dogs while looking at ink blots, cloud formations, or other ambiguous patterns, or when he mistakes some indistinctly seen object for a dog. The behavior of seeing dogs also takes place in the absence of any identifiable external support. He "thinks about dogs," daydreams of dogs, and perhaps even dreams of dogs at night.

Unlike conditioned seeing in the respondent pattern, such behavior is not elicited by current stimuli and does not depend upon the previous pairing of stimuli. The primary controlling variables are operant reinforcement and deprivation. When we make a man hungry, we strengthen practical responses which have in the past been reinforced with food. We also strengthen artistic or verbal responses which produce pictures of food, or generate conditioned stimuli which are effective because they have accompanied food— the individual draws pictures of food or talks about delicious meals he has eaten. At the same time we induce him to "think of food," to daydream of food, or to dream of food. Similarly, it is characteristic of men under strong sexual deprivation, not only that they indulge in sexual behavior as soon as an occasion presents itself or concern themselves with the production or enjoyment of sexual art or engage in sexual self-stimulation, but that they also see sexual objects or activities in the absence of relevant stimuli. That all these forms of activity are traceable to a common variable is shown by eliminating the deprivation, whereupon we eliminate all forms of the behavior.

A discriminative response which can be made when the appropriate stimulus is absent has certain advantages. It does not require the sometimes troublesome precurrent behavior which generates an external stimulus, and it can occur when such behavior is impossible— as when we daydream of a lost love or an opportunity which is wholly out of the question. Also, the private response is not punished by society, even though the overt form may be. There are, however, certain disadvantages. Such behavior does not alter the state of deprivation. The fantasies of the hungry or sexually deprived man do not alter the situation in such a way as to reduce the strength of the behavior through satiation. We often appeal to a reduction in deprivation to account for the effectiveness of a reinforcement, but, as we saw in Chapter V, the relation explains only why such stimuli are currently reinforcing in a given species. The reinforcing effect is carried by private as well as public stimuli. To one who is interested in dogs, simply seeing dogs is automatically reinforcing. The hungry or sexually deprived man is reinforced by the appearance or presence of relevant objects, as well as by seeing them when they are absent. Such reinforcement is not dependent upon an actual reduction in the state of deprivation.

Operant seeing at the private level may be reinforced in other ways. The private response may produce discriminative stimuli which prove useful in executing further behavior of either a private or public nature. In the following problem, for example, behavior is usually facilitated by private seeing. "Think of a cube, all six surfaces of which are painted red. Divide the cube into twenty-seven equal cubes by making two horizontal cuts and two sets of two vertical cuts each. How many of the resulting cubes will have three faces painted red, how many two, how many one, and how many none?" It is possible to solve this without seeing the cubes in any sense— as by saying to oneself, "A cube has eight corners. A corner is defined as the intersection of three faces of the cube. There will therefore be eight pieces with three painted faces. . . ." And so on. But the solution is easier if one can actually see the twenty-seven small cubes and count those of each kind. This is easiest in the presence of actual cubes, of course, and even a sketchy drawing will provide useful support; but many people solve the problem visually without visual stimulation.

Private problem-solving usually consists of a mixture of discriminative and manipulative responses. In this example one may *see* the larger cube, *cut it* covertly, *separate* the smaller cubes covertly, *see* their faces, *count* them subvocally, and so on. In mental arithmetic one multiplies, divides, transposes, and so on, seeing the result in each case, until a solution is reached. Presumably much of this covert behavior is similar in form to the overt manipulation of pencil and paper; the rest is discriminative behavior in the form of seeing numbers, letters, signs, and so on, which is similar to the behavior which would result from overt manipulation.

There are great individual differences in the extent to which private seeing is used. Few people can equal the performance of one of Galton's correspondents who could multiply by visualizing the appropriate section of a slide rule, setting it at the appropriate position, and reading off the answer. As in conditioned seeing, such differences may be traced either to differences in the extent to which private seeing has been established or to differences in the ability to describe the resulting self-stimulation or use it as a basis for further behavior.

There are also differences in the kind of private event preferred. In solving a chess problem, one may have an idea, in the sense of Chapter XVI, in several ways. The solution may come as the overt response of moving a piece. It may come in overt verbal form ("Move the knight to bishop seven") or in the same form covertly. It may also come as covert nonverbal behavior, although it is admittedly hard to determine the dimensions of such a response. We commonly say, "I said to myself, 'Move the knight,'" but we have no comparable idiom of the form, "I moved the knight *to myself*." The solution may also come in the form of a discriminative reaction: we may suddenly see the knight in its new position.

Even when covert behavior is mainly verbal, other types of private responding frequently occur. Some writers report that they first *hear* sentences, which they then record just as they would record the speech of another person. Others execute sentences subvocally in an obviously muscular form. There are instances in which, particularly in dreams, a writer first *reads* a poem or story, which he then transcribes. The poet deals primarily in verbal behavior, but he may be a "seer" who resorts to words only to describe what he has seen, just as he would describe a public event.

Similar differences arise when there is some measure of external stimulation. In the Verbal Summator experiment, for example, some subjects, listening to faint speech patterns, hear the *phonograph* saying something. Others find *themselves* saying something, in which case they may also, of course, "hear" their own verbal behavior. There is commonly no parallel in the nonverbal projective tests. In the Rorschach Test, the effect of the ink blot is primarily to supplement a visual discriminative response. What is revealed is the strength of seeing X, not of saying "X." The verbal report is usually a response to the discriminative visual response.

The verbal repertoire which describes private events may fail to distinguish between these cases. If we ask someone to think of the

number seven and he reports that he has done so, he may be reporting a discriminative response in which he has seen the form 7 or
the word "seven," or some spatial arrangement of seven spots, seven
subdivisions of a line, and so on. But the same report may describe
the fact that he has said "seven" to himself or has drawn the form 7
covertly. In this case the report may also include the fact that he has
heard himself saying "seven" or has seen the result of the nonverbal
response. It is possible that more than one, or even all, of these
activities may occur when one "thinks of the number seven." The
community does not insist upon a distinction among them because a
distinction is usually of little importance. Usually the variables which
strengthen the discriminative response of seeing an object are also
those which strengthen the covert or overt responses which produce
the object. If hearing X is strong, saying X will probably be strong
also, since saying X is a precurrent response which makes hearing X
possible. This is obvious but none the less important. It is often
reinforcing to hear oneself praised. A simple expedient is, therefore,
to praise oneself. Boasting is, so to speak, reinforced by the praise
which one hears. Under the same conditions of motivation one may
also demonstrate a high probability of hearing praise—for example,
one may simply listen closely when one is being praised, or interpret
an overheard flattering remark as applying to oneself, or misinter-
pret a neutral remark as praise.

Private discriminative responses are also reinforced by their effect
in self-control. With the exception of physical restraint all the variables which one may manipulate in self-control are available at the
private level (Chapter XV). One may generate an emotional response
by recounting an emotional event or by simply seeing or hearing it.
One may generate an aversive condition through a verbal description
of punishment or through seeing or hearing the punishment again.

TRADITIONAL TREATMENT
OF THE PROBLEM

We account for verbal behavior which describes the discriminative
response of seeing X in the following way. Such behavior is acquired
when the organism is not only in the presence of X but actually

making a discriminative response to X. A similar discriminative response may come to occur in the absence of X as the result of respondent or operant conditioning. The verbal response which describes the discriminative response is not inevitable, but whenever it occurs, the same variables may be assumed to be active. We have not altered the inaccessibility of the private event by this treatment, but we have succeeded in bringing the behavior which describes the event under some sort of functional control.

This is not, of course, the traditional solution to the problem of private seeing. It is usually held that one does not see the physical world at all, but only a nonphysical copy of it called "experience." When the physical organism is in contact with reality, the experienced copy is called a "sensation," "sense datum," or "percept"; when there is no contact, it is called an "image," "thought," or "idea." Sensations, images, and their congeries are characteristically regarded as psychic or mental events, occurring in a special world of "consciousness" where, although they occupy no space, they can nevertheless often be seen. We cannot now say with any certainty why this troublesome distinction was first made, but it may have been an attempt to solve certain problems which are worth reviewing.

There are often many ways in which a single event may stimulate an organism. Rain is something we see outside our window or hear on the roof or feel against our face. Which form of stimulation *is* rain? It must have been difficult to suppose that any one discriminative response could identify a physical event. Hence it may have been tempting to say that it identified a transient but unitary sensation or perception of the event. Eventually the least equivocal form—stimulation through contact with the skin—became most closely identified with reality. A form vaguely seen in a darkened room was not "really there" until one could touch it. But this was not a wholly satisfactory solution. Stimulation arising from contact may not agree perfectly with that arising visually or audibly, and we may not be willing to identify one form with reality to the exclusion of the others. There still are psychologists, however, who argue for the priority of one form of stimulation and, hence, insist upon a distinction between experience and reality. They are surprised to find that "things are not what they seem" and that a room which looks square from a given angle may be found upon tactual or visual exploration to be askew. This difficulty offers no particular problem here. It is obvious that a single event may stimulate an organism in many ways, depending upon the construction of the organism and its capacity to be stimulated by different forms of energy. We are much less inclined today to ask which form of energy *is* the thing itself or correctly represents it.

Another problem which the distinction between physical and non-physical worlds may have been an attempt to solve arises from the fact that more than one kind of response may be made to stimulation arising from a physical event. Rain is something you may run to escape from, catch in your hands to drink, prepare crops to receive, or call "rain." Which response is made to "rain in itself"? The solution was to construct a passive comprehension of rain, which was supposed to have nothing to do with practical responses. So far as we are concerned here, the problem is disposed of by recognizing that many verbal and nonverbal responses may come under the control of a given form of stimulation. With the possible exception of the abstract verbal response, no behavior need be singled out as "knowing rain."

The process of abstraction raises another difficulty from which the concept of experience may have provided escape. We saw in Chapter VIII that the referent or meaning of the response "rain" could not be identified by examining a single occasion upon which the response was made. Certain properties of a *class* of stimuli control such a response, and they can be revealed only by a systematic investigation of many instances. Upon any given occasion, the response appears to be relatively free of the exigencies of the physical world and to deal with a single dimension abstracted from it. The fact that the process of abstraction appears to generate a world composed of general properties, rather than of particular events, has led, however, to inconsistent interpretations. On the one hand the particular event has been regarded as immediate experience, while the process of abstraction has been said to *construct* a physical world which is never directly experienced. On the other hand the single occasion has been viewed as a momentary unanalyzed contact with reality, while systematic knowledge of the world has been identified with experience.

Still another difficulty which must have encouraged the distinction between two worlds was the inadequacy of early physical science. How could the individual make contact with a world which lay well beyond his skin? It was some comfort to suppose that one never knew more than one's own experience, which could be conceived of as existing within one's body. And if one never sees the real world but only an imaginal copy of it, then it is not difficult to account for instances in which the something seen is not there in the real world at all. We have only to assume that experience is independent of reality. To say that one sees the sensation of a thing when the thing itself is far away appears to solve the problem of the location of what is seen. To say that one sees an image of the thing when the thing itself is absent appears to solve the problem of the existence of what is seen. But the solutions are spurious. One still has to explain how the distant thing can generate the sensation or how an image can occur when the thing is not present. Modern physical science solved the first of these problems by bridging the gap between the distant object and the organism. A study of behavior solved the second by pointing to variables which lead the organism to see X in the absence of X.

Objections to the traditional view. There is scarcely any need to point out the disadvantages of terms which refer to supposed non-physical events. Even if it were possible to define "sensation" and "image" in dimensions acceptable in a natural science, they would appear as intervening concepts comparable to "drive," "habit," "instinct," and so on, and would be subject to the criticism of such concepts presented in Section II. As usual the fictional explanation has offered unwarranted consolation in the face of difficult problems. By suggesting a type of causal event the practice has discouraged the search for useful variables. Contrary to the usual view, the special contact between the individual and the events which occur within his own body does not provide him with "inside information" about the causes of his behavior. Because of his preferred position with respect to his own *history*, he may have special information about his readiness to respond, about the relation of his behavior to controlling variables, and about the history of these variables. Although this information is sometimes erroneous and, as we shall see in Chapter XVIII, may even be lacking, it is sometimes useful in a science of behavior. But the private event is at best no more than a link in a causal chain, and it is usually not even that. We may think before we act in the sense that we may behave covertly before we behave overtly, but our action is not an "expression" of the covert response or the consequence of it. The two are attributable to the same variables.

A recent book on abnormal behavior contains the sentence, "A system of emancipated ideas temporarily seizes control of behavior." The facts are as well described by saying, "A system of responses is temporarily prepotent." In either case we have still to ask, "Why?" Even though something which may properly be called an idea precedes the behavior in a causal chain, we must go back farther than the idea to find the relevant variables. If the individual himself reports, "I have had the idea for some time but have only just recently acted upon it," he is describing a covert response which preceded the overt. Since someone who reports "having an idea" is likely to be someone who will execute the overt form, we may find the report of an idea helpful. But the report does not complete a functional account. As we saw in Chapter X, to say that a man strikes another because he feels angry still leaves the feeling of anger unexplained. When we have once identified the relevant variables, we find the feeling of anger much less important by way of explanation. Similarly, it has often been argued that the conditioned reflex is inadequate because it omits mention of a link traditionally described as the "association of ideas." To report that a man salivates when he hears the dinner bell may be to overlook the fact that the dinner bell first "makes him think of dinner" and that he then salivates *because* he thinks of dinner. But there is no evidence that thinking of dinner, as that expression has been defined here, is more than a collateral effect of the bell and the conditioning process. We cannot demonstrate that thinking of dinner will lead to salivation regardless of any prior event, since a man will not think of dinner in the absence of such an event.

One is still free, of course, to assume that there are events of a nonphysical nature accessible only to the experiencing organism and therefore wholly private. Science does not always follow the principle of Occam's razor, because the simplest explanation is in the long run not always the most expedient. But our analysis of verbal behavior which describes private events is not wholly a matter of taste or preference. We cannot avoid the responsibility of showing how a private event can ever come to be described by the individual or, in the same sense, be known to him. Our survey of the ways in which a community may impart a subjective vocabulary did not reveal any means of setting up a discriminative response to *privacy as such*. A world of experience which is by definition available only to the individual, wholly without public accompaniment, could never become the discriminative occasion for self-description.

OTHER PROPOSED SOLUTIONS

Studying one's own private world. It is sometimes suggested that the psychologist can avoid the problem of privacy by limiting his study to his own private share of the universe. It is true that psychologists sometimes use themselves as subjects successfully, but only when they manipulate external variables precisely as they would in studying the behavior of someone else. The scientist's "observation" of a private event is a response to that event, or perhaps even a response to a response to it. In order to carry out the program of a functional analysis, he must have independent information about the event. This means he must respond to it in some other way. For a similar reason he cannot solve the problem of private events in the behavior of others by asking them to describe such events. It has often been proposed that an objective psychology may substitute the verbal report of a private event for the event itself. But a verbal report is a response of the organism; it is part of the behavior which a science must analyze. The analysis must include an independent treatment of the events of which the report is a function. The report itself is only half the story.

The physiology of sensation. The solution which follows from a functional analysis of behavior is to be distinguished from two others which are currently proposed within the framework of a natural science. One of these is closely identified with the study of the physiology of receptors in the nervous system, the other with a logical or "operational" analysis of the data of sensation and perception. Such concepts as "sensation" and "image" are designed to carry the pattern of the environment into the organism as far as possible and thus to bridge the gap between the knower and the known. The task of bringing the world to the surface of the organism is properly within the scope of physics. Beyond this point it is within the field of psychophysiology. The modern counterpart of the study of mental events in a world of consciousness is the study of the action of receptors and of the afferent and central nervous systems. The rainbow in the sky or some correlated pattern of energy is brought to the outer surface of the eye, then to the retina, then to the optic tract, and eventually to certain parts of the brain—preferably with as little distortion as possible. This makes it more plausible to say that the organism directly experiences the principal features of the rainbow. It is even tempting to suppose that at some stage (presumably the last) the pattern in the brain *is* the sensation or image. But seeing is a *response* to a stimulus rather than a mere camera-like registering. In carrying the pattern of the rainbow into the organism, almost no progress is made toward understanding the behavior of *seeing* the rainbow. It is of little moment whether the individual sees the actual rainbow or the sensation of a rainbow or some terminal neural pattern in the brain. At some point he must *see*, and this is more than recording a similar pattern. Apart from the mode of action of receptors and other organs, the physiology of sensation is concerned with the question of *what* is seen. The question may be a spurious one arising from an idiom or figure of speech. If we say that the rainbow (either as an objective event in the environment or as a corresponding pattern within the organism) is not "what is seen" but simply the commonest variable which controls the behavior of seeing, we are much less likely to be surprised when the behavior occurs as a function of other variables.

Operational definitions of sensation and image. Another proposed solution to the problem of privacy argues that there are public and private events and that the latter have no place in science because science requires agreement by the members of a community. Far from avoiding the traditional distinction between mind and matter, or between experience and reality, this view actually encourages it. It assumes that there is, in fact, a subjective world, which it places beyond the reach of science. On this assumption the only business of a science of sensation is to examine the public events which may be studied in lieu of the private.

The present analysis has a very different consequence. It continues to deal with the private event, even if only as an inference. It does not substitute the verbal report from which the inference is made for the event itself. The verbal report is a response to the private event and may be used as a source of information about it. A critical analysis of the validity of this practice is of first importance. But we may avoid the dubious conclusion that, so far as science is concerned, the verbal report or some other discriminative response *is* the sensation.

The private made public. One other way of attacking the problem within the framework of a natural science is compatible with the present analysis. The line between public and private is not fixed. The boundary shifts with every discovery of a technique for making private events public. Behavior which is of such small magnitude that it is not ordinarily observed may be amplified. Covert verbal behavior may be detected in slight movements of the speech apparatus. Deaf-mutes who speak with their fingers behave covertly with their fingers, and the movements may be suitably amplified. There is no reason why covert behavior could not be amplified so that the individual himself could make use of the additional information—for example, in creative thinking. After all, this is only what the individual does when he thinks publicly by scratching notes on paper or by manipulating an artistic medium. The problem of privacy may, therefore, eventually be solved by technical advances. But we are still faced with events which occur at the private level and which are important to the organism without instrumental amplification. How the organism reacts to these events will remain an important question, even though the events may some day be made accessible to everyone.

CHAPTER XVIII

THE SELF

What is meant by the "self" in self-control or self-knowledge? When a man jams his hands into his pockets to keep himself from biting his nails, *who* is controlling *whom*? When he discovers that a sudden mood must be due to a glimpse of an unpleasant person, *who* discovers *whose* mood to be due to *whose* visual response? Is the self which works to facilitate the recall of a name the same as the self which recalls it? When a thinker teases out an idea, is it the teaser who also eventually has the idea?

The self is most commonly used as a hypothetical cause of action. So long as external variables go unnoticed or are ignored, their function is assigned to an originating agent within the organism. If we cannot show what is responsible for a man's behavior, we say that he himself is responsible for it. The precursors of physical science once followed the same practice, but the wind is no longer blown by Aeolus, nor is the rain cast down by Jupiter Pluvius. Perhaps it is because the notion of personification is so close to a conception of a behaving individual that it has been difficult to dispense with similar explanations of behavior. The practice resolves our anxiety with respect to unexplained phenomena and is perpetuated because it does so.

Whatever the self may be, it is apparently not identical with the physical organism. The organism behaves, while the self initiates or directs behavior. Moreover, more than one self is needed to explain the behavior of one organism. A mere inconsistency in conduct from one moment to the next is perhaps no problem, for a single self could dictate different kinds of behavior from time to time. But there appear to be two selves acting simultaneously and in different ways when one self controls another or is aware of the activity of another.

The same facts are commonly expressed in terms of "personalities." The personality, like the self, is said to be responsible for features of behavior. For example, delinquent behavior is sometimes attributed to a psychopathic personality. Personalities may also be multiple. Two or more personalities may appear in alternation or concurrently. They are often in conflict with each other, and one may or may not be aware of what the other is doing.

Multiple selves or personalities are often said to be systematically related to each other. Freud conceived of the ego, superego, and id as distinguishable agents within the organism. The id was responsible for behavior which was ultimately reinforced with food, water, sexual contact, and other primary biological reinforcers. It was not unlike the selfish, aggressive "Old Adam" of Judeo-Christian theology, preoccupied with the basic deprivations and untouched by similar requirements on the parts of others. The superego—the "conscience" of Judeo-Christian theology—was responsible for the behavior which controlled the id. It used techniques of self-control acquired from the group. When these were verbal, they constituted "the still small voice of conscience." The superego and the id were inevitably opposed to each other, and Freud conceived of them as often in violent conflict. He appealed to a third agent—the ego—which, besides attempting to reach a compromise between the id and the superego, also dealt with the practical exigencies of the environment.

We may quarrel with any analysis which appeals to a self or personality as an inner determiner of action, but the facts which have been represented with such devices cannot be ignored. The three selves or personalities in the Freudian scheme represent important characteristics of behavior in a social milieu. Multiple personalities which are less systematically related to each other serve a similar function. A concept of self is not essential in an analysis of behavior, but what is the alternative way of treating the data?

THE SELF AS AN ORGANIZED SYSTEM OF RESPONSES

The best way to dispose of any explanatory fiction is to examine the facts upon which it is based. These usually prove to be, or suggest, variables which are acceptable from the point of view of scientific method. In the present case it appears that a self is simply a device for representing *a functionally unified system of responses.* In dealing with the data, we have to explain the functional unity of such systems and the various relationships which exist among them.

The unity of a self. A self may refer to a common *mode of action.* Such expressions as "The scholar is Man Thinking" or "He was a better talker than plumber" suggest personalities identified with *topographical subdivisions* of behavior. In a single skin we find the man of action and the dreamer, the solitary and the social spirit.

On the other hand, a personality may be tied to a particular type of occasion—when a system of responses is organized around a given *discriminative stimulus.* Types of behavior which are effective in achieving reinforcement upon occasion A are held together and distinguished from those effective upon occasion B. Thus one's personality in the bosom of one's family may be quite different from that in the presence of intimate friends.

Responses which lead to a common reinforcement, regardless of the situation, may also comprise a functional system. Here the principal variable is *deprivation.* A motion to adjourn a meeting which has run through the lunch hour may show "the hungry man speaking." One's personality may be very different before and after a satisfying meal. The libertine is very different from the ascetic who achieves his reinforcement from the ethical group, but the two may exist side by side in the same organism.

Emotional variables also establish personalities. Under the proper circumstances the timid soul may give way to the aggressive man.

The hero may struggle to conceal the coward who inhabits the same skin.

The effects of *drugs* upon personality are well known. The euphoria of the morphine addict represents a special repertoire of responses the strength of which is attributable to an obvious variable. The alcoholic wakes on the morrow a sadder and wiser man.

It is easy to overestimate the unity of a group of responses, and unfortunately personification encourages us to do so. The concept of a self may have an early advantage in representing a relatively coherent response system, but it may lead us to expect consistencies and functional integrities which do not exist. The alternative to the use of the concept is simply to deal with demonstrated covariations in the strength of responses.

Relations among selves. Organized systems of responses may be related to each other in the same way as are single responses and for the same reasons (Chapters XIV, XV, XVI). For example, two response systems may be incompatible. If the relevant variables are never present at the same time, the incompatibility is unimportant. If the environment of which behavior is a function is not consistent from moment to moment, there is no reason to expect consistency in behavior. The pious churchgoer on Sunday may become an aggressive, unscrupulous businessman on Monday. He possesses two response systems appropriate to different sets of circumstances, and his inconsistency is no greater than that of the environment which takes him to church on Sunday and to work on Monday. But the controlling variables may come together; during a sermon, the churchgoer may be asked to examine his business practices, or the businessman may engage in commercial transactions with his clergyman or his church. Trouble may then arise. Similarly, if an individual has developed different repertoires with family and friends, the two personalities come into conflict when he is with both at the same time. Many of the dramatic struggles which flood the literature on multiple personalities can be accounted for in the same way.

More systematic relations among personalities arise from the controlling relations discussed in Chapters XV and XVI. In self-control, for example, the responses to be controlled are organized around certain immediate primary reinforcements. To the extent that competition for reinforcement makes this behavior aversive to others—and to this extent only—we may refer to an anti-social personality, the id or Old Adam. On the other hand, the controlling behavior engendered by the community consists of a selected group of practices evolved in the history of a particular culture because of their effect upon anti-social behavior. To the extent that this behavior works to the advantage of the community—and again to this extent only—we may speak of a unitary conscience, social conscience, or superego. These two sets of variables account, not only for the membership of each group of responses, but for the relation between them which we describe when we say that one personality is engaged in controlling the other. Other kinds of relations between personalities are evident in the processes of making a decision, solving a problem, or creating a work of art.

An important relation between selves is the self-knowledge of Chapter XVII. The behavior which we call knowing is due to a particular kind of differential reinforcement. In even the most rudimentary community such questions as "What did you do?" or "What are you doing?" compel the individual to respond to his own overt behavior. Probably no one is completely unselfconscious in this sense. At the other extreme an advanced and relatively nonpractical society produces the highly introspective or introverted individual, whose repertoire of self-knowledge extends to his covert behavior—a repertoire which in some cultures may be almost nonexistent. An extensive development of self-knowledge is common in certain Eastern cultures and is emphasized from time to time in those of the West—for example, in the *culte du moi* of French literature. An efficient repertoire of this sort is sometimes set up in the individual for purposes of therapy. The patient under psychoanalysis may become highly skilled in observing his own covert behavior.

When an occasion arises upon which a report of the organism's own behavior, particularly at the covert level, is likely to be reinforced, the personality which makes the report is a specialist trained by a special set of contingencies. The self which is concerned with self-knowing functions concurrently with the behavioral system which it describes. But it is sometimes important to ask whether the selves generated by other contingencies "know about each other." The literature on multiple personalities raises the question as one of "continuity of memory." It is also an important consideration in the Freudian scheme: to what extent, for example, is the superego aware of the behavior of the id? The contingencies which set up the superego as a controlling system involve stimulation from the behavior of the id, but they do not necessarily establish responses of knowing about the behavior of the id. It is perhaps even less likely that the id will know about the superego. The ego can scarcely deal with conflicts between the other selves without responding to the behavior attributed to them, but this does not mean that the ego possesses a repertoire of knowing about such behavior in any other sense.

THE ABSENCE OF SELF-KNOWLEDGE

One of the most striking facts about self-knowledge is that it may be lacking. Several cases deserve comment.

A man may not know that *he has done something*. He may have behaved in a given way, perhaps energetically, and nevertheless be unable to describe what he has done. Examples range all the way from the unnoticed verbal slip to extended amnesias in which large areas of earlier behavior cannot be described by the individual himself. The possibility that the behavior which cannot be described may be covert raises an interesting theoretical problem, since the existence of such behavior must be inferred, not only by the scientist, but by the individual himself. We have seen that a mathematician frequently cannot describe the process through which he solves a problem. Although he may report the preliminary stages of his investigation, his arrangement of materials, and many tentative solutions, he may not be able to describe the self-manipulation which presumably preceded the required response which he suddenly emits. It is not always necessary to infer that other behavior has actually occurred, but under certain circumstances this inference may be justified. Since authenticated overt behavior sometimes cannot be reported by the individual, we have no reason to question the possibility of a covert parallel.

A man may not know that *he is doing something*. Absent-minded conduct, unconscious mannerisms, and mechanically habitual behavior are common examples. More dramatic is automatic writing, in which behavior taking place at the moment cannot be described by the "rest of the organism."

A man may not know that *he tends to, or is going to, do something*. He may be unaware of aggressive tendencies, of unusual predilections, or of the high probability that he will follow a given course of action.

A man may not recognize *the variables of which his behavior is a function*. In the Verbal Summator, for example, the subject often supposes himself to be repeating a verbal stimulus when it is easy to identify variables lying elsewhere in his environment or history which account for the behavior (Chapter XIV). Projective tests are used for diagnostic purposes just because they reveal variables which the individual himself cannot identify.

These phenomena are often viewed with surprise. How can the individual fail to observe events which are so conspicuous and so important? But perhaps we should be surprised that such events are observed as often as they are. We have no reason to expect discriminative behavior of this sort unless it has been generated by suitable reinforcement. Self-knowledge is a special repertoire. The crucial thing is not whether the behavior which a man fails to report is actually observable by him, but whether he has ever been given any reason to observe it.

Self-knowledge may, nevertheless, be lacking where appropriate reinforcing circumstances have prevailed. Some instances may be dismissed without extended comment. For example, the stimuli supplied by behavior may be weak. One may be "unaware" of a facial expression because of the inadequacy of the accompanying self-stimulation. The subject in an experiment on muscle-reading may not be aware of the slight responses which the reader detects and uses in getting the subject to "tell" him the location of a hidden object. The functional relation between behavior and a relevant variable is especially likely to be of subtle physical dimensions. A face in the crowd may be clear enough as a stimulus to generate a mood, but the fact that it has done so may still not be noted. This does not mean that the stimuli are below threshold, for they may be brought into control in other ways. When we point out some part of the behavior of an individual, an occasion is established under which special reinforcement is accorded a discriminative reaction. The fact that the individual then responds to his behavior is what we mean by saying that he was "able to do so" in the first place.

Another case of "not knowing what one is doing" is explained by the principle of prepotency. In the heat of battle there may be no time to observe one's behavior, since strong responses conflict with the discriminative response. Self-knowledge may also be lacking in certain states of satiation and in sleep. One may talk in one's sleep or behave in other ways "without knowing it." Behavior under the influence of drugs—for example, alcohol—may also occur with a minimum of self-observation. The effect of alcohol in reducing the behavior of self-knowledge may be similar to that in reducing the response to the conditioned aversive stimuli characteristic of guilt or anxiety.

It has been argued that one cannot describe behavior after the fact which one could not have described at the time. This appears to explain our inability to recall the events of infancy, since the behavior of the infant occurs before a repertoire of self-description has been set up and therefore too soon to control such a repertoire. The same explanation should apply to behavior unnoticed in the heat of battle. However, it is possible that the rearousal of response on the pattern of the conditioned reflex may supply the basis for a description. In any case it is sometimes impossible to describe earlier behavior which could have been described, and perhaps was described, at the time it was emitted. An important reason why a description may be lacking has still to be considered.

Repression. We have seen that punishment makes the stimuli generated by punished behavior aversive. Any behavior which reduces that stimulation is subsequently reinforced automatically. Now, among the kinds of behavior most likely to generate conditioned aversive stimuli as the result of punishment is the behavior of *observing* the punished act or of observing the occasion for it or any tendency to execute it. As the result of punishment, not only do we engage in other behavior to the exclusion of punished forms, we engage in other behavior to the exclusion of *knowing about* punished behavior, in the sense of Chapter XVII. This may begin simply as "not liking to think about" behavior which has led to aversive consequences. It may then pass into the stage of not thinking about it and eventually reach the point at which the individual denies having behaved in a given way, in the face of proof to the contrary.

The result is commonly called repression. As we saw in Chapters XII and XIV, the individual may repress behavior simply in the sense of engaging in competing forms, but we must now extend the meaning of the term to include the repression of knowing about punished behavior. This is a much more dramatic result, to which the term "repression" is sometimes confined. The same formulation applies, however. We do not appeal to any special act of repression but rather to competing behavior which becomes extremely powerful because it avoids aversive stimulation.

It is not always knowledge of the form of a response which is repressed, because punishment is not always contingent upon form. Aggressive behavior, for example, is not punished in warfare. Imitative behavior is not often punished so long as it is actually under the control of similar behavior on the part of others. For example, when we emit obscene or blasphemous behavior in testifying to an instance of it on the part of someone else, our testimony may not be entirely free of conditioned aversive consequences, and we may avoid testifying if possible; but the aversive stimulation will be much less than that aroused by the same behavior when it is not imitative. In experiments with the Verbal Summator a subject will often emit aggressive, ungrammatical, obscene, or blasphemous responses so long as he remains convinced that he is correctly repeating speech patterns on a phonograph record. He has been told to repeat what he hears and punishment is not contingent upon the form of his behavior under these circumstances, especially if a few objectionable samples are first presented clearly. As soon as he is told that there are no comparable speech patterns on the record, however, this type of response usually becomes much less frequent. The individual must now, so to speak, take the responsibility for the aggression, obscenity, and so on. In other words, his behavior is now of a form and under a controlling relation upon which punishment is contingent. In such a case the subject will often refuse to acknowledge that earlier stimuli were not of the form he reported.

A variation on the repression of a controlling relationship is sometimes called "rationalization." The aversive report of a functional relation may be repressed by reporting a fictitious relationship. Instead of "refusing to recognize" the causes of our behavior, we invent acceptable causes. If an aggressive attack upon a child is due to emotional impulses of revenge, it is usually punished by society; but if it is emitted because of supposed consequences in shaping the behavior of the child in line with the interests of society, it goes unpunished. We may conceal the emotional causes of our aggressive behavior, either from ourselves or from others, by arguing that the child ought to learn what sort of effect he is having on people. We spank the child "for his own good." In the same way we may delight in carrying bad news to someone we dislike "because the sooner he knows it the better." It is not the aggressive response which is repressed, but the response of knowing about the aggressive tendency. The rationalization is the repressing response which is successful in avoiding the conditioned aversive stimulation generated by punishment.

SYMBOLS

In Chapter XIV, we saw that a group of responses strengthened by a common variable might not all have the same aversive consequences and that as a result of the principle of summation the response with the least aversive consequence would emerge. In more general terms, we may note that the property of a response which achieves reinforcement need not coincide with the property upon which punishment is based. A response may appear, therefore, which achieves reinforcement while avoiding punishment. For example, the visual stimulation of a nude figure may be reinforcing because of previous connection with powerful sexual reinforcement. But in many societies the behavior of looking at such figures is severely punished. Under special circumstances—as, for example, in an art museum—it is possible to engage in this behavior and escape punishment. The behavior of the artist may show a similar compromise. His art must not be pornographic or too sensual, but while staying within certain limits which avoid punishment, it may nevertheless be successfully reinforcing for biological reasons. In fantasy the individual makes a similar compromise between seeing certain objects or patterns and avoiding aversive stimulation: he daydreams in a given area but in such a way that he does not generate too much guilt.

A symbol, as the term was used by Freud in the analysis of dreams and art, is any temporal or spatial pattern which is reinforcing because of similarity to another pattern but escapes punishment because of differences. Thus an abstract sculpture is symbolic of the human form if it is reinforcing because of resemblances and if the artist would, in the absence of punishment, have emphasized the resemblances. A musical composition symbolizes sexual behavior if it is reinforcing because of a similarity in temporal pattern and if it is emitted in place of such behavior because it is different enough to escape punishment.

The principal realm of the symbol is the dream which occurs when we are asleep. This is a species of private event which is extremely difficult to study and is, therefore, the subject of much conflicting discussion. In a dream the individual engages in private discriminative behavior, in the sense of Chapter XVII. He sees, hears, feels, and so on, in the absence of the usual stimuli. Controlling variables may sometimes be discovered in the immediate environment or in the recent history of the individual. In the perseverative dream, for example, one may dream of driving a car if one has been driving for many hours. More often, however, the relevant variables are harder to identify. The attempt to do so is commonly called the interpretation of dreams. Freud could demonstrate certain plausible relations between dreams and variables in the life of the individual. The present analysis is in essential agreement with his interpretation. The individual is strongly disposed to engage in behavior which achieves such reinforcements as sexual contact or the infliction of damage upon others. These kinds of behavior, however, are precisely the sort most likely to be punished. As a result the individual not only does not overtly engage in such behavior, he cannot engage in it covertly or see himself engaging in it covertly without automatic aversive self-stimulation. In the symbolic dream and in artistic or literary behavior, however, he may engage in discriminative behavior which is strengthened through stimulus- or response-induction by the same variables but which is not liable to punishment. It is often said or implied that some skillful agent engages in a sort of "dream-work" to produce this result, but the result follows automatically from the discrepancy between the properties of behavior upon which reinforcement and punishment are contingent.

THE BEHAVIOR OF
PEOPLE IN GROUPS

CHAPTER XIX

SOCIAL BEHAVIOR

Social behavior may be defined as the behavior of two or more people with respect to one another or in concert with respect to a common environment. It is often argued that this is different from individual behavior and that there are "social situations" and "social forces" which cannot be described in the language of natural science. A special discipline called "social science" is said to be required because of this apparent break in the continuity of nature. There are, of course, many facts—concerning governments, wars, migrations, economic conditions, cultural practices, and so on—which would never present themselves for study if people did not gather together and behave in groups, but whether the basic data are fundamentally different is still a question. We are interested here in the methods of the natural sciences as we see them at work in physics, chemistry, and biology, and as we have so far applied them in the field of behavior. How far will they carry us in the study of the behavior of groups?

Many generalizations at the level of the group need not refer to behavior at all. There is an old law in economics, called Gresham's Law, which states that bad money drives good money out of circulation. If we can agree as to what money is, whether it is good or bad, and when it is in circulation, we can express this general principle without making specific reference to the use of money by individuals. Similar generalizations are found in sociology, cultural anthropology, linguistics, and history. But a "social law" must be generated by the behavior of individuals. It is always an individual who behaves, and he behaves with the same body and according to the same processes as in a nonsocial situation. If an individual possessing two pieces of money, one good and one bad, tends to spend the bad and save the good—a tendency which may be explained in terms of reinforcing contingencies—and if this is true of a large number of people, the phenomenon described by Gresham's Law arises. The individual behavior explains the group phenomenon. Many economists feel the need for some such explanation of all economic law, although there are others who would accept the higher level of description as valid in its own right.

We are concerned here simply with the extent to which an analysis of the behavior of the individual which has received substantial validation under the favorable conditions of a natural science may contribute to the understanding of social phenomena. To apply our analysis to the phenomena of the group is an excellent way to test its adequacy, and if we are able to account for the behavior of people in groups without using any new term or presupposing any new process or principle, we shall have revealed a promising simplicity in the data. This does not mean that the social sciences will then inevitably state their generalizations in terms of individual behavior, since another level of description may also be valid and may well be more convenient.

THE SOCIAL ENVIRONMENT

Social behavior arises because one organism is important to another as part of its environment. A first step, therefore, is an analysis of the social environment and of any special features it may possess.

Social reinforcement. Many reinforcements require the presence of other people. In some of these, as in certain forms of sexual and pugilistic behavior, the other person participates merely as an object. We cannot describe the reinforcement without referring to another organism. But social reinforcement is usually a matter of personal mediation. When a mother feeds her child, the food, as a primary reinforcer, is not social, but the mother's behavior in presenting it is. The difference is slight—as one may see by comparing breast-feeding with bottle-feeding. Verbal behavior always involves social reinforcement and derives its characteristic properties from this fact. The response, "A glass of water, please," has no effect upon the mechanical environment, but in an appropriate verbal environment it may lead to primary reinforcement. In the field of social behavior special emphasis is laid upon reinforcement with attention, approval, affection, and submission. These important generalized reinforcers are social because the process of generalization usually requires the mediation of another organism. Negative reinforcement—particularly as a form of punishment—is most often administered by others in the form of unconditioned aversive stimulation or of disapproval, contempt, ridicule, insult, and so on.

Behavior reinforced through the mediation of other people will differ in many ways from behavior reinforced by the mechanical environment. Social reinforcement varies from moment to moment, depending upon the condition of the reinforcing agent. Different responses may therefore achieve the same effect, and one response may achieve different effects, depending upon the occasion. As a result, social behavior is more extensive than comparable behavior in a nonsocial environment. It is also more flexible, in the sense that the organism may shift more readily from one response to another when its behavior is not effective.

Since the reinforcing organism often may not respond appropriately, reinforcement is likely to be intermittent. The result will depend upon the schedule. An occasional success may fit the pattern of *variable-interval* reinforcement, and the behavior will show a stable intermediate strength. We might express this by saying that we respond to people with less confidence than we respond to the inanimate environment but are not so quickly convinced that the reinforcing mechanism is "out of order." The persistent behavior which we call teasing is generated by a *variable-ratio* schedule, which arises from the fact that the reinforcer responds only when a request has been repeated until it becomes aversive—when it acquires nuisance value.

The contingency established by a social reinforcing system may slowly change. In teasing, for example, the mean ratio of unreinforced to reinforced responses may rise. The child who has gained attention with three requests on the average may later find it necessary to make five, then seven, and so on. The change corresponds to an increasing tolerance for aversive stimulation in the reinforcing person. Contingencies of positive reinforcement may also drift in the same direction. When a reinforcing person becomes harder and harder to please, the reinforcement is made contingent upon more extensive or highly differentiated behavior. By beginning with reasonable specifications and gradually increasing the requirements, very demanding contingencies may be made effective which would be quite powerless without this history. The result is often a sort of human bondage. The process is easily demonstrated in animal experimentation where extremely energetic, persistent, or complicated responses which would otherwise be quite impossible may be established through a gradual change in contingencies. A special case arises in the use of piecework pay. As production increases, and with it the wages received, the piecework scale may be changed so that more work is required per unit of reinforcement. The eventual result may be a much higher rate of production at only a slight increase in pay— a condition of reinforcement which could not have become effective except through some such gradual approach.

We have already noted another peculiarity of social reinforcement: the reinforcing system is seldom independent of the behavior reinforced. This is exemplified by the indulgent but ambitious parent who withholds reinforcement when his child is behaving energetically, either to demonstrate the child's ability or to make the most efficient use of available reinforcers, but who reinforces an early response when the child begins to show extinction. This is a sort of combined ratio-and-interval reinforcement. Educational reinforcements are in general of this sort. They are basically governed by ratio schedules, but they are not unaffected by the level of the behavior reinforced. As in piecework pay, more and more may be demanded for each reinforcement as performance improves, but remedial steps may be needed.

Schedules of reinforcement which adjust to the rate of the behavior reinforced do not often occur in inorganic nature. The reinforcing agent which modifies the contingency in terms of the behavior must be sensitive and complex. But a reinforcing system which is affected in this way may contain inherent defects which lead to unstable behavior. This may explain why the reinforcing contingencies of society cause undesirable behavior more often than those apparently comparable contingencies in inanimate nature.

The social stimulus. Another person is often an important source of stimulation. Since some properties of such stimuli appear to defy physical description, it has been tempting to assume that a special process of intuition or empathy is involved when we react to them. What, for example, are the physical dimensions of a smile? In everyday life we identify smiles with considerable accuracy and speed, but the scientist would find it a difficult task. He would have to select some identifying response in the individual under investigation—perhaps the verbal response, "That is a smile"—and then investigate all the facial expressions which evoked it. These expressions would be physical patterns and presumably susceptible to geometric analysis, but the number of different patterns to be tested would be very great. Moreover, there would be borderline instances where the stimulus control was defective or varied from moment to moment.

That the final identification of the stimulus pattern called a smile would be much more complicated and time-consuming than the identification of a smile in daily life does not mean that scientific observation neglects some important approach available to the layman. The difference is that the scientist must identify a stimulus with respect to the behavior of someone else. He cannot trust his own personal reaction. In studying an objective pattern as simple and as common to everyone as "triangle," the scientist may safely use his own identification of the pattern. But such a pattern as "smile" is another matter. A social stimulus, like any other stimulus, becomes important in controlling behavior because of the contingencies into which it enters. The facial expressions which we group together and call "smiles" are important because they are the occasions upon which certain kinds of social behavior receive certain kinds of reinforcement. Any unity in the stimulus class follows from these contingencies. But these are determined by the culture and by a particular history. Even in the behavior of a single individual there may be several groups of patterns all of which come to be called smiles if they all stand in the same relation to reinforcing contingencies. The scientist may appeal to his own culture or history only when it resembles that of the subject he is studying. Even then he may be wrong, just as the layman's quick practical reaction may be wrong, especially when he attempts to identify a smile in a different culture.

This issue is far reaching because it applies to many descriptive terms, such as "friendly" and "aggressive," without which many students of social behavior would feel lost. The nonscientist working within his own culture may satisfactorily describe the behavior of others with expressions of this sort. Certain patterns of behavior have become important to him because of the reinforcements based upon them: he judges behavior to be friendly or unfriendly by its social consequences. But his frequent success does not mean that there are objective aspects of behavior which are as independent of the behavior of the observer as are such geometrical forms as squares, circles, and triangles. He is observing an objective event—the behavior of an organism; there is no question here of physical status, but only of the significance of classificatory terms. The geometrical properties of "friendliness" or "aggressiveness" depend upon the culture, change with the culture, and vary with the individual's experience within a single culture.

Some social stimuli are also frequently set apart because a very slight physical event appears to have an extremely powerful effect. But this is true of many nonsocial stimuli as well; to one who has been injured in a fire a faint smell of smoke may be a stimulus of tremendous power. Social stimuli are important because the social reinforcers with which they are correlated are important. An example of the surprising power of an apparently trivial event is the common experience of "catching someone's eye." Under certain circumstances the change in behavior which follows may be considerable, and this has led to the belief that some nonphysical "understanding" passes from one person to another. But the reinforcing contingencies offer an alternative explanation. Our behavior may be very different in the presence or absence of a particular person. When we simply see such a person in a crowd, our available repertoire immediately changes. If, in addition, we catch his eye, we fall under the control of an even more restrictive stimulus—he is not only present, he is watching us. The same effect might arise without catching his eye if we saw him looking at us in a mirror. When we catch his eye, we also know that he knows that we are looking at him. A much narrower repertoire of behavior is under the control of this specific stimulus: if we are to behave in a way which he censures, it will now be not only in opposition to his wishes but brazen. It may also be important that "we know that he knows that we know that he is looking at us" and so on. (What is meant by "know" in these statements is in accord with the analysis in Chapters VIII and XVI.) In catching someone's eye, in short, a social stimulus suddenly arises which is important because of the reinforcements which depend upon it. The importance will vary with the occasion. We may catch someone's eye in a flirtation, under amusing circumstances, at a moment of common guilt, and so on— with an appropriate degree of control in each case. The importance of the event is seen in the use we make of the behavior of "looking someone in the eye" as a test of other variables responsible for such characteristics of behavior as honesty, brazenness, embarrassment, or guilt.

Social stimuli are important to those to whom social reinforcement is important. The salesman, the courtier, the entertainer, the seducer, the child striving for the favor of his parents, the "climber" advancing from one social level to another, the politically ambitious—all are likely to be affected by subtle properties of human behavior, associated with favor or disapproval, which are overlooked by many people. It is significant that the novelist, as a specialist in the description of human behavior, often shows an early history in which social reinforcement has been especially important.

The social stimulus which is least likely to vary from culture to culture is that which controls the imitative behavior described in Chapter VII. The ultimate consequences of imitative behavior may be peculiar to the culture, but the correspondence between the behavior of the imitator and that of the imitatee is relatively independent of it. Imitative behavior is not entirely free of style or convention, but the special features of the imitative repertoire characteristic of a group are slight. When a sizable repertoire has once been developed, imitation may be so skillful, so easy, so "instinctive," that we are likely to attribute it to some such special mode of interpersonal contact as empathy. It is easy to point to a history of reinforcement, however, which generates behavior of this sort.

THE SOCIAL EPISODE

We may analyze a social episode by considering one organism at a time. Among the variables to be considered are those generated by a second organism. We then consider the behavior of the second organism, assuming the first as a source of variables. By putting the analyses together we reconstruct the episode. The account is complete if it embraces all the variables needed to account for the behavior of the individuals. Consider, for example, the interaction between predator and prey called "stalking." We may limit ourselves to that behavior of the predator which reduces the distance between itself and its prey and that behavior of the prey which increases the distance. A reduction in the distance is positively reinforcing to the predator and negatively reinforcing to the prey; an increase is negatively reinforcing to the predator and positively reinforcing to the prey. If the predator is stimulated by the prey, but not vice versa, then the predator simply reduces the distance between itself and the prey as rapidly as possible. If the prey is stimulated by the predator, however, it will respond by increasing the distance. This need not be open flight, but simply any movement sufficient to keep the distance above a critical value. In the behavior called stalking the predator reduces the distance as rapidly as possible without stimulating the prey to increase it. When the distance has become short enough, the predator may break into open pursuit, and the prey into open flight. A different sort of interaction follows.

A similar formulation may be applied where "distance" is not so simple as in movement in space. In conversation, for example, one speaker may approach a topic from which another moves away uneasily. The first may be said to stalk the second if he approaches the topic in such a way as to avoid stimulating the second to escape. We eliminate the figure of speech in "approaching a topic" by analyzing the reinforcing and aversive properties of verbal stimuli.

Another example of a social episode is leading and following. This generally arises when two or more individuals are reinforced by a single external system which requires their combined action—for example, when two men pull on a rope which cannot be moved by either one alone. The behavior of one is similar to that of the other, and the interaction may be slight. If the timing is important, however, one man will pace the other. The first sets a rhythmic pattern relatively independent of the second; the second times his behavior by that of the first. The first may facilitate this by amplifying the stimuli which affect the second—as by saying, "All together now, one, two, three, *pull!*" Collateral behavior with a marked temporal pattern —for example, a sea chanty—may reduce the importance of the leader but will not eliminate it.

The nature of leading and following is clearer when the two kinds of behavior differ considerably and the contingency of reinforcement is complex. A division of labor is usually then required. The leader is primarily under the control of external variables, while the follower is under the control of the leader. A simple example is ballroom-dancing. The reinforcing consequences—both positive and negative —depend upon a double contingency: (1) the dancers must execute certain sequences of steps in certain directions with respect to the available space and (2) the behavior of one must be timed to correspond with that of the other. This double contingency is usually divided between the dancers. The leader sets the pattern and responds to the available space; the follower is controlled by the movements of the leader and responds appropriately to satisfy the second contingency.

It is easy to set up cooperative situations with two or more experimental organisms and to observe the emergence of leading and following. In a demonstration experiment two pigeons are placed in adjacent cages separated by a glass plate. Side by side near the glass are two vertical columns of three buttons each, one column being available to each pigeon. The apparatus is set to reinforce both pigeons with food but only when they peck corresponding buttons simultaneously. Only one pair of buttons is effective at any one time. The situation calls for a rather complicated cooperation. The pigeons must explore the three pairs to discover which is effective, and they must strike both buttons in each pair at the same time. These contingencies must be divided. One bird—the leader—explores the buttons, striking them in some characteristic order or more or less at random. The other bird—the follower—strikes the button opposite whichever button is being struck by the leader. The behavior of the follower is controlled almost exclusively by the behavior of the leader, whose behavior in turn is controlled by the apparatus which randomizes the reinforcements among the three pairs of buttons. Two followers or two leaders placed together can solve the problem only accidentally. The function of leader may shift from one bird to another over a period of time, and a temporary condition may arise in which both are followers. The behavior then resembles that of two people who, meeting under circumstances where the convention of passing on the right is not strongly observed, oscillate from side to side before passing.

Between such an experiment and the relation of leader to follower in politics, for example, there is more than a simple analogy. Most cultures produce some people whose behavior is mainly controlled by the exigencies of a given situation. The same cultures also produce people whose behavior is controlled mainly by the behavior of others. Some such division of the contingencies in any cooperative venture seems to be required. The leader is not wholly independent of the follower, however, for his behavior requires the support of corresponding behavior on the part of others, and to the extent that cooperation is necessary, the leader is, in fact, led by his followers.

Verbal episodes. Verbal behavior supplies many examples in which one person is said to have an effect upon another beyond the scope of the physical sciences. Words are said to "symbolize" or "express" ideas or meanings, which are then "communicated" to the listener. An alternative formulation would require too much space here,[1] but a single example may suggest how this sort of social behavior may be brought within range of a natural science. Consider a simple episode in which A asks B for a cigarette and gets one. To account for the occurrence and maintenance of this behavior we have to show that A provides adequate stimuli and reinforcement for B and vice versa. A's response, "Give me a cigarette," would be quite ineffective in a purely mechanical environment. It has been conditioned by a verbal community which occasionally reinforces it in a particular way. A has long since formed a discrimination by virtue of which the response is not emitted in the absence of a member of that community. He has also probably formed more subtle discriminations in which he is more likely to respond in the presence of an "easy touch." B has either reinforced this response in the past or resembles someone who has. The first interchange between the two is in the direction of B to A: B is a discriminative stimulus in the presence of which A emits the verbal response. The second interchange is in the direction A to B: the response generates auditory stimuli acting upon B. If B is already disposed to give a cigarette to A—for example, if B is "anxious to please A" or "in love with A," the auditory pattern is a discriminative stimulus for the response of giving a cigarette. B does not offer cigarettes indiscriminately; he waits for a response from A as an occasion upon which a cigarette will be accepted. A's acceptance depends upon a condition of deprivation in which the receipt of a cigarette is reinforcing. This is also the condition in which A emits the response, "Give me a cigarette," and the contingency which comes to control B's behavior is thus established. The third interchange is A's receipt of the cigarette from B. This is the reinforcement of A's original response and completes our account of it. If B is reinforced simply by evidence of the effect of the cigarette upon A, we may consider B's account closed also. But such behavior is more likely to remain a

[1] See footnote reference, page 210.

stable part of the culture if these evidences are made conspicuous. If A not only accepts the cigarette but also says, "Thank you," a fourth interchange takes place: the auditory stimulus is a conditioned reinforcer to B, and A produces it just because it is. B may in turn increase the likelihood of future "Thank you's" on the part of A by saying, "Not at all."

When B's behavior in responding to A's verbal response is already strong, we call A's response a "request." If B's behavior requires other conditions, we have to reclassify A's response. If "Give me a cigarette" is not only the occasion for a particular response but also a conditioned aversive stimulus from which B can escape only by complying, then A's response is a "demand." In this case, B's behavior is reinforced by a reduction in the threat generated by A's demand, and A's "Thank you" is mainly effective as a conspicuous indication that the threat has been reduced.

Even such a brief episode is surprisingly complex, but the four or five interchanges between A and B can all be specified in physical terms and can scarcely be ignored if we are to take such an analysis seriously. That the complete episode occupies only a few seconds does not excuse us from the responsibility of identifying and observing all its features.

Unstable interaction. Although many of these interlocking social systems are stable, others show a progressive change. A trivial example is the behavior of a group of people who enter an unfamiliar room containing a sign which reads, "Silence, please." Such a verbal stimulus is generally effective only in combination with the behavior of other members of the group. If many people are talking noisily, the sign may have little or no effect. But let us assume that our group enters silently. After a moment two members least under the control of the sign begin to whisper. This slightly alters the situation for other members so that they also begin to whisper. This alters the situation for the two who are least under the control of the sign, and they then begin to speak in a low voice. This further changes the situation for the others, who also begin to speak in low voices. Eventually the conversation may be quite noisy. This is a simple "autocatalytic" process arising from a repeated interchange between the members of the group.

Another example is a practice common on sailing ships in the eighteenth century. Sailors would amuse themselves by tying several boys or younger men in a ring to a mast by their left hands, their right hands remaining free. Each boy was given a stick or whip and told to strike the boy in front of him whenever he felt himself being struck by the boy behind. The game was begun by striking one boy lightly. This boy then struck the boy ahead of him, who in turn struck the boy next ahead, and so on. Even though it was clearly in the interest of the group that all blows be gentle, the inevitable result was a furious lashing. The unstable elements in this interlocking system are easy to identify. We cannot assume that each boy gave precisely the kind of blow he received because this is not an easy comparison to make. It is probable that he underestimated the strength of the blows he gave. The slightest tendency to give a little harder than he received would produce the ultimate effect. Moreover, repeated blows probably generate an emotional disposition in which one naturally strikes harder. A comparable instability is seen when two individuals engage in a casual conversation which leads to a vituperative quarrel. The aggressive effect of a remark is likely to be underestimated by the man who makes it, and repeated effects generate further aggression. The principle is particularly dangerous when the conversation consists of an exchange of notes between governments.

SUPPORTING VARIABLES IN
THE SOCIAL EPISODE

Although the interchange between two or more individuals whose behavior is interlocked in a social system must be explained in its entirety, certain variables may remain obscure. For example, we often observe merely that one person is predisposed to act with respect to another in certain ways. The mother caring for her child is a familiar case in point. The social emotions are by definition observed simply as predispositions to act in ways which may be positively or negatively reinforcing to others. Such terms as "favor" and "friendship" refer to tendencies to administer positive reinforcement, and love might be analyzed as the mutual tendency of two individuals to reinforce each other, where the reinforcement may or may not be sexual.

Sometimes a reciprocal interchange explains the behavior in terms of reinforcement. Each individual has something to offer by way of reinforcing the other, and once established, the interchange sustains itself. We may detect mutual reinforcement in the case of mother and child. Instead of tendencies to behave in certain ways, they may illustrate tendencies to be reinforced by certain social stimuli. Aside from this, the group may manipulate special variables to generate tendencies to behave in ways which result in the reinforcement of others. The group may reinforce the individual for telling the truth, helping others, returning favors, and reinforcing others in turn for doing the same. The Golden Rule is a generalized statement of the behavior thus supported by the group. Many important interlocking systems of social behavior could not be maintained without such conventional practices. This is an important point in explaining the success of the cultural practices characteristic of a group (Chapter XXVIII).

To the extent that prior reinforcement by the group determines the suitability of the behavior of the individual for an interlocking system, the system itself is not wholly self-sustaining. The instability is demonstrated when an individual who is not adequately controlled by the culture gains a temporary personal advantage by exploiting the system. He lies, refuses to return a favor, or breaks a promise, but this exploitation of the system eventually leads to its deterioration. The boy in the fable cries, "Wolf!" because certain patterns of social behavior have been established by the community and he finds the resulting behavior of his neighbors amusing. The aggressive door-to-door salesman imposes upon the good manners of the housewife to hold her attention in the same way. In each case the system eventually breaks down: the neighbors no longer respond to the cry of "Wolf!" and the housewife slams the door.

The behavior of two individuals may be related in a social episode, not primarily through an interchange between them, but through common external variables. The classic example is competition. Two individuals come into competition when the behavior of one can be reinforced only at the cost of the reinforcement of the other. Social behavior as here defined is not necessarily involved. Catching a rabbit before it runs away is not very different from catching it before someone else does. In the latter case, a social interchange may occur as a by-product if one individual attacks the other. Cooperation, in which the reinforcement of two or more individuals depends upon the behavior of both or all of them, is obviously not the opposite of competition, for it appears to require an interlocking system.

THE GROUP AS A BEHAVING UNIT

It is common to speak of families, clans, nations, races, and other groups as if they were individuals. Such concepts as "the group mind," "the instinct of the herd," and "national character" have been invented to support this practice. It is always an individual who behaves, however. The problem presented by the larger group is to explain why many individuals behave *together*. Why does a boy join a gang? Why does a man join a club or fall in with a lynching mob? We may answer questions of this sort by examining the variables generated by the group which encourage the behavior of joining and conforming. We cannot do this simply by saying that two individuals will behave together cooperatively if it is "in their common interest to do so." We must point to specific variables affecting the behavior of each of them. From a practical point of view, as in setting up cooperative behavior in the pigeon demonstration just described, an analysis of the relevant variables is also essential. The particular contingencies controlling the behavior of the cooperators must be carefully maintained.

Some progress toward explaining participation in a group is made by the analysis of imitation. In general, behaving as others behave is likely to be reinforcing. Stopping to look in a store window which has already attracted a crowd is more likely to be reinforced than stopping to look in store windows which have not attracted crowds. Using words which have already been used by others, rather than strange terms, is more likely to be reinforced positively or to be free of aversive consequences. Situations of this sort multiplied a thousandfold generate and sustain an enormous tendency to behave as others are behaving.

To this principle we must add another of perhaps greater importance. If it is always the individual who behaves, it is nevertheless the group which has the more powerful effect. By joining a group the individual increases his power to achieve reinforcement. The man who pulls on a rope is reinforced by the movement of the rope regardless of the fact that others may need to be pulling at the same time. The man attired in full uniform, parading smartly down the street, is reinforced by the acclaim of the crowd even though it would not be forthcoming if he were marching alone. The coward in the lynching mob is reinforced when his victim writhes in terror as he shouts at him—regardless of the fact that a hundred others are, and must be, shouting at him also. The reinforcing consequences generated by the group easily exceed the sums of the consequences which could be achieved by the members acting separately. The total reinforcing effect is enormously increased.

The interchanges within a group and the heightened effect of the group upon the environment may be studied within the framework of a natural science. They need to be explored further before we accept the proposition that there are social units, forces, and laws which require scientific methods of a fundamentally different sort.

CHAPTER XX

PERSONAL CONTROL

Let us look at a social episode from the point of view of one of the participants. We have seen that A may generate important variables affecting the behavior of B. The change in B may not have a return effect upon A. For example, B may look in a shop window because he sees A doing so although A may be unaffected by B's action. Usually, however, as in many of the examples already analyzed, the resulting change in B's behavior has an effect upon A. In the important case now to be considered the effect is one of reinforcement. A behaves in a way which alters B's behavior because of the consequences which B's behavior has for A. We say, colloquially, that A is *deliberately* controlling B. This does not mean that A is necessarily able to identify the cause or effect of his action. When a baby cries for his mother's attention, he generates an aversive stimulus which he withdraws when the mother pays attention. As a result, the behavior of the mother in paying attention is reinforced. Neither the baby nor the mother may understand the processes involved, but we may still say that the baby has learned how to control his mother in this respect. It is this asymmetrical social relation which we have now to investigate. Our task is to evaluate the various ways in which one person controls another.

CONTROL OF VARIABLES

The power to manipulate the conditions affecting another individual may be delegated to the controlling individual by one of the organized agencies to be discussed in Section V. The controller's relation to the controllee may then be characterized as that of governor to governed, priest to communicant, therapist to patient, employer to employee, teacher to pupil, and so on. But almost everyone controls some relevant variables, apart from such a rôle, which he may employ to his own advantage. This we may speak of as *personal control*. The kind and extent depend upon the personal endowment and skill of the controller. The strong man uses the variables which derive from his strength. The wealthy man resorts to money. The pretty girl uses primary or conditioned sexual reinforcement. The weakling becomes a sycophant. The shrew controls through aversive stimulation.

When compared with the practices of organized agencies, personal control is nevertheless weak. A man of great wealth, a gangster with a gun, or an extremely beautiful woman is the occasional exception to the rule that the individual is rarely, simply as an individual, able to alter the variables affecting other people in very important ways. But he may to some extent offset this shortcoming because he is in an especially favorable position in dealing with the idiosyncrasies of the controllee. Organized agencies manipulate variables common to groups of people, but the individual can ask whether a particular controllee is sensitive to certain kinds of stimuli, whether he responds to certain kinds of reinforcement, whether at the moment he exhibits certain states of deprivation, and so on. Whatever variables are available may be more wisely selected and used.

The limitations of personal control have led to a standard practice in which available variables are first manipulated in order to establish and maintain contact between controller and controllee. If this move is successful, further possibilities of control may then be developed. The first task of the salesman is to keep his prospect within range—to keep the housewife at the door or the customer in the shop. If he has sufficient control to achieve this, he may then safely develop other lines. The counselor, whether he is simply a friend or a professional therapist, faces a similar problem. His first task is to make sure that the man he is counseling continues to listen and to return for further counsel. If this can be done, other lines of control may then be opened.

The preliminary stage of maintaining contact with the controllee is best seen in the career of the entertainer or, somewhat less obviously, the writer, artist, or musician. People of this sort exploit their relatively poor sources of control almost exclusively to increase the probability that the controllee will come back for more. The principal technique is reinforcement. We might say, in fact, that it is the business of the entertainer, writer, artist, or musician to create reinforcing events. In the process of creation, as we saw in Chapter XVI, a medium may be manipulated to reveal *self*-reinforcing properties, but the "universality" of a work of art is measured by the number of other people who also find it reinforcing. If the artist has no further message, this is the extent of the personal control he wields. The propagandist, however, advances to a more specific assignment when the attention, interest, or patronage of his audience has once been assured.

TECHNIQUES OF CONTROL

The techniques available in controlling behavior were reviewed in Chapter XV in connection with self-control, but there are several special features which call for comment in the application to the control of others. Physical force is the most immediately effective technique available to those who have the necessary power. In its most immediately personal form it is exemplified by the wrestler who suppresses the behavior of his opponent through sheer physical restraint. The most extreme form of restraint is death: the individual is kept from behaving by being killed. Less extreme forms include the use of handcuffs, strait jackets, jails, concentration camps, and so on. These all suggest violent control, often for extremely selfish purposes, but even highly civilized societies use physical restraint in the control of children, criminals, and the dangerously insane.

The use of force has obvious disadvantages as a controlling technique. It usually requires the sustained attention of the controller. It is almost exclusively concerned with the prevention of behavior, and hence is of little value in increasing the probability of action. It generates strong emotional dispositions to counterattack. It cannot be applied to all forms of behavior; handcuffs restrain part of a man's rage but not all of it. It is not effective upon behavior at the private level, as we suggest when we say that one cannot imprison a man's thoughts.

For all these reasons, control through physical restraint is not so promising a possibility as it may at first appear. It is, of course, never available to those who lack the necessary power. In the long run the use of force usually gives way to other techniques which employ genuine processes of behavior. Here the controller need not have the power to coerce or restrain behavior directly but may affect it indirectly by altering the environment.

Manipulating stimuli. Most of the techniques of self-control through the manipulation of stimuli may be directly extended to the behavior of others. We present unconditioned or conditioned stimuli to *elicit* reflex responses when we give an emetic to induce vomiting; and we arrange *discriminative occasions* for behavior when we display merchandise in a store in such a way that the customer is more likely to purchase it. We use stimuli to *eliminate* behavior by evoking incompatible responses. When women employed in a factory created a hazard by hurrying down a corridor at the end of the day, the manager put mirrors along the corridor to evoke responses of adjusting wearing apparel and applying cosmetics. This behavior proved to be incompatible with hurrying. We use *supplemental stimuli* to induce behavior when we "interpret a situation favorably," as when the salesman assures the potential buyer that he will enjoy or profit from a purchase, or when we encourage someone to join us on a given occasion by assuring him of enjoyable consequences. A particularly effective mode of stimulation evokes the imitative repertoire discussed in Chapters VII and XIX: the businessman who is resorting to alcohol as a technique of control induces his prospect to have another drink by ordering another himself. The imitative repertoire is the basis of testimonial advertising. People are shown using various products and engaging in various activities, and the effect is to strengthen comparable behavior in the viewer. The whole field of verbal behavior exemplifies the use of stimuli in personal control. The speaker generates auditory patterns which are effective because of the listener's history in a given verbal community.

Reinforcement as a technique of control. If the individual possesses money or goods, he may use them for purposes of reinforcement in the form of wages, bribes, or gratuities. If he is in a position to do someone a favor, he can reinforce accordingly. He may also be able to offer his own physical labor, either to an employer in return for wages or to a friend in return for a particular action. Sexual stimulation is a common form of reinforcement and is widely used in personal control.

In practice many of these reinforcers are preceded by more immediate conditioned reinforcers. Money is itself a conditioned reinforcer, but primary reinforcement may be further postponed when a check is given which is later converted into cash. Contracts and verbal promises are other forms of conditioned reinforcers available in personal control. Minor examples include praise and thanks. These deferred reinforcements are likely to be unreliable, however. Praise may give way to flattery, checks may not be honored, and promises may be made in bad faith. But it may be some time before the interlocking social system deteriorates to the point at which there is no longer a reinforcing effect.

Aversive stimulation. Negative reinforcement is employed in personal control in the aversive cry of the child and the nuisance value of the behavior of an adult. Control is achieved by making the withdrawal of these aversive stimuli contingent upon the response to be strengthened. Forgiveness and acquittal are similarly reinforcing. The bully who pommels another boy until he cries "Uncle!", the police who employ the third degree to obtain a confession, and the nation which makes war until the enemy surrenders, exemplify the same use of aversive stimulation. *Conditioned* aversive stimulation used in the same way is exemplified by the "dare" or by other ways of shaming someone into acting.

Punishment. The individual who is able to present a positive rein-forcement or withdraw a negative is usually also able to present the negative or withdraw the positive and is therefore able to punish. Punishment is not to be confused with physical restraint or the use of aversive stimulation. All three forms of control are usually avail-able to the same individual because of the nature of the power of control, but confining a man in jail to keep him from behaving in a certain way or to induce him to behave in a certain way in order to be released is not the same as confining him in order to reduce his tendency to behave in a given way in the future. In the control of psy-chotic patients confinement is a means of restraint rather than pun-ishment; and, conversely, some forms of punishment involve at best only momentary restraint. Punishment as a technique of control has all the disadvantages of physical restraint and, in addition, all the weaknesses pointed out in Chapter XII. Moreover, it generates emo-tional dispositions which may be disadvantageous or even dangerous to both controller and controllee, as we shall see in discussing psycho-therapy in Chapter XXIV.

Punishment as the removal of positive reinforcers, conditioned or unconditioned, is exemplified by cutting a dependent off "without a cent," refusing to supply food or shelter previously given, imposing economic sanctions, and refusing customary sexual contact. Another important example is withholding customary social stimulation, as in snubbing an acquaintance or "putting a schoolboy on silence." Lesser degrees of such punishments are social neglect and inattention. None of these are punishments in their own right, but only when made contingent upon behavior.

Punishment in the form of presenting aversive stimuli is commoner. Physical injury is exemplified by spanking a child, striking an adult, and attacking a nation. Conditioned aversive stimuli, many of them verbal, are exemplified by disapproval and criticism, by damning and cursing, by ridicule, and by the carrying of bad news. These again are punishments only when contingent upon behavior. We have seen that it is questionable whether they permanently reduce any tendency to behave. They all generate emotional dispositions which are particularly disorganizing and which may in turn call for further remedial control.

Pointing up contingencies of reinforcement. It is possible to use techniques based upon reinforcement and punishment without being able to control the events in question. A considerable effect may be achieved simply by clarifying the relation between behavior and its consequences. The instructor in sports, crafts, or artistic activities may directly reinforce the behavior he is trying to establish, but he may also simply point up the contingency between a given form of behavior and the result—"Notice the effect you get when you hold the brush this way," "Strike the key this way and see if it isn't easier," "If you swing the club this way, you won't slice the ball," and so on. The controller may make use of reinforcing events which have occurred without his intervention by making the contingencies more likely to modify the behavior of the controllee. Punishing consequences are pointed up by such expressions as "Now, see what you've done," "This is costing you money," or "You are responsible for all this." Other techniques of emphasizing reinforcing contingencies consist of arranging various schedules of reinforcement—"Play this passage until you can play it without a mistake"—and programs of differential reinforcement—"When you can clear the bar at this height, move it one inch higher."

Deprivation and satiation. If we are controlling a child's behavior through reinforcement with candy, it is well to make sure that little candy is received at other times. Deprivation may also be used to control behavior which has been strengthened by generalized reinforcers. To evoke behavior which has been reinforced with money, one procedure is to deprive the individual in such a way as to strengthen behavior which can be executed only with money. For example, a man is made susceptible to bribery by encouraging him to follow a mode of living in which money is an important requirement. Satiation is a common technique of control which is particularly effective in eliminating unwanted behavior. A child stops teasing for candy when he is given all he will eat. One may satiate an aggressor by submitting to him—by "turning the other cheek."

Emotion. We are sometimes interested in controlling the reflex responses characteristic of emotion, as in making someone laugh, blush, or cry. We are more likely to be interested in establishing emotional *predispositions*. We have noted the important case in which someone is "favorably inclined" toward a particular person or set of circumstances. Building morale is usually concerned with generating such a predisposition. The effect often follows from the same events which reinforce behavior. Gratuities, for example, serve as a mode of control not only through reinforcement but by generating "favorable attitudes." More specific predispositions are also generated with appropriate stimuli—as when Christmas music is played in a store to encourage "good will toward men" and the purchase of gifts. Other techniques of altering emotional predispositions are suggested by terms like "jollying," "cajoling," "haranguing," "seducing," "inciting," "allaying fear," and "turning away wrath." The actual variables responsible for a given predisposition need to be analyzed in each case.

The use of drugs. The drug most commonly used in personal control is alcohol. Like certain emotional operations it is often used to dispose an individual toward favorable action. It appears also to act directly in reducing anxieties or alarm and may be used for that reason—for example, in closing a business deal or in getting someone to talk about a confidential matter. It is also used as a positive reinforcer. As a habit-forming drug it makes possible a special form of deprivation, in which behavior which has been reinforced with alcohol may be made so powerful that the individual will "do anything" for a drink. Such drugs as morphine and cocaine have, as we have seen, been used to create the possibility of using other powerful deprivations for the same purpose. Other drugs are employed in the control of psychotic behavior and in connection with governmental or police functions—for example, the so-called truth serums.

OBJECTIONS TO PERSONAL CONTROL

Students of human behavior often avoid the issue of control and even regard it as in bad taste to suggest that deliberate control is ever undertaken. The codification of controlling practices is left to the Machiavellis and Lord Chesterfields. Psychologists, sociologists, and anthropologists usually prefer theories of behavior in which control is minimized or denied, and we shall see that proposed changes in governmental design are usually promoted by pointing to their effect in maximizing freedom. All this appears to be due to the fact that control is frequently aversive to the controllee. Techniques based upon the use of force, particularly punishment or the threat of punishment, are aversive by definition, and techniques which appeal to other processes are also objectionable when, as is usually the case, the ultimate advantage to the controller is opposed to the interest of the controllee.

One effect upon the controllee is to induce him to engage in countercontrol. He may show an emotional reaction of anger or frustration including operant behavior which injures or is otherwise aversive to the controller. Such behavior may have been reinforced by the reduction in similar aversive consequences. The importance of reinforcement is seen in the fact that we are much more likely to respond in this way to social than to nonsocial control. If we are forced to step off the sidewalk by a large branch blown down by the wind, we shall probably not exhibit a strong emotional reaction, but if we are forced to step off in the same way by a group of idle people, aggressive behavior—verbal and nonverbal—may be generated. The aggressive behavior has probably alleviated similar social conditions but has had little or no effect upon branches of trees. It is not necessarily more "natural" to react emotionally to social than to nonsocial restraint.

Because of the aversive consequences of being controlled, the individual who undertakes to control other people is likely to be countercontrolled by all of them. The power which "other people" generate when they act as a group is discussed in Chapter XXI. Part of such countercontrol is assigned to specific religious or governmental agencies which possess the power to manipulate important variables. The opposition to control is likely to be directed toward the most objectionable forms—the use of force and conspicuous instances of exploitation, undue influence, or gross misrepresentation—but it may extend to any control which is "deliberately" exerted because of the consequences to the controller. As a result of the principal technique employed in countercontrol, the individual who engages in control automatically generates conditioned aversive self-stimulation—he "feels guilty" about exerting control. He is then automatically reinforced for doing something else, for giving up any attempt to control, and for declaring himself opposed to personal control in general.

The countercontrol exercised by the group and by certain agencies may explain our hesitancy in discussing the subject of personal control frankly and in dealing with the facts in an objective way. But it does not excuse such an attitude or practice. This is only a special case of the general principle that the issue of personal freedom must not be allowed to interfere with a scientific analysis of human behavior. As we have seen, science implies prediction and, insofar as the relevant variables can be controlled, it implies control. We cannot expect to profit from applying the methods of science to human behavior if for some extraneous reason we refuse to admit that our subject matter can be controlled. The advantage of this general principle is well illustrated by the present point: those who are most concerned with restricting personal control have most to gain from a clear understanding of the techniques employed.

CHAPTER XXI

GROUP CONTROL

The individual is subjected to a more powerful control when two or more persons manipulate variables having a common effect upon his behavior. This will happen if two or more persons are moved to control him in the same way. The condition is usually fulfilled when the members of a group compete for limited resources. A social system, in the sense of Chapter XIX, is then established in which one man's positive reinforcement is another man's negative. In the expression, "the spoils of war," the reinforcement of the conqueror is named for its aversive effect upon the conquered. The child who takes a toy from another is thereby reinforced, but the loss of the toy is aversive to the other child. The successful suitor inevitably creates an aversive condition for other suitors.

Since an individual may affect all other members of a group in this way, their countercontrol may be undertaken in concert. All the other members become what we may designate as the controlling group. The group acts as a unit insofar as its members are affected by the individual in the same way. It need not be highly organized, but some sort of organization usually develops. Controlling practices acquire a certain uniformity from the cohesive forces which lead individuals to take part in group action (Chapter XIX) and from their mode of transmission from one generation to another.

The principal technique employed in the control of the individual by any group of people who have lived together for a sufficient length of time is as follows. The behavior of the individual is classified as either "good" or "bad" or, to the same effect, "right" or "wrong" and is reinforced or punished accordingly. We need not seek far for a definition of these controversial terms. The behavior of an individual is usually called good or right insofar as it reinforces other members of the group and bad or wrong insofar as it is aversive. The actual practices of the group may not be completely consistent with these definitions. The initial classification may have been accidental: a conspicuous bit of behavior which was only adventitiously correlated with reinforcing or aversive events came to be classed as good or bad accordingly. Our definition applies literally to the origin of such a superstitious practice but does not fit any current effect. A classification of behavior may also continue in force long after it is out of date: behavior often continues to be branded good or bad although, through some change in conditions, it is no longer reinforcing or aversive.

The classification may also be defective because of the faulty structure of the group. All members may not participate to the same extent. Since an act may have different effects upon different members, some of whom may, therefore, classify it as good and others as bad, subdivisions of the group may conflict with each other in the direction of their control. For example, the use of physical force is generally aversive to others and hence called bad, but it may be classified as good by those who exhibit similar behavior in controlling a third party, either within or outside the group. Behavior which is immediately reinforcing may have a long-term aversive effect. The behavior of seduction or of exerting "undue influence" is often effective through positive reinforcement, but the ultimate consequences may lead the victim, as well as others, to classify it as bad.

The group as a whole seldom draws up a formal classification of behavior as good or bad. We infer the classification from our observations of controlling practices. A sort of informal codification takes place, however, when the terms themselves come to be used in reinforcement. Perhaps the commonest generalized reinforcers are the verbal stimuli "Good," "Right," "Bad," and "Wrong." These are used, together with unconditioned and other conditioned reinforcers such as praise, thanks, caresses, gratuities, favors, blows, blame, censure, and criticism, to shape the behavior of the individual.

The actual controlling practices are usually obvious. Good behavior is reinforced, and bad behavior punished. The conditioned aversive stimulation generated by bad behavior as the result of punishment is associated with an emotional pattern commonly called "shame." The individual responds to this when he "feels ashamed of himself." Part of what he feels are the responses of glands and smooth muscles recorded by the so-called lie detector (Chapter X). The relevance of this instrument to lie detection is based upon the fact that lying is frequently punished. Another part of the reaction of shame is a conspicuous change in normal dispositions—the social offender acts in a shamefaced manner. Any or all of these emotional conditions may be directly or indirectly aversive, in which case they combine with other conditioned aversive stimulation in providing for the reinforcement of behavior which displaces or otherwise reduces the probability of the punished response. The best example of such behavior is self-control. The group also directly reinforces practices of self-control.

WHY THE GROUP EXERTS CONTROL

In explaining any given instance of group control we have to show how the behavior of the controller is interlocked with that of the controllee in a social system. We must also show that both are adequately accounted for by the specified variables. In a given instance, good behavior on the part of A may be positively reinforced by B because it generates an emotional disposition on the part of B to "do good" to A. This explanation is not very satisfactory because it simply appeals to a standing tendency to do good. But it seems clear, simply as a matter of observation, that the behavior of favoring another is modified by appropriate emotional circumstances and that good behavior on the part of another is a case in point. The mother reinforces her child in a burst of affection when the child's behavior is especially good or right.

Another possibility is that the group appropriately reinforces good behavior just because the probability of similar behavior in the future is thus increased. The gratuity may be given to guarantee similar service in the future; it then has nothing to do with gratitude as an emotional disposition to favor others. The community also teaches each member to thank or praise the individual who has behaved well and to do so even when the member himself is not directly affected. An act of heroism is acclaimed by many people who have not, in this instance, been positively reinforced. The educational practice generates good behavior in the individual by assuring the proper reinforcing behavior on the part of the group.

The emotional dispositions which lead the members of a group to punish bad behavior are, unfortunately, more obvious. Anyone who injures others, deprives them of property, or interferes with their behavior generates a heightened inclination toward counterattack. This statement is again merely an appeal to an observed increase in the tendency of individuals to act aggressively under certain circumstances, but there are variables outside the field of emotion which work in the same direction. If A's aggression is momentarily reduced through B's counteragression (we have seen, of course, that the long-term effect is different), B will be reinforced. B's behavior in punishing A may thus be due simply to operant reinforcement. It is sometimes argued that an emotional disposition to counterattack is the basic variable—that we always "strike a child in anger," and that any interpretation of the behavior as "intellectual" is a mere rationalization (Chapter XVIII). But the practice could arise in the absence of an emotional variable; one could punish objectionable behavior simply to reduce the probability that it will recur. Educational agencies also encourage the use of punishment to control bad behavior, and they generate a tendency to exert the control even though the individual himself is not at the moment involved. The agency may work through emotional variables—for example, by generating resentment or indignation with respect to dishonesty, theft, or murder —or through operant reinforcement by appeal to the consequences.

THE EFFECT OF GROUP CONTROL

The control exercised by the group works to at least the temporary disadvantage of the individual. The man who has been positively reinforced for giving his possessions and services to others may find himself thoroughly despoiled. The group has generated behavior which, although it achieves the positive reinforcement accorded good behavior, also creates strongly aversive conditions for the individual. Among the forms of good behavior strengthened by the community are practices of self-control in which behavior which might result in extensive reinforcement is weakened. That the individual suffers when bad behavior is punished is more obvious. Punishment itself is aversive, and behavior which works to the advantage of the individual at the expense of others is, temporarily at least, suppressed. Punishment is also the principal variable responsible for the behavior of self-control, which, as we have just seen, also reduces primary reinforcement.

In short, the effect of group control is in conflict with the strong primarily reinforced behavior of the individual. Selfish behavior is restrained, and altruism encouraged. But the individual gains from these practices because he is part of the controlling group with respect to every other individual. He may be subject to control, but he engages in similar practices in controlling the behavior of others. Such a system may reach a "steady state" in which the individual's advantages and disadvantages strike some sort of balance. In such a state a reasonable control over the selfish behavior of the individual is matched by the advantages which he gains as a member of a group which controls the same selfish behavior in others.

The power of the group is, of course, great. Even the political tyrant, the despotic father, the bully in the street gang, or any other exceptionally strong individual usually yields eventually to the group as a whole. The less talented may be wholly submerged by it. In discussing psychotherapy in Chapter XXIV we shall consider some of the consequences of excessive control. Fortunately, the group seldom acts efficiently enough to press its advantage to the limit, and its full power is probably never felt. Classifications of behavior as "good," "bad," "right," or "wrong" are seldom clear-cut. And they are not consistently supported by all members of a group. Certain organized subdivisions of the group, however, may make better use of their power, as we shall see in Section V.

JUSTIFICATION OF GROUP CONTROL

Certain familiar questions in the field of ethics may have occurred to the reader. What do we mean by the Good? How may we encourage people to practice the Good Life? And so on. Our account does not answer questions of this sort in the spirit in which they are usually asked. Within the framework of a natural science certain kinds of behavior are observed when people live together in groups—kinds of behavior which are directed toward the control of the individual and which operate for the advantage of other members of the group. We define "good" and "bad," or "right" and "wrong," with respect to a particular set of practices. We account for the practices by noting the effects which they have upon the individual and in turn upon the members of the group, according to the basic processes of behavior.

Ethics is usually concerned with *justifying* controlling practices rather than with merely describing them. Why is a particular bit of behavior classed as good or bad? The question is sometimes answered by asserting that "good" and "bad" have been defined by supernatural authorities. Although a science of behavior might help in designing educational practices which would encourage people to be good and dissuade them from being bad according to a given authority, it can scarcely pass upon the validity of such a definition. When it can be shown that a classification leads to results which are positively reinforcing to the individual who reveals the word of authority, another sort of explanation is available. Such an explanation need not question the ultimate, possibly beneficial, effect of a classification.

Attempts have been made to avoid an appeal to authority by finding other bases for a definition. It has been argued that a particular form of individual behavior, or the controlling practice which produces it, is to be recommended if it can be shown to work for the "greatest good of the greatest number," to increase the "sum total of human happiness," to maintain the "equilibrium" of a group, and so on. The original problem remains, however, because we still have to justify the criteria. Why do we choose the greatest good or the sum total of human happiness or equilibrium as a basis for a definition? A science of behavior might be able to specify behavior which would or would not make for happiness, but the question remains whether it can decide that happiness is "best" in the ethical sense. Here again we may be able to show that practices which are justified in terms of happiness have consequences which are reinforcing to the proponents of such a justification. It is *their* happiness which is primarily affected. But this is also irrelevant to the ultimate effect of the classification.

Such a criterion as the "greatest good of the greatest number" represents a type of explanation, based upon the principle of maxima and minima, which has often proved useful in the physical sciences. In the field of behavior, however, the definition of what is being maximized or minimized is unsatisfactory—as we might suspect from the enormous amount of discussion which terms like "the greatest good" have provoked. Even if these terms could be defined, the practice of characterizing a controlling practice as maximizing or minimizing some such entity is very different from an analysis in terms of relevant variables. It is not impossible that the two could be shown to be compatible if physical dimensions could be assigned to the thing maximized, but this has not been done in the traditional study of ethics. The program of a functional analysis offers a course of action in which the problem of the definition of such entities may be avoided.

Obviously an important feature of any group is the extent to which it exercises control over each of its members. We shall return in Section VI to the question of whether a science of human behavior provides any basis for determining the most expedient extent of such control. This problem is quite independent of an analysis of actual controlling practices.

CONTROLLING AGENCIES

CHAPTER XXII

GOVERNMENT AND LAW

CONTROLLING AGENCIES

The group exercises an ethical control over each of its members mainly through its power to reinforce or punish. The power is derived from sheer number and from the importance of other people in the life of each member. Usually the group is not well organized, nor are its practices consistently sustained. Within the group, however, certain *controlling agencies* manipulate particular sets of variables. These agencies are usually better organized than is the group as a whole, and they often operate with greater success.

The agencies to be considered in this section are chosen from the fields of *government, religion, psychotherapy, economics,* and *education.* These are very broad areas, of course, which cannot be adequately treated here. Fortunately, for our present purposes we do not need an exhaustive account of the historical and comparative facts about particular religions, governments, economic systems, and so on. We are concerned only with the conceptions of the behaving individual which are encountered in these fields. Theology usually has much to say of man in his relation to the universe. Theories of government frequently describe man as a political animal or as a responsible agent under the law. Psychotherapy is particularly rich in "systems" of human behavior, and "economic man" has figured prominently in economic theory. A special psychology has been developed in the field of education.

These theories of human behavior are seldom, if ever, satisfactory even in their appropriate fields, and a broader objection may be urged against them. Each conception is based upon a particular set of facts and is developed and used primarily to explain these facts alone. The conception developed in one field is seldom applied, and never effectively applied, to another. What the political scientist has to say about man proves to be of little value to the psychotherapist, while the individual who emerges from educational psychology bears no familial resemblance to economic man. It is not likely that the human organism is compartmentalized in this way. We might arrive at a formulation of behavior which could be applied to any field by considering all the historical and comparative facts at once. There is a simpler way, however. Our conception of human behavior need not be *deduced* from the complex facts which it must eventually explain. We are not required, for example, to discover the characteristics of the political animal through a study of the facts of government. If the political animal is man himself, we may study him elsewhere and often under better conditions. A functional analysis of behavior provides us with a basic conception with which we may approach each of these fields in turn. We may be interested primarily in testing such an analysis by discovering whether it yields a plausible account of the behavior of the individual in each case, but if we can achieve such an account, then a considerable advantage may be claimed over traditional formulations. Not only will our analysis in each case have the support of the scientific study of the individual under optimal conditions of observation, it will be common to all fields. It will then be possible to consider the effect upon the individual of the *total culture*, in which all our controlling agencies and all the other features of the social environment work together simultaneously and with a single effect.

In discussing controlling agencies we are concerned specifically with certain kinds of power over variables which affect human behavior and with the controlling practices which can be employed because of this power. Possibilities which are as yet unrealized may be as important as the practices of which history has already provided examples. A controlling agency, together with the individuals who are controlled by it, comprises a *social system* in the sense of Chapter XIX, and our task is to account for the behavior of all participants. We must identify the individuals composing the agency and explain why they have the power to manipulate the variables which the agency employs. We must also analyze the general effect on the controllee, and show how this leads to a return reinforcement which explains the continuing existence of the agency. All the preceding analysis is needed in doing this. The classification of controlling variables, the study of basic processes, and the analysis of complex arrangements of variables and of the interaction of two or more individuals in a social system are all indispensable.

THE GOVERNMENTAL AGENCY

Perhaps the most obvious type of agency engaged in the control of human behavior is government. Traditional studies in political science deal with the history and properties of actual governments, with various types of governmental structure, and with the theories and principles which have been offered to justify governmental practices. We shall be concerned here principally with the behavioral processes through which a government exercises control. We have to examine the resulting behavior of the governed and the effect of this behavior which explains why the agency continues to control.

Narrowly defined, government is the use of the power to punish. Although this definition is sometimes offered as exhaustive, governmental agencies often resort to other kinds of control. The source of the power to punish determines the composition of the agency in the stricter sense. The strong or clever man is a sort of personal government whose power derives from his strength or skill. He may acquire henchmen who exercise the actual control over the group but who are in turn controlled by him through personal strength or skill. The underworld gang often shows a governmental structure of this sort. In the organized government of a modern state the specific task of punishment is assigned to special groups—the police and military. Their power is usually sheer physical force, amplified by special equipment, but the power of the ultimate governmental agency may be of a different nature. For example, the police and military may be recruited after appropriate *education*, they may be controlled through *economic* measures, or they may act under *religious* pressure.

Power which is derived from the "consent of the governed" also determines the composition of the appropriate agency. To say that power is "delegated" does not describe the actual process. An adequate analysis of such a government would include a study of the techniques used by the individual in becoming a member of the agency and in maintaining himself as such. This is roughly the field of practical politics. The individual must induce the group to assign governmental power to him, and once in office he must maintain his connection with this source. The techniques employed by an individual will be similar to those of a political machine or party.

In the long run the power of a government which has the consent of the governed derives from a congruence of function between governmental and ethical control (Chapter XXI). If the police or military are controlled through economic means, the group supplies the necessary money through taxation. Members of the group may volunteer or be conscripted to serve in the police or military. Since religious control often derives support from the same source (Chapter XXIII), it is not unusual to find a considerable overlap in the composition of religious and governmental agencies. Once an agency with a particular membership is in power, however, it may insure its own support through the use of the power to punish rather than through appeal to the congruence of its function with that of the ethical group. Not everyone pays taxes simply because of group pressure. We are not concerned here, however, with the various kinds of ultimate power in government or with the internal control which maintains the structure of the agency or makes it function smoothly. The effect upon the governed is the point at issue.

TECHNIQUES IN GOVERNMENTAL CONTROL

Where the group classifies behavior as "right" or "wrong" for purposes of ethical reinforcement, the governing agency adopts a distinction between "legal" and "illegal." The terms are defined roughly in relation to the source of power of the agency. Under an absolute ruler behavior is illegal if it has aversive consequences for the agency. To the extent that the power of the government derives from the group, the definitions approach those of "right" and "wrong." Since the governmental agency operates principally through the power to punish, however, the emphasis is upon "wrong." A government uses its power to "keep the peace"—to *restrain* behavior which threatens the property and persons of other members of the group. A government which possesses only the power to punish can *strengthen* legal behavior only by making the removal of a threat of punishment contingent upon it. This is sometimes done, but the commoner technique is simply to punish illegal forms of behavior.

Some governmental punishments consist of removing positive reinforcers—for example, dispossessing a man of property, fining him, taxing him punitively, or depriving him of contact with society through incarceration or banishment. Other common punishments consist of presenting negative reinforcers—for example, inflicting physical injury as in flogging, threatening injury or death, imposing a sentence at hard labor, exposing the individual to public ridicule in the stocks, and aversively stimulating the individual in minor ways as by requiring him to report in person to a police station where the principal punishment is simply the time and labor consumed in reporting. In practice, these punishments are made contingent upon particular kinds of behavior in order to reduce the probability that the behavior will occur again. A direct weakening as the opposite effect of reinforcement is, as we have seen, unlikely. Instead, conditioned aversive stimuli are produced, one effect of which resembles the "sense of shame" of group control. When this results from governmental punishment, the commoner term is "guilt." The process provides for the automatic reinforcement of responses which are incompatible with illegal behavior. As the net effect of governmental control, then, illegal behavior comes to generate aversive stimuli which make the individual "feel guilty" and which provide for the automatic positive reinforcement of behaving legally.

A controlling technique usually associated with an emphasis upon punishment is the establishment of *obedient* behavior. This is often a characteristic of personal control—for example, in the relation between parent and child. It is seen as a by-product of auxiliary techniques in the field of education when the pupil is taught obedience to his teacher. It is a staple product of governmental control. In the broadest sense the controlled individual is obedient to the dictates of the agency if he behaves in conformity with its controlling practices, but there is a special form of obedience in which a particular response is brought under the control of a verbal command. As a verbal stimulus a command serves a double function. It specifies behavior to be carried out, and it generates an aversive condition from which only that behavior will bring escape. The command is, of course, a familiar feature of military training. A selected repertoire of responses is brought under the control of appropriate verbal stimuli, which may then be used to time or otherwise coordinate the behavior of the members of a group. The civilian shows a comparable repertoire when he obeys traffic signals or a traffic policeman. But obedience to the government is more than a selected repertoire. Any behavior commanded by the government—in actual fact by "persons in authority" who are able to exert governmental control—is eventually carried out within the range of the verbal history of the individual. The group exercises a control of this sort to the extent that the imperative mood prevails in everyday discourse. By establishing obedient behavior, the controlling agency prepares for future occasions which it cannot otherwise foresee and for which an explicit repertoire cannot, therefore, be prepared in advance. When novel occasions arise to which the individual possesses no response, he simply does as he is told.

LAW

An important point in the development of a governmental agency is the codification of its controlling practices. The study of law or jurisprudence is usually concerned with the codes and practices of specific governments, past or present. It is also concerned with certain questions upon which a functional analysis of behavior has some bearing. What is a law? What role does a law play in governmental control?

In particular, what effect does it have upon the behavior of the controllee and of the members of the governmental agency itself?

A law usually has two important features. In the first place, it specifies behavior. The behavior is usually not described topographically but rather in terms of its effect upon others—the effect which is the object of governmental control. When we are told, for example, that an individual has "committed perjury," we are not told what he has actually said. "Robbery" and "assault" do not refer to specific forms of response. Only properties of behavior which are aversive to others are mentioned—in perjury the lack of a customary correspondence between a verbal response and certain factual circumstances, in robbery the removal of positive reinforcers, and in assault the aversive character of physical injury. In the second place, a law specifies or implies a consequence, usually punishment. A law is thus a *statement of a contingency of reinforcement maintained by a governmental agency.* The contingency may have prevailed as a controlling practice prior to its codification as a law, or it may represent a new practice which goes into effect with the passage of the law. Laws are thus both descriptions of past practices and assurances of similar practices in the future. A law is a *rule* of conduct in the sense that it specifies the consequences of certain actions which in turn "rule" behavior.

The effect of a law upon the controllee. To show how the individual actually comes to abide by a code, we should have to analyze how he learns not to lie, not to steal, not to assault others, and so on. The governmental agency may codify its controlling practices and maintain the contingencies thus set forth, but it seldom attempts to make the code effective in any other way. The individual is directly affected by only a small fraction of prevailing contingencies. In asserting that "ignorance of the law is no excuse," the governmental agency leaves the actual conditioning of the individual to others. Parents and friends establish minor contingencies which keep behavior within legal bounds, and the governmental function may also be actively supported by the ethical group and by religious and educational institutions with their appropriate techniques.

The governmental agency often conceals its neglect of this important step in control by claiming to have an educational effect. The individual is said to be affected by witnessing the punishment of others. But the effect of punishment as a deterrent to those who are not themselves punished is neither simple nor inevitable. The question is not peculiar to governmental contingencies. A boy may see a companion fall from a tree and may then see that the companion behaves in a manner characteristic of strong aversive stimulation. Through at least two stages of respondent conditioning any subsequent move on the part of the boy himself to climb trees generates conditioned aversive stimulation, a reduction in which reinforces competing behavior. The process is the same, although the effect is not of the same magnitude, as when the boy himself falls and is hurt. The same aversive stimulation—from trees and from boys in trees— explains why the boy may stop others who start to climb trees and why he may call climbing trees "wrong" or "bad." In the same way a man who has observed illegal behavior and the punishment contingent upon it may act to keep himself from such behavior and to prevent others from behaving in the same way. In doing so, he supports governmental control. But it is rare that an individual witnesses both the behavior and the punishment of another person. The effect of the contingency expressed in a law is usually mediated by complex verbal processes, which cannot be fully analyzed here. The law itself is a verbal device, and it is in furthering these intermediate processes that codification of governmental practices helps most. A code supports the verbal behavior which bridges the gap between instances of punishment and the behavior of others. Nevertheless, it is only a slight step toward a recognition of the behavioral processes through which governmental control is usually exerted.

The effect of a law upon the controlling agency. The government of a large group requires an elaborate organization, the practices of which may be made more consistent and effective by codification. How codes of law affect governmental agents is the principal subject of jurisprudence. The behavioral processes are complex, although presumably not novel. In order to maintain or "enforce" contingencies of governmental control, an agency must establish the fact that an individual has behaved illegally and must interpret a code to determine the punishment. It must then carry out the punishment. These labors are usually divided among special subdivisions of the agency. The advantages gained when the individual is "not under man but under law" have usually been obvious, and the great codifiers of law occupy places of honor in the history of civilization. Codification does not, however, change the essential nature of governmental action nor remedy all its defects.

TRADITIONAL INTERPRETATIONS

Until fairly recently it was customary to accept a mode of government, and the law which embodied it, as derived from unquestionable authority and permanently fixed. In the Divine Law of the Middle Ages, "legal" and "illegal" were held to be immutable classifications laid down by absolute decree. Such a view was strengthened by the absence of historical and comparative facts regarding other governmental and legal practices, and it was probably to some extent encouraged by the very codification of law. But the inevitable consequence was that any analysis of human behavior had to adjust itself to a particular set of established practices. Behavior had to be accepted, not for what it was observed to be, but for what it was decreed to be. If there was any discrepancy between the two, conformity to the decree prevailed.

The modern view, which is of surprisingly recent date, accepts the fact that government and law depend upon the circumstances of a given culture or epoch. It recognizes the fact that there is an English law, a French law, a Chinese law, a law of the sixteenth century, a law of the twentieth century, and so on. The modern lawmaker and the modern jurist are more likely to interpret governmental and legal practices in terms of their current effects upon the individual and the state. As a result of this change the observation of human behavior is no longer bound by authoritarian pronouncements, and a scientific study is under no obligation to justify a given set of practices. There remains, however, a great discrepancy between legal and scientific conceptions of human behavior.

In the tradition which led to modern English and American law, man was regarded as a "responsible" creature, who was born with or quickly acquired a "knowledge of right and wrong." He was held to be "accountable" for his actions, and if he violated a law, it was considered just that he be punished. Punishment was explained in different ways, depending upon the source of power of the government. When the power was derived from the strength of the governor or was asserted to be of divine or other absolute origin, a crime was regarded as an offense against the state. Punishment of the offender "vindicated" the state. This interpretation appears to be a rationalization of emotional dispositions on the part of governors to act aggressively toward those who "disturb the peace" or otherwise threaten their power. When the power was derived, at least in part, from the governed, the state was said to act in the interest of the more immediately aggrieved. Its function was then to "even a score," and the problem of penology was to make the punishment fit the crime. Justice had been done when the aversive stimulation received by the criminal precisely matched that of the aggrieved member of the group: an eye for an eye and a tooth for a tooth. This interpretation also seems to be related to an emotional tendency to take revenge.

Another interpretation of punishment appeals to constructive behavioral processes: It is said that a man is punished so that he will be less likely to misbehave in the future and so that others will be deterred from similar misbehavior. This effect may have nothing to do with emotional dispositions on the part of an offended ruler or an aggrieved citizen. At the same time, it is not appropriate to a conception of man as a responsible free agent with a knowledge of right and wrong. The difficulty is currently evident in conflicting theories of penology. It is now generally recognized that punishment is ineffective simply as a means of making behavior less probable. To take advantage of a better understanding of the process requires a change of practice, but this is difficult in the face of traditional views of human nature which presuppose another result. We may restate governmental and legal practices, however, in a way which is consistent with the behavioral processes involved in punishment.

As we saw in Chapter VII, operant behavior is closely associated with "volition." A "deliberate act," undertaken to obtain a "desired end," is an operant. The traditional way of describing it is unfortunate because it emphasizes a future event which can have no contemporary effect. It is necessary to endow the individual with a "knowledge of consequences" or some sort of "expectation" to bridge the gap between the past and the future. But we are always dealing with a *prior* history of reinforcement and punishment. The practices of government and law are clearly designed to construct or supplement such histories, and we can describe the individual who has come under governmental control wholly in such terms. The "reasons" or "grounds" for an "end-seeking action" are simply some of the variables of which behavior is a function. "Deliberation" and "desire" are others. A history of punishment is still another. To say that a person is "held responsible" for an act is simply to say that he is usually punished for it.

The question of the death penalty for murder supplies an example of the necessary change in interpretation. There is little doubt that death is an effective way of reducing a probability of response, but if capital punishment is simply a way of removing a dangerous individual from society, it has only an economic advantage over life imprisonment, which might be preferred for other reasons. Whether the execution of a murderer is a deterrent to others could presumably be decided with available techniques. It has often been pointed out that when pickpockets were hanged publicly, the crowds which gathered to witness the hangings proved to be easy marks for pickpockets, although it is difficult to conceive of circumstances under which the death penalty should be a more effective deterrent. Any decision concerning capital punishment appears to be a practical one, involving the weighing of advantages and disadvantages to society. But if the decision is to eliminate the death penalty, it may be opposed by those to whom punishment is a form of retribution and who may argue that in order to "equal the score" or "maximize justice" one who has killed must be killed.

A similar conflict arises in other forms of punishment. Is imprisonment a form of aversive stimulation or an opportunity to re-educate the individual? The fixing in advance of a given period of imprisonment presupposes the former, since the time needed for re-education is not necessarily closely related to the nature of a crime or to its magnitude. Any attempt to adopt practices which presuppose the latter may be opposed by those to whom punishment is a form of revenge.

The same transitional stage is evident in other discussions of responsibility. In current practice a murderer who is judged insane does not receive the death penalty; he is merely incarcerated to prevent further criminal behavior. The traditional view is that since he is not "responsible," it is not "just" that he be killed. But the same practice may be defended more consistently in terms of controllability. We cannot deter the insane or correct their behavior because they are *by definition* out of control. Physical restraint is the only available technique and may be frankly adopted for this reason. Lesser degrees of "irresponsibility" prove upon analysis to be simply lesser degrees of "uncontrollability." When it can be demonstrated by adequate testimony that a man is incapable of changing his conduct as the result of repeated legal punishment, he is permanently incarcerated. We do not commonly regard this as retribution; incarceration is required because other governmental techniques have failed. Sometimes psychotherapy, rather than legal punishment, is recognized as appropriate.

The responsibility of even the normal or legally sane citizen is acknowledged to have certain limits. This is again the question of the effectiveness of governmental controls. Illegal behavior is sometimes not punished, or is punished less severely, because it is committed in "the heat of passion," or in obeying an "irresistible impulse," or "under extenuating circumstances." In the traditional view the individual is not held responsible for his actions under such circumstances. In the present terms we may simply say that certain techniques of governmental control are recognized to be ineffective in competition with strong emotional or motivational variables. There is no point in attempting to apply governmental control, other than incarceration, to the behavior to which these variables lead. When such circumstances are not likely to occur frequently, the individual is permitted to remain at large. A philosophy of retribution, on the other hand, would still demand that justice be done.

OTHER TYPES OF GOVERNMENTAL CONTROL

It is not only the weight of tradition which is responsible for current inconsistencies in our philosophies of government and law. The ultimate weakness of punishment as a technique of control has been known for a long time. Unfortunately, alternative techniques require a different kind of governmental power and a better understanding of human behavior. Ethical control by the group has moved only very slowly from coercive techniques, in which the individual is forced to behave in conformity with the interests of others, to techniques in which "good" is more important than "bad." Religious agencies have, as we shall see, moved only slowly from an emphasis upon the punishments of Hell and the anger of jealous gods to the positive inducements of Heaven or the present satisfactions of the good life. Since governmental agencies have been particularly committed to the use of punishment, the change to other forms of control has been especially slow.

Modern governments, however, have it in their power to use other techniques and do so extensively. If wealth is accumulated—through taxation, for example—economic control is then available (Chapter XXV). This is used as a form of positive reinforcement in subsidies and bonuses. The citizen is thus induced to act legally rather than deterred from acting illegally. Although it is theoretically possible to control agricultural production through punishment by making the cultivation of certain crops illegal, a government with economic power achieves the same effect through positive reinforcement with subsidies. The educational control of legal behavior is another alternative technique. Where it is theoretically possible to induce a soldier to fight entirely through coercion—by arranging matters so that he must fight or be still more severely punished than in battle—a modern government is likely to generate an inclination to fight through educational devices. Variables in the fields of respondent conditioning, motivation, and emotion are arranged to increase a disposition to fight. These practices lead eventually to far more effective behavior than coercion. Unfortunately, educational techniques in the field of government are represented most conspicuously by propaganda, where variables are manipulated for an effect which is concealed or disguised, often in a way which is aversive to many people. But education may be effective even when the result is clearly indicated.

Similar alternative techniques are available in preventing illegal behavior, but the processes are more complicated and are not yet well explored. A start has been made at the level of minor offenses. Motorists are usually induced to obey traffic signals by a familiar process. A certain percentage of those who go through stop signs, for example, are punished. An alternative procedure which has been tried successfully is to commend or otherwise reinforce motorists who obey signs. This is clearly not an adequate technique for all drivers, but it has a measurable effect upon many who might otherwise be only partially controlled by traffic signals. Educational programs which point up the contingencies between reckless driving and its consequences—injury or death—should in the long run be more effective than a program of arrests and fines.

When a governmental agency turns to auxiliary techniques which are not based upon punishment, the concept of man as a "responsible agent" falls into disuse. This is additional proof that the concept serves merely to rationalize the use of punishment as a technique of control.

COUNTERCONTROL OF GOVERNMENTAL AGENCIES

Government and governed compose a social system in the sense of Chapter XIX. The questions which have just been raised concern the reciprocal interchange between the participants. The government manipulates variables which alter the behavior of the governed and is defined in terms of its power to do so. The change in the behavior of the governed supplies a return reinforcement to the government which explains its continuing function. A given system may be as simple as a strong man taking property from the weaker members of a group or as complex as a modern government embarking upon an educational program which will generate the skilled manpower it needs.

Such a system is inherently unstable, again in the sense of Chapter

XIX, since the power of the agency increases with each interchange. In fact, the growth of power accelerates as control becomes more and more effective. Other things being equal, governments grow stronger in the act of governing. When the strong man coerces others to engage in control in his interest, his total power is increased. When a government uses force to acquire wealth, it can then also exercise economic control.

The process cannot go on indefinitely, however. One limit, which arises within the system itself, is the simple exhaustion of the resources of the governed. This is exemplified in the ultimate failure of the tyrannical exploitation of a people. Excessive control also generates behavior on the part of the controllee in the form of escape, revolt, or passive resistance, as we shall see in Chapter XXIV. Other limits may be imposed from outside the system through competition with other would-be governing agencies.

The codification of controlling practices often has the effect of stabilizing the system. In stating a contingency between behavior and punishment, for example, a law imposes a restriction upon the governing agency. The social system of government and governed cannot deteriorate appreciably unless the law is changed. A more explicit countercontrol is represented by a constitution, in which a government which derives its power from the consent of the governed is constrained to use that power within specified areas. A constitution may specify the composition of the governing agency, the channels through which it receives its power, and the procedures according to which laws are to be made, interpreted, and enforced. With these specifications the system is prevented from deteriorating through an asymmetrical interchange.

A nation which has been completely defeated in warfare may, for a time at least, be governed by its conquerors. No constitution specifies the kinds or limits of power to be wielded. So far as immediate power is concerned, there is nothing to prevent the mass slaughter of the whole population, a practice of which history supplies many examples. But even when governmental power is not derived from the consent of the governed, it is now recognized that a government is not strengthened by excessive exploitation of a people. Mass murder is obviously not an effective way to use the human resources of the conquered country. The practice also generates extreme measures of countercontrol on the part of other countries in danger of a similar fate, and it plunges the government into serious trouble in controlling its own citizens.

We shall consider other undesirable by-products of excessive control in Chapter XXIV.

JUSTIFICATION OF GOVERNMENTAL PRACTICES

Governments have traditionally been evaluated in terms of their effects in promoting several principles. We have seen that one of these—justice—is appropriate to the narrower definition of government as the power to punish. It is punishment which is administered *with justice*, and a government which is successful in balancing aversive consequences is said to "maximize justice." Our practical support of such a government is probably not due to any such principle, however, but rather to the fact that a just government, in comparison with other governments, is more likely to reinforce the behavior of supporting it.

Another principle commonly appealed to is freedom. That government is said to be best which governs least. The freedom which is maximized by a good government is not, however, the freedom which is at issue in a science of behavior. Under a government which controls through positive reinforcement the citizen feels free, though he is no less controlled. Freedom from government is freedom from aversive consequences. We choose a form of government which maximizes freedom for a very simple reason: aversive events are aversive. A government which makes the least use of its power to punish is most likely to reinforce our behavior in supporting it.

Another principle currently in fashion is security. Security against aversive governmental control raises the same issue as freedom. So does security from want, which means security from aversive events which are not specifically arranged by the governing agency—from hunger, cold, or hardship in general, particularly in illness or old age. A government increases security by arranging an environment in which many common aversive consequences do not occur, in which positive consequences are easily achieved, and in which extreme states of deprivation are avoided. Such a government naturally reinforces the behavior of supporting it.

The "right" of a ruler was an ancient device for explaining his power to rule. "Human rights" such as justice, freedom, and security are devices for explaining the countercontrol exercised by the governed. A man has his rights in the sense that the governing agency is restricted in its power to control him. He asserts these rights along with other citizens when he resists control. "Human rights" are ways of representing certain effects of governing practices—effects which are in general positively reinforcing and which we therefore call good. To "justify" a government in such terms is simply an indirect way of pointing to the effect of the government in reinforcing the behavior of the supporting group.

It is commonly believed that justice, freedom, security, and so on refer to certain more remote consequences in terms of which a form of government may be evaluated. We shall return to this point in Section VI, where we shall see that an additional principle is needed to explain why these principles are chosen as a basis for evaluation.

CHAPTER XXIII

RELIGION

We have no reason to be disturbed by the fact that the basic practice through which an efficient government "keeps the peace" is exemplified under far less admirable circumstances in the use which the bully or gangster makes of his power to punish. It is not the technique of control but the ultimate effect upon the group which leads us to approve or disapprove of any practice. There is a similar discrepancy between the kinds of uses to which the basic technique of religious control may be put. The place of religion in modern life cannot be clearly understood without considering certain processes which are employed outside the field of religion proper for very different purposes.

Usually such terms as "superstition" and "magic" are aversive because they are commonly associated with exploitation for selfish purposes or with ineffective or poorly organized behavior. There is, however, no absolute distinction between a superstitious and a non-superstitious response. In respondent conditioning we saw that a single pairing of stimuli could result in a conditioned reflex. A neutral stimulus which has merely happened to accompany a fearful event may subsequently evoke an emotional response, and the effect may survive for a long time in spite of repeated presentations of the neutral stimulus alone. In operant behavior a single instance of a response which is followed by a reinforcing event may be strengthening, and the effect may survive for a long time even though the same consequence never occurs again. Verbal behavior is especially likely to show this sort of "magic" because of the lack of a mechanical connection between response and reinforcement. The child acquires an elaborate verbal repertoire which produces certain effects. Through the process of induction he also exhibits verbal responses which cannot have more than an occasional "accidental" effect. Having successfully told people to stop, he may cry "Stop!" to a ball rolling out of reach. Though we may prove that his response can have no effect upon the ball, it is in the nature of the behavioral process that the response nevertheless acquires strength. As we have already seen, the tendency to behave superstitiously necessarily increases as the individual comes to be more sensitively affected by single contingencies. Between the contingency which is observed only once in the life of the individual and the contingency which is inevitably observed there is a continuum which we cannot divide sharply at any point to distinguish between "superstition" and "fact."

A prototype of religious control arises when rare or accidental contingencies are used in controlling the behavior of others. For example, we may "blame" someone for an unfortunate event which was not actually the result of his behavior, although the temporal relation was such that a contingency can be asserted. "If you hadn't dawdled so, we should have started earlier, and the accident never would have happened." We blame him in order to alter his future behavior—to make him less likely to dawdle, and we achieve this by converting an unrelated event into an effective punishing consequence through certain verbal processes. We use the event as a punishment, even though we did not actually arrange the contingency. It is only a short step to claiming the ability to arrange such contingencies. This is the underlying principle of witchcraft. Unless the controllee behaves according to command, the controller will bring bad luck to him. The threat to do so may be as powerful as the infliction of comparable physical punishment.

We also affect the behavior of others by using accidental reinforcing consequences of a positive sort. "You see, if you hadn't followed my advice, you would have missed this pleasant surprise." It is only a short step to the claim to be able to mediate future positive reinforcements—to be able to "bring good luck." The claim may be used to induce another person to grant favors, to pay money, and so on. Thus, to sell a spurious device for locating water underground it is only necessary to establish the claim that by using the device the well-digger will be reinforced by finding water. Good-luck charms have economic value when their power to mediate positive reinforcement is made convincing to the buyer.

Perhaps it is a far cry from these selfish practices to those of the organized religious agency, but the same techniques appear to be exemplified. The control which defines a religious agency in the narrowest possible sense derives from a claimed connection with the supernatural, through which the agency arranges or alters certain contingencies involving good or bad luck in the immediate future or eternal blessedness or damnation in the life to come. Such a controlling agency is composed of those who are able to establish their claim to the power to intervene supernaturally. The agency may consist of a single individual, such as the tribal medicine man, who resorts to demonstrations of magic to prove his power to bring good luck or bad, or of a well-organized church with documented proof that the power to intervene in the arrangement of reinforcing contingencies has been vested in it by supernatural authority. We are concerned here, not with the actual structure of the agency nor with the internal techniques of control which make it an effective instrument, but with the practices through which it controls the members of the group.

TECHNIQUES OF RELIGIOUS CONTROL

The principal technique is an extension of group and governmental control. Behavior is classified, not simply as "good" and "bad" or "legal" and "illegal," but as "moral" and "immoral" or "virtuous" and "sinful." It is then reinforced or punished accordingly. Traditional descriptions of Heaven and Hell epitomize positive and negative reinforcement. The features vary from culture to culture, but it is doubtful whether any well-known positive or negative reinforcer has not been used. To a primitive people who depend upon forest and field for their food, Heaven is a happy hunting ground. To a poverty-stricken people primarily concerned with the source of the next meal, it is a perpetual fish fry. To the unhappy it is relief from pain and sorrow or a reunion with departed friends and loved ones. Hell, on the other hand, is an assemblage of aversive stimuli, which has often been imaginatively portrayed. In Dante's *Inferno*, for example, we find most of the negative reinforcers characteristic of social and nonsocial environments. Only the electric shock of the psychological laboratory is missing.

The reinforcers portrayed in Heaven and Hell are far more powerful than those which support the "good" and "bad" of the ethical group or the "legal" and "illegal" of governmental control, but this advantage is offset to some extent by the fact that they do not actually operate in the lifetime of the individual. The power achieved by the religious agency depends upon how effectively certain verbal reinforcements are conditioned—in particular the promise of Heaven and the threat of Hell. Religious education contributes to this power by pairing these terms with various conditioned and unconditioned reinforcers which are essentially those available to the ethical group and to governmental agencies. The relation between the agency and the communicant, or between God and man, is often made more effective by being characterized as such a familiar mundane relation as that between a father and his sons, a king and his subjects, or a military commander and his men—where again the primary reinforcing contingencies do not differ greatly from those used in ethical and governmental control.

In actual practice a threat to bar from Heaven or to consign to Hell is made contingent upon sinful behavior, while virtuous behavior brings a promise of Heaven or a release from the threat of Hell. The last is a particularly powerful technique. The agency punishes sinful behavior in such a way that it automatically generates an aversive condition which the individual describes as a "sense of sin." The agency then provides escape from this aversive condition through

expiation or absolution and is thus able to supply a powerful reinforcement for pious behavior.

Other techniques are, of course, encountered in religious control.
Insofar as the agency controls other variables, it can use other processes. It may acquire wealth and operate eventually through *economic*
control (Chapter XXV). It may train and support teachers to achieve
educational control (Chapter XXVI). It may utilize *ethical* or *governmental* techniques in addition to those within its own sphere
(Chapters XXI and XXII). This is especially likely when its controlling practices coincide with those of the group as a whole. In short, all
the techniques described under self-control in Chapter XV and under
personal control in Chapter XX are available to the agency possessing
the necessary power.

The use of physical restraint by a religious agency is exemplified by
actual incarceration, as in the treatment of women in Moslem countries. Relevant environmental conditions are manipulated when the
stimuli which elicit or set the occasion for sinful behavior are weakened or removed and when the stimuli which elicit or serve as the
occasion for virtuous behavior are pointed up. Suggested regimens of
simple fare, unseductive clothing, limited personal contact, and the
other features of the cloister or the "sheltered life" follow this pattern. Religious agencies are likely to favor censorship of movies,
plays, and books, the enforcement of laws governing modesty of
dress, the prohibition of the sale of alcoholic beverages, and so on,
because these measures reduce occasions for sinful behavior. Satiation and deprivation also are manipulated. St. Paul defended marriage as a measure which reduces licentious behavior, and periods of
fasting and regimens of exercise may be employed for the same
effect. Ritualistic techniques which affect the physiology of the
organism are common—in Hindu practices, for example. Some religions encourage substitute forms of behavior to reduce sexual or
other tendencies; the practice is based upon the transferred satiation
discussed in Chapter IX. Since emotion is usually an important means
of religious control, respondent conditioning is important. Religious
art, music, and pageantry generate emotional responses by portraying
the suffering of martyrs, the torments of the damned, the tender

emotions of the family, and so on. These responses are transferred to stimuli, verbal or nonverbal, which are later used by the agency for purposes of control. Some religious agencies resort to the use of drugs, either to induce appropriate emotional or motivational conditions or to produce effects which seem to support the claim of a supernatural connection.

Other kinds of religious agencies. Many religious agencies make no claim to be able to intervene in the arrangement of reinforcements. The agency may accept the existence of supernatural reinforcing events—for example, Heaven and Hell—but may claim only to be able to *prescribe a course of action* upon which they are contingent. The attainment of Heaven or Hell is said to depend upon the behavior of the individual alone. The agency controls the communicant, not by manipulating contingencies of reinforcement, but by making certain real or claimed contingencies more effective. Its techniques then resemble those of the counselor (Chapter XXIV) or teacher (Chapter XXVI). Such an agency is composed of those who establish their claim to the knowledge of such a way of life and who exercise that claim for purposes of control.

Still other religious agencies make no appeal to supernatural events whatsoever. Their techniques are scarcely to be distinguished from those of the ethical group. The agency simply furthers ethical control in encouraging good behavior and discouraging bad. It functions as counselor or teacher in demonstrating certain contingencies between "good" or "bad" behavior and *natural* consequences. A way of life is set forth which "brings its own reward." Membership in this third type of agency is often not sharply defined.

THE BEHAVIOR CONTROLLED BY THE RELIGIOUS AGENCY

The behavior which comes under religious control depends upon the type of agency. For the medicine man, who uses his magic for his own aggrandizement, "pious" behavior is simply any behavior which reinforces him. On the other hand, the well-developed religious agency which derives much of its power from the group may control largely in accordance with group practice. It works in concert with ethical control in suppressing selfish, primarily reinforced behavior and in strengthening behavior which works to the advantage of others. The control is usually much more stringent, however, than that exercised by the group. Variables are manipulated in ethical control because of some current threat to the welfare of a member of the group, but the religious agency maintains its practices according to more enduring criteria of virtuous and sinful behavior. Where eating and drinking may be restricted by ethical reinforcement only when they work to the momentary disadvantage of others, religious control may establish much narrower limits by classifying gluttony as a deadly sin and temperance as a cardinal virtue. Where sexual behavior is controlled by the group mainly in certain competitive situations, the religious agency may encourage chastity and celibacy as a general program and may tolerate sexual behavior even in marriage only for the purpose of procreation. Acquisitive or possessive behavior which leads to group retribution only in a competitive situation and is elsewhere classified as good may be wholly suppressed, regardless of the circumstances, by the religious agency which demands a vow of poverty or enjoins the communicant not to lay up treasures on earth. The boastful behavior of the Pharisee, which encounters only moderate group censure, is suppressed in favor of humility and modesty. The extremity of this form of religious control is seen in the suppression of the behavior of self-preservation in pacifistic philosophies, acts of martyrdom, and the mortification of the flesh. On the other hand, behavior which benefits others is promoted. Love or charity as a disposition to favor others is encouraged, and the communicant is reminded that he is his brother's keeper and must give all that he has to the poor.

The religious agency usually establishes a repertoire of *obedience* for future use, and it may also set up extremely powerful *self-control* to guarantee a measure of controlled behavior in the absence of the religious agent. The latter is one of the consequences of an emphasis on punishment. Because the control is often exerted more powerfully than by the group, the religious conscience or superego often speaks in a louder voice than the ethical. Extreme measures of self-restraint are sometimes enjoined. The individual may confine himself to restricted diets, enter upon periods of fasting, engage in certain exercises or adopt certain postures, or take certain drugs—all because of the resulting change in his dispositions to act in virtuous or sinful ways. Self-control through the manipulation of stimuli is common. "Temptation" (often personified in religious literature as Satan) embraces all the stimuli which lead to sinful behavior. "Wrestling with the devil" appears to describe the conflict between the controlled and controlling responses of Chapter XV.

EXPLAINING THE AGENCY

The controlling relations which hold the religious agency together as an effective unit do not account for the ultimate form of control, nor would they explain the agency which has only one member. To account for the existence and maintenance of the agency as a whole we turn to external variables. If the agency serves the group by extending ethical control, the agency may be explained by the support which the group gives it. The religious agent may be paid by the group, he may be disposed to control because the group approves this as "right," or he may be coerced into working for the agency because any other course of action would be punished as "wrong."

There is another possible interpretation of the behavior of some religious agents. When an individual is conditioned through ethical and religious practices to "avoid temptation"—to eliminate stimuli which would otherwise be conducive to wrong or sinful behavior—his efforts may be so extensive that they affect other people as well. Freud called the result "reaction formation." If the individual's behavior in this respect resembles religious control, he may simply join the agency. He is reinforced for serving as a religious agent by the effect upon his own behavior. If economic or coercive control appears to be unimportant, his zeal may be unusually conspicuous. Since this explanation presupposes that the religious agent himself has an especially high probability of engaging in sinful behavior, it is generally resisted.

COUNTERCONTROL

An agency always operates within certain limits. The religious agency may come into conflict with other religious agencies attempting to control the same people or with governmental agencies with different programs of control. Religious control is often opposed by economic and educational agencies and, as we shall see in Chapter XXIV, by psychotherapy.

Another limit is internal. It is imposed by the extent to which the controllee will submit to control. The claim to supernatural intercession supplies a powerful technique. Religious agencies, like all other agencies here being considered, have sometimes used their power for personal or institutional advantages—to build organizations, to accumulate wealth, to punish those who do not come under control easily, and so on. From time to time this has given rise to measures of countercontrol which have restricted the scope of the agency. The religious controllee may simply leave the sphere of control of the agency, he may question the reality of claimed contingencies, he may attack the agency by establishing a rival agency, and so on.

JUSTIFICATION OF RELIGIOUS CONTROL

The justification of religious practice is an important part of theology. A particular practice may be recommended because it maximizes some such entity as salvation or the glory of God. Such justifications are presumably beyond the realm of science. An analysis of techniques permits us to account for the behavior of both controller and controllee without raising the question of any ultimate effect of this sort. When a religious practice does not appeal to supernatural events, its traditional justification resembles that of ethical control; a religious practice is supported because it maximizes *piety* or *virtue*. These entities have a function in the field of religion similar to that of the greatest good of the greatest number in ethics, and freedom or justice in government. They are "principles" in terms of which we choose or suggest a given practice. Whether a science of behavior provides us with any basis for explaining why we choose or suggest such a principle will be considered in Section VI.

CHAPTER XXIV

PSYCHOTHERAPY

CERTAIN BY-PRODUCTS OF CONTROL

The control exercised by the group and by religious and governmental agencies, as well as by parents, employers, associates, and so on, restricts the selfish, primarily reinforced behavior of the individual. It is exercised for just that reason. Certain by-products, however, are not to the advantage of the controller and are often harmful both to the individual and to the group. These are especially likely to be encountered when the control is excessive or inconsistent.

Escape. The individual may simply run away from the controller. The hermit escapes from the control of the ethical group by physically withdrawing from it, as the boy runs away from home; but the controllee may be "withdrawn" without being actually separated. Escape from religious control is represented by disbelief and defection, and from various forms of governmental control by desertion, evasion, renunciation of citizenship, and breaking jail.

Revolt. The individual may counterattack the controlling agent. He may respond to criticism from the group by criticizing it in turn; the liberal accuses the group of being reactionary, the libertine accuses it of being prudish. Vandalism is a more concrete example of counteraggression—toward the group as a whole or toward a specific subgroup, as in the willful destruction of school property. Religious revolt may be directed toward a specific agency, as in protestant reform, or against the theological system used in control, as in atheism. Revolt against governmental control is exemplified, not only by political revolution, but, when the structure of the group permits, by impeachment or a vote of no confidence.

Passive resistance. Another result, far less easily described, consists of simply not behaving in conformity with controlling practices. This often follows when the individual has been extinguished in efforts to escape or revolt. The behavior is epitomized by the mule which fails to respond to the aversive stimulation of the whip. The child, unsuccessful in avoiding or revolting against parental control, simply becomes stubborn. The employee, unable to escape (by resigning) or to revolt in vandalism or other acts of violence, simply "slows down," "sits down," or "strikes." Thoreau's civil disobedience, practiced perhaps most conspicuously by Gandhi, is the parallel reaction to governmental control.

The controlling agency usually deals with these by-products by intensifying its practices. The escapee is captured and confined more securely. The revolt is put down, and the revolutionist shot. The apostate is excommunicated. A fire is built under the mule, and Thoreau is jailed. The agency may also meet this problem by preparing the individual in advance to control his own tendencies to escape, revolt, or strike. It classifies these types of behavior as wrong, illegal, or sinful, and punishes accordingly. As a result any tendency on the part of the individual to escape, revolt, or strike generates aversive self-stimulation, a reduction in which may reinforce behavior acceptable to the agency. But in the long run the problem cannot be solved in this way. Intensification of control may simply multiply the difficulties. Physical restraint or death may effectively eliminate behavior, but the individual is no longer useful to the group. Restraint is unsuccessful in controlling the covert behavior in which the individual may plan escape or revolt. Restraint also cannot control many sorts of emotional reactions. Techniques designed to generate additional *self*-control of emotional behavior are, as we have seen, especially inadequate.

The by-products of control which incapacitate the individual or are dangerous either to the individual or to others are the special field of psychotherapy. We shall discuss this as a kind of controlling agency. Among the kinds of behavior which it treats we may distinguish certain effects primarily in the field of emotion and others in operant behavior.

EMOTIONAL BY-PRODUCTS OF CONTROL

Fear. The controlling practice which leads the individual to escape also gives rise to the emotional pattern of fear. Reflex responses in glands and smooth muscles are first elicited by the aversive stimuli used in punishment and later by any stimuli which have occurred at the same time. These responses may be accompanied by a profound change in operant behavior—an increase in the strength of any behavior which has led to escape and a general weakening of other forms. The individual shows little interest in food, sex, or practical or artistic enterprises, and in the extreme case he may be essentially "paralyzed by fear."

When the stimuli which have this effect are supplied by the punishing agent, the individual suffers from an excessive fear of his father, the police, God, and so on. When they arise from the occasion upon which punished behavior has occurred, the individual is afraid of such occasions. Thus if he has been punished for sexual behavior, he may become unduly afraid of anything which has to do with sex; if he has been punished for being unclean, he may become unduly afraid of filth; and so on. When the stimuli are generated by the punished behavior itself, the individual is afraid to act—he is, as we say, afraid of himself. It is often difficult, for either the individual himself or anyone else, to identify the stimulation responsible for the emotional pattern. If the condition recurs frequently, as is especially likely to be the case with self-generated stimuli, the fear may become chronic.

The phobias represent excessive fear reactions to circumstances which are not always clearly associated with control. But the fact that they are "unreasonable" fears—fears for which no commensurate causal condition can be found—suggests that they are primarily responses to punishment and that the fear generated by excessive control has simply been displaced (Chapter X).

Anxiety. A common accompaniment of avoidance or escape is anxiety. As we saw in Chapter XI, fear of a future event may be aroused by specific stimuli which have preceded punishing events or by features of the general environment in which such events have occurred. Anxiety may vary in intensity from a slight worry to extreme dread. The condition includes both responses of glands and smooth muscles and marked changes in operant behavior. We imply that the condition is due to controlling practices when we call it shame, guilt, or a sense of sin.

Anger or rage. The emotional pattern which accompanies revolt includes responses of glands and smooth muscles and a well-marked effect upon operant behavior which includes a heightened disposition to act aggressively toward the controlling agent and a weakening of other behavior. The emotion may be displaced from the controlling agent to other people or to things in general. A mild example is a bad temper; an extreme one, sadism. The temper tantrum appears to be a sort of undirected revolt.

Depression. Emotional responses associated with passive resistance are of several kinds. The stubborn child also sulks; the adult may be depressed, resentful, moody, listless, or bored, depending upon minor details of control. (Boredom arises not simply because there is nothing to do but because nothing can be done—either because a situation is unfavorable for action or because the group or a controlling agency has imposed physical or self-restraint.)

All these emotional patterns may, of course, be generated by aversive events which have nothing to do with social control. Thus a storm at sea may generate fear or anxiety, a door which will not open may engender frustration or rage, and something akin to sulking is the emotional counterpart of protracted extinction, as at the end of a long but fruitless struggle to win an argument or repair a bicycle. By far the greater part of the inciting circumstances of this sort, however, are due to the control of the individual by the group or by governmental or religious agencies.

The effects may be severe. Productive patterns of behavior are distorted by strong emotional predispositions, and the operant behavior which is strengthened in emotion may have disastrous consequences. Frequent or chronic emotional responses of glands and smooth muscles may injure the individual's health. Disorders of the digestive system, including ulcers, and allergic reactions have been traced to chronic responses in fear, anxiety, rage, or depression. These are sometimes called "psychosomatic" disorders. The term carries the unfortunate implication that the illness is the effect of the mind upon the body. As we have seen, it is sometimes correct to say that an emotional state *causes* a medical disability, as when a chronic response of glands or smooth muscles produces a structural change, such as an ulcer, but both cause and effect are somatic, not psychic. Moreover, an earlier link in the causal chain remains to be identified. The emotional state which produces the disability must itself be accounted for and treated. The manipulable variables of which both the somatic cause and the somatic effect are functions lie in the environmental history of the individual. Some psychosomatic "symptoms" are merely parallel effects of such a prior common cause. For example, an asthmatic attack is not the effect of anxiety, it is part of it.

SOME EFFECTS OF CONTROL
UPON OPERANT BEHAVIOR

Control through punishment may also have unforeseen effects upon operant behavior. The process of self-control miscarries when the individual discovers ways of avoiding aversive self-stimulation which prove eventually to be ineffective, troublesome, or dangerous. Emotional reactions may be involved, but we are concerned here with the operant effect only.

Drug addiction as a form of escape. Certain drugs provide a temporary escape from conditioned or unconditioned aversive stimulation as well as from accompanying emotional responses. Alcohol is conspicuously successful. The individual who has engaged in behavior which has been punished, and who therefore feels guilty or ashamed, is reinforced when he drinks alcohol because self-generated aversive stimuli are thus suppressed. A very strong tendency to drink may result from repeated reinforcement, especially if the aversive condition is severe. The word "addiction" is often reserved for the case in which the drug provides escape from the aversive effects called withdrawal symptoms, which are produced by the earlier use of the drug itself. Alcohol may lead to this sort of addiction, but such drugs as morphine and cocaine show it more clearly. Addiction at this stage is a different problem, but the earlier use of the drug can usually be explained by its effect upon the consequences of punishment.

Excessively vigorous behavior. The individual may show an unusually high probability of response which is not "well adapted to reality" in the sense that the behavior cannot be accounted for in terms of current variables. It can sometimes be explained by pointing to an earlier history of control. When effective escape is impossible, for example, a highly aversive condition may evoke ineffective behavior in the form of aimless wandering or searching. Simple "nervousness" is often of this sort. The individual is uneasy and cannot rest, although his behavior cannot be explained plausibly in terms of its current consequences.

Sometimes there are obvious consequences, but we need to appeal to an earlier history to show why they are reinforcing. For example, behavior may provide a measure of escape by generating stimuli which evoke reactions incompatible with the emotional by-products of punishment. Thus in "thrill-seeking" the individual exposes himself to stimuli which evoke responses incompatible with depression or boredom. We explain why the "thrill" is reinforcing by showing that it supplants an aversive result of excessive control. Sometimes the behavior to be explained can be shown to be a form of "doing something else." A preoccupation which does not appear to offer commensurate positive reinforcement is explained by showing that it avoids the aversive consequences of some other course of action. Some compulsions and obsessions appear to have this effect. A preoccupation with situations in which punished behavior is especially unlikely to occur may be explained in much the same way. When the excessive behavior is an extension of a technique of self-control in which the environment is altered so that it becomes less likely to generate punished behavior, the effect is Freud's "reaction formation."

Excessively restrained behavior. The special caution with which one drives a car after an accident or near accident may also be generated by the aversive events used in control. Repeated punishment may produce an inhibited, shy, or taciturn person. In the so-called "hysterical paralyses" the restraint may be complete. The etiology is usually clear when the paralysis is limited to a particular part of the topography of behavior. Thus the individual who is excessively punished for talking may stop talking altogether in "hysterical aphasia." No control, aversive or otherwise, will succeed in generating verbal behavior. Similarly, the individual who has been punished—perhaps only through self-generated aversive consequences—for striking a friend may develop a paralyzed arm. This is different from the paralysis of fear. It is the difference between being too frightened to move and being afraid to move. The first of these conditions can be generated by an event which is not contingent upon behavior, and it is usually not localized topographically. The second is a result of the punishing consequences of previous movement.

Defective stimulus control. When behavior has been severely punished, either by a controlling agency or by the physical environment, the individual may come to make ineffective or inaccurate discriminative responses. A stimulus similar to that which evoked the punished behavior may evoke no response whatsoever. When the stimulus pattern is complex, we say that the individual "refuses to face the facts." When, for example, he does not see a very obvious object, we say that he suffers from a "negative hallucination." All reactions to a given mode of stimulation are absent in *hysterical anesthesia*. A child may begin by "paying no attention" to a nagging parent, but the behavior of "doing something else instead" may be so successful in avoiding aversive stimulation and possibly aversive emotional responses to such stimulation that a complete "functional" deafness may develop.

A commoner result is simply defective discrimination. In projection, for example, the individual reacts incorrectly or atypically to a given state of affairs, and his behavior can often be traced to the avoidance of effects of control. In a "show of bravado" a situation is characterized as nothing to be afraid of and is therefore less likely to generate the fear for which the individual has been punished. In some *hallucinations* a situation in which punishment has been received is "seen" as free of any threat. In a *delusion of persecution* a distorted reaction to the environment permits the individual to escape from the aversive self-stimulation generated by behavior or a failure to behave for which he has been punished.

Defective self-knowledge. The individual may also react defectively to stimuli generated by his own behavior. In simple boasting, for example, he characterizes his own behavior in a way which escapes aversive stimulation. He boasts of achievement to escape the effects of punishment for incompetence, of bravery to escape the effects of punishment for cowardice, and so on. This sort of rationalizing is best exemplified by delusions of grandeur in which all aversive self-stimulation may be effectively masked. It has already been shown that complete lack of self-knowledge—a form of negative hallucination or hysterical anesthesia restricted to self-stimulation—can be attributed to the avoidance of the effects of punishment (Chapter XVIII).

Aversive self-stimulation. One may injure oneself or arrange to be injured by others. One may also deprive oneself of positive reinforcers or arrange to be so deprived by others. These consequences may or may not be contingent upon behavior in the form of punishment, and we have seen that the effect of the contingency is, in any case, not clear. Such self-stimulation is explained if it can be shown that the individual thus avoids even more aversive consequences. If a conditioned aversive stimulus characteristically precedes the unconditioned by an appreciable interval of time, the total effect of the prolonged conditioned stimulus may be more aversive than that of the briefer unconditioned stimulus. The individual can then escape from the anxiety of impending punishment by "getting it over with." The murderer in Dostoevski's *Crime and Punishment* turns himself over to a punishing governmental agent. Religious confession occurs because expiation is less aversive than a sustained sense of sin. It has been argued, particularly by Freud, that "accidents" are sometimes a species of aversive self-stimulation which alleviates a condition of guilt or sin.

It is not always possible to find a specific history of punishment which will explain a given instance of aversive self-stimulation. Why an individual injures himself or arranges to be injured by others "masochistically" may be difficult to explain. In the absence of a more obvious explanation, it may be argued that such behavior reduces a sustained state of shame, guilt, or sin. When many different kinds of responses have been punished under many different circumstances, conditioned aversive stimuli may be widely distributed in the environment, and a condition of anxiety may be chronic. Under these circumstances aversive self-stimulation may be positively reinforcing. Another possible explanation of masochistic self-stimulation is that the process of respondent conditioning has been effective in the wrong direction. In punishment aversive stimuli are paired with the strongly reinforcing consequences of, say, sexual behavior. The expected result is that sexual behavior will automatically generate conditioned aversive stimuli—*but the aversive stimuli used in punishment may become positively reinforcing in the same process.*

PSYCHOTHERAPY AS A
CONTROLLING AGENCY

Behavior which is inconvenient or dangerous to the individual himself or to others often requires "treatment." Formerly this treatment was left to friends, parents, or acquaintances, or to representatives of controlling agencies. In simple "good advice" a course of action which should have advantageous consequences is recommended. A great deal of casual therapy is prescribed in proverbs, folklore, and other forms of lay wisdom.

Psychotherapy represents a special agency which concerns itself with this problem. It is not an organized agency, like a government or religion, but a profession, the members of which observe more or less standardized practices. Psychotherapy has already become an important source of control in the lives of many people, and some account is therefore required here.

Diagnosis. The psychotherapist must of course know something about the patient whom he is treating. He must have certain information about his history, about the behavior which calls for treatment, and about the current circumstances in which the patient lives. The examination of the patient has been heavily emphasized in clinical psychology. How to conduct an interview, how to take a life history, how to analyze trains of thought in free association, how to determine probabilities of response from projective tests or dreams, and how to use these probabilities to infer histories of deprivation, reinforcement, or emotional stimulation have all been studied. Tests of intelligence and other traits have been devised to enable the therapist to predict how readily the patient will react to various kinds of therapy.

It is often implied that diagnosis, merely as the collection of information about the patient, is the only point at which a science of behavior can be helpful in therapy. Once all the facts about an individual have been collected, treatment is left to good judgment and common sense. This is an example of a broad misunderstanding of the application of the methods of science to human behavior. The collecting of facts is only the first step in a scientific analysis. The demonstrating of functional relationships is the second. When the independent variables are under control, such relationships lead directly to control of the dependent variable. In the present case, control means therapy. An adequate science of human behavior should make perhaps a greater contribution to therapy than to diagnosis. Nevertheless, the extension of science to therapy has met with resistance, possibly for certain reasons to be considered in Chapter XXIX.

The steps which must be taken to correct a given condition of behavior follow directly from an analysis of that condition. Whether they can be taken will depend, of course, upon whether the therapist has control over the relevant variables.

Therapy. The initial power of the therapist as a controlling agent arises from the fact that the condition of the patient is aversive and that any relief or promise of relief is therefore positively reinforcing. To explain why the patient turns to the therapist in any given instance requires the analysis of a rather complicated history, much of which is verbal. Assurances of help, various forms of evidence which make such assurances effective, the prestige of the therapist, reports of improvement in other patients, slight signs of early improvement in the patient himself, evidences of the wisdom of the therapist in other matters—all enter into the process but in much too complex a way to be analyzed here. In addition the therapist may use variables which are available to him in personal control or as a member of the ethical group or which derive from his resemblance to members of the patient's family or to governmental or religious agents who have already established control in other ways.

All in all, however, the original power of the therapist is not very great. Since the effect which he is to achieve requires time, his first task is to make sure that the time will be available. The therapist uses whatever limited power he originally possesses to make sure that the patient will remain in contact with him—that the patient will return for further treatment. As treatment progresses, however, his power increases. As an organized social system develops, the therapist becomes an important source of reinforcement. If he is successful in providing relief, the behavior of the patient in turning to him for help is reinforced. The therapist's approval may become especially effective. As his knowledge of the patient grows, he may also use positive reinforcers which are, in a sense, beyond his control by pointing up contingencies between particular forms of behavior and particular consequences. He may demonstrate, for example, that various aversive events actually result from the patient's own behavior. He may suggest modes of action which are likely to be positively reinforced. Once the therapist has acquired the necessary control, he may also suggest schedules or routines which affect levels of deprivation or satiation, which arrange for the presentation of stimuli leading to the conditioning or extinction of emotional reflexes, which eliminate stimulating situations having unfortunate consequences, and so on. These schedules, adopted first because of the verbal control of the therapist, eventually acquire other sources of strength if their effect upon the condition of the patient is reinforcing.

The nonpunishing audience. The commonest current technique of psychotherapy is due to Sigmund Freud. It has been characterized in many different ways in many different theories of behavior. So far as we are concerned here, it may be described simply in this way: the therapist constitutes himself a nonpunishing audience. The process through which he does this may take time. From the point of view of the patient, the therapist is at first only one more member of a society which has exerted excessive control. It is the task of the therapist to establish himself in a different position. He therefore consistently avoids the use of punishment. He does not criticize his patient nor object to his behavior in any way. He does not point out errors in pronunciation, grammar, or logic. In particular, he avoids any sign of counteraggression when the patient criticizes or otherwise injures him. The role of nonpunisher is made clearer if the therapist frequently responds in ways which are incompatible with punishment—for example, if he returns a conspicuous demonstration of friendship for aggressive attack or dismisses the patient's report of punishable behavior with a casual, "That's interesting."

As the therapist gradually establishes himself as a nonpunishing audience, behavior which has hitherto been repressed begins to appear in the repertoire of the patient. For example, the patient may recall a previously forgotten episode in which he was punished. Early experiences in which aversive control was first felt, and which have been long repressed, often supply dramatic examples. The patient may also begin to describe current tendencies to behave in punishable ways—for example, aggressively. He may also begin to behave in punishable ways: he may speak ungrammatically, illogically, or in obscene or blasphemous terms, or he may criticize or insult the therapist. Nonverbal behavior which has previously been punished may also begin to appear: he may become socially aggressive or may indulge himself selfishly. If such behavior has been wholly repressed, it may at first reach only the covert level; the individual may begin to behave verbally or nonverbally "to himself"—as in fantasying punished behavior. The behavior may later be brought to the overt level. The patient may also begin to exhibit strong emotions: he may have a good cry, make a violent display of temper, or be "hysterically" silly.

If, in the face of such behavior, the therapist is successful in maintaining his position as a nonpunisher, the process of reducing the effect of punishment is accelerated. More and more punished behavior makes its appearance. If, however, the therapist becomes critical or otherwise punishes or threatens to punish, or if previously punished behavior begins to be emitted too rapidly, the process may suddenly cease. The aversive condition which arises to reverse the trend is sometimes spoken of as "resistance."

There is a second stage in the therapeutic process. The appearance of previously punished behavior in the presence of a nonpunishing audience makes possible the extinction of some of the effects of punishment. This is the principal result of such therapy. Stimuli which are automatically generated by the patient's own behavior become less and less aversive and less and less likely to generate emotional reactions. The patient feels less wrong, less guilty, or less sinful. As a direct consequence he is less likely to exhibit the various forms of operant behavior which, as we have seen, provide escape from such self-generated stimulation.

PSYCHOTHERAPY VERSUS RELIGIOUS AND GOVERNMENTAL CONTROL

The principal technique of psychotherapy is thus designed to reverse behavioral changes which have come about as the result of punishment. Very frequently this punishment has been administered by religious or governmental agencies. There is, therefore, a certain opposition between psychotherapy and religious and governmental control. The opposition is also seen when the psychotherapist advocates changes in established controlling techniques. For example, he may recommend a modification of police action against young offenders or certain types of psychopathic personalities. This opposition has attracted considerable attention. Representatives of some religious agencies have accused psychotherapists of fostering immoral tendencies, and, for similar reasons, government officials have resisted reforms proposed by psychotherapists.

Although there is a fundamental opposition in the behavioral processes employed, there is not necessarily any difference in the behavior which these three agencies attempt to establish. The psychotherapist is interested in correcting certain by-products of control. Even though he may dispute the efficacy of certain techniques, he will probably not question the need for the behavior which the religious or governmental practice is designed to establish. In avoiding the by-products of excessive control, he may reinstate a certain amount of selfish behavior in the individual by weakening the aversive stimulation which results from religious or governmental control; but he will agree that selfish behavior must be suppressed by the group and by agencies operating within and for the group, and he must prepare his patient to accept this control.

The techniques available to religious and governmental agencies are extremely powerful, and they are frequently misused with disadvantageous results both to the individual and to the group. Some degree of countercontrol on the part of psychotherapy or some similar agency is therefore often needed. Since the variables under the control of the therapist are relatively weak, and since he must operate within certain ethical, religious, and legal limits, he can scarcely be regarded as a serious threat. Whether we can decide ultimately upon the "best" degree of religious or governmental control will be considered in Section VI.

TRADITIONAL INTERPRETATIONS

What is "wrong" with the individual who displays these by-products of punishment is easily stated. A particular personal history has produced an organism whose behavior is disadvantageous or dangerous. In what sense it is disadvantageous or dangerous must be specified in each case by noting the consequences both to the individual himself and to others. The task of the therapist is to supplement a personal history in such a way that behavior no longer has these characteristics.

This is not, however, the traditional view. The field of psychotherapy is rich in explanatory fictions. Behavior itself has not been accepted as a subject matter in its own right, but only as an indication of *something wrong somewhere else*. The task of therapy is said to be to remedy an inner illness of which the behavioral manifestations are merely "symptoms." Just as religious agencies maximize salvation or piety, and governmental agencies justice, freedom, or security, so psychotherapy is dedicated to the maximizing of *mental health* or *personal adjustment*. These terms are usually negative because they are defined by specifying unhealthy or maladjusted behavior which is absent in health or adjustment. Frequently, the condition to be corrected is called "neurotic," and the thing to be attacked by psychotherapy is then identified as a "neurosis." The term no longer carries its original implication of a derangement of the nervous system, but it is nevertheless an unfortunate example of an explanatory fiction. It has encouraged the therapist to avoid specifying the behavior to be corrected or showing why it is disadvantageous or dangerous. By suggesting a single cause for multiple disorders it has implied a uniformity which is not to be found in the data. Above all, it has encouraged the belief that psychotherapy consists of removing certain inner causes of mental illness, as the surgeon removes an inflamed appendix or cancerous growth or as indigestible food is purged from the body. We have seen enough of inner causes to understand why this doctrine has given psychotherapy an impossible assignment. It is not an inner cause of behavior but the behavior itself which—in the medical analogy of catharsis—must be "got out of the system."

The belief that certain kinds of "pent-up" behavior cause trouble until the organism is able to get rid of them is at least as old as the Greeks. Aristotle, for example, argued that tragedy had a beneficial effect in purging the individual of emotional behavior. On the same analogy it has been argued that competitive sports permit both the participant and the spectator to rid themselves of aggressive tendencies. It has been argued that the human infant has a certain amount of sucking behavior which he must eventually get rid of, and that if he does not exhaust this behavior in the normal process of nursing, he will suck his fingers or other objects. We have seen that it is meaningful to say that an organism is disposed to emit behavior of a given form in a given amount. Such behavior spends itself in the process of extinction, for example. But it does not follow that a potential disposition causes trouble or has any other effect upon the organism until it has been spent. There is some evidence that sucking behavior in the infant is *reinforced* by nursing and is then made more rather than less likely to occur. It is also a tenable hypothesis that competitive sports generate rather than relieve aggressive tendencies. In any case, the variables to be considered in dealing with a probability of response are simply the response itself and the independent variables of which it is a function. We have no reason to appeal to pent-up behavior as a causal agent.

On the assumption that the inner causes of neurotic or maladjusted behavior are subject to gross physiological assault, cures are sometimes attempted by administering drugs, by performing surgery upon the nervous system, or by using drugs or electric shock to set off violent convulsions. Such therapy is obviously directed toward a supposed underlying condition rather than toward the behavior itself or the manipulable variables outside the organism to which the behavior may be traced. Even "functional" therapy, in which external variables are manipulated, is often described with the same figure of speech. The therapist is regarded as rooting out a source of trouble. The conception is not far removed from the view—which large numbers of people still hold—that neurotic behavior arises because the Devil or some other intruding personality is in temporary "possession" of the body. The traditional treatment consists of exorcising the Devil—driving him out of the individual by creating circumstances which are appropriately aversive to him—and some treatments of multiple personality differ from this only in avoiding theological implications. The lesser demons of modern theory are anxieties, conflicts, repressed wishes, and repressed memories. Just as pent-up emotion is purged, so conflict is resolved and repressed wishes and memories are released.

This view of mental illness and therapy owes most to Sigmund Freud. It appears to have withstood assault largely because of Freud's contributions in other directions. His great achievement, as a disciple of his said recently, was to apply the principle of cause and effect to human behavior. Aspects of behavior which had hitherto been regarded as whimsical, aimless, or accidental, Freud traced to relevant variables. Unfortunately, he chose to represent the relationships he discovered with an elaborate set of explanatory fictions. He characterized the ego, superego, and id as inhabitants of a psychic or mental world subdivided into regions of conscious, co-conscious, and unconscious mind. He divided among these personalities a certain amount of psychic energy, which flowed from one to the other in a sort of hydraulic system. Curiously enough, it was Freud himself who prepared the way for dismissing these explanatory fictions. By insisting that many mental events could not be directly observed, even by the individual himself, he widened the scope of the psychic fiction. Freud took full advantage of the possibilities, but at the same time he encouraged an analysis of the processes of inference through which such events might be known. He did not go so far as to conclude that references to such events could be avoided altogether; but this was the natural consequence of a further examination of the evidence.

Freud's conceptions of mental disease and therapy were closely related to his conception of a mental life. Psychoanalysis was regarded as *depth* psychology, concerned with discovering inner and otherwise unobservable conflicts, repressions, and springs of action. The behavior of the organism was often regarded as a relatively unimportant by-product of a furious struggle taking place beneath the surface of the mind. A wish which has been repressed as the result of aversive consequences struggles to escape. In doing so it resorts to certain devices which Freud called "dynamisms"—tricks which the repressed wish uses to evade the effects of punishment. Therapy is concerned with discovering the repressed wish and rooting it out, or occasionally repressing it more securely, so that the symptoms will disappear.

The present view of therapy is quite different. The Freudian wish is a device for representing a response with a given probability of occurrence. Any effect of "repression" must be the effect of the variables which have led either to the response itself or to the repressing behavior. We have to ask why the response was emitted in the first place, why it was punished, and what current variables are active. The answers should account for the neurotic behavior. Where, in the Freudian scheme, behavior is merely the symptom of a neurosis, in the present formulation it is the direct object of inquiry.

Let us consider the apparent result of the struggle of a wish to express itself. An example which permits us to observe the principal Freudian dynamisms is sibling rivalry. Let us say that two brothers compete for the affection of their parents and for other reinforcers which must be divided between them. As a result, one brother behaves aggressively toward the other and is punished, by his brother or by his parents. Let us suppose that this happens repeatedly. Eventually any situation in which aggressive action toward the brother is likely to take place or any early stage of such action will generate the conditioned aversive stimulation associated with anxiety or guilt. This is effective from the point of view of the other brother or the punishing parent because it leads to the self-control of aggressive behavior; the punished brother is now more likely to engage in activities which compete with and displace his aggression. In this sense he "represses" his aggression. The repression is successful if the behavior is so effectively displaced that it seldom reaches the incipient state at which it generates anxiety. It is unsuccessful if anxiety is frequently generated. Other possible consequences, which are described by the so-called dynamisms, are as follows:

The same punishment may lead the individual to *repress* any knowledge of his aggressive tendencies (Chapters XVII and XVIII). Not only does he not act aggressively toward his brother, he does not even "know" that he has tendencies to do so.

He may control himself by changing the external environment so that it is less likely to evoke aggressive behavior, not only in himself but in others. As an example of *reaction formation*, he may engage in social work, in campaigns against racial discrimination, or in support of a philosophy of brotherly love. We explain his behavior by showing that it contributes to the suppression of his own aggressive impulses and hence toward a reduction in the conditioned aversive stimulation resulting from punishment (Chapter XV).

He may actually injure his brother but *rationalize* his conduct. For example, he may discipline his brother "for his own good" or may be especially energetic in carrying bad news to him "because he ought to know the worst." These expressions describe the behavior in such a way that punishment is withheld by others and conditioned aversive stimulation fails to be generated in the individual's own behavior (Chapter XVIII).

He may *sublimate* his aggression by taking up an occupation in which such behavior is condoned. For example, he may join the armed services or the police or get employment in an abattoir or wrecking company. This is response induction if different forms of the behavior of striking are strengthened by a variable which strengthens striking his brother (Chapter VI); it is stimulus induction if different stimuli which show any property in common with his brother evoke striking.

He may *fantasy* injuring or killing his brother. If this also generates aversive stimulation, he may fantasy injuring or killing other people. If he has the talent, he may write stories about the murder of a brother, or if there is anxiety in connection with the word "brother," about other murders (Chapter XVIII).

He may *dream* of injuring or killing his brother or, if this generates aversive stimulation, of injuring or killing someone who *symbolizes* his brother—perhaps an animal which in another part of the dream takes on his brother's features (Chapter XVIII).

He may *displace* his aggression by "irrationally" injuring an innocent person or thing (Chapter X). This may occur simply because emotional responses show stimulus induction—a man who is angry with an absent office boy takes it out on another employee—or because the displaced behavior will not be punished, at least so severely—a man who is angry with his boss takes it out on the office boy.

He may engage in aggressive *wit* by saying something which in one sense injures his brother but in another escapes censure. The remark is injurious and punishable if it is attributed to one variable, but not if it is attributed to another. The response is witty simply in the sense of being a function of two variables (Chapter XIV).

He may *identify* himself with prize fighters or with characters in a sadistic movie or in stories about men who injure or kill their brothers, in the sense that he will be highly disposed to imitate their verbal and nonverbal behavior (Chapter XIV). He will be reinforced by such stories and will report this fact, together with the emotional reaction common to positive reinforcers, by saying he "enjoys" them.

He may *project* his aggression by describing a picture in which two men are fighting as a picture of brothers (Chapter XIV), in the sense that he is disposed to imitate such behavior and to suppose that the men in the picture are responding to the same variables.

He may respond aggressively in a Freudian *slip*—for example, by saying, "I never said I didn't hate my brother" instead of "I never said I hated my brother" (Chapter XIV).

He may *forget* to keep an appointment with his brother or with anyone who resembles him (Chapter XIV).

He may escape anxiety about punishment by *"punishing himself"* —by masochistic behavior, by forcing himself to undertake arduous or dangerous work, or by encouraging accidents.

He may develop certain *physical symptoms,* especially when he is with his brother. These may be a characteristic form of competitive behavior from which he gains an advantage, or the presence of his brother may arouse strong responses of glands and smooth muscles which have an injurious effect.

It would be difficult to prove that all these manifestations are due to the early punishment of aggressive behavior toward a brother. But they are reasonable consequences of such punishment, and the early history may be appealed to *if no other variables can be discovered to account for the behavior.* (If the behavior has no connection with such a history, there is so much the less to explain in a scientific analysis.)

Such manifestations are simply the responses of a person who has had a particular history. They are neither symptoms nor the surreptitious expression of repressed wishes or impulses. The dynamisms are not the clever machinations of an aggressive impulse struggling to escape from the restraining censorship of the individual or of society, but the resolution of complex sets of variables. Therapy does not consist of releasing a trouble-making impulse but of introducing

variables which compensate for or correct a history which has produced objectionable behavior. Pent-up emotion is not the cause of
disordered behavior; it is part of it. Not being able to recall an early
memory does not produce neurotic symptoms; it is itself an example
of ineffective behavior. It is quite possible that in therapy the pent-up
emotion and the behavioral symptom may disappear at the same
time or that a repressed memory will be recalled when maladjusted
behavior has been corrected. But this does not mean that one of these
events is the cause of the other. They may both have been products
of an environmental history which therapy has altered.

In emphasizing "neurotic" behavior itself rather than any inner
condition said to explain it, it may be argued that we are committing
the unforgivable sin of "treating the symptom rather than the cause."
This expression is often applied to attempts to remove objectionable
features of behavior without attention to causal factors—for example,
"curing" stammering by a course of vocal exercises, faulty posture
by the application of shoulder braces, or thumb-sucking by coating
the thumb with a bitter substance. Such therapy appears to disregard
the underlying disorder of which these characteristics of behavior
are symptoms. But in arguing that behavior is the subject matter of
therapy rather than the symptom of a subject matter, we are not
making the same mistake. By accounting for a given example of disadvantageous behavior in terms of a personal history and by altering
or supplementing that history as a form of therapy, we are considering the very variables to which the traditional theorist must ultimately turn for an explanation of his supposed inner causes.

OTHER THERAPEUTIC TECHNIQUES

There are many other ways in which behavior which calls for
remedial action may be corrected. When the difficulty cannot be
traced to the excessive use of punishment or to other aversive circumstances in the history of the individual, different therapeutic
techniques must be developed. There is the converse case, for example, in which ethical, governmental, or religious control has been
inadequate. The individual may not have been in contact with controlling agents, he may have moved to a different culture where his

early training is inadequate, or he may not be readily accessible to control. Therapy will then consist of supplying additional controlling variables. When the individual is wholly out of control, it is difficult to find effective therapeutic techniques. Such an individual is called psychotic.

Sometimes the therapist must construct a new repertoire which will be effective in the world in which the patient finds himself. Suitable behavior already in the repertoire of the patient may need to be strengthened, or additional responses may need to be added. Since the therapist cannot foresee all the circumstances in which the patient will find himself, he must also set up a repertoire of self-control through which the patient will be able to adjust to circumstances as they arise. Such a repertoire consists mainly of better ways of escaping from the aversive self-stimulation conditioned by punishment.

Such constructive techniques may be needed after the nonpunishing audience of the therapist has had its effect. If the condition which is being corrected is the by-product of controlling circumstances which no longer exist in the life of the patient, alleviation of the effects of excessive control may be enough. But if the patient is likely to be subjected to continued excessive or unskillful control, therapy must be more constructive. The patient may be taught to avoid occasions upon which he is likely to behave in such a way as to be punished, but this may not be sufficient. An effective repertoire, particularly in techniques of self-control, must be constructed.

As another possible source of trouble, the individual may have been, or may be, strongly reinforced for behavior which is disadvantageous or dangerous. Behavior which violates ethical, governmental, or religious codes is often by its very nature strongly reinforcing. Sometimes, accidental contingencies may also arise. In Sacha Guitry's film, *The Story of a Cheat*, a child is punished for some trivial misbehavior by being denied his supper. But the supper turns out to be poisonous, and the child is the only one of a large family to survive. The implication that the child will then dedicate himself to a life of crime is not entirely fanciful. Positive reinforcement in atypical situations produces other forms of ineffective or even crippling behavior. For example, the social reinforcement supplied by a particular person may become very powerful, and it may be contingent upon behavior which is not effective in the world at large. Thus when a solicitous parent supplies an unusual measure of affection and attention to a sick child, any behavior on the part of the child which emphasizes his illness is strongly reinforced. It is not surprising that the child continues to behave in a similar fashion when he is no longer ill. This may begin as simple malingering, when it is scarcely to be distinguished from the behavior of the malingerer who claims to have been injured in an accident in order to collect damages, but it may pass into the more acute condition of hysterical illness if the child himself becomes unable to identify the relevant variables or correctly appraise the possibilities of his own behavior. Other sorts of social consequences have similar effects. The child who is angry with his parents is reinforced when he acts in any way which injures them—for example, in any way which annoys them. If such a condition is long sustained, a repertoire may be established which will work to the disadvantage of the child in his dealings with other people. One obvious remedial technique for behavior which is the product of excessive reinforcement is to arrange new contingencies in which the behavior will be extinguished. The child is no longer reinforced with affection for feigning illness or with a strong emotional response for being annoying.

Just as the traditional conception of responsibility is abandoned as soon as governments turn to techniques of control other than the use of punishment, so the conception of therapy as the rooting out of inner causes of trouble is not likely to be invoked to explain these constructive techniques. There is, however, a roughly parallel explanation which has been applied to all techniques of therapy. When a therapist encounters a patient for the first time, he is presented with a "problem" in the sense of Chapter XVI. The patient usually shows a novel pattern of disadvantageous or dangerous behavior, together with a novel history in terms of which that behavior is to be understood. The particular course of therapy needed in altering or supplementing this history may not be immediately obvious. However, the therapist may eventually "see what is wrong" and be able to suggest a remedial course of action; this is his *solution* to the problem. Now therapeutic experience has shown that when such a solution is proposed to an individual, it may not be effective even though, so far as we know, it is correct. But if the patient arrives at the solution himself, he is far more likely to adopt an effective course of action. The technique of the therapist takes this fact into account. Just as the psychoanalyst may wait for a repressed memory to make itself manifest, so the nonanalytic therapist waits for the emergence of a solution from the patient. But here again we may easily misunderstand the causal relation. "Finding a solution" is not therapy, no matter who does the finding. Telling the patient what is wrong may make no substantial change in the relevant independent variables and hence may make little progress toward a cure. When the patient himself sees what is wrong, it is not the fact that the solution has come from within him which is important but that, in order to discover his own solution, his behavior with respect to his problem must have greatly altered. It follows from the nature of disadvantageous or dangerous behavior that a substantial change must be accomplished if the individual is to identify the relevant variables. A solution on the part of the patient thus represents a substantial degree of progress. No such progress is implied when the therapist states the solution. Therapy consists, not in getting the patient to discover the solution to his problem, but in changing him in such a way that he is able to discover it.

EXPLAINING THE PSYCHOTHERAPEUTIC AGENCY

The therapist engages in therapy primarily for economic reasons. Therapy is a profession. The services which the therapist renders are reinforcing enough to the patient and others to permit him to exchange them for money (Chapter XXV). Usually the therapist is also reinforced by his success in alleviating the conditions of his patients. This is particularly apt to be true in a culture which reinforces helping others as a standard ethical practice. Frequently another important sort of reinforcement for the therapist is his success in manipulating human behavior. He may have a personal interest, for example, in proving the value of a particular theory of neurotic behavior or of therapeutic practice. These return effects upon the agency will determine in the long run the composition of the profession of psychotherapy and the uniformity of its practices.

At certain stages in psychotherapy the therapist may gain a degree of control which is more powerful than that of many religious or governmental agents. There is always the possibility, as in any controlling agency, that the control will be misused. The countercontrol which discourages the misuse of power is represented by the ethical standards and practices of the organized profession of psychotherapy. The danger of misuse may, as we shall see in Chapter XXIX, explain the current popularity of theories of psychotherapy which deny that human behavior can in the last analysis be controlled or which deliberately refuse to accept responsibility for control.

CHAPTER XXV

ECONOMIC CONTROL

We turn now to the use of positive reinforcement in the practical control of behavior. This consists in general of the presentation of food, clothing, shelter, and other things which we call "goods." The etymology is significant. Like the behavior of the individual which is positively reinforcing to the group, goods are "good" in the sense of being positively reinforcing. We sometimes speak of them also as "wealth." This term has a similar etymological connection with positive reinforcement, but it also includes generalized conditioned reinforcers, such as money and credit, which are effective because they may be exchanged for goods.

REINFORCING BEHAVIOR WITH MONEY

As a simple example of economic control an individual is induced to perform labor through reinforcement with money or goods. The controller makes the payment of a wage contingent upon the performance of work. In actual practice, however, the process is seldom as simple as this. When we tip a man or pay him for performing a small service and thereby increase the probability of his performing a similar service in the future, we do not depart far from the laboratory study of operant reinforcement. Behavior has occurred and has

384

been strengthened by its consequences. This is also roughly true when a man is steadily employed. His performance at a given time is mainly determined by the contingencies of reinforcement which have prevailed up to that time. When an explicit agreement is made, however, prior verbal stimuli must be analyzed in order to account for the effect of the economic contingency. Thus when we agree to pay a man a given amount for a given piece of work, our promise to pay is not far from the command analyzed in Chapter XXII, except that reinforcement is now positive rather than negative. Payment is contingent upon the verbal stimulus of the promise to pay and upon a correspondence between the topography of the behavior and certain verbal specifications. The offer, "I'll pay you two dollars if you mow the lawn" specifies (1) behavior ("mowing the lawn"), (2) a reinforcement ("two dollars"), and (3) a contingency ("if"). To the prospective employee the whole remark serves as an occasion which, if the offer is to be effective, must be similar to other occasions upon which similar contingencies have prevailed.

WAGE SCHEDULES

Fixed-ratio schedules. With the exception of payment "by the job," the economic control of behavior follows certain schedules of reinforcement. When a man is paid in terms of the number of units of work completed, the schedule is essentially that of a fixed ratio. It is usually known in industry as piecework pay. The same principle applies to commission selling, to the craftsman who makes and sells a standard product, to the writer who is paid by the story or book, and to the small private contractor. Fixed ratio is, in general, a very effective schedule of reinforcement. If the ratio is not too high—that is, if the amount of work required per unit of pay is not too great—and if each reinforcement is of a significant amount, the individual will characteristically work at a high rate. This is as true of the pigeon in the laboratory as of the man in industry. An employee who has been paid on some other basis and then transferred to piecework pay will usually show a considerable increase in speed. The increase is partly the automatic result of the increasing frequency of reinforcement which follows on a fixed-ratio schedule as the rate increases. Some of it is due, as we have seen, to the fact that a high rate of responding tends to prevail at the moment of reinforcement under such a schedule. Progress toward the completion of a given number of responses also has the effect of a conditioned reinforcer. The schedule is more effective if this progress is emphasized—for example, by a visible counter.

A fixed-ratio schedule may, in fact, be too effective. It leads not only to high levels of activity, but to long working hours, both of which may be harmful. A bricklayer paid in terms of the number of bricks laid may "burn himself out" in a few years. Another objection to the use of the schedule in industry is that the increased return to the worker which follows conversion to such a schedule often seems to justify increasing the ratio. Let us suppose that an employee producing a hundred items per week is paid fifty dollars on a weekly basis and that the management offers to pay this instead on a piecework basis of one dollar for every two items. The effect upon the employee is a rapid increase in production. Let us suppose that he is able to increase his weekly wage to a hundred dollars. In terms of current rates of pay this may appear to justify increasing the number of items required per dollar to, say, three. As the piecework schedule remains in force, production may continue to rise. In the long run a very much higher rate of work may be generated by only a slight increase in weekly pay. This is precisely the way in which in the laboratory a high rate of responding is generated under a fixed-ratio schedule.

When the ratio is high or the reinforcement trivial, a fixed-ratio schedule characteristically produces a period of inactivity just after each reinforcement. At very high ratios these periods may be greatly prolonged. They represent, as we have seen, a condition of abulia similar to that in complete extinction in which, although the deprivation is severe, the individual simply "has no behavior available." He finds it impossible to start on his next assignment. He may report this by saying that he is discouraged, that he can't face his job, and so on. A typical example of fixed-ratio pay is the salesman selling on commission. When "business is not good," the amount of work which must be done per unit of reinforcement is high, and abulia is common.

The ratio and the magnitude of the reinforcement show a subtle relation. Is a reinforcement of ten dollars per thousand items as effective as one dollar per hundred, or one cent per item? If a man places a fixed economic value upon his labor, there should be no difference, but this is not the case. One can advance to a high ratio only after a long history of reinforcement at lower ratios. Especially with uneducated labor the ratio may be crucial. Thus a contractor who employed peasant labor to move earth with wheelbarrows found it most effective to pay a small amount each time a full wheelbarrow was delivered to the proper point. The use of piecework pay in industry or elsewhere presupposes a considerable history of economic control.

Fixed-interval schedules. Labor is most commonly paid by the day, week, month, or year. These appear to be fixed-interval schedules. The size of the interval, like the size of the ratio, is a rough function of earlier contingencies affecting the individual. The wages of the day laborer are not only calculated on a daily basis, they are often paid daily also. Substantial reinforcement at shorter intervals is needed before payments spaced as much as a month apart are effective. To analyze such a history in detail we should have to investigate certain subsidiary kinds of behavior, some of them verbal, which are generated by schedules of reinforcement and which bridge the gap between working on, say, the first day of the month and being reinforced on the last. Such an analysis would have to include the effect of agreements or contracts between employer and employee.

In any case, however, wages received at fixed intervals do not parallel the intermittent reinforcements described in Chapter VI. In human behavior certain prominent stimuli, commonly correlated with the time of payment, make a temporal discrimination possible. The performance of a pigeon or rat under fixed-interval reinforcement changes dramatically when a stimulus is arranged to vary in some way with the passing of time between reinforcements. Clocks and calendars are verbal devices designed to supply stimuli of this sort to the human subject. When such stimuli are available, the worker—whether human or subhuman—waits until the reading on the clock is very close to that at which behavior is reinforced. If there were no other factors involved, payment for work at the end of each week would generate only a small amount of work just before pay-time.

It is necessary, therefore, to supplement fixed-interval schedules with other techniques of control. The supervisor or "boss" is a source of aversive stimulation contingent upon any behavior which falls below certain specifications, including a minimum rate of production. Some of the power available to the supervisor may be derived from his position in the ethical group—he may condemn laziness or poor work as bad or something to be ashamed of—but insofar as he "can't do any worse than fire a man," his main aversive stimulation is the threat of dismissal. Wages serve in such a case simply to create a standard economic condition which may be withdrawn aversively. The boss threatens dismissal, or some measure which is effective because it is a step toward dismissal, whenever the employee slows down; he removes that threat when the employee speeds up. Eventually the behavior of the employee generates comparable aversive stimulation; he works at a rate just above that at which he feels guilty or threatened. The use of an aversive boss is an excellent example of the general principle that when punishment is abandoned in favor of positive reinforcement, there is a tendency to turn to other forms of aversive control. The threat of withholding an accustomed positive reinforcement is always available for this purpose. Payment of wages is an obvious advance over slavery, but the use of a standard wage as something which may be discontinued unless the employee works in a given manner is not too great an advance.

A production line moving at a set rate makes the contingency between speed of work and aversive stimulation more clear-cut. This "pacing" of behavior is by no means a modern achievement. The galley slave pulled his oar to avoid the whip, which was contingent upon his failing to pull in unison with others. A line of reapers swinging scythes in unison paced each other—the basic rhythm being determined in part by a leader but also in part by the length and mass of the pendulum composed of man and scythe—because any deviation brought aversive stimulation, often dangerous, from the scythes of other reapers. The production line has the effect of reducing some of the personal attributes of aversive stimulation by a boss, but a danger inherent in any pacing system is the temptation on the part of the controller to increase the pace.

Combined schedules. Fixed-interval schedules are also supplemented in industry by various sorts of "incentive pay." These are combinations of fixed-interval and fixed-ratio schedules. Each of the component schedules corrects some of the shortcomings of the other. Supplementary aversive stimulation from a supervisor is not needed if the ratio component is effective. At the same time the ratio component may not be enough to lead to dangerously high rates or long hours of work. When a salesman is paid partly on salary and partly on commission, the combination is designed to correct the abulia which might otherwise follow reinforcement at a high ratio.

Variable schedules. Laboratory studies have shown that variable-interval and variable-ratio schedules are superior to fixed schedules in sustaining performance, but it is not easy to adapt such schedules to the payment of wages. A contract between employer and employee which guarantees a given return, either per interval of time or per unit of work, rules out a genuine variable schedule. Such schedules may be used, however, in the payment of money—such as a bonus—not specified in a contract or contingent upon behavior in any other way. The bonus would usually be classed as an emotional variable which predisposes the individual favorably toward his work or his employer, but it may also act as a reinforcer. Its effect as such is considerably reduced if it is given on a fixed-interval schedule. The standard Christmas bonus, for example, eventually functions primarily as part of the pay which may be withdrawn as a form of aversive stimulation in dismissal. An unpredictable bonus, given in smaller sums on a variable-interval schedule but in approximately the same amount annually, would have a much greater effect.

Differential reinforcement of quality of work. Wages are usually contingent upon specified behavior at a specified level of quality or skill. In general the performance of an employee, like that of the laboratory animal, adjusts quite accurately to the exact contingencies of reinforcement. Both "do no more than they need to do." Additional economic reinforcement may be made contingent upon work which exceeds minimum standards. Bonuses, raises, and promotions, when contingent upon exceptional performance, shape the topography of behavior in the direction of quality or skill (Chapter VI).

Extra-economic factors. It is now generally recognized that the employee seldom works "just for the money." The employer who relies exclusively on economic control overlooks the fact that the average worker is reinforced in other ways. The individual craftsman not only constructs something which he can sell for money, he is reinforced by his success in dominating the medium in which he works and in producing an article for which he receives approval. These additional reinforcements may have a substantial effect in sustaining his level of work. They are often lost in mass-production methods in which the worker receives only an economic reinforcement for his achievement. To say that the craftsman is motivated by "pride in his work" does not help us to understand the problem. In order to deal effectively with the behavior of the employee we must in any given case be able to specify the actual circumstances which are reinforcing, and perhaps how they have come to be reinforcing.

The effect of the reinforcement of the worker is not shown in his rate of production if that rate is determined by an aversive pacing system. Extra-economic factors in industry usually have a more direct effect upon the behavior of the worker either in coming to work or in staying on one job. Quite apart from his rate of production while at work, the worker who "likes his job" shows little absenteeism and a history of few changes of employment. He likes his job in the sense that he is reinforced for coming to work—not only by an effective wage schedule but by the conditions under which he works, by his fellow workers, and so on. He dislikes his job insofar as it has aversive properties. If he is kept at a high level of work through constant aversive stimulation in the form of a threat of dismissal, the whole task will become aversive and, when his economic condition permits, he will remain absent or, if possible, change jobs. Conditioned aversive stimuli associated with sickness, unemployment, or hardship in old age may also have important aversive effects. It does not help much in dealing with these problems to say that the employee wants "freedom" or "security." In the design of optimal working conditions, considered with respect not only to productivity but to absenteeism and labor turnover, we need an explicit analysis of actual reinforcing and aversive events.

THE ECONOMIC VALUE OF LABOR

That part of the behavior of the worker which is under economic control generates aversive stimuli—from the nature of the work itself or from the fact that it prevents the worker from engaging in activities which would be reinforcing in other ways. These aversive consequences are roughly offset by the economic reinforcement which the worker receives. When the worker accepts or rejects the offer of a job, he may be said to be comparing positive and negative reinforcers. A similar comparison is made by the employer. Since those who use economic control must give up the goods or money with which they reinforce behavior, economic reinforcement is by definition aversive to the controller.

If these conflicting consequences are roughly equal, the individual may engage in behavior leading to a decision in the sense of Chapter XIV. Shall a man mow his own lawn or pay someone else to mow it for him? This will depend in part upon the aversive properties of mowing the lawn and the aversive properties of giving up the money needed to hire someone to mow it. It will also depend upon the behavior of making a decision in which the man may review other possible consequences of mowing the lawn himself—the exercise may be good for him—or the kinds of things for which the money which must be paid could otherwise be exchanged, or ways in which he might earn that amount of money less aversively than by mowing a lawn, and so on. The prospective employee may alter similar conditions affecting his behavior in accepting or rejecting an offer.

A "deal" is made in such a case if in avoiding the aversive consequences of mowing the lawn, the employer offers an amount equal to or greater than that which matches the aversive consequences to the employee. The amount offered will also depend upon the aversive consequences of giving up money. The amount offered by the employer is what the job is "worth" to him in his current economic circumstances; the amount accepted by the employee is what the job is "worth" to him in *his* current economic circumstances.

The "economic value" of labor or other personal services thus has to do with the matching of positive and negative reinforcing effects. The reinforcing effects of two tasks could be directly compared, but money provides a single scale on which the economic values of many different types of labor or services may be represented. We have already seen that money has certain advantages as a generalized reinforcer; it has fairly simple dimensions, it can be made contingent upon behavior in a clear-cut way, and its effects are relatively free of the momentary condition of the organism. Money has a special advantage in representing economic value because different amounts can be compared on a single scale; one amount may be equal to another, twice as great as another, and so on. This standard scale is so effective in comparing reinforcers that it is often taken to represent some sort of independent economic value not associated with positive or negative consequences. The monetary scale is regarded as a primary dimension of value. But the scale would have no meaning apart from the comparison of other consequences.

To the employer the economic value of labor is just that amount of money which he will give up in return for that labor. This depends upon the results of the labor. We pay a man for mowing a lawn if a mowed lawn is reinforcing. We pay him for making shoes if shoes are personally reinforcing or can be exchanged for money or goods which are reinforcing for other reasons. Sometimes behavior itself is directly reinforcing, as in entertainment; we have seen that the entertainer is in the business of making his behavior positively reinforcing so that it will have economic value.

To the employee the economic value of labor is just that amount of money for which he will supply that labor. The aversive consequences against which he places a value upon his services may be of many sorts. Hard labor is directly aversive, as is confinement at a given task for long periods of time regardless of the energy required. Some tasks are aversive for special reasons. Thorndike found that people were in general willing to name a price for engaging in a wide variety of aversive tasks—such as letting a snake coil around one's arms and head, eating a dead earthworm, or spitting on a picture of George Washington. Money which is paid for behavior which, although not especially aversive in itself, may possibly lead to punishment, is usually called a bribe. The bribe supplies a measure of the economic value of a given probability of punishment.

Behavior has "nuisance value" when a man is paid for not engaging in it. When a solicitous parent gives an allowance to his son so long as he does not smoke or drink or marry before a given age, the behavior which the son foregoes may have substantial reinforcing properties for him. He "earns" his allowance by accepting the aversive consequences of giving up the stipulated reinforcements. When the behavior which is given up has no substantial reinforcing consequences but would be highly aversive to the man who pays to suppress it, the money paid is referred to as blackmail. When the behavior is verbal—for example, testifying to or otherwise reporting censurable behavior—it is commonly called hush money. A similar controlling relation is exploited by the underworld gang which sells "protection"—in other words, agrees not to damage person or property in return for payment. Blackmail and protection represent unstable social systems in the sense of Chapter XIX. Such control is opposed by the ethical group or by religious and governmental agencies which make aversive consequences contingent upon engaging in such transactions.

BUYING AND SELLING

Buying and selling or exchanging in barter are so commonplace that we are likely to overlook several of the processes involved. The basic transaction or "deal" is expressed by the offer, "I will give you this if you will give me that." As in transactions involving personal labor, such complex stimuli are effective only after extensive economic conditioning. The process is easy to observe as a child learns to swap toys with his playmates or to buy penny candy at the corner store. Before such behavior reaches a relatively stable state, the child must be affected by the full aversive consequences of giving up a toy or a penny and by the reinforcing consequences of obtaining another toy or candy. When such conditioning has taken place, similar behavior with similar objects and similar money may become relatively automatic, and it may be easy to overlook the complex relationships involved. Whether a sale is made quickly or after long deliberation depends upon whether the aversive properties of giving up money or going without the object are matched by the positively reinforcing properties of the money or the object. In "a good bargain" the object bought is more highly reinforcing than the money given up, and the sale takes place quickly. In the doubtful bargain, positive and negative consequences are relatively evenly matched, and the sale may take place only after long deliberation.

The economic value of goods. The use of money in buying and selling permits us to evaluate goods as we evaluated labor—on a simple one-dimensional scale. An object is "worth" to an individual just that amount of money which he will give up in exchange for it, or in exchange for which he will give it up. Before an exchange or a sale can occur, certain critical values must be reached or exceeded. A will give the article to B if the aversive consequences of this act are roughly matched by the positively reinforcing consequences of the money which B will give to A. B will give this amount of money to A if the aversive consequences which are thus involved are matched by the positively reinforcing consequences of receiving the article from A.

Several other conditions affect economic transactions. Since the money which a man will give in exchange for goods is a measure of the reinforcing effect of the goods, it will vary with the level of *deprivation*. The value which a man assigns to food depends upon how hungry he is. By keeping food in short supply he may be induced to pay a high price. In the population as a whole this is reflected by the fact that the price commonly paid for an object can be manipulated by manipulating the supply. But how much a man will pay for food also depends upon the aversive consequences of giving up money, and this depends roughly upon how much money he has. If "money is no object," he may pay a high price. In the population as a whole the price of an object will therefore be determined in part by the supply of money. These two factors, the supply of goods and the supply of money, have, of course, a prominent place in traditional economic theory. They are not, however, the only determiners of economic transactions.

An important consideration is the *history of reinforcement* of the behavior of acquiring or giving up goods or money. The behavior of buying or selling may be strengthened or weakened apart from the particular nature of a given transaction. When the reinforcing consequences to the buyer greatly exceed the aversive consequences of giving up the price of an article, the simple behavior of buying is strengthened. In the technique of the bargain store some objects are sold at a low price so that others, which are not bargains, can also be sold. The "buying habits" of the public often reflect the same principle. Whether an individual readily engages in buying also depends in part upon previous aversive consequences of giving up money. "Learning the value of a dollar" is the effect of the aversive consequences of parting with a dollar.

The reinforcing effect of an article, and hence the price which can be obtained for it, is enhanced by many techniques of *merchandising*. The article is made "attractive" by design, packaging, and so on. Properties of this sort make an object reinforcing as soon as it is seen by the prospective purchaser, so that a previous history with similar objects is not required.

Imitative behavior is relevant in buying and selling. An object may be bought simply because other people are buying objects of the same kind. This is the principle of the bargain crush and the public spending spree. Testimonial advertising sets up imitative patterns for the potential buyer by portraying other buyers or possessors of goods. Imitative nonbuying is characteristic of periods of deflation.

The balancing of positive and negative consequences may be offset by altering the *time* which elapses between these consequences and behavior. Sales are encouraged by promises of immediate delivery. The same effect is felt, in the absence of an agreement, when a mail order house by filling its orders as rapidly as possible gains an advantage over a rival house with a longer average delivery time. The behavior of mailing in an order is probably not, strictly speaking, reinforced by the receipt of goods after, say, four days; any reinforcing effect of such a consequence must be mediated by verbal or nonverbal intervening steps. But these intervening steps need not change the advantage gained by reducing the time which passes between the behavior and the ultimate consequence. Another kind of time relation is manipulated when the purchaser is permitted to buy on credit. In buying on the installment plan, the aversive consequences of giving up the purchase price are postponed and distributed. The effect is to be distinguished from the effect of credit in permitting goods to be purchased before money is available.

Another important factor contributing to the probability that an individual will turn over money, either for other money or for goods, is the schedule on which he is reinforced for doing so. A faulty vending machine or dishonest vendor occasionally fails to complete the exchange of goods for money. The probability of engaging in transactions under similar circumstances is to some extent reduced through extinction. However, if a vendor characteristically offers an especially good bargain whenever the transaction is completed, the probability may remain at a significant value. In general, the greater the reinforcing effect of the object exchanged for money, the more often reinforcements may fail without extinguishing the behavior altogether. This is an example of the type of economic interchange called *gambling*.

One may gamble with money for money, as in playing a roulette wheel or slot machine; with money for goods, as in buying a chance on an automobile; or with goods for money, as in playing a customer double or nothing for the bill. The behavior of the gambler is under very complex control depending upon his history of reinforcement. It is sometimes possible to calculate the "chances" of a given gambling system, and these, if known to the gambler, may determine whether he will place a bet or not. How the probability that a man will place a bet of a given size varies with such factors as the size of the stake or a given history of reinforcement can be studied experimentally. The predisposition to continue betting under a given system, however, depends primarily upon the schedule of reinforcement. Gambling devices in general observe a variable-ratio schedule. From the point of view of the gambling establishment this is a safe schedule because the percentage profit in the long run is fixed. It is also an unusually effective schedule in generating gambling behavior. The gambling establishment selects a mean ratio which is a compromise between two consequences. Too high a ratio yields a large mean profit per play but a loss of patronage. Too low a ratio yields too small a profit in spite of a ready patronage. The professional gambler "leads his victim on" by building a favorable history of reinforcement. He begins with a low mean ratio under which reinforcement occurs so frequently that the victim wins. The mean ratio is then increased, either slowly or rapidly depending upon how long the gambler plans to work with a particular victim. This is precisely the way in which the behavior of a pigeon or rat is brought under the control of a variable-ratio schedule. A mean ratio can be reached at which reinforcements occur so rarely that the pigeon or rat spends more energy in operating the device than he receives from the reinforcement with food, while the human subject steadily loses money. All three subjects, however, continue to play.

Gambling devices make an effective use of conditioned reinforcers which are set up by pairing certain stimuli with the economic reinforcers which occasionally appear. For example, the standard slot machine reinforces the player when certain arrangements of three pictures appear in a window on the front of the machine. By paying off very generously—with the jack pot—for "three bars," the device eventually makes two bars plus any other figure strongly reinforcing. "Almost hitting the jack pot" increases the probability that the individual will play the machine, although this reinforcer costs the owner of the device nothing.

Gambling, then, is a system of economic control in which the individual is induced to pay money in return for a reinforcement the value of which is too small to lead to exchange under other schedules. If a man cannot sell a car to one man for $3,000, he may still sell it to 3,000 men for $1.00 if the culture has provided the necessary history of variable-ratio reinforcement when its members have "taken chances." If the gambling establishment cannot persuade a patron to turn over money with no return, it may achieve the same effect by returning part of the patron's money on a variable-ratio schedule.

In summary, then, the probability that a transaction will take place is a function of the levels of deprivation of buyer and seller with respect to goods and money, upon the history of both participants with respect to good and bad bargains, upon the temporary characteristics of the object or the situation involved in merchandising, upon the behavior of others engaged in similar transactions, upon the temporal contingencies which govern the receipt of goods or the giving up of money, and upon a history of certain schedules of reinforcement. All these conditions follow from an analysis of human behavior; they are also familiar features in traditional discussions of economic behavior. They obviously affect the usefulness and precision of the concept of economic value. The reinforcing effect of either goods or money cannot be stated without taking into account many different characteristics of the history of the individual buyer or seller, as well as the external circumstances under which a given economic transaction takes place.

"ECONOMICS"

When millions of people engage in buying and selling, lending and borrowing, renting and leasing, and hiring and working, they generate the data which are the traditional subject matter of the science of economics. The data include the quantities and locations of goods, labor, and money, the numbers of economic transactions in a given period, certain characteristics of transactions expressed as costs, prices, interest rates, and wages, together with changes in any of these as functions of time or other conditions.

Statements about goods, money, prices, wages, and so on, are often made without mentioning human behavior directly, and many important generalizations in economics appear to be relatively independent of the behavior of the individual. A reference to human behavior is at least implied, however, in the definition of all key terms. Physical objects are not goods apart from their reinforcing value. More obviously, money cannot be defined without reference to its effect upon human behavior. Although it may be possible to demonstrate valid relationships among the data generated by the economic transactions of large numbers of people, certain key processes in the behavior of the individual must be considered. The traditional procedure has been to *deduce* the behavior of the individual engaging in economic transactions from the data derived from the group. This procedure led to the Economic Man of nineteenth-century economic theory, who was endowed with just the behavior needed to account for the over-all facts of the larger group. This explanatory fiction no longer plays a prominent role in economic theorizing.

Some attention to the individual transaction is often required when generalizations at the level of the group prove invalid. We have already noted many special conditions which affect economic value. In the data generated by millions of people the effects of these special conditions may strike an average or cancel each other out. But when a given condition holds for a large number of people, it cannot be disposed of in this way. Economists frequently explain the failure to predict a particular consequence from a broad generalization by appealing to special conditions of this sort. Although the supply of money and goods may suggest inflation, for example, some external condition, not otherwise related to the supply of money or goods, may generate undue caution on the part of a large number of buyers. If the science of economics were to take all such extra-economic variables into account, it would become a complete science of human behavior. But economics is concerned with only a small number of the variables of which the behavior of the individual is a function. There are many practical reasons why this limited area needs to be studied in relative isolation. This means that the economist will always need to appeal from time to time to the behavior of the real economic man.

Economic theory has been especially inclined to use the principle of maxima and minima. The freedom, justice, and security of the governmental agency, the salvation and piety of the religious agency, and the mental health and adjustment of psychotherapy have their parallels in "wealth," "profits," "utility," and many other concepts in terms of which economic transactions have been evaluated. Since quantification is encouraged in economic theorizing by the useful dimensions of money as a generalized reinforcer, it may appear that these entities are more easily adapted to a functional analysis. But it has not been shown that they are, in fact, any more useful in predicting or controlling a given economic transaction than are their counterparts in the other fields. The conception of economic behavior which emerges from a functional analysis offers an alternative possibility. The present chapter has, of course, dealt with only a small fraction of the many kinds of economic transactions to be observed in any large group of people, but an adequate science of behavior should supply a satisfactory account of the individual behavior which is responsible for the data of economics in general.

THE ECONOMIC AGENCY

The power to wield economic control naturally rests with those who possess the necessary money and goods. The economic agency may consist of a single individual, or it may be as highly organized as a large industry, foundation, or even government. It is not size or structure which defines the agency as such, but the use to which the economic control is put. The individual uses his wealth for personal reasons, which may include the support of charities, scientific activities, artistic enterprises, and so on. The eleemosynary foundation is engaged in disposing of wealth in support of specified activities. Religious and governmental agencies frequently, as we have seen, use this supplementary technique for their special purposes.

If there is any special economic agency as such, it is composed of those who possess wealth and use it in such a way as to preserve or increase this source of power. Just as the ethical group is held together by the uniformity of the aversive effect of the behavior of the individual, so those who possess wealth may act together to protect wealth and to control the behavior of those who threaten it. To that extent we may speak of the broad economic agency called "capital." The study of such an agency requires an examination of the practices which represent concerted economic control and of the return effects which support these practices.

COUNTERCONTROL

As in religious, governmental, or psychotherapeutic control, economic power may be used to further the special interests of those who possess it. Excessive control generates behavior on the part of the controllee which imposes a practical limit. The group as a whole usually condemns the excessive use of wealth as bad or wrong, and classifies the charitable use of wealth as good or right. Some counter-control is also exerted by religious and governmental agencies. Under most modern governments, for example, the individual cannot legally control many sorts of behavior through economic power. Laws concerning prostitution, child labor, fraudulent practices, gambling, and so on all impose limits. Particular economic transactions are restricted, or rendered more or less probable, by tariffs, levies, taxes on profits and on transactions, price controls, changing the supply of money, government spending, and so on. All these measures alter the balance between those possessing labor or goods and those possessing money; hence they alter the frequency with which certain kinds of economic transactions take place. The effect is usually to reduce the extent to which the possessor of wealth is able to employ it in controlling others.

CHAPTER XXVI

EDUCATION

In an American school if you ask for the salt in good French, you get an A. In France you get the salt. The difference reveals the nature of educational control. Education is the establishing of behavior which will be of advantage to the individual and to others at some future time. The behavior will eventually be reinforced in many of the ways we have already considered; meanwhile reinforcements are arranged by the educational agency for the purposes of conditioning. The reinforcers it uses are artificial, as such expressions as "drill," "exercise," and "practice" suggest.

Education emphasizes the acquisition of behavior rather than its maintenance. Where religious, governmental, and economic control is concerned with making certain kinds of behavior more probable, educational reinforcement simply makes special forms more probable under special circumstances. In preparing the individual for situations which have not as yet arisen, discriminative operants are brought under the control of stimuli which will probably occur in these situations. Eventually, noneducational consequences determine whether the individual will continue to behave in the same fashion. Education would be pointless if other consequences were not eventually forthcoming, since the behavior of the controllee at the moment when he is being educated is of no particular importance to any one.

EDUCATIONAL AGENCIES AND THEIR
TECHNIQUES OF CONTROL

The immediate family functions as an educational agency in teaching the child to walk, to talk, to play, to eat in a given way, to dress himself, and so on. It uses the primary reinforcers available to the family: food, drink, and warmth, and such conditioned reinforcers as attention, approval, and affection. The family sometimes engages in education for obvious reasons—for example, because the child is converted into a useful member. The "pride" which a parent takes in the achievements of his children does not provide an explanation, since the term simply describes the fact that the achievement of a child is reinforcing. This fact appears to depend upon the culture. The individual continues to receive many forms of casual instruction from members of the group outside his family, where the variables available to the group are similar to those in ethical control (Chapter XXI). Certain forms of behavior are classified as good or right and others as bad or wrong and are reinforced accordingly. It is not always clear why this is done, however. An extension of ethical control to education may, like family pride, have special advantages for the group, in which case it can be explained only through an analysis of cultural practices (Section VI).

The artisan teaches an apprentice because in so doing he acquires a useful helper, and industries teach those who work for them for a similar reason. The reinforcers are usually economic. When a government engages in military training to improve the efficiency of its armed forces, the techniques are usually based upon punishment or the threat of punishment. When religious agencies turn to education to supplement other techniques, they also use the variables peculiarly under their control. The educational agency, then, is not distinguished by the nature of its variables but in the use to which they are put. There is a difference between the use of economic power to induce an apprentice to work and to induce him to acquire effective forms of behavior, between the use of the threat of punishment to induce a soldier to fight and to induce him to fight effectively, and between the use of the power peculiarly available to the religious agency to reinforce pious behavior and to teach a catechism.

The educational institution. A more explicit educational agency requires special treatment. Education is a profession, the members of which engage in education primarily because of economic reinforcement. As in many other professions, reinforcements supplied by the ethical group are also often important: teaching is not only a way of earning a living, it is "a good thing to do." In explaining the presence of educational institutions in a given community, then, we have to explain the behavior of those who pay for or approve those who teach. What is received by them in return?

The private tutor extends family education, and the family pays for his services for the same reason it educates its children directly. The private school is a collaborative effort of the same sort. Religious or trade schools are similar extensions of the activities of other agencies. In explaining public education, certain immediate benefits to the group as a whole may be pointed out. The lower grades of the public schools take over the educational function of the family, supervise the children during part of the day, generate behavior which is useful to the family and the community and which permits the family to escape censure. Comparable results from the education of older children are not always clear, and this fact raises a practical as well as a theoretical difficulty. The explicit educational agency is not found in every culture, and the extent to which a given group supports it may vary widely from time to time. When those who supply the ultimate power, economic or otherwise, do not receive sufficient reinforcement for doing so, they withdraw their support. Yet educators seldom attempt to increase the return benefits or to make them more effective as reinforcers.

Aside from any immediate return we have to note the possible long-term effect of education. Like family pride or education by members of the group, the explicit educational institution may be explained by a different sort of consequence to the group to be considered in Section VI.

EDUCATIONAL REINFORCEMENT

The reinforcers used by established educational institutions are familiar: they consist of good grades, promotions, Phi Beta Kappa keys, diplomas, degrees, and medals, all of which are associated with the generalized reinforcer of approval. The spelling bee is a familiar device which makes approval or other social reinforcers explicitly contingent upon scholastic behavior. The same technique is represented by modern quiz programs in which "knowledge is reinforced for its own sake." A certain exchange value is evident when the recently educated individual is offered a job or is automatically admitted to membership in certain controlling groups. The educational agency usually wields no economic power itself, however, except for prizes, fellowships, and scholarships. Some reinforcers may be available in the form of privileges. The institution may also have the support of the family which makes primary or conditioned reinforcers contingent upon a level of scholastic achievement—for example, by granting a special allowance to the student who maintains a certain average. During World War II some military education was taken over by educational institutions, and a new and important reinforcer then became available to the teacher in the form of military advancement.

The venerable place of punishment in educational control is represented by the birch rod and the cane, as well as by the condoning of certain forms of disciplinary violence—for example, hazings. Extreme forms of physical punishment have now been generally abandoned, but we have noted the general rule that when one aversive consequence is dropped, another is often created to take its place. Just as wages paid on a fixed-interval schedule may eventually be used to supply aversive stimulation in the form of a threat of dismissal, so the teacher of small children who does not spank may nevertheless threaten to withdraw approval or affection in a form of aversive control. In the same way, the positive reinforcers available to schools and colleges are often used as the basis for conditioned aversive stimulation in the form of a threat of failure or dismissal.

By-products of control through punishment have always been conspicuous features of educational institutions. Hell-raisings, riots, hazings, and truancy are forms of counteraggression or escape which follow the analysis of Chapter XXIV. Somewhat more neurotic by-products are common. The advantages to be gained in turning to other techniques of control are therefore obvious. But one mode of control cannot be given up until something else is ready to take its place, and there is evidence that the educational institution at the moment lacks adequate control. Not only has the educator relinquished the birch rod; he can no longer borrow discipline from family practices based on aversive control. As more and more people are educated, the honorific reinforcements of education are weakened; fewer special advantages are now contingent upon education. With increasing social security the economic consequences of an education are also less important; relatively fewer students are out to "make good" in amassing wealth or at least in escaping the threat of a destitute old age.

Educational institutions have, therefore, turned to alternative methods of control. The teacher, often unwillingly, uses the sources of power available to him in personal control to make himself or his teaching interesting; in other words, he becomes an entertainer. Textbooks are supplied with pictures and diagrams which resemble expositions of the subject matter in magazines or the press, and lectures are supplemented with demonstrations and "visual aids." Especially favorable circumstances for the execution of the behavior to be controlled by the educational institution are arranged: libraries are designed to make books more readily accessible, laboratories are expanded and improved, facilities are provided for field trips and periods of study in especially favorable locations. Subjects which are not easily adapted to these techniques are often minimized or discarded.

The term "progressive education" roughly describes a concerted effort to find substitutes for the spurious reinforcements of educational control. Consequences of the sort which will eventually govern the behavior of the student are brought into the educational situation. Under the traditional system the student who is reinforced for speaking French correctly by an A is eventually reinforced, if at all, when he enjoys books written in French or communicates effectively in a French-speaking community. In progressive education, these "natural" or "functional" reinforcements are employed by the educational agency as soon as possible. Similarly, the student who is studying science is reinforced as soon as possible by his increasing competence in dealing with nature. By permitting a wider choice of what is to be studied, the probability is increased that scholastic behavior will receive such noneducational reinforcement at an early date. It has perhaps always been characteristic of good education to introduce "real" consequences, but progressive education has made an effort to do this as often and as soon as possible. A common objection has been that certain fields of study are thus unduly emphasized at the expense of others in which disciplinary training with merely educational reinforcement cannot be avoided.

The conditioned reinforcers of the educational agency may be made more effective by pointing up the connection with natural contingencies to be encountered later. By informing the student of the advantages to be gained from education, education itself may be given reinforcing value. Many educational institutions have therefore turned to counseling and various forms of therapy as auxiliary techniques.

THE BEHAVIOR RESULTING FROM
EDUCATIONAL CONTROL

When educational reinforcements are made contingent upon topographical or intensive properties of behavior, the result is called *skill*. The differentiation discussed in Chapter VI is characteristic of training in painting, music, handwriting, speaking, sports, and crafts. The noneducational reinforcements which eventually take control are the special consequences of skilled behavior. In teaching a man to play tennis some such educational reinforcer as the verbal stimulus "Good!" or "That's right!" is made contingent upon the proper grip, the proper stroke, the proper timing, and so on. The resulting "good form" is eventually maintained by the natural consequences of the flight of the ball. Similarly, the educational reinforcement of good technique in painting is eventually replaced by the production of pictures which are in themselves reinforcing. Technical skill in the operation of tools and machines leads first to the approval of the instructor and then to the successful production of objects which are reinforcing.

Knowledge. The entity which is traditionally said to be maximized by education is called "knowledge." The term refers to some of the most complex kinds of human behavior, and it is therefore not surprising that it has seldom been clearly defined or effectively employed in evaluating educational practices. We sometimes use the term to represent simply the probability of skilled behavior. A man "knows how to write" in the sense that he possesses behavior with pen and paper which will be emitted under suitable circumstances and will generate certain kinds of marks. In a similar sense he knows how to hit a tennis ball or sing a tune or draw a straight line. Usually, however, knowledge refers to a controlling relation between behavior and discriminative stimuli. The response may be skilled, but we are concerned primarily with whether it will be made upon the proper occasion. Thus, skilled movements are needed in driving a car, but knowing how to drive a car is making the proper responses at appropriate times. One knows how to repair a radio in the sense, not of being able to manipulate pliers, screw driver, and soldering iron, but of manipulating them in appropriate places.

Most knowledge acquired in education is verbal. The stimuli which constitute the appropriate occasions may be verbal or nonverbal. A child "knows the alphabet," not because he can pronounce the names of the letters, but because he can do so in the proper order. One letter or group of letters is the occasion for pronouncing the letter which follows. He "knows the capital of Peru" in the sense that he will correctly answer when asked what the capital is or will make statements about the capital in discussing Peru, and so on. A man "knows his table of integrals" in the sense that under suitable circumstances he will recite it, make corresponding substitutions in the course of a calculation, and so on. He "knows his history" in the sense of possessing another highly complex repertoire. In rare instances parts of the historical repertoire are controlled by nonverbal

EDUCATION 409

stimuli—the primary data of history; but historical knowledge is largely verbal behavior in response to verbal stimuli. The repertoire is useful primarily when the individual is in contact with other individuals possessing similar knowledge. In other kinds of knowledge, particularly in science, a greater part of the discriminative stimuli may be nonverbal, and the repertoire is useful primarily in enabling the individual to act effectively with respect to nature. We need not regard such repertoires as "signs" of knowledge but rather as knowledge itself. Knowledge enables the individual to react successfully to the world about him just because it is the very behavior with which he does so.

The contention that a knowledge of history, for example, is simply a verbal repertoire does not mean that education is merely rote learning. The student comes also to *understand* the facts of history. An adequate explanation of what this means would require an exhaustive analysis of verbal behavior which cannot be given here.[1] The individual agrees with a statement about a historical event in the sense that he shows a high probability of making the statement himself. The growing understanding with which he reads and rereads a passage describing a period in history may also be identified with the growing probability that he will emit verbal responses similar to those which comprise the passage. But the high probability which characterizes agreement or understanding may have many sources; knowledge of a given field is coherent and well integrated to the extent that these multiple sources of strength are generally consistent. So far as the present point is concerned, we may note simply that the supplementary sources of strength which distinguish "understanding" from "tending to say" do not require us to modify the view that knowledge is a repertoire of behavior. Understanding is a collateral issue which concerns the variables of which such a repertoire is a function.

A verbal repertoire also gains importance from the fact that it may have concurrent effects upon other behavior of the individual. One such effect is most easily observed when the verbal repertoire and the change in behavior are located in different organisms. The speaker

[1] Cf. footnote on page 210.

has many effects upon the listener. One of these may conveniently be called "instruction." The verbal stimulus generated by the speaker alters the probability of a verbal or nonverbal response in the listener. Let us assume, for example, that a man is familiar with electrical apparatus and possesses a set of avoidance responses controlled by parts of such an apparatus which are electrically charged or "hot." In working with a new piece of apparatus, he acquires, perhaps apart from any verbal instruction, appropriate avoidance behavior with respect to certain features. The process is naturally aversive and may not be necessary if the individual is *instructed* in the use of the apparatus. When he is told, for example, that certain terminals are hot, he avoids them even though he has not received aversive stimulation from them. But the process of being told is complex. The instruction involves the pairing of two stimuli—a complex verbal stimulus generated as the speaker says "this terminal" and points to a part of the apparatus and the verbal stimulus "hot." The occurrence of these stimuli together has an effect similar to that of respondent conditioning; the object identified as "this terminal" subsequently evokes the avoidance behavior appropriate to objects designated "hot." As we observe in the behavior of children, the capacity to be affected by verbal behavior in this way develops only very slowly.

An educational institution often directly instructs the student in this sense, but it usually functions by establishing a complex verbal repertoire which the student later uses in what may be called self-instruction. The speaker and the listener now inhabit the same skin. Upon a given occasion verbal behavior is evoked which instructs the student himself in nonverbal behavior. In a simple example, the student memorizes a set of instructions and then later correctly operates the device to which they are appropriate. In a far more complex example, he acquires an extensive historical repertoire and then deals effectively with a current situation when some of the responses in that repertoire instruct him appropriately.

If we take knowledge to include not only a repertoire as such, but all the effects which the repertoire may have upon other behavior, then the acquisition of knowledge in education is obviously far more than rote learning. Moreover, the educational institution does more than impart knowledge even in this broad sense. It teaches the student to *think*, in the sense of Chapter XVI. It establishes a special repertoire which has as its effect the manipulation of variables which encourage the appearance of solutions to problems. The student learns to observe, to assemble relevant materials, to organize them, and to propose tentative solutions. Such a practice is essential in preparing him for some kinds of future occasions. We saw that the ethical group and religious and governmental agencies cannot simply establish good, pious, or legal forms of behavior, but must also set up processes of self-control which will enable the individual himself to arrive at good, pious, or legal behavior on novel occasions in the absence of members of the group or agency. In the same way the educational institution cannot be content merely with establishing standard repertoires of right answers but must also establish a repertoire with which the student may, so to speak, arrive at the right answer under novel circumstances in the absense of any representative of the agency.

COUNTERCONTROL

Since the power over variables available to the educational institution is in general weak, we might not expect to find that it is often misused or that anyone is interested in countercontrol. There are, however, several ways in which the control exercised by the educator is commonly restricted. An educational institution is usually set up and supported in terms of a particular curriculum. A child is sent to a particular school largely because of what the school will teach. Those who are in ultimate control—for example, those who supply the institution with money—may insist that the curriculum be closely followed. The college supported by a religious agency engages in appropriate religious instruction and must not establish behavior opposed to the interests of the agency. Schools supported by a government may be asked to apply their educational techniques in supporting the government and to avoid any education which conflicts with governmental techniques of control or threatens the sources of governmental power.

Since other types of agencies also engage in educational control, they often enlist the services of the educational institution. Economic and religious agencies sometimes supply materials for school use which encourage education in line with economic or religious control. It may be necessary for a governmental agency to restrict the extent to which public schools serve other agencies in this way.

THE CONTROL OF HUMAN BEHAVIOR

CHAPTER XXVII

CULTURE AND CONTROL

MANNERS AND CUSTOMS

In addition to the ethical behavior discussed in Chapter XXI the individual acquires from the group an extensive repertoire of *manners* and *customs.* What a man eats and drinks and how he does so, what sorts of sexual behavior he engages in, how he builds a house or draws a picture or rows a boat, what subjects he talks about or remains silent about, what music he makes, what kinds of personal relationships he enters into and what kinds he avoids—all depend in part upon the practices of the group of which he is a member. The actual manners and customs of many groups have, of course, been extensively described by sociologists and anthropologists. Here we are concerned only with the kinds of processes which they exemplify.

Behavior comes to conform to the standards of a given community when certain responses are reinforced and others are allowed to go unreinforced or are punished. These consequences are often closely interwoven with those of the nonsocial environment. The way in which a man rows a boat, for example, depends in part upon certain mechanical contingencies; some movements are effective and others ineffective in propelling the boat. These contingencies depend upon the construction of the boat and oars—which are in turn the result

415

of other practices observed by the boatmakers in the group. They also depend upon the type of water, which may be peculiar to a group for geographical reasons, so that the manner in which a boat is rowed in an inland lake district is different from that along the seacoast even when boat and oars are of the same type. The educational contingencies established by the group are still another source of difference. The individual is reinforced with approval when he adopts certain grips, postures, kinds of strokes, and so on, and punished with criticism when he adopts others. These variables are especially important in determining the "style" which eventually becomes characteristic of a group.

The contingencies to be observed in the social environment easily explain the behavior of the conforming individual. The problem is to explain the contingencies. Some of these are arranged for reasons which have no connection with the effect of customs or manners upon the group. The community functions as a reinforcing environment in which certain kinds of behavior are reinforced and others punished, but it is maintained as such through other return benefits. Verbal behavior is a good example. In a given community certain vocal responses are characteristically reinforced with food, water, and other services or objects. These responses become part of a child's repertoire as naturally as nonverbal responses reinforced by the same consequences. It does not greatly matter whether a child gets a drink by bending over a pool or by saying, "I want a drink of water." To explain why the water is forthcoming in the latter case, however, requires a rather elaborate analysis of the verbal environment. It is enough to note here that a verbal environment may maintain itself through its effects upon all participants, quite apart from its function in teaching the language to new members of the community. An adult in a new verbal environment may receive no explicit educational reinforcement but may nevertheless acquire an adequate vocabulary. Some nonverbal customs and manners can be explained in the same way. Moreover, when a custom is perpetuated by a governmental, religious, or educational agency, we may point to the usual return benefits.

But there remains the fact that the community as a whole often establishes conforming behavior through what are essentially educational techniques. Over and above the reciprocal reinforcements which sustain verbal behavior, for example, the community extends the classification of "right" and "wrong" to certain forms of that behavior and administers the generalized reinforcements of approval and disapproval accordingly. In many groups a mistake in grammar or pronunciation is followed by more aversive consequences than, say, minor instances of lying or stealing. The group also supports educational agencies which supply additional consequences working in the same direction. But why is such deviant behavior aversive? Why should the group call an ungrammatical response "wrong" if the response is not actually ambiguous? Why should it protest unconventional modes of dress or rebuke a member for unconventional table manners?

One classical answer is to show that a given form of deviant behavior must have been aversive for good reason under an earlier condition of the group. Foodstuffs are in general selected by contingencies which follow from their physical and chemical properties. Foods which are unpalatable, inedible, or poisonous come to be left alone. A child who starts to eat such a food receives powerful aversive stimulation from the group. "Good" and "bad" foods are eventually specified in ethical, religious, or governmental codes. When, now, through a change in climate or living conditions, or as the result of changing practices in the preparation and preservation of food, a "bad" food becomes safe, the classification may nevertheless survive. There is no longer any current return advantage to the group to explain why eating a particular food is classified as bad. The classification may be especially puzzling if the group has meanwhile invented an explanation for it.

We may also show indirect, but presumably none the less effective, current consequences. In his *Theory of the Leisure Class*, Thorstein Veblen demonstrated that customs or manners which seemed to have no commensurate consequences, and which were explained in terms of doubtful principles of beauty or taste, had an important effect upon other members of the group. According to Veblen we do not necessarily wear "dress" clothes or speak useless languages because the clothes are beautiful or the languages "cultured," but because we are then accepted by a group in which these achievements are a mark of membership and because we gain prestige in controlling those who are unable to behave in the same way. According to this theory, a modern American university builds Gothic buildings not because the available materials resemble those which were originally responsible for this style of architecture, or because the style is beautiful in itself, but because the university then commands a more extensive control by resembling medieval educational institutions. The practices of the group which perpetuate a "good" style of architecture are thus as easy to explain as those which perpetuate modes of construction which are "good" for mechanical reasons.

Perhaps the simplest explanation of the differential reinforcement of conforming behavior is the process of induction. The forces which shape ethical behavior to group standards are powerful. The group steps in to suppress lying, stealing, physical assault, and so on, because of immediate consequences to its members. Its behavior in so doing is eventually a function of certain characteristic features of the "good" and "bad" behavior of the controlled individual. Among these is lack of conformity to the general behavior of the group. There is thus a frequent association of aversive properties of behavior with the property of nonconformance to a standard. Nonconforming behavior is not always aversive, but aversive behavior is always nonconforming. If these properties are paired often enough, the property of nonconformance becomes aversive. "Right" and "wrong" eventually have the force of "conforming" and "nonconforming." Instances of behavior which are nonconforming but not otherwise aversive to the group are henceforth treated as if they were aversive.

No matter how we ultimately explain the action of the group in extending the ethical classification of "right" and "wrong" to manners and customs, we are on solid ground in observing the contingencies by virtue of which the behavior characteristic of a particular group is maintained. As each individual comes to conform to a standard pattern of conduct, he also comes to support that pattern by applying a similar classification to the behavior of others. Moreover, his own conforming behavior contributes to the standard with which the behavior of others is compared. Once a custom, manner, or style has arisen, therefore, the social system which observes it appears to be reasonably self-sustaining.

THE SOCIAL ENVIRONMENT
AS CULTURE

A social environment is usually spoken of as the "culture" of a group. The term is often supposed to refer to a spirit or atmosphere or something with equally nonphysical dimensions. Our analysis of the social enviroment, however, provides an account of the essential features of culture within the framework of a natural science. It permits us not only to understand the effect of culture but, as we shall see later, to alter cultural design.

In the broadest possible sense the culture into which an individual is born is composed of all the variables affecting him which are arranged by other people. The social environment is in part the result of those practices of the group which generate ethical behavior and of the extension of these practices to manners and customs. It is in part the accomplishment of all the agencies considered in Section V and of various subagencies with which the individual may be in especially close contact. The individual's family, for example, may control him through an extension of religious or governmental techniques, by way of psychotherapy, through economic control, or as an educational institution. The special groups to which he belongs—from the play group or street gang to adult social organizations—have similar effects. Particular individuals may also exert special forms of control. A culture, in this broad sense, is thus enormously complex and extraordinarily powerful.

It is not, however, unitary. In any large group there are no universally observed contingencies of control. Divergent customs and manners often come into conflict—for example, in the behavior of the child of immigrants, where social reinforcements supplied by the family may not coincide with those supplied by acquaintances and friends. Different institutions or agencies of control may operate in conflicting ways; secular education often conflicts with religious education, and government with psychotherapy, while economic control is characteristically divided among many groups which wield their power in different ways.

A given social environment may change extensively in the lifetime of a single individual, who is then subjected to conflicting cultures. In America, important changes have recently taken place in the techniques used to control sexual behavior. The unmarried female was formerly subjected to strict control by the ethical group and by governmental, religious, and educational agencies. Access to the world at large was forbidden or permitted only in the company of a chaperon who might use physical restraint if necessary. Stimuli leading to sexual behavior were, so far as possible, eliminated from the immediate environment. The anatomy and physiology of reproductive organs, particularly of the male, remained obscure, and any behavior which might alter this condition was severely punished. Such punishment, supplemented by other procedures, generated behavior which reflected "purity" or "modesty" as a form of self-control. Facts related to sexual behavior which could not be concealed were explained in fictitious ways. Incipient sexual behavior was, of course, severely punished, not only with aversive stimulation, but with such powerful conditioned punishments as disapproval, shaming, and threats of ostracism. As a result any incipient sexual behavior gave rise to aversive self-stimulation. This provided for the reinforcement of further acts of self-control and elicited emotional responses with which sexual behavior was incompatible.

Such severe measures could be justified only by arguing that sexual behavior was wrong, that it was nevertheless very powerful, and that aggressive sexual behavior on the part of the male must be met with exceptional defenses on the part of the female. There were often objectionable by-products, however. Although the control was intended to apply mainly to premarital sexual behavior, the effect commonly extended into the marital state, and the individual was prevented from enjoying sexual relations in a normal fashion. The resulting repression of sexual impulses had many of the neurotic effects outlined in Chapter XXIV—from perverted sexual activity to the behavior of the common scold. These consequences, doubtless in company with many other factors, led to a substantial change in practice.

The modern version of sexual control is very different. Although there is no one clearly formulated program, it is recognized that anxiety with respect to sexual behavior is unnecessary. Instead of removing from the environment all stimuli which could possibly lead to sexual behavior, a knowledge of the anatomy and function of sex is supplied. Friendly relations with the opposite sex are more freely permitted, and severe punishment of sexual behavior is avoided in favor of instruction in the consequences of such behavior. It is possible that these techniques are not so effective as earlier measures. Sexual behavior is probably not so deeply repressed, and it is also probably commoner at the overt level. The net result may or may not be to the advantage of the individual and the group.

In any case, the adolescent of today is affected by conflicting techniques which show a transition from one cultural practice to the other. In general, religious and governmental controls still follow the earlier pattern. Within the family, members of different ages frequently differ in their controlling techniques. The family as a whole may differ substantially from other groups of which the individual is a member. We cannot say that a single set of practices with respect to the control of sexual behavior is characteristic of the culture of such a person.

THE EFFECT OF CULTURE
UPON BEHAVIOR

It is often said that "human nature is the same the world over." This may mean that behavioral processes are the same wherever they are encountered—that all behavior varies in the same way with changes in deprivation or reinforcement, that discriminations are formed in the same way, that extinction takes place at the same rate, and so on. Such a contention may be as correct as the statement that human respiration, digestion, and reproduction are the same the world over. Undoubtedly there are personal differences in the rates at which various changes take place in all these areas, but the basic processes may have relatively constant properties. The statement may also mean that the independent variables which determine behavior are the same the world over, and this is another matter. Genetic endowments differ widely, and environments are likely to show more differences than similarities, a large number of which may be traced to cultural variables. The result is, of course, a high degree of individuality.

The effect of a social environment upon the behavior of the individual may be inferred point for point from an analysis of that environment. Let us consider an individual at the age of thirty. To what extent may his behavior reasonably be traced to the cultural variables with which he has come into contact?

Work level. In the sense that particular parts of our subject's repertoire show given probabilities as the result of reinforcement, we say that he shows a given level of interest, enthusiasm, or freedom from "mental fatigue." We are likely to find a high level of relevant behavior if the physical environment includes a favorable climate, an adequate food supply, and other resources. It is also important that abundant positive reinforcement is supplied by the family, the group as a whole, and various subgroups, as well as by governmental, religious, psychotherapeutic, economic, and educational agencies.

Motivation. Whether an individual is frequently hungry will depend, not only upon the availability of food in the nonsocial environment, but upon cultural practices which control what he eats, when he eats it, whether he observes periods of fasting, and so on. His sexual behavior will depend, not only upon the availability of members of the opposite sex, but upon the ethical control of sexual relations, upon governmental and religious restrictions, upon sex education, and so on. Other kinds of deprivation and satiation are also controlled by both social and nonsocial conditions.

Emotional dispositions. The social environment is mainly responsible for the fact that our subject may have grown up in an atmosphere of love, hate, anger, or resentment, and that various emotional patterns may therefore characterize his behavior.

Repertoire. The inanimate world builds an elaborate repertoire of practical responses. It may also set up behavior which is effective in extending such a repertoire: our subject will show a strong "curiosity about nature" if exploratory responses have frequently been reinforced, and special skills in research and invention if self-manipulative behavior of the sort discussed in Chapter XVI has been conditioned. But the comparable repertoire generated by the culture is usually much more extensive. Verbal problem-solving and the social skills employed in personal control are important examples. All controlling agencies are concerned in part with the creation of behavior of this sort, although it is the special concern, of course, of education. The competence of the individual in dealing with things, as well as men, will depend largely upon the extent to which such agencies have characterized the social environment.

Self-control. The inanimate environment may establish some degree of self-control—for example, the individual may learn not to eat a delicious but indigestible food—but by far the greater part of self-control is culturally determined, particularly by ethical, religious, and governmental agencies. The amoral individual who escapes this influence shows the effect of too little control, while the completely "inhibited" or restrained individual stands at the other extreme. Whether our subject conspicuously displays the other effects of his culture which we have just considered will often depend upon this one effect. For example, he may behave readily in an emotional fashion or show a stoical restraint depending upon the extent to which his emotional behavior has been reinforced or punished as right or wrong, legal or illegal, or pious or sinful.

Self-knowledge. Discriminative responses to one's own behavior and to the variables of which it is a function appear to be the exclusive product of the social environment. Whether or not our subject will be self-conscious and introspective depends upon the extent to which the group has insisted upon answers to questions such as "What are you doing?" or "Why did you do that?"

Neurotic behavior. A purely physical enviroment could no doubt generate behavior which was so ineffective, disadvantageous, or dangerous that it would be called neurotic. By far the greater source of trouble, however, is social. Whether or not our subject is well balanced, in good contact with the environment, or free of crippling emotional reactions will depend mainly upon the controlling practices of the group into which he was born.

CULTURAL CHARACTER

When certain features of the social environment are peculiar to a given group, we expect to find certain common characteristics in the behavior of its members. A common culture should lead to a common "character." Russian and American children learn to throw stones and to keep from stubbing their toes in essentially the same way because the relevant variables are principally in the physical environment. They do not speak in the same way because their verbal environments are different. Other kinds of behavior which are socially reinforced are also different. The two groups follow different classifications in shaping the behavior of the individual as right or wrong. Religious, governmental, psychotherapeutic, economic, and educational agencies differ widely in the power and extent of their control. The effects of the family and of business and social organizations are also different. As a result Russians and Americans show very different behavioral repertoires or "characters."

The concept of a group or cultural character, however, has all the dangers inherent in any system of typology. There is always a tendency to argue that, because individuals are similar in one respect, they are similar in others also. Although certain features of behavior may differ consistently between cultures, there are also great differences among the individuals in a given group. We have seen that a social environment is never wholly consistent. It is also probably never the same for two individuals. Only those characteristics of the social environment which are common to the inhabitants of Russia and which differ from the characteristics of any other social environment may be spoken of as "Russian culture." The Russian language fulfills these conditions fairly well, and it should be possible to detect certain corresponding features of "Russian thought" as part of the Russian "character." It is not easy to find other instances, especially of manners and customs, which satisfy these conditions so well.

It is difficult to demonstrate a relation between a given cultural practice and a characteristic of behavior on the empirical evidence obtained by studying a particular group. Recently certain aspects of national character have been attributed to practices in the care of infants. In some national or cultural groups a baby is held essentially immobile throughout the greater part of the first year through the use of swaddling clothes or a cradle board. It has been argued that, especially in the last three months of the year, this physical restraint is highly frustrating and leads to powerful emotional predispositions. If the baby submits to restraint, the effect may be evident in the behavior of the adult, who becomes a "follower." If the restraint strengthens a typical pattern of rage or revolt, the effect may be observed when he becomes a "leader." A particular practice in caring for infants is thus said to produce two types of adult character. The types fit nicely into an interpretation of a particular political pattern, but the evidence is not satisfactory. The extent to which such a cultural practice as swaddling characterizes a group, and is absent from other groups with which a comparison is being made, can presumably be determined by field observation or other forms of inquiry. Whether the adult members of any group fall into two classes showing, respectively, submissive and aggressive behavior can also presumably be established, although this has not been done. Even if we were to accept these facts as proved, a relation between them would not therefore be established. By the very nature of the cultural group as a sample, many other practices will be associated with any one practice chosen for study. Some other practice may therefore be responsible for any demonstrated aspect of group character.

The anthropologist is interested in groups of people as such, and he pays particular attention to the customs, manners, and other features of behavior peculiar to a given group. So long as we are not interested in any particular set of cultural practices, the issue of a national or cultural character will not have the same urgency. We may agree that if a group is characterized by a unique set of practices, it may also be characterized by unique modes of behavior, but the causal connection between the practice and the mode of behavior may be left to a functional analysis of relevant variables under the conditions characteristic of an experimental science.

CHAPTER XXVIII

DESIGNING A CULTURE

The social environment of any group of people is the product of a complex series of events in which accident sometimes plays a prominent role. Manners and customs often spring from circumstances which have little or no relation to the ultimate effect upon the group. The origins of more explicit controlling practices may be equally adventitious. Thus the pattern of control exercised by a strong leader, reflecting many of his personal idiosyncrasies, may result in an established governmental classification of behavior as legal or illegal and may even set the pattern for a highly organized agency. The techniques which a saint employs to control himself may become part of the established practices of a religious agency. Economic control is determined in part by the resources available to the group, which are ultimately a matter of geography. Other fortuitous factors are introduced when different cultures intermingle or when a culture survives important changes in the nonsocial environment. A cultural practice is not the less effective in determining the behavior characteristic of a group because its origins are accidental. But once the effect upon behavior has been observed, the source of the practice may be scrutinized more closely. Certain questions come to be asked. Why should the design of a culture be left so largely to accident? Is it not

426

possible to change the social environment deliberately so that the human product will meet more acceptable specifications?

In many cultural groups we observe practices which might be described as "making changes in practice." The great religious books supply many examples of the deliberate construction of a social environment. The Ten Commandments were a codification of existing and proposed practices according to which, henceforth, behavior was to be reinforced or punished by the group or by the religious agency. The teachings of Christ were more clearly in the nature of a new design. In governmental control, the enactment of a law usually establishes new cultural practices, and a constitution is a similar undertaking on a broader scale. Experimental curricula in schools and colleges and books on child care which recommend substantial changes in family practices are attempts to manipulate important parts of a culture. The social environment is changed to some extent when a new technique of psychotherapy is derived from a theory or from an experimental study of human behavior. Social legislation creates an experimental environment in which behavior is more often reinforced with food, clothing, housing, and so on, and in which certain kinds of deprivation are less likely to occur. Planning the structure of a large industry or governmental agency is an experiment in cultural design. These are all examples of the manipulation of small parts of the social environment; what is called "Utopian" thinking embraces the design of a culture as a whole.

The deliberate manipulation of the culture is therefore itself a characteristic of many cultures—a fact to be accounted for in a scientific analysis of human behavior. Proposing a change in a cultural practice, making such a change, and accepting such a change are all parts of our subject matter. Although this is one of the most complex of human activities, the basic pattern seems clear. Once a given feature of an environment has been shown to have an effect upon human behavior which is reinforcing, either in itself or as an escape from a more aversive condition, constructing such an environment is as easily explained as building a fire or closing a window when a room grows cold. A doctor tells his patient to stop eating a certain food so that he will no longer be troubled by an allergy because he has observed a connection between the food and the allergy. The psychotherapist tells his patient to change to a job to which he is better suited so that he will suffer less from a sense of failure because a similar connection has been established. An economist advises a government to impose heavy taxes in order to check inflation because still another relation has been observed. All these examples involve many detailed steps, many of them verbal, and we should need a more detailed analysis of scientific thinking than can be undertaken here to give a reasonable account of particular instances. But the basic process is clear enough to permit some interpretation.

When we speak of the "deliberate" design of a culture, we mean the introduction of a cultural practice "for the sake of its consequences." But as we saw in discussing "voluntary behavior" in Chapter VII, it is never a future consequence which is effective. A change in practice is made because similar changes have had certain consequences in the past. When the individual describes his own behavior, he may speak of past consequences as the "goal" of his current action, but this is not very helpful. We can best understand the cultural designer, not by guessing at his goals or asking him to guess at them for us, but by studying the earlier environmental events which have led him to advocate a cultural change. If he is basing a given proposal upon scientific experiments, we want to know how closely the experimental and practical situations correspond. We may also want to examine other "reasons for making a change" which are to be found in his personal history and in the recorded history of those who have investigated similar areas.

VALUE JUDGMENTS

Such an interpretation of the behavior of the cultural designer brings us to an issue of classical proportions. Eventually, a science of human behavior may be able to tell the designer what kind of culture must be set up in order to produce a given result, but can it ever tell him what kind of result he *should* produce? The word "should" brings us into the familiar realm of the value judgment. It is commonly argued that there are two kinds of knowledge, one of fact and the other of value, and that science is necessarily confined to the first. Does the design of a culture demand the second? Must the cultural designer eventually abandon science and turn to other ways of thinking?

It is not true that statements containing "should" or "ought" have no place in scientific discourse. There is at least one use for which an acceptable translation can be made. A sentence beginning "You ought" is often a prediction of reinforcing consequences. "You ought to take an umbrella" may be taken to mean, "You will be reinforced for taking an umbrella." A more explicit translation would contain at least three statements: (1) Keeping dry is reinforcing to you; (2) carrying an umbrella keeps you dry in the rain; and (3) it is going to rain. All these statements are properly within the realm of science. In addition to this, of course, the word "ought" plays a large part in the control exercised by the ethical group and by governmental and religious agencies. The statement, "You ought to take an umbrella," may be emitted, not as a prediction of contingencies, but to induce an individual to take an umbrella. The "ought" is aversive, and the individual addressed may feel guilty if he does not then take an umbrella. This exhortatory use may be accounted for in the usual way. It is nothing more than a concealed command and has no more connection with a value judgment than with a scientific statement of fact.

The same interpretation is possible when the reinforcing consequences are of an ethical nature. "You ought to love your neighbor" may be converted into the two statements: (1) "The approval of your fellow men is positively reinforcing to you" and (2) "loving your fellow men is approved by the group of which you are a member," both of which may be demonstrated scientifically. The statement may also be used, of course, to coerce an individual into behaving in a fashion which resembles loving his neighbor, and indeed is probably most often used for this reason, but again this is not what is meant by a value judgment.

When a given change in cultural design is proposed primarily to induce people to make the change, we may account for it as in the exhortatory example above. The proposal may also be a prediction of consequences. Sometimes these are easily specified, as when it is said that the group "ought" to approve of honesty because its members will thus avoid being deceived or that it "ought" to disapprove of theft because its members will then avoid the loss of property. Sometimes the implied consequences are less obvious, as when a study of behavior leads someone to propose that we "ought" to deal with criminals in a certain way or that we "ought" to avoid aversive control in education. It is at this point that the classical values of freedom, security, happiness, knowledge, and so on are usually appealed to. We have seen that these often refer indirectly to certain immediate consequences of cultural practices. But the crucial issue concerning value hinges upon another meaning of the word "ought" in which a more remote consequence is implied. Is there a scientific parallel for this kind of value?

THE SURVIVAL OF A CULTURE

We have seen that in certain respects operant reinforcement resembles the natural selection of evolutionary theory. Just as genetic characteristics which arise as mutations are selected or discarded by their consequences, so novel forms of behavior are selected or discarded through reinforcement. There is still a third kind of selection which applies to cultural practices. A group adopts a given practice—a custom, a manner, a controlling device—either by design or through some event which, so far as its effect upon the group is concerned, may be wholly accidental. As a characteristic of the social environment this practice modifies the behavior of members of the group. The resulting behavior may affect the success of the group in competition with other groups or with the nonsocial environment. Cultural practices which are advantageous will tend to be characteristic of the groups which survive and which therefore perpetuate those practices. Some cultural practices may therefore be said to have survival value, while others are lethal in the genetic sense.

A given culture is, in short, an experiment in behavior. It is a particular set of conditions under which a large number of people grow and live. These conditions generate the patterns or aspects of behavior—the cultural character—which we have already examined. The general interest level of members of the group, their motivations

and emotional dispositions, their behavioral repertoires, and the extent to which they practice self-control and self-knowledge are all relevant to the strength of the group as a whole. In addition the culture has an indirect effect upon other factors. The general health of the group will depend upon birth rate, hygiene, methods of child care, general living conditions, and hours and kinds of work, upon whether many men and women of talent go into medicine and nursing, and upon what proportion of the wealth of the group goes into the construction of hospitals, public health services, and so on. All these conditions, in turn, depend upon the culture. Cultural practices are also largely responsible for the use which is made of the genetic material born into the group, since they determine whether the individual will be able to develop his talents fully, whether educational institutions will be open to him regardless of class or other distinction, whether educational policies are progressive or reactionary, whether he will be subject to political or economic favoritism in the selection of a profession, and so on. The culture also determines the extent to which the members of the group are preoccupied with food or sex or with escape from minor aversive stimulation in the search for "comfort" or from such major aversive stimulation as hard labor or combat, as well as the extent to which they are subject to exploitation by powerful agencies. In turn, therefore, it determines the extent to which they are able to engage in productive activities in science, art, crafts, sports, and so on. The experimental test of a given culture is provided by competition between groups under the conditions characteristic of a particular epoch.

Is survival, then, a criterion according to which a given cultural practice may be evaluated? Those who are accustomed to appealing to more traditional values are usually not willing to accept this alternative. Survival value is a difficult criterion because it has perhaps even less obvious dimensions than happiness, freedom, knowledge, and health. It is not an unchanging criterion, for what may in this sense be a "good" culture in one period is not necessarily "good" in another. Since survival always presupposes competition, if only with the inanimate environment, it does not appear to define a "good" culture in the absence of competition. There appears to be no way

in which we can test the survival value of a culture *in vacuo* to determine its absolute goodness. Conversely, the temporary survival of a culture is no proof of its goodness. All present cultures have obviously survived, many of them without very great change for hundreds of years, but this may not mean that they are better cultures than others which have perished or suffered drastic modification under more competitive circumstances. The principle of survival does not permit us to argue that the status quo must be good because it is here now.

Another difficulty is that survival is often in direct conflict with traditional values. There are circumstances under which a group is more likely to survive if it is not happy, or under which it will survive only if large numbers of its members submit to slavery. Under certain circumstances the survival of a culture may depend upon the unrestricted exercise of sexual behavior, while under other circumstances severely repressive control may strengthen advantageous behavior of other sorts. In order to accept survival as a criterion in judging a culture, it thus appears to be necessary to abandon such principles as happiness, freedom, and virtue. Perhaps the commonest objection to survival is essentially an aversive reaction to the practices which have, thus far in the history of mankind, had survival value. Aggressive action has usually been most successful in promoting the survival of one group against another or of one individual against another.

These difficulties appear to explain why those who are accustomed to the traditional values hesitate to accept survival as an alternative. We have no reason to urge them to do so. We need not say that anyone *chooses* survival as a criterion according to which a cultural practice is to be evaluated. Human behavior does not depend upon the prior choice of any value. When a man jumps out of the way of an approaching car, we may say that he "chooses life rather than death." But he does not jump because he has so chosen; he jumps because jumping is evoked by certain stimulating circumstances. This fact is explained in turn by many earlier contingencies of reinforcement in which quick movement has reduced the threat of impending aversive stimulation or has, in the sense of Chapter XI, avoided aversive consequences. Now, the fact that the individual responds or can

be conditioned to respond in this way is not wholly unrelated to the issue of life or death. It is obvious, after the fact, that the behavior has worked to his advantage. But this particular advantage could not have operated before he jumped. Only past advantages could have had an effect upon his behavior. He was likely to jump or to learn to jump because his ancestors were selected from a large population just because they jumped or learned to jump quickly from the paths of moving objects. Those who did not jump or could not learn to jump are probably not represented by contemporary descendants. The "value" which the individual appears to have chosen with respect to his own future is therefore nothing more than that condition which operated selectively in creating and perpetuating the behavior which now seems to exemplify such a choice. An individual does not choose to live or die; he behaves in ways which work toward his survival or death. Behavior usually leads to survival because the behaving individual has been selected by survival in the process of evolution.

In the same sense, the behavior of making a constructive suggestion about a cultural practice does not involve the "choice of a value." A long biological and *cultural* history has produced an individual who acts in a particular way with respect to cultural conditions. Our problem is not to determine the value or goals which operate in the behavior of the cultural designer; it is rather to examine the complex conditions under which design occurs. Some changes in culture may be made because of consequences which are roughly described as happiness, freedom, knowledge, and so on. Eventually, the survival of the group acquires a similar function. The fact that a given practice is related to survival becomes effective as a *prior* condition in cultural design. Survival arrives late among the so-called values because the effect of a culture upon human behavior, and in turn upon the perpetuation of the culture itself, can be demonstrated only when a science of human behavior has been well developed. The "practice of changing practice" is accelerated by science just because science provides an abundance of instances in which the consequences of practices are shown. The individual who is familiar with the results of science is most likely to set up comparable conditions in cultural design, and we may say, if the expression will not be misunderstood, that he is using survival as a criterion in evaluating a practice.

CAN WE ESTIMATE SURVIVAL VALUE?

The evolution of cultures appears to follow the pattern of the evolution of species. The many different forms of culture which arise correspond to the "mutations" of genetic theory. Some forms prove to be effective under prevailing circumstances and others not, and the perpetuation of the culture is determined accordingly. When we engage in the deliberate design of a culture, we are, so to speak, generating "mutations" which may speed up the evolutionary process. The effect could be random, but there is also the possibility that such mutations may be especially adapted to survival.

But there is one difficulty and it is a very serious one. Survival will not have a useful effect upon the behavior of the cultural designer unless he can actually calculate survival value. A number of current issues suggest that this is not always possible. We may change the pattern of family life and of educational institutions so that children will grow up to be happier people, but are we sure that happy people are most likely to survive in the world today? The psychotherapist faces a comparable problem which is best exemplified by the writings of Freud himself. Freud was, on the one hand, interested in curing neuroses and, on the other, in demonstrating the importance of the achievements of neurotic men. Would a group of nonneurotic people lack scientific and artistic initiative, and if so, could they compete with a group of moderately neurotic people? Similarly, in governmental design, it may be possible to give everyone a considerable measure of security, but will the government which does so then be supported by an energetic, productive, and inventive people?

Practical situations are almost always more complex than those of the laboratory since they contain many more variables and often many unknowns. This is the special problem of technology as against pure science. In the field of human behavior, particularly in the design of culture, we must recognize a kind of complexity in the face of which the rigor of a laboratory science cannot be maintained. But this does not mean that science cannot contribute to the solution of crucial problems. It is in the spirit of science to insist upon careful observation, the collection of adequate information, and the formulation of conclusions which contain a minimum of wishful thinking. All of this is as applicable to complex situations as to simple. In addition, a rigorous science of human behavior offers the following kinds of practical help.

A demonstration of basic behavioral processes under simplified conditions enables us to see these processes at work in complex cases, even though they cannot be treated rigorously there. If these processes are recognized, the complex case may be more intelligently handled. This is the kind of contribution which a pure science is most likely to make to technology. For example, a behavioral process frequently occupies a considerable period of time and often cannot be observed at all through casual observation. When the process is revealed with proper recording techniques under controlled conditions, we may recognize it and utilize it in the complex case in the world at large. Punishment gives quick results, and casual observation recommends its use, but we may be dissuaded from taking this momentary advantage if we know that progress towards a better solution is being made in some alternative course of action. It is difficult to resist punishing a child for conduct which it will eventually outgrow without punishment until we have adequate evidence of the process of growth. Only when developmental schedules have been carefully established by scientific investigation are we likely to put up with the inconvenience of foregoing punishment. The process of extinction also requires a good deal of time and is not clear to casual inspection. We are not likely to use the process effectively until the scientific study of simpler instances has assured us that a given end-state will indeed be reached. It is the business of science to make clear the consequences of various operations performed upon a system. Only when we have seen these consequences clearly set forth are we likely to be influenced by their counterparts in complex practical situations.

A rigorous science of behavior makes a different sort of remote consequence effective when it leads us to recognize survival as a criterion in evaluating a controlling practice. We have seen that happiness, justice, knowledge, and so on are not far removed from certain immediate consequences which reinforce the individual in selecting one culture or one practice against another. But just as the immediate advantage gained through punishment is eventually matched by later disadvantages, these immediate consequences of a cultural practice may be followed by others of a different sort. A scientific analysis may lead us to resist the more immediate blandishments of freedom, justice, knowledge, or happiness in considering the long-run consequence of survival.

Perhaps the greatest contribution which a science of behavior may make to the evaluation of cultural practices is an insistence upon experimentation. We have no reason to suppose that any cultural practice is always right or wrong according to some principle or value regardless of the circumstances or that anyone can at any given time make an absolute evaluation of its survival value. So long as this is recognized, we are less likely to seize upon the hard and fast answer as an escape from indecision, and we are more likely to continue to modify cultural design in order to test the consequences.

Science helps us in deciding between alternative courses of action by making past consequences effective in determining future conduct. Although no one course of action may be exclusively dictated by scientific experience, the existence of any scientific parallel, no matter how sketchy, will make it somewhat more likely that the more profitable of two courses will be taken. To those who are accustomed to evaluating a culture in terms of absolute principles, this may seem inadequate. But it appears to be the best we can do. The formalized experience of science, added to the practical experience of the individual in a complex set of circumstances, offers the best basis for effective action. What is left is not the realm of the value judgment; it is the realm of *guessing*. When we do not know, we guess. Science does not eliminate guessing, but by narrowing the field of alternative courses of action it helps us to guess more effectively.

CHAPTER XXIX

THE PROBLEM OF CONTROL

There are certain rules of thumb according to which human behavior has long been controlled which make up a species of prescientific craft. The scientific study of behavior has reached the point where it is supplying additional techniques. As the methods of science continue to be applied to behavior, we may expect technical contributions to multiply rapidly. If we may judge from the application of science to other practical problems, the effect upon human affairs will be tremendous.

We have no guarantee that the power thus generated will be used for what now appear to be the best interests of mankind. As the technology of modern warfare clearly shows, scientists have not been able to prevent the use of their achievements in ways which are very far from the original purposes of science. A science of behavior does not contain within itself any means of controlling the use to which its contributions will be put. Machiavelli's prescientific insight into human behavior was dedicated to preserving the power of a governmental agency. In Nazi Germany the results of a more exact science were applied to similarly restricted interests. Can this be prevented? Are we to continue to develop a science of behavior without

437

regard to the use which will be made of it? If not, to whom is the control which it generates to be delegated?

This is not only a puzzling question, it is a frightening one; for there is good reason to fear those who are most apt to seize control. To the suggestion that science would eventually be able to "control man's thoughts with precision" Winston Churchill once replied, "I shall be very content if my task in this world is done before that happens." This is not, however, a wholly satisfactory disposition of the problem. Other kinds of solutions may be classified under four general headings.

Denying control. One proposed solution is to insist that man is a free agent and forever beyond the reach of controlling techniques. It is apparently no longer possible to seek refuge in that belief. The freedom which is at issue in the evaluation of governments is related to the countercontrol of aversive techniques. A doctrine of personal freedom appeals to anyone to whom the release from coercive control is important. But behavior is determined in noncoercive ways; and as other kinds of control are better understood, the doctrine of personal freedom becomes less and less effective as a motivating device and less and less tenable in a theoretical understanding of human behavior. We all control, and we are all controlled. As human behavior is further analyzed, control will become more effective. Sooner or later the problem must be faced.

Refusing to control. An alternative solution is the deliberate rejection of the opportunity to control. The best example of this comes from psychotherapy. The therapist is often clearly aware of his power over the individual who turns to him for help. The misuse of that power requires, as we have seen, unusual ethical standards. Carl R. Rogers has written, "One cannot take responsibility for evaluating a person's abilities, motives, conflicts, needs; for evaluating the adjustment he is capable of achieving, the degree of reorganization he should undergo, the conflicts which he should resolve, the degree of dependence which he should develop upon the therapist, and the goals of therapy, without a significant degree of control over the individual being an inevitable accompaniment. As this process is

extended to more and more persons, as it is for example to thousands
of veterans, it means a subtle control of persons and their values and
goals by a group which has selected itself to do the controlling. The
fact that it is a subtle and well-intentioned control makes it only
less likely that people will realize what they are accepting." [1] Rogers'
solution is to minimize the contact between patient and therapist to
the point at which control seems to vanish.

Philosophies of government which arise from a similar fear of control are represented in an extreme form by anarchy and more con-
servatively by the doctrine of laisser faire. "He governs best who
governs least." This does not mean that moderate governmental
techniques are especially effective, for if that were true the moderate
government would govern most. It means that a government which
governs least is relatively free from the dangers of misuse of power.
In economics a similar philosophy defends the normal stabilizing
processes of a "free" economy against all forms of regulation.

To refuse to accept control, however, is merely to leave control in
other hands. Rogers has argued that the individual holds within himself the solution to his problems and that *for this reason* the therapist
need not take positive action. But what are the ultimate sources of
the inner solution? If the individual is the product of a culture in
which there is marked ethical and religious training, in which governmental control and education have been effective, in which economic
reinforcement has worked in an acceptable way, and in which there
is a substantial lay wisdom applicable to personal problems, he may
very well "find a solution," and a therapist may not be necessary. But
if the individual is the product of excessive, unskillful, or otherwise
damaging control, or has received atypical ethical or religious training, or is subject to extreme deprivations, or has received powerful economic reinforcements for asocial behavior, no acceptable solution may
be available "within himself." In government a philosophy of laisser
faire is effective if the citizen is in contact with religious, educational,
and other types of agencies, which supply the control which the government refuses to accept. The program of anarchy, which argues
that man will flourish as soon as governmental control is withdrawn,

[1] *Harvard Educational Review*, Fall 1948, page 212.

usually neglects to identify the other controlling forces which adapt man to a stable social system. A "free society" is one in which the individual is controlled by agencies other than government. The "faith in the common man" which makes a philosophy of democracy possible is actually a faith in other sources of control. When the governmental structure of the United States was being designed, the advocates of a minimal government could point to effective religious and ethical controls; if these had been lacking, a program of laisser faire would have left the people of the country to other controlling agencies with possibly disastrous results. Similarly, in an uncontrolled economy, prices, wages, and so on are free to change as functions of variables which are not arranged by a governmental agency; but they are not free in any other sense.

To refuse to accept control, and thus to leave control to other sources, often has the effect of diversifying control. Diversification is another possible solution to our problem.

Diversifying control. A rather obvious solution is to distribute the control of human behavior among many agencies which have so little in common that they are not likely to join together in a despotic unit. In general this is the argument for democracy against totalitarianism. In a totalitarian state all agencies are brought together under a single superagency. A state religion conforms to governmental principles. Through state ownership the superagency acquires complete economic control. Schools are used to support governmental practices and to train men and women according to the needs of the state, while education which might oppose the governmental program is prevented through control of speech and the press. Even psychotherapy may become a function of the state, as in Nazi Germany, where, because there were no opposing agencies, extreme measures were adopted.

A unified agency is often said to be more efficient, but it makes a solution to the problem of control very difficult. It is the inefficiency of diversified agencies which offers some guarantee against the despotic use of power. A simple example of the beneficial effect of diversification is provided by American advertising. Large sums of money are spent annually to induce people to purchase particular brands of goods. A large part of the control attempted by each company is counteracted by the control attempted by others. Insofar as advertising is directed toward the choice of brand only, the net effect is probably slight. If all the money used to promote particular brands of cigarettes, for example, were devoted to increasing the number of cigarettes smoked per day regardless of brand, the effect might well be more marked. This fact is recognized by industries which pool their advertising funds to promote a type of product rather than individual brands.

In a democracy there is a similar, but much more important, canceling out of the effects of control: economic control is often opposed by education and by governmental restrictions; governmental and religious control is often opposed by psychotherapy; there is often some opposition between government and religion; and so on. So long as the opposing forces remain in some sort of balance, excessive exploitation by any one agency is avoided. This does not mean that control is never misused. Proceeds from control tend to be less conspicuous when thus divided, and no one agency increases its power to the point at which the members of the group take alarm. It does not follow, however, that diversified control does more than diversify the proceeds.

The great advantage of diversification is not closely related to the problem of control. Diversification permits a safer and more flexible experimentation in the design of culture. The totalitarian state is weak because if it makes a mistake, the whole culture may be destroyed. Under diversification, new techniques of control may be tested locally without a serious threat to the whole structure.

Those who accept diversification as a solution to the problem of control find it possible to adopt several appropriate measures. One controlling agency is explicitly opposed to another. Legislation against monopolistic practices, for example, prevents the development of the unlimited economic power of a single agency. It often has the effect of setting up two or three powerful agencies among which a given sort of economic control is distributed. In education an explicit diversification is implied in any opposition to standardized practices. By maintaining many different kinds of educational institutions, working in different ways and achieving different results, we gain the advantages of safe experimentation and avoid excessive emphasis on any one program. In America diversification in government is exemplified by the coexistence of federal, state, and local governments, while religious control is distributed among many sects.

To those who fear the misuse of a science of human behavior this solution dictates an obvious step. By distributing scientific knowledge as widely as possible, we gain some assurance that it will not be impounded by any one agency for its own aggrandizement.

Controlling control. In another attempt to solve the problem of control a governmental agency is given the power to limit the extent to which control is exercised by individuals or by other agencies. The possibility of controlling men through force, for example, is all too evident. One strong man governing through force alone is a small totalitarian state. When the force is distributed among many men, the advantages of diversification ensue: there is some cancellation of effect, exploitation is less conspicuous, and the strength of the group does not depend so critically upon the continuing strength of one man. But an advance over the mere diversification of force is achieved by a government which functions to "keep the peace"—to prevent any sort of control through the use of force. Such a government may be extended to other forms of control. In modern democracies, for example, the man in possession of great wealth is not permitted to control behavior in all the ways which would otherwise be open to him. The educator is not permitted to use the controls at his disposal to establish certain kinds of behavior. Religion and psychotherapy are not permitted to encourage or condone illegal behavior. Personal control is restricted by giving the individual redress against "undue influence."

In this solution to the problem there is no doubt where the ultimate control rests. But if such a government is to operate efficiently, it must be assigned superior power, and the problem of preventing its misuse remains. The problem has apparently been solved with respect to control through force whenever a government has successfully kept the peace without otherwise interfering in the lives of its citizens. But this result is not inevitable. Governments which are assigned force in order to keep the peace may use it to control citizens in other ways and to fight other governments. Other sorts of control may also be misused. A government which is able to restrict the control exercised by a particular agency may coerce that agency into supporting its own program of expansion. The totalitarian state begins perhaps by merely restricting the control of the agencies under it, but it can eventually usurp their functions. This has happened in the past. Does a science of behavior necessarily make it less likely to happen again?

A POSSIBLE SAFEGUARD
AGAINST DESPOTISM

The ultimate strength of a controller depends upon the strength of those whom he controls. The wealth of a rich man depends upon the productivity of those whom he controls through wealth; slavery as a technique in the control of labor eventually proves nonproductive and too costly to survive. The strength of a government depends upon the inventiveness and productivity of its citizens; coercive controls which lead to inefficient or neurotic behavior defeat their own purpose. An agency which employs the stupefying practices of propaganda suffers from the ignorance and the restricted repertoires of those whom it controls. A culture which is content with the status quo—which claims to know what controlling practices are best and therefore does not experiment—may achieve a temporary stability but only at the price of eventual extinction.

By showing how governmental practices shape the behavior of those governed, science may lead us more rapidly to the design of a government, in the broadest possible sense, which will necessarily promote the well-being of those who are governed. The maximal strength of the manpower born to a group usually requires conditions which are described roughly with such terms as freedom, security, happiness, and knowledge. In the exceptional case in which it does not, the criterion of survival also works in the interests of the governed as well as those of the government. It may not be purely wishful thinking to predict that this kind of strength will eventually take first place in the considerations of those who engage in the design of culture. Such an achievement would simply represent a special case of self-control in the sense of Chapter XV. It is easy for a ruler, or the designer of a culture, to use any available power to achieve certain immediate effects. It is much more difficult to use power to achieve certain ultimate consequences. But every scientific advance which points up such consequences makes some measure of self-control in the design of culture more probable.

Government for the benefit of the governed is easily classified as an ethical or moral issue. This need not mean that governmental design is based upon any absolute principles of right and wrong but rather, as we have just seen, that it is under the control of long-term consequences. All the examples of self-control described in Chapter XV could also be classified as ethical or moral problems. We deal with the ethics of governmental design and control as we deal with the ethics of any other sort of human behavior. For obvious reasons we call someone bad when he strikes us. Later, and for as obvious reasons, we call him bad when he strikes others. Eventually we object in more general terms to the use of physical force. Countermeasures become part of the ethical practices of our group, and religious agencies support these measures by branding the use of physical force immoral or sinful. All these measures which oppose the use of physical force are thus explained in terms of the immediate aversive consequences. In the design of government, we can, however, evaluate the use of physical force by considering the ultimate effect upon the group. Why should a particular government not slaughter the entire population of a captured city or country? It is part of our cultural heritage to call such behavior wrong and to react, perhaps in a violently emotional way, to the suggestion. The fact that the members of a group do react in this way could probably be shown to contribute ultimately to the strength of the group. But quite apart from such a reaction we may also condemn such a practice because it would eventually weaken the government. As we have seen, it would lead to much more violent resistance in other wars, to organized counterattack by countries afraid of meeting the same fate, and to very serious problems in the control of the government's own citizens. In the same way, although we may object to slavery because aversive control of one individual is also aversive to others, because it is "wrong," or because it is "incompatible with our conception of the dignity of man," an alternative consideration in the design of culture might be that slavery reduces the effectiveness of those who are enslaved and has serious effects upon other members of the group. Similarly, we defend a way of life which we believe to be superior to others by listing those characteristics which are immediately reinforcing to us and which we call ethically or morally good; but in evaluating a particular cultural experiment we may, instead, ask whether that way of life makes for the most effective development of those who follow it.

Ethical and moral principles have undoubtedly been valuable in the design of cultural practices. Presumably those principles which are with us today have been most valuable in this respect. However, the ultimate survival value of any given set is not thereby guaranteed. What science can tell us about the effect of a given practice upon behavior, and the effect of that behavior upon the survival of the group, may lead more directly to recognition of the ultimate strength of government in the broadest sense. Eventually the question must be asked with respect to mankind in general. Much has been written recently of the need to return to "moral law" in deliberations concerning human affairs. But the question, "*Whose* moral law?" frequently proves embarrassing. Faced with the problem of finding a moral law acceptable to all the peoples of the world, we become more acutely aware of the shortcomings of the principles proposed by any one group or agency. The possibility of promoting such principles, either through education or military conquest, is not promising. If a science of behavior can discover those conditions of life which make for the ultimate strength of men, it may provide a set of "moral values" which, because they are independent of the history and culture of any one group, may be generally accepted.

WHO WILL CONTROL?

Although science may provide the basis for a more effective cultural design, the question of who is to engage in such design remains unanswered. "Who *should* control?" is a spurious question—at least until we have specified the consequences with respect to which it may be answered. If we look to the long-term effect upon the group, the question becomes, "Who should control if the culture is to survive?" But this is equivalent to asking, "Who *will* control in the group which does survive?" The answer requires the kind of prediction which cannot be made with any certainty because of the extremely complex circumstances to be taken into account. In the long run, however, the most effective control from the point of view of survival will probably be based upon the most reliable estimates of the survival value of cultural practices. Since a science of behavior is concerned with demonstrating the consequences of cultural practices, we have some reason for believing that such a science will be an essential mark of the culture or cultures which survive. The current culture which, on this score alone, is most likely to survive is, therefore, that in which the methods of science are most effectively applied to the problems of human behavior.

This does not mean, however, that scientists are becoming self-appointed governors. It does not mean that anyone in possession of the methods and results of science can step outside the stream of history and take the evolution of government into his own hands. Science is not free, either. It cannot interfere with the course of events; it is simply part of that course. It would be quite inconsistent if we were to exempt the scientist from the account which science gives of human behavior in general. Science can, however, supply a description of the kind of process of which it itself is an example. A reasonable statement of our present position in the evolution of culture might take this form: We find ourselves members of a culture in which science has flourished and in which the methods of science have come to be applied to human behavior. If, as seems to be the case, the culture derives strength from this fact, it is a reasonable prediction that a science of behavior will continue to flourish and that our culture will make a substantial contribution to the social environment of the future.

THE FATE OF THE INDIVIDUAL

Western thought has emphasized the importance and dignity of the individual. Democratic philosophies of government, based upon the "rights of man," have asserted that all individuals are equal under the law, and that the welfare of the individual is the goal of government. In similar philosophies of religion, piety and salvation have been left to the individual himself rather than to a religious agency. Democratic literature and art have emphasized the individual rather than the type, and have often been concerned with increasing man's knowledge and understanding of himself. Many schools of psychotherapy have accepted the philosophy that man is the master of his own fate. In education, social planning, and many other fields, the welfare and dignity of the individual have received first consideration.

The effectiveness of this point of view can scarcely be denied. The practices associated with it have strengthened the individual as an energetic and productive member of the group. The individual who "asserts himself" is one to whom the social environment is especially reinforcing. The environment which has characterized Western democratic thought has had this effect. The point of view is particularly important in opposition to despotic control and can, in fact, be understood only in relation to such control. The first step in the countercontrol of a powerful agency is to strengthen the controllee. If the governing agency cannot be made to understand the value of the individual to the agency itself, the individual himself must be made to understand his own value. The effectiveness of the technique is evident in the fact that despotic governments have eventually been countercontrolled by individuals acting in concert to build a world which they find more reinforcing, and in the fact that governing agencies which recognize the importance of the individual have frequently become powerful.

The use of such concepts as individual freedom, initiative, and responsibility has, therefore, been well reinforced. When we turn to what science has to offer, however, we do not find very comforting support for the traditional Western point of view. The hypothesis that man is not free is essential to the application of scientific method to the study of human behavior. The free inner man who is held responsible for the behavior of the external biological organism is only a prescientific substitute for the kinds of causes which are discovered in the course of a scientific analysis. All these alternative causes lie *outside* the individual. The biological substratum itself is determined by prior events in a genetic process. Other important events are found in the nonsocial environment and in the culture of the individual in the broadest possible sense. These are the things which make the individual behave as he does. For them he is not responsible, and for them it is useless to praise or blame him. It does not matter that the individual may take it upon himself to control the variables of which his own behavior is a function or, in a broader sense, to engage in the design of his own culture. He does this only because he is the product of a culture which generates self-control or cultural design as a mode of behavior. The environment determines the individual even when he alters the environment.

This prior importance of the environment has slowly come to be recognized by those who are concerned with changing the lot of mankind. It is more effective to change the culture than the individual because any effect upon the individual as such will be lost at his death. Since cultures survive for much longer periods, any effect upon them is more reinforcing. There is a similar distinction between clinical medicine, which is concerned with the health of the individual, and the science of medicine, which is concerned with improving medical practices which will eventually affect the health of billions of individuals. Presumably, the emphasis on culture will grow as the relevance of the social environment to the behavior of the individual becomes clearer. We may therefore find it necessary to change from a philosophy which emphasizes the individual to one which emphasizes the culture or the group. But cultures also change and perish, and we must not forget that they are created by individual action and survive only through the behavior of individuals.

Science does not set the group or the state above the individual or vice versa. All such interpretations derive from an unfortunate figure of speech, borrowed from certain prominent instances of control. In analyzing the determination of human conduct we choose as a starting point a conspicuous link in a longer causal chain. When an individual conspicuously manipulates the variables of which the behavior of another individual is a function, we say that the first individual controls the second, but we do not ask who or what controls the first.

When a government conspicuously controls its citizens, we consider this fact without identifying the events which control the government. When the individual is strengthened as a measure of counter-control, we may, as in democratic philosophies, think of him as a starting point. Actually, however, we are not justified in assigning to anyone or anything the role of prime mover. Although it is necessary that science confine itself to selected segments in a continuous series of events, it is to the whole series that any interpretation must eventually apply.

Even so, the conception of the individual which emerges from a scientific analysis is distasteful to most of those who have been strongly affected by democratic philosophies. As we saw in Chapter I, it has always been the unfortunate task of science to dispossess cherished beliefs regarding the place of man in the universe. It is easy to understand why men so frequently flatter themselves—why they characterize the world in ways which reinforce them by providing escape from the consequences of criticism or other forms of punishment. But although flattery temporarily strengthens behavior, it is questionable whether it has any ultimate survival value. If science does not confirm the assumptions of freedom, initiative, and responsibility in the behavior of the individual, these assumptions will not ultimately be effective either as motivating devices or as goals in the design of culture. We may not give them up easily, and we may, in fact, find it difficult to control ourselves or others until alternative principles have been developed. But the change will probably be made. It does not follow that newer concepts will necessarily be less acceptable. We may console ourselves with the reflection that science is, after all, a cumulative progress in knowledge which is due to man alone, and that the highest human dignity may be to accept the facts of human behavior regardless of their momentary implications.

INDEX

451